EU COMPETITION AND INTERNAL MARKET LAW IN THE HEALTH CARE SECTOR

LEIGH HANCHER

WOLF SAUTER

OXFORD
UNIVERSITY PRESS

OXFORD
UNIVERSITY PRESS

Great Clarendon Street, Oxford, OX2 6DP,
United Kingdom

Oxford University Press is a department of the University of Oxford.
It furthers the University's objective of excellence in research, scholarship,
and education by publishing worldwide. Oxford is a registered trade mark of
Oxford University Press in the UK and in certain other countries

First Edition published in 2012
Impression: 1

British Library Cataloguing in Publication Data
Data available

Library of Congress Cataloging in Publication Data
Library of Congress Control Number: 2012942993

ISBN 978–0–19–964217–5

Printed by in Great Britain by
CPI Group (UK) Ltd, Croydon, CR0 4YY

Internal market and health care

In principle the TFEU provisions on free movement apply to all goods and services that form part of the national economies of the Member States. The mere fact that a good or service forms part of a national health care system is not sufficient in itself to remove it from the application of EU law. The ECJ has applied the TFEU rules on free movement of services to the provision of health care in hospital and non-hospital settings, those on the freedom of establishment to providers of health and social care, those on free movement of goods to pharmaceuticals and medical devices, and finally those on free movement of persons—potentially even citizenship—to health care. As stated in *Van Delft* (2010) in accordance with Article 21 TFEU, every citizen of the EU has the 'right to move and reside freely within the territory of the Member States', which right may be undermined if obstacles are placed in his way solely due to the fact he has used those opportunities.[34] Such obstacles may include a refusal to cover the costs of treatment enjoyed in other Member States. 1.48

As we shall see in Chapter 6, the EU has adopted a raft of legislation on the last category of measures listed in Article 168(4) TFEU, medicinal products and medical devices, and it has substantially restricted the scope for national measures as a result. Furthermore the principle that EU internal market law applies to all goods and services is reflected in a significant body of legislation regulating public procurement by government authorities (although within the system of public procurement rules a light regime applies to contracting authorities in the health care sector), as discussed in Chapter 5. 1.49

In addition, the TFEU incorporates a general competence to adopt the necessary measures to harmonize many areas affecting health care provision, beyond Article 168 TFEU in the interests of achieving an internal market while at the same time protecting more specific public interests. Even before the adoption of a specific power to regulate tobacco advertising in Article 168(5) TFEU the EU institutions had adopted secondary legislation on this matter on the basis of Article 114 TFEU (then Article 95 EC), as is discussed in some more detail below.[35] Similarly, the 1.50

[34] Case C-345/09 *J.A. van Delft and others v College voor zorgverzekeringen* [2010] judgment of 14 October 2010 (nyr). With reference to Case C-208/07 *Petra von Chamier-Glisczinski v Deutsche Angestellten-Krankenkasse* [2009] ECR I-6095.

[35] Dir 98/43/EC of the European Parliament and of the Council of 6 July 1998 on the approximation of the laws, regulations and administrative provisions of the Member States relating to the advertising and sponsorship of tobacco products [1998] OJ L213/9; Dir 2003/33/EC of the European Parliament and of the Council of 26 May 2003 on the approximation of the laws, regulations and administrative provisions of the Member States relating to the advertising and sponsorship of tobacco products [2003] OJ L152/16. Both these Directives were subject to litigation. The first was struck down in Case C-376/98 *Germany v European Parliament and Council (Tobacco Advertising I)* [2000] ECR I-8419. The new Directive was upheld in Case C-380/03 *Germany v European Parliament and Council (Tobacco Advertising II)* [2006] ECR I-11573.

Patients' Rights Directive—that in contrast to tobacco advertising concerns a subject-matter not listed in Article 168 TFEU—was based both on Articles 168 and 114 TFEU.

1.51 Specific provisions, Articles 53 and 59 TFEU, give the EU institutions power to adopt internal market legislation (on person, and services respectively) which can also have implications for national health care systems. Although the final version of the Directive on Services in the Internal Market does not apply to health care services, earlier proposals did do so and in principle this Directive could apply to services in the health care sector, so long as the services in question meet the definition of a 'service' for the purposes of EU law, and do not concern services rendered directly to consumers.[36] Article 53 TFEU on the freedom of establishment is the basis for the non-life insurance Directives,[37] which have had significant implications for health insurance structures in Member States with 'mixed systems', as will be explained in Chapter 5. Article 48 TFEU provides for the coordination of social security systems in order to promote the free movement of workers. This provision led to secondary legislation that regulates rights to medical treatment in other Member States (and reimbursement of the costs involved),[38] and did so exclusively until the emergence of patient mobility case law with *Kohll* and *Decker* in 1998.

1.52 Exceptions to the internal market rules may be based on Articles 36, 45 and 52 TFEU, which explicitly mention public health (and Articles 51, 52, 62 and 65 TFEU which list other public policy grounds) as well as on the open-ended category of overriding requirements in the public interest. The latter are meant to be taken into account only when the state measures concerned are non-discriminatory (both formally and in effect), but the ECJ has ignored this prescript in health care cases. Overriding requirements are also supposedly non-economic in nature. However as we have seen above, taking into account the financial balance of the social security system with regard to planning considerations is considered legitimate.[39] Finally these various exceptions are relevant only to the extent that they have not been foreclosed (or pre-empted) by harmonization measures that may in

[36] Dir 2006/123/EC of the European Parliament and of the Council of 12 December 2006 on services in the internal market [2006] OJ L376/36.

[37] Dir 92/49/EEC of 18 June 1992 on the coordination of laws, regulations and administrative provisions relating to direct insurance other than life assurance and amending Dirs 73/239/EEC and 88/357/EEC (third non-life insurance Directive) [1992] OJ L228/1.

[38] Reg (EC) 883/2004 of the European Parliament and of the Council of 29 April 2004 on the coordination of social security systems [2004] OJ L166/1. Formerly Reg (EEC) 1408/71 of the Council of 14 June 1971 on the application of social security schemes to employed persons and their families moving within the Community [1971] OJ L149/2, last amended by Reg (EC) 1992/2006 of the European Parliament and of the Council of 18 December 2006 amending Council Reg (EEC) 1408/71 on the application of social security schemes to employed persons, to self-employed persons and to members of their families moving within the Community [2006] OJ L392/1.

[39] Case C-157/99 *Smits and Peerbooms*, supra n 12; Case C-385/99 *Müller-Fauré*, supra n 12.

fact codify the exceptions involved. Before moving on to the competition rules we will briefly consider the rules on tobacco advertising.

The Tobacco Advertising Directives

Although the distinction is not always clear-cut, generally health care (which is patient oriented and curative in nature) is distinguished from public health (largely preventative and systematic in nature). In this book we do not aim to deal with the activities of the EU in the area of public health. By way of example and because this topic has been the subject of a significant controversy in EU law we will however briefly cover the Tobacco Directives. This particular controversy also illustrates the flexibility of the constitutional framework. **1.53**

Since the 1980s the EU has contributed to the promotion of public health by participating in programmes for fighting cancer, in particular where related to the use of tobacco.[40] Already in 1989 a first Directive on the labelling of tobacco products was adopted,[41] which was subsequently revised repeatedly, to include a prohibition on the marketing of tobacco products for oral use.[42] This last provision was contested in several court cases, but was upheld.[43] In all these cases, just as in the *Tobacco advertising* cases I and II, the legal basis of the measure concerned was at issue, as was the proportionality of the ban. **1.54**

Television advertising for tobacco products was prohibited—also in 1989—in the Television Without Borders Directive.[44] This was followed in 1998 by a specific Directive prohibiting other forms of tobacco advertising which found its legal basis in the internal market (harmonization) provisions of Article 114 TFEU (then Article 100a EEC).[45] This Directive was eventually struck down by the ECJ in an **1.55**

[40] cf T Hervey and J McHale, supra n 7, pp 368–84.

[41] Council Dir 89/622/EEC of 13 November 1989 on the approximation of the laws, regulations and administrative provisions of the Member States concerning the labelling of tobacco products [1989] OJ L359/1.

[42] Council Dir 92/41/EEC of 15 May 1992 amending Dir 89/622/EEC on the approximation of the laws, regulations and administrative provisions of the Member States concerning the labelling of tobacco products [1992] OJ L158/30; Dir 2001/37/EC of the European Parliament and of the Council of 5 June 2001 on the approximation of the laws, regulations and administrative provisions of the Member States concerning the manufacture, presentation and sale of tobacco products [2001] OJ L194/26.

[43] Case C-210/03 *The Queen, ex parte Swedish Match AB and Swedish Match UK Ltd v Secretary of State for Health (Swedish Match)* [2004] ECR I-11893; Case C-491/01 *The Queen v Secretary of State for Health, ex parte British American Tobacco (Investments) Ltd en Imperial Tobacco Ltd (BAT)* [2002] ECR I-11453; Case C-434/02 *Arnold André GmbH & Co. KG v Landrat des Kreises Herford* [2004] ECR I-11825.

[44] Council Dir 89/552/EEC of 3 October 1989 on the coordination of certain provisions laid down by Law, Regulation or Administrative Action in Member States concerning the pursuit of television broadcasting activities [1989] OJ L298/23.

[45] Dir 98/43/EC of the European Parliament and of the Council of 6 July 1998 on the approximation of the laws, regulations and administrative provisions of the Member States relating to the advertising and sponsorship of tobacco products [1998] OJ L213/9.

appeal filed by Germany on constitutional grounds,[46] because Article 114 TFEU served to remove significant barriers to interstate trade as well as appreciable restrictions of competition, but did not regulate minor barriers or non-appreciable restrictions.[47]

> If the Community legislature were permitted to harmonise national legislation even where there was no appreciable effect on the internal market, it could adopt directives in any area whatsoever and judicial review of the legislation's compliance with Article 100a [EEC now Article 114 TFEU] would become superfluous.[48]

Because this question touched on a principle of EU law it has given rise to abundant commentary.[49]

1.56 However, the Court also stated the following:

> Furthermore, provided that the conditions for recourse to Articles 100a, 57(2) and 66 EEC [now Articles 114, 53 and 62 TFEU] as a legal basis are fulfilled, the Community legislature cannot be prevented from relying on that legal basis on the ground that public health protection is a decisive factor in the choices to be made.[50]

Hence, if a real free movement problem or appreciable restriction of competition is involved the EU may take harmonization measures, even if public health is an important motivating factor for the action concerned.

1.57 This was followed in 2003[51] by a new Directive that did survive a new appeal by Germany (except on a few minor aspects).[52] Remarkably enough the differences between the earlier Directive that was struck down and that which was confirmed were relatively slight: such as the fact that in the meantime ten new Member States had entered which increased the risk of diverging regulation; the increased role of the Internet; the shift in public opinion; and the stricter policies in Member States regarding the risks of tobacco smoke, as well as the fact that the Commission had investigated the differences between the Member States further. Hence the cases

[46] Case C-376/98 *Tobacco advertising I*, supra n 35, para 60.

[47] ibid, paras 29–31; with reference to inter alia Case C-300/89 *Commission v Council (Titaniumdioxide)* [1991] ECR I-2867, para 25.

[48] Case C-376/98 *Tobacco advertising I*, supra n 35, para 29.

[49] cf eg S Crosby, 'The new Tobacco Control Directive: an illiberal and illegal disdain for the law' [2002] *European Law Review*, 177; R Gosalbo Bono, 'L'arrêt "Tabac" ou l'apport de la Cour de justice au débat sur la délimitation des compétences' [2001] *Revue trimestrielle de droit européen*, 790; TK Hervey, 'Up in smoke? Community (anti)-tobacco law and policy' [2001] *European Law Review*, 101; M Hilf and K Frahm, 'Nichtigerklärung der Richtlinie zum Tabakwerbeverbot: Das letzte Wort?' [2001] *Recht der internationalen Wirtschaft*, 128; S Weatherill, 'European private law—Is there a future after the Tobacco Advertising decision' [2003] *Europäisches Integrationsrecht im Querschnitt*, 93.

[50] Case C-380/03 *Tobacco advertising II*, supra n 35, para 95; Case C-491/01 *BAT*, supra n 43, para 62; Case C-210/03 *Swedish Match*, supra n 43, para 31.

[51] Dir 2003/33/EC of the European Parliament and of the Council of 26 May 2003 on the approximation of the laws, regulations and administrative provisions of the Member States relating to the advertising and sponsorship of tobacco products [2003] OJ L152/16.

[52] Case C-380/03 *Tobacco advertising II*, supra n 35.

revolved around a marginally changed set of facts and not around the application of a different norm. Nevertheless this led the ECJ to conclude that, unlike before in the second case, barriers were removed and restraints on competition lifted—hence reliance on the harmonization provision was justified.

We now move on to consider, first, EU competition law and, second, EU social and employment law. **1.58**

Competition law, state aid, and services of general economic interest

The TFEU rules on the four freedoms are complemented by the provisions on competition law. EU law prohibits anti-competitive agreements between firms and abuse of a dominant position by monopolies or close oligopolies—groups of firms acting as one. The TFEU also prohibits the grant of state aids to undertakings that distort competition. As with the free movement provisions, the mere fact that an agreement, abuse of a dominant position, or the grant of a state aid involves part of a national health system is not in itself sufficient to remove it from the application of EU competition law: there is no health care specific exception to EU competition law. Nevertheless the application of these rules can be tempered by the TFEU Articles guaranteeing the provision of services of general economic interest (SGEI). Given that health care is a public good where market failures are widespread, national health care systems within the EU may charge undertakings with carrying out such SGEIs. Hence Articles 14 and 106(2) TFEU are of particular relevance. The interaction between the state aid and SGEI provisions have led to the adoption of the so-called *Altmark* regulatory package that has been recently updated by the Commission, this is discussed further in Chapter 9. **1.59**

EU social and employment law

Article 153 TFEU gives the EU power to adopt Directives in various employment-related fields, in particular health and safety at work and working conditions. (Note that free movement of workers includes the coordination of social security systems based on Article 48 TFEU, as mentioned above.) This coordination includes granting certain rights to health care in host (as opposed to home) Member States across the EU. In principle and provided that health care professionals satisfy the status of 'employee' or 'worker' then they are treated in the same way as all other workers. Consequently certain Directives in this field do not cater to the specific features of health care employment, as in the case of the Working Time Directive (see Chapter 5).[53] **1.60**

[53] Dir 2003/88/EC of the European Parliament and of the Council of 4 November 2003 concerning certain aspects of the organisation of working time [2003] OJ L299/9. Formerly Council Dir 93/104/EC of 23 November 1993 concerning certain aspects of the organization of working time [1993] OJ L307/18.

1.61 All three of these areas of EU law—internal market, competition and social and employment law—have significant implications for national health care systems and underline the multiple aspects of EU law concerning health care that are important for the arrangements at national level. These will be discussed in detail in the second section of the book on the internal market (Chapters 3 and 4) and the third section on competition (Chapters 8 and 9). We now move on to describe, first, the different EU secondary legal instruments and second, institutional arrangements and related governance issues in health care.

E. The Instruments of EU Law

Types of EU legislation

1.62 The following types of EU legislation can be distinguished: Regulations, Directives, Decisions and Recommendations. Article 288 TFEU reads:

> To exercise the Union's competences, the institutions shall adopt regulations, directives, decisions, recommendations and opinions.
>
> A regulation shall have general application. It shall be binding in its entirety and directly applicable in all Member States.
>
> A directive shall be binding, as to the result to be achieved, upon each Member State to which it is addressed, but shall leave to the national authorities the choice of form and methods.
>
> A decision shall be binding in its entirety upon those to whom it is addressed.
>
> Recommendations and opinions shall have no binding force.

These legal instruments will each be discussed in turn.

Regulations

1.63 Regulations are the most centralising form of all EU instruments and are used where there is a need for uniformity. Regulations are directly applicable in that from the date they enter into force they automatically become part of the domestic legal order of each Member State and require no further transposition. A number of examples can be found in the various domains of the EU health care law, in particular in relation to marketing of medicinal products.[54] Regulations are also typically used to determine the procedures to be applied by the EU institutions.[55]

---

[54] Council Reg 1768/92/EEC concerning the creation of a supplementary protection certificate for medicinal products [1992] OJ L182/1.

[55] For example, the European Medicines Agency (EMEA) is governed by Reg (EC) 726/2004 of the European Parliament and of the Council of 31 March 2004 laying down Community procedures for the authorisation and supervision of medicinal products for human and veterinary use and establishing a European Medicines Agency [2004] OJ L136/1.

Directives

A Directive is binding on Member States as to the result to be achieved, 'but shall leave to the national authorities the choice of form and methods'. The role of national authorities is to ensure a faithful transposition of the Directive into national law in accordance with Articles 5 and 288 TFEU. **1.64**

In this context the ECJ has conceded that there are considerable differences between the types of obligations that the various types of Directives place on Member States. Some require legislation and compliance whereas others set out broad objectives without specifying the necessary measures. In other cases very precise and specific results must be achieved within a specific timeframe.[56] **1.65**

Furthermore the ECJ has set out that: **1.66**

> ... the transposition of a Directive into domestic law does not necessarily require that its provisions be incorporated formally and verbatim in express, specific legislation; a general legal context may, depending on the content of the Directive, be adequate for the purpose provided that it does indeed guarantee the full application of the Directive in a sufficiently clear and precise manner so that, where the Directive is intended to create rights for individuals, the persons concerned can ascertain the full extent of their rights and, where appropriate, rely on them before the national courts.[57]

As a consequence, it may well be that in some cases no legislative action is required at national level. However the ECJ has recognized that the legal position under national law should be sufficiently precise and clear for individuals to be aware of their rights and to be able to rely on them in court. This is especially important regarding the rights of nationals of other Member States.[58]

Exceptions and derogations

A degree of flexibility is preserved for the Member States with respect to key national interests and policies; hence exceptions to the internal market freedoms are found both in TFEU and in overriding reasons of public interest as discussed above. In principle, reliance on these exceptions may be pre-empted (foreclosed) by the existence of harmonization measures—although this may depend on whether the harmonization measures concerned involve maximum or minimum harmonization (see below), and the relevant EU rules may themselves codify exceptions that the Member States may apply. **1.67**

In addition, powers to take protective measures that go beyond harmonization are granted to national authorities—but they are constrained by EU law. **1.68**

---

[56] Case C-32/05 *Commission v Luxembourg (environment)* [2006] ECR I-11323, paras 37–39.

[57] Case C-58/89 *Commission v Germany (drinking water)* [1991] ECR I-498, para 13.

[58] Case C-144/99 *Commission v the Netherlands (consumer contracts)* [2001] ECR I-3541, paras 17–18.

- Article 169(4) TFEU on consumer protection provides that the measures adopted: 'shall not prevent any Member State from maintaining or introducing more stringent protective measures. Such measures must be compatible with the Treaties. The Commission shall be notified of them.'
- Moreover Article 114 TFEU provides a derogation from harmonization measures for individual Member States in cases of major needs subject to Commission authorization via Articles 114(4) and following. The Commission is notified and starts a procedure to determine whether the measures concerned are acceptable or whether they are a means of arbitrary discrimination, a disguised restriction on trade, or whether they constitute an obstacle to the functioning of the internal market. TFEU does not offer a ready answer to the question whether measures adopted under Article 114 TFEU may permit stricter national rules than the agreed norm other than via the limited sphere of authorized variation conceded by this Article itself.

Altogether this means that there is significant scope for national exceptions under EU law, although this is constrained when harmonization measures are in place.

Types and degrees of harmonization

1.69 Both the level and the scope of harmonization employed in the EU may differ by subject matter and over time.[59] The terminology used is as follows: maximum and minimum harmonization is to be distinguished from full versus limited harmonization. Maximum and minimum refer to the *level* of harmonization achieved (in a vertical dimension) while full versus limited refers to the *scope* covered by the harmonization instrument (in a horizontal dimension: covering the ground fully or not). However both minimum harmonization and limited harmonization leave room for additional measures to be taken at national level. The normal approach in the harmonization of rules applicable to the economic interest of consumers, for example, was originally minimum harmonization,[60] but since 2006 the Commission has preferred maximum harmonization as an instrument for market-making.[61] The Green Paper on the Review of the Consumer Acquis excluded the then current model of 'minimum harmonization' as an option for the future, given the inadequacy of the minimum model as a tool of market-making. Furthermore once a legislative framework has developed in a specific field, for example the rules

[59] cf S Weatherill, 'Harmonisation: How much, how little?' [2005] *European Business Law Review* 533; and P Slot, 'Harmonisation of law' [2006] *European Law Review* 378.

[60] cf Case 382/87 *R. Buet and Educational Business Services (EBS) v Ministère public (doorstep selling)* [1989] ECR 1235.

[61] Commission, Green Paper on the Review of the Consumer Acquis, COM (2006) 744 final. cf earlier Dir 2005/29/EC of the European Parliament and of the Council of 11 May 2005 concerning unfair business-to-consumer commercial practices in the internal market and amending Council Dir 84/450/EEC, Dir 97/7/EC, 98/27/EC and 2002/65/EC of the European Parliament and of the Council and Reg (EC) 2006/2004 of the European Parliament and of the Council [2005] OJ L149/22.

governing the authorization and marketing of medicinal products, maximum harmonization tends to become the rule. Whether or not minimum harmonization is involved is relevant to the degree to which adopting distinctive national measures and invoking exceptions are pre-empted. The difference between minimum versus maximum harmonization can be illustrated by reference to the *Gintec* case.[62]

The Gintec *case*

1.70 This 2007 case concerned a reference made in the context of proceedings between *Gintec*, an undertaking which marketed over-the-counter medicinal products and the German Association for the Defence of Free Competition, concerning advertising that *Gintec* had distributed concerning medicinal products based on ginseng root. The association claimed that *Gintec* was not allowed to use either a consumer survey evaluation or a prize draw in its advertising, because the use of third party statements and advertising by means of competitions, prize draws and similar procedures outside professional circles was generally prohibited under the German law on advertising for medicinal products (Heilmittelwerbegesetz).

1.71 The German Federal Court of Justice decided to stay the proceedings and to refer several questions to the ECJ for a preliminary ruling, including the following, on the Community code relating to medicinal products for human use (Directive 2001/83/EC):[63]

> Do the provisions of Directive 2001/83/EC, concerning a reference to statements of third parties who lack professional knowledge of the subject and advertising with a prize draw, set not only a minimum standard for the prohibition on advertising of a medicinal product to the general public, but also a definitive maximum standard?

In response the ECJ held that Directive 2001/83/EC has brought about complete harmonization in the field of advertising of medicinal products and expressly listed the cases in which Member States remain authorized to adopt provisions departing from the rules laid down by that Directive:

> The Directive must therefore be interpreted to the effect that a Member State may not provide, in its national legislation, for an absolute and unconditional prohibition, in the advertising of medicinal products to the general public, on the use of statements from third parties, whilst their use can be limited, under that same directive, only by reason of their specific content or the type of person making the statement.

[62] Case C-374/05 *Gintec International Import-Export GmbH v Verband Sozialer Wettbewerb eV* [2007] ECR I-9517. cf M Campolini, 'ECJ Ruling Confirms Complete Harmonisation of Drug Advertising Rules in Europe' [2008] *RAJ Pharma* 519.

[63] Dir 2001/83/EC of the European Parliament and of the Council of 6 November 2001 on the Community code relating to medicinal products for human use [2001] OJ L311/67.

Hence the Member States must respect the degree of freedom left (or not) by EU Directives. This ruling is also in line with the decision that the ECJ had rendered two months earlier in the *Netherlands v Antroposana* where it decided that the procedures for obtaining a marketing authorization laid down in the Community code relating to medicinal products are exhaustive, preventing the Member States from implementing additional procedures.[64]

Decisions

1.72 Decisions are binding on those to whom they are addressed although the majority are addressed to Member States as opposed to private parties, with almost all of the latter being in the field of competition where the Commission can impose fines on private parties or require them to desist from certain practices. Decisions on state aids are addressed to the Member States.

'Soft law'

1.73 Recommendations and opinions have no binding force and form a body of soft law which includes resolutions and declarations, action programmes and plans, guidelines and other communications by the Commission. Action plans set out objectives and timetables for particular EU policies, and may be used to justify specific legislation on EU public health. Over time, elements of soft law may spill over into hard law, and hard law may also make inroads into policy areas that were initially governed exclusively by soft law.[65]

F. Governance

EU law and health care governance

1.74 The main EU institutions are well-known as being the legislature, consisting of the directly elected European Parliament and the Council (made up, according to the subject matter under discussion, of the relevant ministers from the 27 Member States), the judicature, consisting of the General Court and the ECJ (as well as the less familiar Court of Auditors) whereas the Commission fulfils the roles of executive, policy initiator and enforcement agency. These are not health care specific bodies and we will not refer to their institutional roles except in passing.[66] Instead we will briefly look at health care governance and EU law.

---

[64] Case C-84/06 *The Netherlands v Antroposana, Patiëntenvereniging voor Antroposofische Gezondheidszorg* et al [2007] ECR I-7609.

[65] cf S Greer and B Vanhercke, supra n 9; L Senden, *Soft Law in European Community Law* (Oxford: Hart Publishing, 2004).

[66] For an overview cf eg D Chalmers et al, *European Union Law: Text and Materials* (Cambridge: Cambridge University Press, 2010); K Bradley, *A Handbook of EU Institutional Law* (Oxford: Hart Publishing, 2012).

As explained above, EU legislative competence in the health care sector goes far beyond its limited competences to address 'public health' issues, and in particular its competences in relation to the internal market, competition and (to a lesser extent) social protection of workers. Although it therefore has a major impact on the health sector, it is not possible to conclude that this results in a stable or coherent legal or policy framework. A main reason is a lack of agreement among the Member States. 1.75

- First, even where competence to adopt secondary legislation concerning health care exists, it may be difficult to harness the political will necessary to achieve the (near) consensus required for decision making at Council level.
- Second, nevertheless extensive EU regulation of specific health care domains such as the regulation of pharmaceutical products has not just been adopted but has in turn necessitated the creation of powerful centralized regulatory agencies with far-reaching competence. In the case of pharmaceuticals this was always an internal market dominated area where industry pushed for harmonization from early years. Experience proved that the only way to allow new innovative products to compete on same scale as in US, for example, was to have a centralized authorization procedure, coordinated by a centralized agency.

These two features lead to a variety of governance issues and accountability problems, known in the academic literature as the EU democratic deficit and the joint decision making trap.[67] The idea behind this approach is that federal or EU level decision making is caught between powerlessness on the one hand and a lack of accountability where it is able to act on the other. 1.76

To address the first issue the EU institutions have resorted to a variety of soft law instruments and specific policy coordination methods which fall short of hierarchical binding legal rules but which nevertheless determine the impact of EU law on national health systems. Given that EU law, and especially the internal market and competition law, have had a potentially far reaching impact on health care provision, and in particular in the context of solidarity-based systems of health care, it has become apparent that even if secondary legislation may not be an option, a policy response is needed. Consequently EU policy makers have established various types of EU-level health care governance. These vary from initiatives to promote the exchange of information and best practices and other means of benchmarking, to monitoring and knowledge dissemination. Even though they may not be formally hierarchical, such measures contain an important normative dimension. They are fashioned through a variety of informal consultation processes, often 1.77

[67] cf Y Meny, 'De la democratie en Europe: Old Concepts and New Challenges' [2003] *Journal of Common Market Studies* 1; A Moravcsik, 'In defence of the democratic deficit: reassessing legitimacy in the European Union' [2002] *Journal of Common Market Studies* 603; F Scharpf, 'The Joint-Decision Trap. Lessons From German Federalism and European Integration' [1988] *Public Administration*, 239; F Scharpf, 'The Joint-Decision Trap Revisited' [2006] *Journal of Common Market Studies* 845.

under the auspices of a group of senior representatives of the Member States and draw on an increasingly wide range of stakeholders. Examples are the High Level Group on Innovation and Provision of Medicines in the EU, the High Level Committee on Health and the EU Health Policy Forum, the EU Patients' Forum, and the High Level Process of Reflection on Patient Mobility and Healthcare Developments in the EU.[68]

1.78 The second issue, the governance of centralized regulatory competence and the need for closer collaboration between the Member States, has been addressed by the creation of specialized agencies. In step with the extension of the Commission's competences in social affairs (albeit more slowly than on internal market issues), the use of agencies has further spread in health care, to include the European Agency for Safety and Health at Work, the European Monitoring Centre for Drugs and Drug Addiction, the European Centre of Disease Prevention and Control, as well as the European Medicines Evaluation Agency (EMEA). As this book focuses on substantive law of the internal market and competition regarding health care the following section briefly describes the role of the EMEA which has been assigned specific powers and duties in this respect.

EU agencies: EMEA

1.79 Certain agencies are only mandated to collect and disseminate information and have merely advisory powers. The main tasks of the European Drugs and Drug Addiction Monitoring Centre are the provision and supervision of information, along with creating and coordinating relevant networks. On the other hand, the EMEA, created in 1993, issues expert opinions on the market access of new drugs in the EU and monitors their post-approval safety.[69] The EMEA does not take legally binding decisions on the authorization of new medicines. Given the limited legal scope for the EU institutions to delegate executive powers which has resulted from the so-called *Meroni* doctrine,[70] final decisions rests with the Commission. The EMEA provides scientific advice and effectively prepares the final decision on a particular application which will then be adopted by the Commission as a matter of formality. With national medicines agencies directly involved in the decision

[68] G Permanand and E Vos, 'EU regulatory agencies and health protection', in E Mossialos et al (eds), supra n 7.

[69] Council Reg (EEC) 2309/93 of 22 July 1993 laying down Community procedures for the authorization and supervision of medicinal products for human and veterinary use and establishing a European Agency for the Evaluation of Medicinal Products [1993] OJ L214/1. This regime was updated and replaced by Reg (EC) 726/2004 of the European Parliament and of the Council of 31 March 2004 laying down Community procedures for the authorisation and supervision of medicinal products for human and veterinary use and establishing a European Medicines Agency [2004] OJ L136/1. Cf G Permanand and E Vos, supra n 68.

[70] Case 9–56 *Meroni & Co., Industrie Metallurgiche, SpA v High Authority of the ECSC* [1958] ERC English Special Edn 133.

making process, the regulation of medicines is often referred to as a 'hub and spoke' model and indeed the regulation of medicines remains a joint-EU competence.

The EMEA cannot therefore be characterized as an independent regulatory agency because it remains firmly linked to the Commission who not only influences its operations through its appointment, budgetary and supervisory powers but also takes the final binding decision on whether a medicine will receive a marketing authorization. In *Schering Plough* (2007) the ECJ ruled that in so far as the relevant EU regulations provide only advisory powers for the EMEA, a decision relating to variations on the terms of an authorization must be deemed to emanate from the Commission itself,[71] hence the EMEA's decision was not a reviewable act. However, at the same time, its decision was deemed to emanate from the Commission and as such would be reviewable by the ECJ. **1.80**

How are wider public concerns taken on board in the EMEA's assessment process? In the 2003 *Olivieri* case a clinical investigator who had been involved in assessing a drug which has been given a favourable opinion by the EMEA complained that although subsequent new information on the potential toxicity and inefficacy emerged, the opinion was revised and an application was nevertheless granted.[72] She attempted to have the Commission decision and underlying EMEA revised opinion overturned. However, the ECJ held that as a third party she did not have an interest in bringing an action in order to protect public health and therefore her complaint was inadmissible. The EMEA procedure was a purely bilateral one—that is to say limited to the applicant for authorization and the agency. **1.81**

However Regulation 726/2004 now requires EMEA to develop its contacts with consumer organizations.[73] Article 78(1) of the Regulation reads: **1.82**

> The Management Board shall, in agreement with the Commission, develop appropriate contacts between the Agency and the representatives of the industry, consumers and patients and the health professions. These contacts may include the participation of observers in certain aspects of the Agency's work, under conditions determined beforehand by the Management Board, in agreement with the Commission.

Consequently in 2005 the EMEA internalized external consumer interests to some extent by creating a Human Scientific Committees Working Party with Patients and Consumers Organisations (PCWP) that advises on transparency, product information, pharmacovigilance and interaction between the EMEA scientific committees and patients' organizations. Signalling these developments wraps up our short overview on EU law on health care.

---

[71] Case T-133/03 *Schering-Plough Ltd v Commission and EMEA* [2008] OJ C37/32.
[72] Case T-326/99 *Nancy Fern Olivieri v Commission and EMEA* [2003] ECR II-6053.
[73] Reg 726/2004, supra n 69.

G. Conclusion

1.83 Below we summarize our findings in this introductory chapter and sketch the structure of the book as a whole.

The substantive impact of EU law on health care

1.84 Having surveyed these various aspects it is, paradoxically, the issues listed in Article 168(7) TFEU that correspond most closely to our field of study on the substantive impact of EU law in health care: meaning the organization, management and delivery of health services and medical care and the allocation of the resources assigned to them. This may appear puzzling as this Article seems to delineate the competences of the EU from those of the Member States. It is noteworthy however that 'Union action shall respect the responsibilities of the Member States' with respect to health care delivery. This is not to say that EU action is excluded. For one, the Patients' Rights Directive included Article 168 TFEU as one of its two legal bases (alongside Article 114 TFEU on internal market harmonization). Moreover it is with respect to the limitations that general EU law imposes on the exercise of these responsibilities, including financing, that EU law can have its most profound impact.

1.85 In order to understand this statement it is necessary to consider what may be referred to as the EU law toolbox that lawyers have to work (and contend) with when invoking EU law. This is reviewed in the next chapter (Chapter 2).

Structure

1.86 We have chosen to limit the coverage of this book to the substantive law both because, in our view, this is most useful in practice, and because any remaining gaps may be easily dealt with by referring to general works on institutional law. With this in mind our book is divided into three main sections.

- The first section is introductory in nature and covers the present chapter (Chapter 1) and Chapter 2 on the EU law toolbox.
- The second section deals with the internal market, and covers:
  - First, the primary (Treaty) law in Chapter 3 on services and Chapter 4 on establishment, goods and capital.
  - Second, the secondary law (the relevant Regulations and Directives), with Chapter 5 on horizontal rules of general application and Chapter 6 on vertical rules applicable specifically to health care, and finally Chapter 7 on new rules for health care covering the newly adopted Patients' Rights Directive and proposed Regulation concerning pharmaceuticals advertising.
- The third section deals with competition law, divided between a Chapter 8 on the rules for undertakings (the cartel and dominance abuse prohibitions as well as

merger control) and Chapter 9 on the rules for public involvement, that is state aid and services of general economic interest.

Together these three sections cover all relevant substantive rules, including the relevant case law of the EU courts. The concluding Chapter 10 draws together some of the general trends highlighted in the individual chapters. 1.87

2

THE EU LAW TOOLBOX

A. The EU Law Toolbox—What Is It and Who Can Use It?

The EU legal toolbox consists of the instruments that shape the contours of EU law on health care but at the same time constitutes the tools that interested parties can use to challenge the behaviour of undertakings, Member States, and/or national rules based on EU law. It is unique, in being more restricted than any comparable national toolbox, but of higher rank in that EU law can trump national rules. The range and scope of the toolbox is certainly more extensive than that at the disposal of any other international or inter-governmental organization. **2.01**

It is important to note that due to the EU legal doctrines of supremacy and direct effect, the use of this toolbox is not solely the preserve of EU institutions. Concerning the internal market freedoms and the legislation based on these TFEU principles, as well as legislation on social issues, we see: **2.02**

- individual rights, in particular the right of consumers to challenge national measures, to demand access to health care provision, or reimbursement of costs;
- guarantees of individual EU rights:
  - against the Member State—the concept of vertical direct effect; and
  - to some extent, against other private actors—the concept of horizontal direct effect.

2.03 The competition and state aid rules are aimed at undertakings but also give rights to undertakings to enforce these rules against their competitors and incumbent providers. Moreover the Member States are barred from denying the competition rules their useful effect ('*effet utile*'); and national rules that cause the competition rules to be infringed must be disapplied by state competition authorities, regulators, and courts.

2.04 To a certain extent the EU law toolbox is oriented to individual rights as opposed to collective rights but various incumbent interest groups and professional associations have not been slow to invoke the public interest exceptions to the TFEU rules to protect their private spoils. At the same time new interest groups (such as market entrants) may avail themselves of the free movement and competition rules to try to break down national barriers to change. In this way interested parties can invoke their EU rights to contribute to the process of negative or market integration. At an even earlier stage in the process of positive or policy harmonization, we see lobbying at Member State and EU level aimed at influencing the legislative process ('rent seeking'). This is not something that we deal with in this book, as this seems more pertinent to a political science based analysis than a legal one. However when discussing individual court cases we come across both types of private action: change seeking and protecting entrenched interests. In colloquial terms, EU law is at once a sword and a shield.

2.05 It is also important to stress that that no right in the EU law toolbox is absolute, for example:

- For the free movement rules there are explicit Treaty exceptions and overriding reasons of public interest which may be invoked provided they are proportionate and, in principle, non-discriminatory. The category of overriding reasons is moreover open-ended.
- The competition rules allow for an efficiency defence as well as a proportionate exception for services of general economic interest (SGEI). The latter holds for the state aid rules too; whereas both sets of rules exclude their application to entities that are not undertakings (but solidarity-based).

2.06 These exceptions act as a corrective factor enabling not only market failures to be addressed but also bringing back national values into the equation. They also mean that actual cases in EU law are almost never based on a simple binary application of the rules, but often depend on a complex balancing process between the competing interests concerned and their claims in EU law. Consequently the role of the European Court of Justice (ECJ) as the ultimate arbiter in the system is of utmost importance.

2.07 Furthermore it is important to emphasize that the EU law in and of itself is not intended to replace or displace national powers and prerogatives, or to lead to deregulation of a particular sector: it merely imposes certain EU level limits on the relevant national competencies. Although it does place sometimes invasive constraints on the exercise of those competencies, this stems from legislative and Treaty making processes that are based on Member State representation and participation in accordance with the constitutional order of the EU. Hence the results are normally legitimate in a formal legal sense.

The toolbox can be invoked to shape and sometimes limit the exercise of national powers by various public authorities, and in this way it has potentially has a major impact on the scope for national choices in the health sector. **2.08**

The nature of the 'toolbox'

The EU law toolbox can best be understood and explained by examining the following three factors: **2.09**

- fundamental principles which aim to operationalize EU law but which also determine the scope and reach of the very tools employed;
- specific principles of relevance to health care systems; and
- general and specific instruments.

B. Fundamental Principles

In order to understand why EU law can have such an impact despite the apparent constraints imposed by Article 168 TFEU it is important to underline the key importance of two intertwined legal concepts. That is two fundamental principles of EU law which are of equal importance as the principle of subsidiarity (acting at the lowest effective level)[1] that Article 168 TFEU enshrines in a sector-specific manner: these are the general EU law principles of supremacy and direct effect. Arguably it is these two qualities that have the most wide ranging implications for the impact of EU law on national health care systems. **2.10**

Supremacy

The supremacy or primacy principle in which EU law takes precedence over national law was first proclaimed by the ECJ in the 1964 *Costa v ENEL* case and was reiterated in the 1970 case *Internationale Handelsgesellschaft* where the ECJ also confirmed that EU law takes precedence over all forms of national law.[2] **2.11**

---

[1] Art 5(3) TEU: Under the principle of subsidiarity, in areas which do not fall within its exclusive competence, the Union shall act only if and insofar as the objectives of the proposed action cannot be sufficiently achieved by the Member States, either at central level or at regional and local level, but can rather, by reason of the scale or effects of the proposed action, be better achieved at Union level.

[2] Case 6/64 *Flaminio Costa v ENEL* [1964] ECR English Special Edn 585; Case 11/70 *Internationale Handelsgesellschaft mbH v Einfuhr- und Vorratsstelle für Getreide und Futtermittel* [1970] ECR 1125.

The primacy principle applies not only to substantive conflicts, when a domestic norm conflicts with EU law, both primary and secondary; it also applies to jurisdictional issues.

2.12 As the ECJ ruled in *Simmenthal* in 1978:

> Every national court must in a case within its jurisdiction apply Union law in its entirety and protect the rights which the latter confers on individuals (…). Accordingly any provision of a national legal system and any legislative, administrative or judicial practice which might impair the effectiveness of Union law by withholding from the national court (…) the power to do everything necessary at the moment of its application to set aside national legislative provisions which might prevent Union rules from have full force and effect are incompatible with those requirements which are the very essence of Community law.[3]

2.13 'Union law' in the sense used above refers not only to the Treaty rules but also to secondary legislation adopted to further the objectives of those same rules. This means that EU law places considerable power in the hands of the national judiciary and that the question of whether provisions of EU law can be directly invoked by individuals—direct effect—is key (see immediately below).

Direct effect

2.14 The doctrine of direct effect is the reverse side of the coin to that of supremacy and if cases such as *Costa v ENEL* affirmed the distinct quality of EU law as a new sovereign legal order, the principle of direct effect concerns those Treaty provisions which contain clear and unconditional prohibitions, such as the TFEU Articles establishing the four fundamental freedoms, and leads to the effective enforcement of this legal order.[4] Indeed the requirement that a Treaty provision should be unconditional was subsequently relaxed in later case law,[5] so that the substance of the test has become focused on whether the provision in question is precise. In effect most Treaty articles can meet this test and hence can be invoked in national courts by individuals to assert their EU law rights and to require national judges to set aside conflicting national legal measures—see in detail Chapters 3 and 4 of this book.

2.15 However, not all Treaty Articles are susceptible to this doctrine. For example, in the case law on Article 107(1) TFEU, which prohibits the grant of state aids, the courts have repeatedly stated that this provision does not have direct effect because the prohibition is not absolute—a state aid may be found to be compatible with the Treaty in accordance with Article 107(3) TFEU. At the same time Article 108(3)

---

[3] Case 106/77 *Amministrazione delle Finanze dello Stato v Simmenthal SpA* [1978] ECR 629, paras 21–22.

[4] Case 26/62 *NV Algemene Transport- en Expeditie Onderneming van Gend & Loos v Netherlands Inland Revenue Administration* [1962] ECR English Special Edn 1.

[5] Case 41/74 *Yvonne van Duyn v Home Office* [1974] ECR 1337.

TFEU, requiring notification of every aid, creates directly effective rights if aid has not been notified—and is therefore per se illegal.

Moreover, the doctrine allows individuals to assert not only rights against public authorities but, in certain situations, also against other undertakings. The TFEU competition rules are addressed to undertakings and their competitors as well as the consumers of their products and services may be entitled to rely upon these rules to challenge certain anti-competitive practices. **2.16**

The doctrine of direct effect has gradually been extended to secondary legislation—first to Regulations and, although more hesitantly, to Directives. The latter in so far as the Court was prepared to recognize that Directives could have 'vertical direct effect' whereas Regulations would always have both 'vertical' and 'horizontal' direct effect (the latter between two private parties). If a Member State fails to implement a Directive within the stated deadline or fails to do so correctly, then it may not rely on its failure to do so and deny an individual the rights guaranteed under that Directive. **2.17**

Vertical direct effect

It should be stressed here that for the purposes of the doctrine of 'vertical direct effect', the concept of the 'state' is wide and the test is largely a functional one: that is to say the ECJ does not look at the formal categories and classifications of national law. It is sufficient that the body in question is carrying out a public service, and for that reason, has special legal powers. In the 2006 health care case *Vasallo,* the Court held that an EU Directive providing that successive fixed term contractual relationships should be converted into a permanent contract could be invoked against an Italian hospital, which although it received public funding was not run by the Italian state: **2.18**

> (...) a directive may be relied on not only against State authorities, but also against organisations or bodies which are subject to the authority or control of the State or have special powers beyond those which result from the normal rules applicable to relations between individuals, such as local or regional authorities or other bodies which, irrespective of their legal form, have been given responsibility, by the public authorities and under their supervision, for providing a public service.[6]

The referring national court had already ruled that the hospital was part of the public sector and performed a public service.

In other cases the ECJ will look at the degree of state control. Private hospitals which (i) do not receive funding from the state and (ii) are not subject to control by a public authority will probably not be subject to this doctrine—see further **2.19**

[6] Case C-180/04 *Andrea Vassallo v Azienda Ospedaliera Ospedale San Martino di Genova e Cliniche Universitarie Convenzionate* [2006] ECR I-7251, para 26 with reference to Case 103/88 *Fratelli Costanzo SpA v Comune di Milano* [1989] ECR 1839, para 31; Case C-188/89 *A. Foster* et al *v British Gas plc* [1990] ECR I-3313, para 19; Case C-157/02 *Rieser Internationale Transporte GmbH v Autobahnen- und Schnellstraßen-Finanzierungs- AG (Asfinag)* [2004] ECR I-1477, para 24.

Chapters 3–7. The mere fact that a (private) body is subject to regulatory control is probably insufficient for a Directive to be invoked against it. Regulatory agencies themselves (including national medicines approval agencies) are however considered 'emanations of the state' and their actions—or inactions—can be reviewed accordingly. As a result, the doctrine of vertical direct effect has important implications in a sector where state involvement is extensive as is the case for health care.

Horizontal direct effect

2.20 Whether horizontal direct effect of the Treaty provisions can be invoked depends on the specific objective and the relevant provision and its place in the overall scheme of the Treaty. Horizontal direct effect of Treaty provisions has been accepted with regard to equal treatment[7] and in employment relations more generally, as well as in relation to the competition rules.[8] The position with respect to the four freedoms, discussed in section 2 of this book (Chapters 3–7), is somewhat more complex. These Articles contain duties for the state authorities but certain 'state-like' regulation by private organizations, such as professional associations, may also be caught by these rules. In its recent case law the ECJ has applied these Treaty obligations to trade unions and to private banks.[9] Horizontal direct effect of Regulations is also accepted,[10] but the doctrine has not been extended to directives.

2.21 The ECJ takes a restricted approach to the doctrine of horizontal direct effect in relation to directives. The rights guaranteed by the directives can be invoked against public authorities or other emanations of the state, however vaguely defined, but not against private actors. Directives are addressed to Member States and failing implementation, private actors cannot be held responsible for the failure of the state. The result it is not however entirely logical. The case law developed in the 1993 health care case *Marshall*, involving compensation for discriminatory dismissal by a health authority, rests on the assumption that if a state fails properly to implement a directive, it should not be entitled to rely on its own failure to deny EU law rights to individuals.[11] This so-called doctrine of estoppel appears difficult to justify in the case of public health authorities. Certainly, the state is responsible

[7] Case 149/77 *Gabrielle Defrenne v Société anonyme belge de navigation aérienne Sabena* [1978] ECR 1365.

[8] Case C-415/93 *Union royale belge des sociétés de football association ASBL v Jean-Marc Bosman, Royal club liégeois SA v Jean-Marc Bosman* et al *and Union des associations européennes de football (UEFA) v Jean-Marc Bosman* [1995] ECR I-4921; Case C-281/98 *Roman Angonese v Cassa di Risparmio di Bolzano SpA* [2000] ECR I-4139.

[9] Case C-438/05 *International Transport Workers' Federation and Finnish Seamen's Union v Viking Line ABP and OÜ Viking Line Eesti* [2007] ECR I-10779; Case C-341/05 *Laval un Partneri Ltd v Svenska Byggnadsarbetareförbundet, Svenska Byggnadsarbetareförbundets avdelning 1, Byggettan and Svenska Elektrikerförbundet* [2007] ECR I-11767; Case C-281/98 *Angonese*, supra n 8.

[10] Case C-253/00 *Antonio Muñoz y Cia SA and Superior Fruiticola SA v Frumar Ltd and Redbridge Produce Marketing Ltd* [2002] ECR I-7289.

[11] Case C-271/91 *M. Helen Marshall v Southampton and South-West Hampshire Area Health Authority* [1993] ECR I-4367.

for implementing directives and public health authorities are part of the state; but at the same time the latter are not responsible for transposing directives into national law. Despite this the ECJ has ruled that directives are enforceable against such public authorities. Treating the emanations of the state as a whole creates legal certainty and effective protection for private actors who incur harm as a result of a breach of its implementing duties.

Triangular direct effect

While a straightforward endorsement of the doctrine of horizontal direct effect of directives by the ECJ remains elusive, the Court has developed supplementary concepts such as 'indirect' and 'incidental' direct effect as well as 'triangular' direct effect which effectively expand the possibilities of private parties to invoke directives against other private actors. As a result these doctrines achieve essentially the same result as if horizontal direct effect had been recognized. **2.22**

The idea of a triangular situation is that a dispute between two parties may affect the legal rights of a third party or impose a financial burden upon them. The ECJ addressed this problem in the 2004 *Wells* case concerning an environmental impact assessment as required by Directive 85/337/EEC.[12] It was ruled that the UK government had failed to implement the Directive properly and as a result Mrs Wells was unable to oppose the granting of a mining authorization for a quarry opposite her home. The ECJ ruled that Mrs Wells could in fact invoke the Directive stating that the failure to implement the Directive had adverse repercussions on a third party. In *Arcor* (2008) the ECJ went on to confirm that additional costs or removal of benefits for a third party (in this case an additional connection charge to offset the costs of the telecommunications local loop) were not a reason to prevent an individual invoking a directive in the national courts.[13] Hence a directive can in fact, under certain conditions, impose obligations on third parties.[14] **2.23**

The Constanzo *doctrine*

The duty to apply the doctrine of direct effect is an obligation for national courts and 'other authorities'. In *Constanzo* (1989) the ECJ stated that when the conditions are met under which the Court has held that individuals may rely on the provisions of a directive before the national courts, then all organs of the administration are obliged to apply these provisions, including decentralized authorities **2.24**

[12] Case C-201/02 *The Queen, ex parte Delena Wells v Secretary of State for Transport, Local Government and the Regions (Wells)* [2004] ECR I-723; Council Dir 85/337/EEC of 27 June 1985 on the assessment of the effects of certain public and private projects on the environment [1985] OJ L175/40.

[13] Joined Cases C-152/07 to C-154/07 *Arcor AG & Co. KG (C-152/07) Communication Services TELE2 GmbH (C-153/07) and Firma 01051 Telekom GmbH (C-154/07) v Bundesrepublik Deutschland* [2008] ECR I-5959.

[14] See A Dashwood, 'From Van Duyn to Mangold via Marshall' [2006] *Cambridge Yearbook of European Legal Studies*, 81, 94ff.

such as municipalities.[15] This means that in the EU law context, administrative authorities are put under a duty to enforce directly effective norms of EU law and to set aside conflicting national legislation even though they cannot use the mechanism of the preliminary ruling (Article 267 TFEU) to request guidance from the ECJ on whether the EU norm has direct effect and whether there is a conflict with national law. Twenty years later, in the 2009 *German pharmacies* case (discussed further in Chapter 4), a German court referred a preliminary question to the ECJ inviting it to reconsider its *Constanzo* doctrine. The Court however refused to answer the question as not being strictly relevant to the case.[16] The facts of the *German pharmacies* judgment show how an administrative authority (the regional government) had erred in disapplying a German federal statue for alleged conflict with EU law, whereas the ECJ found that there was no such conflict at all.

C. Consistent Interpretation

2.25 Even if a directive does not confer clear and unconditional rights, the ECJ has nevertheless required national courts to interpret national law in accordance with EU law. In its 1990 ruling in *Marleasing* the Court required that all national legislation should be interpreted in the light of EU law, irrespective of whether it is implementing legislation or not, and irrespective of whether it was enacted prior or subsequent to the provisions of EU law in question.[17]

2.26 In other words national courts are required as far as possible to interpret their national law in the light of the wording and the purpose of a directive in order to achieve the result pursued by the latter. The ECJ has also ruled that national courts should set aside national rules that conflict with general principles of EU law in 'horizontal situations' in litigation between private parties, as in the *Mangold* case (2005), thus causing considerable controversy.[18] (The ECJ may be required to return to this jurisprudence in the context of the application of the Charter of Fundamental Rights of the European Union to disputes between private parties.)

2.27 As a result of the *Mangold* ruling it was no longer sufficient for a national court to turn to EU law only if a national provision is 'ambiguous'. Its duty is to establish the meaning of the EU obligation and only then to conclude whether it is possible to

[15] Case 103/88 *Fratelli Costanzo SpA v Comune di Milano* [1989] ECR 1839. A competition law equivalent is found in Case C-198/01 *Consorzio Industrie Fiammiferi (CIF) v Autorità Garante della Concorrenza e del Mercato (CIF)* [2003] ECR I-8055.

[16] Joined Cases C-171/07 and C-172/07 *Apothekerkammer des Saarlandes and Others (C-171/07) and Helga Neumann-Seiwert (C-172/07) v Saarland and Ministerium für Justiz, Gesundheit und Soziales (German pharmacies)* [2009] ECR I-4171, paras 15–62.

[17] Case C-106/89 *Marleasing SA v La Comercial Internacional de Alimentacion SA* [1990] ECR I-4135.

[18] Case C-144/04 *Werner Mangold v Rüdiger Helm* [2005] ECR I-9981.

achieve the necessary reconciliation with national law. The duty of 'consistent interpretation' allows directives to govern disputes between private parties. The ECJ has however recognized that the duty of consistent interpretation does not require *contra legem* interpretations of national law: the national courts cannot be required to give an interpretation of national law that flatly contradicts its ordinary meaning. Furthermore the ECJ has been particularly careful to apply this doctrine in the field of criminal law, where the liberties of individuals are at stake.[19] The current debate is about whether national law that pre-dates the directive at issue must still be subject to consistent interpretation; an issue too specialized to be dealt with further here.

The impact of the general doctrine of consistent interpretation on the health care sector can be illustrated by the 2004 *Pfeiffer* case.[20] The Deutsches Rotes Kreuz (the German Red Cross) operated land-based emergency services which are manned round the clock, and stations which are manned for 12 hours per day. Land-based emergency rescue is carried out by means of ambulances and emergency medical vehicles. Mr Pfeiffer and the other complainants were formally employed by the Deutsches Rotes Kreuz as emergency workers. The parties to the main proceedings were at odds in essence over whether, in calculating the period of maximum weekly working time, account should be taken of periods of duty time when the workers were on call ('Arbeitsbereitschaft') and which they were required to do in the course of their employment. **2.28**

The ECJ held that the Working Time Directive at issue applied to all sectors of activity, both public and private, which include services as a whole and further to that the activity of emergency workers run by a body such as the Deutsche Rotes Kreuz were not covered by the exceptions provided in that Directive. The Court then went on to consider whether Article 6(2) of the Directive, which requires Member States to take measures necessary to ensure that the maximum working week did not exceed 48 hours per week, had direct effect. The Court held that on a proper interpretation, Article 6(2) imposed a maximum upper limit on the average working week from which every worker must benefit and a provision of national law which allowed that limit to be exceeded was incompatible with the Directive. The Court then turned to the ensuing consequences of its finding for the case before the national court. It held that Article 6(2) met all the relevant conditions, as it **2.29**

[19] Joined Cases C-387/02, C-391/02 and C-403/02 *Criminal proceedings against Silvio Berlusconi (C-387/02), Sergio Adelchi (C-391/02) and Marcello Dell'Utri and Others (C-403/02)* [2005] ECR I-3565; Case C-168/95 *Criminal proceedings against Luciano Arcaro* [1996] ECR I-4705.

[20] Joined Cases C-397/01 to C-403/01 *Bernhard Pfeiffer (C-397/01)* et al *v Deutsches Rotes Kreuz, Kreisverband Waldshut eV* [2004] ECR I-8835. cf the case note by S Prechal, 'Joined Cases C-397/01 to C-403/01 Bernhard Pfeiffer et al' [2005] *Common Market Law Review* 1445; S Prechal, 'Direct Effect, Indirect Effect, Supremacy and the Evolving Constitution of the European Union' in C Barnard (ed), *The Fundamentals of EU Law Revisited: Assessing the Impact of the Constitutional Debate?* (Oxford: Oxford University Press, 2007) 35.

imposed a precise and unconditional obligation on Member States but also went on to recall that such a provision could not of itself apply in proceedings between private parties. Nonetheless it was the responsibility of national courts to provide the legal protection which individuals derive from the rules of EU law and to ensure those rules are fully effective. They must therefore interpret national law in conformity with EU law and consider national law as a whole in order to assess to what extent it can be applied so as not to produce a result contrary to the Directive and to achieve an outcome which is consistent with that Directive's objectives. It followed that the national court must do whatever lies within its jurisdiction to ensure that the maximum working week of 48 hours was not exceeded. This line of case law has been confirmed in numerous recent cases on direct effect and consistent interpretation.[21]

D. State Liability

State liability for non-implementation

2.30 There can be situations where the doctrine of indirect effect only partially addresses the 'gap' left by directives just having vertical direct effect. In particular it will not help individuals where there is no national law to interpret or where national law directly contradicts the directive. This scenario arose in the key case of *Francovich* (1991) where Italy had persistently failed to implement a directive intended to guarantee a minimum level of protection for employees in the event of the insolvency of their employer.[22] The Commission had successfully brought an enforcement action against the Italian government for its failure to transpose the directive but even after that ruling, there was still no transposition. *Francovich* concerned an action against the Italian state brought by a number of employees who were owed compensation by employers who had gone bankrupt. They claimed for the losses they had suffered as a result of the state's liability to transpose the directive. The ECJ confirmed that the state would be liable to pay damages in such a situation, albeit subject to three conditions:

- the result prescribed by the directive should entail the grant of rights to individuals;
- it should be possible to identify the content of those rights on the basis of the provisions of the directive; and
- a causal link must be established between the breach of the state's obligations and the damage or loss suffered by the injured parties.

[21] See further, M Dougan, 'When Worlds Collide: Competing visions of the relationship between Direct Effect and Supremacy' [2007] *Common Market Law Review* 931.

[22] Joined Cases C-6/90 and C-9/90 *Andrea Francovich and Danila Bonifaci and others v Italian Republic* [1991] ECR I-5357.

In the 1995 cases *Brasserie de Pecheur* and *Factortame*, the ECJ went on to establish state liability on the basis of Article 340 TFEU where a Member State has infringed a Treaty provision (in this case Articles 34 and 49 TFEU).[23] Again the Court attached conditions to this liability, essentially in the same terms as in *Francovich*. These are that: (i) the provision in question must be intended to confer rights on individuals; (ii) the breach must be sufficiently serious; and (iii) there must be a causal link between the damage sustained by the injured parties and the breach of the obligation resting on the state. Moreover, in cases where the provision in question leaves no discretion to the Member State there is no requirement for the breach to be sufficiently serious. Hence Member States will be deemed to have no discretion where they have totally failed to implement a directive. (More recently, the ECJ has indicated that these are not the only circumstances where this condition may be waived.)[24] **2.31**

The health care sector has not been immune to the 'state liability' or 'non-contractual' liability doctrine. In the 2008 *Synthon* case, the UK government was held liable for initially refusing to recognize the marketing authorization of a medicinal product for the treatment of depression, that had been certified by the Danish authorities, on the grounds that the breach was a sufficiently serious one—this in spite the fact that the United Kingdom subsequently granted the licence on re-submission of Synthon's application.[25] The UK government refused to grant a marketing authorization in the first instance on the ground that the product was not 'essentially similar' to that authorized in Denmark. The United Kingdom did not rely on public health arguments in this situation but argued that the so-called mutual recognition procedures (see Chapters 5 and 6) did not apply in this type of case, which concerned a so-called abridged procedure. The original marketing authorization holder—SmithKline Beecham—had in fact challenged the Danish authorization. However the ECJ confirmed that the Danish authorization was properly granted under the abridged procedure.[26] **2.32**

The ECJ held that this refusal was sufficiently serious as the provision in the Directive at issue in this case, albeit not entirely clear in its terminology, allowed Member States no discretion to refuse mutual recognition unless they followed a special procedure, which had not been invoked by the UK government in this case. This breach was capable of rendering the United Kingdom liable in damages and indeed the UK government agreed on an informal cash settlement of some £34 million. **2.33**

[23] Joined Cases C-46/93 and C-48/93 *Brasserie du Pêcheur SA v Bundesrepublik Deutschland and The Queen v Secretary of State for Transport, ex parte: Factortame Ltd and others* [1996] ECR I-1029.

[24] cf eg Case C-470/03 *AGM-COS.MET Srl v Suomen valtio and Tarmo Lehtinen* [2007] ECR I-2749 and Case C-452/06 *The Queen, ex parte Synthon BV v Licensing Authority of the Department of Health (Synthon)* [2008] ECR I-7681.

[25] Case C-452/06 *Synthon*, supra n 24.

[26] See Case C-74/03 *SmithKline Beecham plc v Lægemiddelstyrelsen* [2005] ECR I-595.

2.34 Liability will probably be easy to establish if there has been a complete failure to transpose a directive, or there is breach of an order of the ECJ, or there has been a breach of settled case law. In other circumstances, for example where a directive has been inadequately transposed, or the case law is not completely settled, the court looks at the clarity of the legal provisions concerned. If there is no consensus on the meaning of the provision then no liability will be found; but liability may well be established if the Member State is breaching EU law in a manner that must be obvious to them and which leaves little room for doubt.[27] State liability can therefore be seen as a back stop measure which is intended to penalize the state rather than to guarantee redress for individuals, even though the latter often drive the legal process.

2.35 Liability may also arise where a Member State has failed to implement a directive correctly and this same directive has been the subject of case law clarifying its interpretation. The persistent failure of Germany to fully implement the Working Time Directive in the health care sector has led the Court to consider this to be a sufficiently serious breach which can be remedied in damages (as discussed in Chapter 5).

Useful effect

2.36 Above we have mainly discussed the direct effect of secondary EU law. As was mentioned at the outset however the primary provisions of the Treaty also have vertical direct effect, and can additionally have horizontal direct effect. This last holds true for the competition rules which, because they are targeted at undertakings, must by definition be capable of being invoked horizontally. In EU competition law therefore the reverse problem has been tackled: invoking the competition rules against the Member States (that is to say vertically) where they impose or abet competition law infringements by undertakings. Such a rule is necessary because under the so-called 'state action doctrine' undertakings are not liable for competition law infringements that are the result of obligations imposed by the Member States—that is, not of the free will of the private parties involved. The key case in this respect is *Van Eycke*.[28] Here the ECJ held that:

> (...) Articles 85 and 86 of the Treaty [now Articles 101 and 102 TFEU], in conjunction with Article 5 [now Article 4 TFEU], require the Member States not to introduce or maintain in force measures, even of a legislative nature, which may render ineffective the competition rules applicable to undertakings. Such would be the case, the Court has held, if a Member State were to require or favour the adoption of agreements, decisions or concerted practices contrary to Article 85 [now Articles 101 TFEU] or to reinforce their effects, or to deprive its own legislation of its official character by delegating to private traders responsibility for taking decisions affecting the economic sphere.[29]

[27] cf Case C-452/06 *Synthon*, supra n 24, Opinion of AG Sharpston.
[28] Case 267/86 *Pascal Van Eycke v ASPA NV* [1988] ECR 4769.
[29] ibid, para 16.

Hence, based on the principle of loyal cooperation under the Treaties, Member States are barred from condoning or imposing anti-competitive conduct. Undertakings will remain liable to the extent that they restrict the remaining scope for competition of their own accord.[30] Once state action has been withdrawn the undertakings concerned are fully liable for their conduct from that point on. **2.37**

Finally in the *CIF* (2003) case the ECJ confirmed the duty of Member States' authorities (including not only competition authorities as in *CIF* but also regulatory authorities and courts) not to apply national legislation that caused infringements of EU competition law.[31] **2.38**

> (...) where undertakings engage in conduct contrary to Article 101 TFEU and where that conduct is required or facilitated by national legislation which legitimises or reinforces the effects of the conduct, specifically with regard to price-fixing or market-sharing arrangements, a national competition authority, one of whose responsibilities is to ensure that Article 101 TFEU is observed:
> - has a duty to disapply the national legislation;
> - may not impose penalties in respect of past conduct on the undertakings concerned when the conduct was required by the national legislation;
> - may impose penalties on the undertakings concerned in respect of conduct subsequent to the decision to disapply the national legislation, once the decision has become definitive in their regard.[32]

Hence, in line with what was stated above, the liability of the undertakings involved only begins from the time when the national measures concerned are disapplied. This case law provides what is potentially a powerful new tool to decentralized national authorities and complainants invoking EU law alike. However, in spite of the clarity of the EU doctrine involved, these types of authorities may be reluctant to set aside democratically legitimized measures in order to enforce EU law based claims and it is to be expected that before a full-blown practice evolves in this respect they may require backing by further prejudicial decisions of the ECJ. At the same time it should be recalled that only judicial bodies, and not regulatory institutions or competition authorities, can refer cases to the ECJ. **2.39**

E. Enforcement and EU Law Venues

It is a matter of the national law of each individual Member State to designate the courts that control access to EU law remedies and to determine the procedures by which they function. This ground rule was determined by the ECJ in its *Rewe* and **2.40**

[30] cf eg Joined Cases C-359/95 P and C-379/95 P *Commission of the European Communities and French Republic v Ladbroke Racing Ltd* [1997] ECR I-6265.

[31] Case C-198/01 *CIF*, supra n 15.

[32] ibid, para 58.

Comet judgments in 1976.[33] So far, competition law is the main exception in the EU system—here there is some harmonization but this is by no means complete. This is discussed in the next section. Public procurement is another exception given the partial harmonization of legal remedies involved (see Chapter 6).

Decentralized enforcement

2.41 The administrative application of EU antitrust law was originally highly centralized with a notification requirement for possibly anti-competitive agreements and the European Commission having a legal monopoly on exemption from the cartel prohibition. National courts have of course always played an independent role, given the direct effect of Articles 101 and 102 TFEU, but it was quite different because the prohibition of restrictive agreements in Article 101(1) TFEU was strictly applied and only the Commission had the power to grant exemptions based on Article 101(3) TFEU. That meant that where Article 101(3) TFEU was at issue, clearance by the Commission was required (although in time collective, or block exemptions, were issued for particular types of agreements). This no longer applies.

2.42 With the coming into force of Regulation 1/2003 in May 2004 a new decentralized system of EU competition law enforcement came into being.[34] All Member States must have independent national competition authorities (NCAs) that are competent to apply the cartel and abuse of dominance prohibitions in Articles 101 and 102 TFEU and to adopt cease and desist orders, impose fines, and so forth. If such behaviour has an EU dimension—effect on trade between the Member States[35]—the application of these EU provisions is mandatory. The NCAs, like the European Commission, may act either on their own accord, based on a complaint, or based on a referral from another competition authority. The NCAs and the Commission collaborate in the European Competition Network (ECN) which aims to pool experience and identify best practice.

2.43 Merger cases are covered not by Regulation 1/2003 but by the Merger Control Regulation that allocates cases based on a complex threshold system that is described in Chapter 8: only mergers with an EU dimension are vetted at EU level.[36] This allocation of cases is not absolute. At the request of the NCA (or NCAs) concerned, a merger that falls below the threshold can be dealt with at EU level, just as a merger

[33] Case 33/76 *Rewe-Zentralfinanz eG and Rewe-Zentral AG v Landwirtschaftskammer für das Saarland* [1976] ECR 1989; Case 45/76 *Comet BV v Produktschap voor Siergewassen* [1976] ECR 2043.

[34] Council Reg (EC) No 1/2003 of 16 December 2002 on the implementation of the rules on competition laid down in Articles 81 and 82 of the Treaty [2003] OJ L1/1.

[35] Commission Notice—Guidelines on the effect on trade concept contained in Articles 81 and 82 of the Treaty [2004] OJ C101/81.

[36] Council Reg (EC) No 139/2004 of 20 January 2004 on the control of concentrations between undertakings (the EC Merger Regulation) [2004] OJ L24/1.

with an EU dimension that predominantly has effects within a single Member State may be referred down to an NCA.

Finally because the cartel and abuse of dominance prohibitions are directly effective they may be invoked by interested (private) parties before national courts. If an agreement is found to be restrictive a national court may determine which parts of it (or the whole) are, as a consequence, legally void. Interested (private) parties may also file a complaint with their NCA and/or with the European Commission. Chapter IV of Regulation 1/2003, on cooperation, also provides for the decentralized coordination of judicial enforcement and for a limited encroachment into national procedural autonomy. National courts cannot take decisions concerning the application of Articles 101 and 102 TFEU running counter to a decision that has already been adopted by the Commission. National courts must also avoid giving decisions which would conflict with a decision that the Commission intends to take in proceedings it has initiated. This may require the national court to stay its proceedings.[37] **2.44**

Venues for the application of EU law

Due to the direct effect of many Treaty provisions (including those on free movement and competition), as well as Regulations, vertical direct effect of directives and the various ways discussed above that create near horizontal direct effect for directives, almost all EU law that is relevant to health care can be invoked in proceedings between national courts and tribunals. In addition, competition law based complaints are possible before NCAs and the European Commission. **2.45**

Similarly, private parties may complain to the Commission of infringements of both the Treaty rules and secondary legislation in an attempt to trigger the launch of Treaty infringement proceedings by the Commission against the Member State concerned. In practice recourse to national judicial proceedings where EU law is invoked either by way of justification of certain private practices, to attack public strictures, or both, is likely to be more effective in individual cases. The reason why judicial action may be more effective is that infringement procedures require prioritization by the Commission, and are to some extent politicized and time-consuming, and will not result in a remedy for the complaining individual as infringement proceedings concern a general failure to apply EU law correctly, and do not aim to resolve a particular private dispute. **2.46**

Finally we should mention prejudicial proceedings—also called preliminary rulings—under Article 267 TFEU—in which a national court (often the highest **2.47**

[37] Council Reg (EC) 1/2003, supra n 34. Art 16 on the uniform application of Community competition law. cf Commission Notice on the co-operation between the Commission and the courts of the EU Member States in the application of Articles 81 and 82 EC [2004] OJ C101/54; Commission Notice on cooperation within the Network of Competition Authorities [2004] OJ C101/43.

court responsible for hearing a particular type of case at national level) stays its proceedings and addresses a question to the ECJ on one or more points of EU law that must be interpreted correctly in order to decide the case. Needless to say this prejudicial procedure, although frequently time-consuming, is a key process in ensuring the unity of EU law. The ECJ can only be addressed by a private party by means of a direct action if the proceedings relate to an act of an EU institution (see below). The prejudicial procedure ensures that at least the questions raised by private parties before their national courts can be brought to the highest EU judicial level.

2.48 At the same time, recourse to so-called direct actions against acts of the EU institutions is restricted for 'non-privileged' actors, as provided for in Article 263(4) TFEU. These institutions include the Commission, the Parliament, the Council, the General Court and the ECJ as well as the Court of Auditors. Their roles and powers are set out in the Treaties. It is only where the applicant can establish that it is directly and individually affected by an EU act that it can have a right to challenge the act in question. Similarly, although the Treaty makes provision for non-privileged actors to bring an action for failure to act against the EU institutions, the legal hurdles are considerable and the results, even if successful, are usually meagre.

F. Conclusion

2.49 The EU toolbox is complex, varied, and dynamic, as we have seen. In this concluding section we summarize five of its main features—features which will be developed in the subsequent chapters.

Direct effect and state liability

2.50 First, it should be recalled that primary Treaty law, and in particular the rules on free movement and competition, apply in full to the health care sector and to national health care systems. The Treaty provides no general exception for the sector as such. These rules form part of the EU's economic and social constitution, and are underpinned by the principles of supremacy and direct effect. This allows individuals to invoke the rights guaranteed by the TFEU to challenge not only restrictions on the exercise of those rights imposed by governments but also, in certain cases, by third parties.

2.51 Second, as we have shown, the doctrines of vertical direct effect, as well as indirect effect and the related doctrine of triangular direct effect, and the doctrine of consistent interpretation allow individuals to invoke the rights given to them under the relevant directives and to challenge national laws which do not properly implement EU directives. This particular tool is an important complement to the right of the Commission, as guardian of the Treaties, to bring infringement actions against errant Member States. It is also an important gateway for individuals and associations to raise actions in their national courts and to have those courts refer questions of interpretation to the European courts. Even if the doctrine of direct effect has certain limits and the European courts continue to refuse to endorse the concept of full horizontal direct effect, the doctrine of state liability may function as a back stop.

It should be noted that as a result, the fundamental principles discussed in this chapter are more likely to be of use for parties seeking to challenge elements of their national health care systems than to be of use as a basis for challenging EU action, or for the very failure of EU action (and by implication a failure of the Member States to reach consensus on such action) in the health care field. **2.52**

Exceptions

Third, *no rights are absolute*. The TFEU Articles on the four freedoms, competition, and on state aid, all make provision for those defending a restriction on the right in question to invoke an exception. For example, Article 36 TFEU provides that the Treaty does not preclude restrictions on imports of goods justified on the grounds of protecting the health and the life of humans. A similar exemption is available for restrictions on freedom to provide services, freedom of establishment and freedom of persons, on the basis of 'protection of public health', although the European courts have interpreted these exemptions restrictively. **2.53**

In addition the European courts have recognized that non-discriminatory restrictions on freedom to provide services, freedom of establishment and the free movement of goods can be justified in pursuance of an objective public interest ('overriding reason of public interest'). This so-called 'rule of reason' approach has led the ECJ to recognize that various national interests are directly relevant in health care contexts; for instance, the application of professional rules, including rules relating to the organization of professions, the social protection provided by national social security systems and the financial viability of these systems. The European courts have been relatively stalwart in their deference to national concerns, especially in relation to a national state's right to determine how it organizes its health care system, how it finances it and the level of health protection it seeks to aspire to. This topic is further explored in detail in section 2 of this book (Chapters 3–7). **2.54**

Furthermore, the EU courts have not been prepared to allow the internal market objective to maintain the upper hand and have often been sensitive to national petitions in the name of social cohesion. Member States are entitled to protect undertakings providing universal service (or SGEI) from the 'stiff winds' of competition and to finance providers of services of general economic interest (we shall explore this in detail in Chapter 9). **2.55**

At the same time the EU courts have not been prepared to give carte blanche to the Member States' prerogatives at the expense of either internal market goals or the **2.56** goal of ensuring proper implementation of secondary legislation to guarantee a genuinely uniform application of the law. New legal principles have been fashioned—including the overriding principles of transparency, non-discrimination, and consistency—and imposed as requirements on Member States if they try to invoke these various exceptions provided for in the Treaty, as will be discussed in the following chapters. That said it should not be overlooked that the procedural autonomy of Member States, although subject to the ECJ's requirements of equivalence and effectiveness,[38] is still a potential hurdle to the enforcement of the rights discussed in this Chapter.[39]

Negative and positive integration

2.57 Taken together these various aspects of the EU toolbox have proved an important force for the process of what is often called negative integration (or market integration)—using Treaty provisions to remove disparities in national regimes. As such they provide an important counter-balance to the relative lack of momentum for, as well as progress on, positive or policy integration in recent years. Market integration—or negative integration—has been propelled by the ECJ's assertive case law requiring states to refrain from interfering with free trade and free movement of persons and services by removing barriers: striking down national rules. However it was often thought that policy integration—or positive integration—could not be brought about by judicial fiat alone: new common norms cannot be set by judges. It must now be recognized that this imbalance is no longer so obvious. Once policy integration based on common norms is introduced in a certain sector, and often as a response to judicial activism striking down barriers, then in a further stage, primacy and direct effect will give teeth to such secondary legislation.

2.58 This results in broader relevance of EU law: in fact today *policy* integration norms are more often invoked by individuals before national courts than *market* integration norms. This may well justify the claim that EU law has become a charter not just of economic rights but also of consumer rights, social rights, and citizenship rights, all of which are of considerable importance to the health care sector.[40] An obvious example of this trend is the Patients' Rights Directive which codifies, but also expands on, the case law on the freedom to provide and receive services.[41]

---

[38] Case 33/76 *Rewe*, supra n 33.

[39] For a further discussion see, M Dougan, 'Remedies and Procedures for Enforcing Union Law' in P Craig and G De Burca (eds), *The Evolution of EU Law* (2nd edn, Oxford: Oxford University Press, 2011), 408.

[40] See N Reich, 'A European Constitution for Citizens. Reflections on Rethinking of Union and Community Law' [1997] *European Law Journal* 131; B De Witte, 'Direct Effect, Primacy and the Nature of the Legal Order' in P Craig and G De Burca (eds) supra n 39, 359.

[41] Directive 2011/24/EU of the European Parliament and of the Council of 9 March 2011 on the application of patients' rights in cross-border healthcare [2011] OJ L88/45.

Fourth, there are key legal principles which limit progress on positive integration: notably subsidiarity—acting at the lowest effective level of government; and proportionality—meaning that measures must be suitable, necessary in the sense of the least intrusive effective means and applied after balancing the interests involved. **2.59**

Fifth, and finally, secondary legislation varies in scope in terms of its impact on the residual powers of Member States; although soft law is gradually making room for hard law in health care and maximum harmonization is now generally preferred over minimum harmonization for market building purposes. **2.60**

3

THE PRIMARY LAW OF THE INTERNAL MARKET: SERVICES

A. Introduction

The internal market has long been the core project of the EU (see Chapter 1). With the more recent emergence of EU economic and monetary policy; EU citizenship; and the creation of an area of freedom, security and justice without internal frontiers, the internal market has become one among multiple EU objectives—albeit, arguably, still the basis of European integration—as was reaffirmed in the Lisbon Treaty that came into force on 1 December 2009 (amending the TEU and TFEU, it is the latter to which we will generally refer as it contains the main material provisions of primary EU law regarding the internal market and competition). The internal market is based on the interplay between the abolition of national barriers (negative or market integration, also known as liberalization) and the creation of common norms at EU level (positive or policy integration, also known as harmonization). **3.01**

In this context health care is just one economic sector among many and it is subject to horizontal rules that apply broadly across sectors, such as the primary law, Treaty freedoms themselves, and the secondary law of EU legislation. The latter consists of **3.02** general (or horizontal) rules on areas such as services, insurance and coordination of social security which are not health care specific but apply across economic sectors. In addition there is a small but growing body of sector specific (or vertical) law concerning health care, notably the recent Patients' Rights Directive,[1] but also on tobacco products, pharmaceuticals and medical devices. This secondary law, both general and sector-specific, will be dealt with in Chapters 5 and 6 respectively, followed by Chapter 7 on new health care legislation which is consumer based. In Chapter 7 we will also examine whether in the health care sector, as in others, negative (market) integration has triggered positive (policy) integration, and whether liberalization and harmonization are operating in tandem as the internal market rules spill over into areas that were hitherto considered to be excluded from the scope of EU law.

3.03 First however we will see what the effect of the Treaty freedoms—and of the individual rights that are based upon them—has been on the rights of EU citizens and on market access in the health care sector.

3.04 This chapter focuses on the freedom to provide and receive services, which has been the most significant of the four freedoms to come into play in the health care sector so far. This freedom is one of the most significant instruments in the European legal toolbox. The next chapter covers the remaining three freedoms: establishment, goods, and capital.

B. The Role of the Treaty Freedoms

3.05 As regards primary law, the legal framework for the discussion of health care consists of the freedoms of services, establishment, goods, and capital; and (to a lesser extent) Article 168 TFEU (Title XIV) on public health. The Treaty also contains secondary references to public health and health in the context of proposals for harmonization in Articles 52 and 114(3) TFEU, as well as concerning complementary action to protect workers' health and safety in Article 153(1).[2] Finally, Article 6(a) TFEU includes among the activities of the EU 'the protection and improvement of human health'. These have already been discussed in the introductory chapter and that discussion will not be repeated here. This brings us to the discussion of the directly effective provisions of the TFEU that do not specifically concern health care but are of general application and therefore also include health care.

---

[1] Directive 2011/24/EU of the European Parliament and the Council of 9 March 2011 on the application of patients' rights in cross-border healthcare.

[2] For a general overview of EU health law see T Hervey and J McHale, *Health Law and the European Union* (Cambridge: Cambridge University Press, 2004). Also T Hervey, 'Mapping the contours of European Union health law and policy' [2002] *European Public Law 2002* 69.

Direct effect of Treaty provisions means they can be invoked by individuals before a court of law (see Chapter 2).

The context to this discussion is the following. The European ambitions in the Member States have gradually evolved to include the creation of EU citizenship, an area of freedom, security and justice, a common foreign policy, and an economic and monetary union. From the outset however the internal market has been the heart—and thereby the engine—of European integration. Incidentally, this internal market is not a goal in and of itself but serves to realise the broader social and economic objectives such as that are now set out in Article 3(3) TEU: 3.06

> The Union shall establish an internal market. It shall work for the sustainable development of Europe based on balanced economic growth and price stability, a highly competitive social market economy, aiming at full employment and social progress, and a high level of protection and improvement of the quality of the environment. It shall promote scientific and technological advance.

This internal market concerns creating an area, spanning all 27 Member States, that does not have internal legal boundaries in the sense of quantitative restrictions (tariffs), measures of equivalent effect, or barriers to market access—with or without distinction by nationality (direct or indirect discrimination). This area consists of different dimensions, the four so-called 'freedoms'. These freedoms respectively concern the free movement of goods, of persons (which includes the free movement of workers and freedom of establishment), of services, and of capital (and of payment). 3.07

In order to realise the internal market these freedoms must be promoted effectively. This is possible because they have vertical direct effect: a citizen can invoke one or more of the Treaty freedoms in court, against the government, in order to have a judge strike down the legal measure that is at odds with this freedom. In addition, it has gradually become generally recognized that certain freedoms may have horizontal direct effect as well (so far with the exception of the free movement of goods, presumably given the existence of a regime of competition law in the Treaty).[3] This means that citizens will also be able to invoke the Treaty freedoms against each other—in a health care context, for instance, patients may invoke them against insurers or health care providers, or the latter may invoke the freedoms against each other (see Chapter 2). The courts have a duty to uphold rights derived from the Treaty principles. 3.08

[3] Case 36/74 *B.N.O. Walrave, L.J.N. Koch v Association Union Cycliste internationale, Koninklijke Nederlandsche Wielren Unie and Federación Española Ciclismo* [1974] ECR 1405; Case 149/77 *Gabrielle Defrenne v de Belgische luchtvaartmaatschappij NV Sabena* [1978] ECR 1365; Case C-415/93 *Union royale belge des sociétés de football association ASBL v Jean-Marc Bosman (Bosman)* [1995] ECR I-4921; Case C-176/96 *Jyri Lehtonen and Castors Canada Dry Namur-Braine ASBL v Fédération royale belge des sociétés de basket-ball ASBL (FRBSB)* [2000] ECR I-2681; Case C-281/98 *Roman Angonese v Cassa di Risparmio di Bolzano SpA.* [2000] ECR I-4139; Case C-519/04P *David Meca-Medina and Igor Majcen v Commission* [2006] ECR I-6991.

3.09 In this book our emphasis will be on the freedom to provide (and receive) services and the freedom of establishment (see Chapter 4). This is because these are the freedoms that have been most contested in the health care context so far. To the extent that it is effective in removing market barriers this process generates a demand for EU solutions (of which the Patients' Rights Directive is the foremost example) in a policy area where the Member States had earlier deliberately attempted to foreclose EU involvement (Article 168(7) TFEU). As we will see this appears broadly consistent with a view that sees negative integration (removing national barriers) triggering positive integration (the adoption of common norms).

3.10 The freedoms interdict both direct and indirect discrimination. Direct discrimination involves an explicit distinction based on nationality, while indirect discrimination involves rules that are formally indistinct (that is to say a seemingly 'neutral' criterion, such as a language requirement, is used and applied to everyone indistinctly) yet, in their effect, impact on parties from other Member States disproportionately. Another relevant aspect is that over time the ECJ has fashioned a general prohibition of barriers to trade from the Treaty freedoms, which are originally prohibitions of discrimination (the freedom of capital already followed directly from the Treaty). For services and establishment, the *Säger* (1991) and *Gebhard* (1995) cases are generally cited in this context. In the health care context, the main reference is *Deutsche Paracelsus Schulen* (2002). The latter case concerned the free movement of services and freedom of establishment with respect to natural healers. With regard to the free movement of goods, reference is generally made to the earlier, landmark cases of the 1970s: *Dassonville* (1974) and *Cassis de Dijon* (1979).[4] The ECJ often immediately applies a prohibition of barriers without examining discrimination. It should be noted however there is only a slight difference between the prohibition of indirect discrimination and a prohibition of barriers to trade.

3.11 The application of EU law is generally examined using the following three parts:

1. What legal rule is applicable?
2. Is a breach of this rule involved?
3. Is there an exception that is applicable?

This means that for the protection of legitimate public interests that involve a breach of one of the Treaty freedoms an appeal can usually be made to one of the limited set of Treaty exceptions set out in the sections that deal with goods, respectively services and capital in Titles II and IV of Part Three of the TFEU (such

[4] Case C-76/90 *Manfred Säger v Dennemeyer & Co. Ltd* [1991] ECR I-4221; Case C-55/94 *Reinhard Gebhard v Consiglio dell'Ordine degli Avvocati e Procuratori di Milano* [1995] ECR I-4165; Case C-294/00 *Deutsche Paracelsus Schulen für Naturheilverfahren GmbH v Kurt Gräbner* [2002] ECR I-6515; Case 8/74 *Procureur des Konings v Benoît and Gustave Dassonville* [1974] ECR 837; Case 120/78 *Rewe-Zentral AG v Bundesmonopolverwaltung für Branntwein (Cassis de Dijon)* [1979] ECR 649.

as public policy, public security and public health in Articles 36, 52 and 62). These cover measures both with distinction (also known as directly discriminatory measures) and measures without distinction (not directly discriminatory, but indirectly discriminatory or involving barriers to trade between the Member States). However only the latter are covered by the unwritten overriding reasons of public interest.[5] In both cases benefitting from the exceptions involves invoking a legitimate public interest (subject to limited judicial review) that cannot serve a purely economic motive (that is to say the EU interest prevails by definition in the economic realm). However, as we will see in subsequent health care cases that the ECJ does not always apply this dogmatic distinction between discriminatory and non-discriminatory restrictions in a consistent manner. (Nor does it strictly exclude economic arguments: overriding reasons based on planning considerations and protecting the financial balance of the social security system are acceptable.) This is in line with a view that concentrates on market barriers. Both Treaty exceptions and overriding reasons of public interest are subject to a proportionality test, which likewise comes in three parts. This means verifying whether:

1. the measure is suitable to attain the goal set;[6]
2. the measure is necessary (the least restrictive means);[7] and
3. an adequate balancing of the national interest invoked against the EU interest of the internal market has been carried out.[8]

Hence the restrictions of free movement have to be proportional to the public interest invoked in the abovementioned sense. The case law shows how the tensions between the private individual seeking recourse against public measures based on the EU rules on the one hand and the appeal by the national authorities to public interest exceptions on the other hand play out in practice. Whenever possible the EU courts tend to favour procedural solutions and, as will be seen below, so far they tend to favour individual consumers/patients over health care providers. This also explains why the freedom to receive services is more advanced than the freedom of establishment, as can be seen from the fact that EU legislation has been adopted to codify this case law—the Patients' Rights Directive.[9] What adds greatly to the force of the Treaty freedoms is that the rights involved can be invoked by citizens against their own Member State: there is no need for an 'out of state' test.[10] **3.12**

[5] Case 120/78 *Cassis de Dijon*, supra n 4.

[6] Case C-189/95 *Criminal proceedings against Harry Franzén* [1997] ECR I-5909.

[7] Case 120/78 *Cassis de Dijon*, supra n 4.

[8] Case 302/86 *Commission v Denmark (Danish bottles)* [1988] ECR 4607.

[9] Dir 2011/24/EU of the European Parliament and of the Council of 9 March 2011 on the application of patients' rights in cross-border healthcare [2011] OJ L88/45.

[10] Case C-451/03 *Servizi Ausiliari Dottori Commercialisti Srl v Giuseppe Calafiori* [2006] ECR I-2941.

3.13 Finally, it should be noted that the exception for services of general economic interest (SGEI) found in Article 106(2) TFEU, which is generally invoked with respect to the competition rules, also forms an exception to the four freedoms.[11] This provision is dealt with in detail in Chapter 9. Unlike the free movement exceptions mentioned above, which are not valid if economic considerations predominate, SGEI explicitly concern economic services. They obtain the privileged status of SGEI if they serve to provide universal services designated by the competent public authorities. Here too a proportionality test applies, alongside the need of a clear statement of what the SGEI involves.

C. Services

3.14 The category of services is defined in Article 57 TFEU by means of exclusion with reference to the scope of the other freedoms:

> Services shall be considered to be 'services' within the meaning of the Treaties where they are normally provided for remuneration, in so far as they are not governed by the provisions relating to freedom of movement for goods, capital and persons.

3.15 It is clear from this definition that consideration is a key dimension. As we will see, this even played a role in national health service (NHS) cases such as *Watts*: here the focus was on the consideration exchanged for services received outside the NHS system, sidestepping the issue that within the NHS services were fully tax-funded.[12] What remained to be clarified in the case law was whether the service provider, the service, or the consumer of the service would have to cross national borders, or a combination of these three possibilities. The case law on services in health care is also known as 'patient mobility' case law.

3.16 Originally, the case law on patient mobility was limited entirely to interpretations of then Regulation 1408/71 (now Regulation 883/2004)[13] on the coordination of

---

[11] eg Case C-209/98 *Entreprenørforeningens Affalds/Miljøsektion (FFAD) v Københavns Kommune* [2000] ECR I-3743; and the electricity cases: Case C-157/94 *Commission v The Netherlands* [1997] ECR I-5699; Case C-158/94 *Commission v Italy* [1997] ECR I-5789; Case C-159/94 *Commission v France* [1997] ECR I-5815; Case C-160/94 *Commission v Spain* [1997] ECR I-5851.

[12] Case C-372/04 *The Queen, ex parte Yvonne Watts v Bedford Primary Care Trust and Secretary of State for Health* [2006] ECR I-4325. cf Communication from the Commission, Implementing the Community Lisbon programme: Social services of general interest in the European Union (SEC(2006) 516) COM(2006) 177 final, pp 6–7; with reference to Case 352/85 *Bond van Adverteerders* et al *v the Netherlands* [1988] ECR 2085.

[13] Reg (EEC) No 1408/71 of the Council of 14 June 1971 on the application of social security schemes to employed persons and their families moving within the Community [1971] OJ L149/2. Last amended by Reg (EC) No 1992/2006 of the European Parliament and of the Council of 18 December 2006 [2006] OJ L392/1 (hereinafter Reg 1408/71). Replaced by Reg (EC) 883/2004 of the European Parliament and of the Council of 29 April 2004 on the coordination of social security systems [2004] OJ L166/1. cf F Pennings, *European Social Security Law* (5th edn, Antwerp: Intersentia, 2010).

social security schemes, which was grounded in the free movement of workers.[14] For several decades having recourse to this Regulation was the only way in which reimbursement for cross-border health care could be claimed until the scope of the freedom to provide and receive services had been clarified in relation to health care.

In this context the ECJ opted for sometimes extensive readings of the definition of worker, and of the related workers' rights under Regulation 1408/71, notably including the finding in the two *Pierik* (1978–79) judgments that there was an obligation to grant authorization for 'necessary and effective' treatment in another Member State even where such treatment was not covered by national social security legislation in the Member State of affiliation.[15] Hereby the Court directly threatened national control over the scope of social security entitlements. This case law in turn triggered various amendments to Regulation 1408/71 that aimed to reassert Member State control.[16] Thus the original provision in Article 22(2) that authorization may not be refused 'where the treatment in question cannot be provided for the person concerned within the territory of the Member State in which he resides' was eventually replaced by: **3.17**

> (...) where the treatment in question is among the benefits provided for by the legislation of the Member State on whose territory the person concerned resided and where he cannot be given such treatment within the time normally necessary for obtaining the treatment in question in the Member State of residence taking account of his current state of health and the probable course of the disease.

Similarly the concept of 'worker' was replaced with 'employed or self-employed person'. Otherwise, the impact of this early case law was limited.

Following this case law on workers' rights and social security coordination were the initial rulings on the interpretation of the Treaty in relation to health care. In cases concerning the combination of a tourist visit with unspecified medical treatment in *Luisi and Carbone* (1984),[17] and the medical termination of pregnancy (abortion) **3.18**

[14] eg Case 117/77 *Bestuur van het Algemeen Ziekenfonds Drenthe-Platteland v G. Pierik (Pierik I)* [1978] ECR 825; Case 182/78 *Bestuur van het Algemeen Ziekenfonds Drenthe-Platteland v G. Pierik (Pierik II)* [1979] ECR 1977. Both Pierik cases concerned the rights to cross-border health care of pensioners. More recently on pensioners' rights to health care under Reg 1408/71 (now Reg 883/2004), supra n 13: Case C-326/00 *Idryma Koinonikon Asfaliseon (IKA) v Vasileios Ioannidis* [2003] ECR I-1703; Case C-156/01 *R.P. van der Duin v Onderlinge Waarborgmaatschappij ANOZ Zorgverzekeringen UA and Onderlinge Waarborgmaatschappij ANOZ Zorgverzekeringen UA v T.W. van Wegberg-van Brederode* [2003] ECR I-7045; Case C-345/09 *J.A. van Delft* et al *v College van zorgverzekeringen* [2010] judgment of 14 October 2010 (nyr).

[15] Case 117/77 *Pierik I*, supra n 14, para 22; Case 182/78 *Pierik II*, supra n 14, para 13.

[16] V Hatzopolous, 'Health Law and Policy: the Impact of the EU' in G De Burca (ed), *EU Law and the Welfare State: In Search of Solidarity* (Oxford: Oxford University Press, 2005), 125–27.

[17] Joined Cases 286/82 and 26/83 *Luisi and Carbone v Ministero del Tesoro* [1984] ECR 377, para 16.

in *SPUC v Grogan* (1991),[18] the ECJ established the fundamental principle that health care falls within the scope of the freedom to provide services, and that, in this context, Article 56 TFEU (then Article 49 EC) concerns the freedom not only to provide but to receive services. Substantively however, the immediate impact of these cases on national health care systems was a limited one as well.

3.19 This changed quickly with the third generation of case law, starting with the landmark rulings in *Kohll* (1998) and *Decker* (1998),[19] and culminating in *Watts* (2006).[20] It spelled out the implications of free movement for hospital services and outpatient services, and for the various types of Member States health systems (reimbursement, benefits in kind, and NHS). It is this latter case law that is primarily relevant to the development of EU law in relation to patient mobility, as recently codified in the Patients' Rights Directive,[21] and that will now be dealt with in more detail.

D. The Patient Mobility Case Law

Kohll and *Decker*

3.20 The *Kohll* and *Decker* Cases were decided in parallel on 28 April 1998. (Case C-158/96 *Kohll* and Case C-120/95 *Decker* formed the subject of a joint Opinion by Advocate General Tesauro, the ECJ's arguments in both cases are in track, and they were decided on the same day—but separately.) *Kohll* concerned a claim for reimbursement of the costs of dental treatment received by his daughter in Germany by Mr Kohll, a Luxembourg national who had not obtained prior authorization based on Article 22 of Regulation 1408/71. *Decker* concerned the purchase by another Luxembourg national of spectacles in Belgium, likewise without prior authorization. In *Kohll* the applicability of the freedom to provide services of Article 56 TFEU was invoked, in *Decker* it was the free movement of goods under Articles 34 and 36 TFEU.

3.21 At issue were the questions of whether the free movement provisions of the Treaty precluded such authorization requirements, even if (in *Kohll*) their professed aim was to maintain a balanced medical and hospital service available to everyone in a

---

[18] Case C-159/90 *Society for the protection of unborn children Ireland Ltd v Stephen Grogan* [1991] ECR I-4685, para 18.

[19] Case C-158/96 *Raymond Kohll v Union des caisses de maladie (Kohll)* [1998] ECR I-1931; Case C-120/95 *Nicolas Decker v Caisse de maladie des employés privés (Decker)* [1998] ECR I-1831. Annotation by R Giesen, 'Case C-120/95, Nicolas Decker v. Caisse de maladie des employes prives, Judgment of 28 April 1998, Case C-158/96, Raymond Kohll v. Union des caisses de maladie, Judgment of 28 April 1998' [1999] *Common Market Law Review* 841; P Cabral, 'Cross-border medical care in the European Union—bringing down a first wall' [1999] *European Law Review* 387.

[20] Case C-372/04 *Watts*, supra n 12.

[21] Dir 2011/24/EU, supra n 9.

given region. Closely following the reasoning of the Advocate General, both in *Kohll* and in *Decker* the Court construed the applicability of the free movement provisions in three steps:

- The first step was for the ECJ to decide that although, in the absence of harmonization, the Member States remained in control of determining the scope of social security benefits and the conditions for entitlements, they must nevertheless comply with EU law and the national rules at issue were subject to the Treaty rules on free movement. In *Kohll*, citing *Webb* (1981), it held that 'the special nature of certain services does not remove them from the ambit of the fundamental principle of freedom of movement'.[22]
- Next the ECJ ruled that the free movement rules continued to apply in spite of the fact that the national measures concerned might be consistent with a provision of secondary legislation, in this case Article 22 of Regulation 1408/71.
- Third, the ECJ observed that Article 22 of Regulation 1408/71 is only intended to allow an insured person, following authorization, to receive treatment in another Member State with a right to receiving reimbursement at the level established in the Member State of treatment. From this it concluded that Regulation 1408/71 does not regulate or prevent the reimbursement at the level established in the Member State of affiliation (where the person is insured), even without prior authorization.

By taking this approach the ECJ in effect sidestepped the existing secondary legislation in this field. The scope of the latter is under the control of the Member States collectively in the Council, and individually as they determine the coverage of their respective social security regimes. Instead it opened the alternative and parallel route of recourse to the directly effective Treaty provisions themselves, out of reach of the Member States. Thus 'the Court treats Regulation 1408/71 as a specific application of the general Treaty rules on free movement and not as the only occasion in which social security funds may be called upon to reimburse expenses incurred in other Member States', thereby greatly reduced the relevance of Regulation 1408/71 to the reimbursement of health expenditure.[23] Moreover, the resulting two regimes were logically quite distinct. The Council Regulation 1408/71 construed authorization and hence patient mobility not as a right (apart from exceptional cases) but as a privilege. The reverse held for patient mobility based on Article 49 EC (Article 56 TFEU). As this was based on the Treaty freedom to provide services it would come to be seen as constituting a right that **3.22**

[22] Case C-158/96 *Kohll*, supra n 19, para 20; citing Case 279/80 *Criminal proceedings against Alfred John Webb* [1981] ECR 3305, para 10.

[23] V Hatzopoulos, 'Killing national health and insurance systems but healing patients? The European market for healthcare services after the judgments of the ECJ in Vanbraekel and Peerbooms' [2002] *Common Market Law Review* 683, 696.

could only be subjected to a prior authorization requirement under exceptional circumstances.[24]

3.23 Next the ECJ noted that although the prior authorization requirement for reimbursement does not preclude patients from purchasing medical services or medical products in another Member State, they are denied reimbursement if they have not obtained that authorization. Because no similar authorization requirement existed for the reimbursement of medical services or medical products purchased in the Member State of affiliation, this deterred patients from seeking cross-border services and products, as well as the provision to them of such services and products. It therefore constituted a barrier to free movement in both directions.[25]

3.24 In *Decker*, concerning the free movement of goods, the ECJ examined two defences to this finding:

- First, that a barrier might be justified as an overriding reason in the general interest by the risk of seriously undermining the financial balance of the social security system. It is noteworthy that the Court raised this possibility in view of the fact that overriding reasons in the general interest can in principle only be invoked with respect to non-discriminatory measures, whereas the authorization requirement was explicitly discriminatory. Meanwhile, the justification of maintaining the financial balance of the health insurance system had already been accepted in *Duphar* (1984).[26] Under this heading the Court might be condoning the limitation of 'supply-induced demand'.[27] In line with the reasoning provided by the Advocate General,[28] the Court accepted that this did not form an aim of a purely economic nature and could therefore constitute an overriding reason of general interest. In particular in relation to protecting the national hospital infrastructure, the Advocate General held that prior authorization might be legitimate to ensure forward-planning so an adequate number of medical facilities would be available throughout the national territory. The Advocate General had suggested that a prior authorization requirement would be justified in relation to hospital treatment (without further qualification) as opposed to outpatient treatment.[29] He made a similar distinction between reimbursement in full and flat-rate reimbursement, which (unlike the distinction between hospital

[24] cf A van der Mei, 'Cross-border access to medical care: Non-hospital care and waiting lists' [2004] *Legal Issues of Economic Integration* 57, 58; A Kaczorowska, 'A review of the creation by the European Court of Justice of the right to effective and speedy medical treatment and its outcomes' [2006] *European Law Journal* 345.

[25] Case C-158/96 *Kohll*, supra n 19, para 35.

[26] Case 238/82 *Duphar BV and others v The Netherlands* [1984] ECR 523, para 16.

[27] cf Giesen, supra n 19, p 848.

[28] Case 120/95 *Decker*, supra n 19, Opinion of AG Tesauro, para 53. With reference to Case C-275/92 *Her Majesty' s Customs and Excise v Gerhart Schindler and Joerg Schindler* [1994] ECR I-1039, para 60; Case C-415/93 *Bosman*, supra n 3, paras 106–7.

[29] ibid, para 60. Critical, P Cabral, supra n 19, p 394.

and outpatient services) has not played a significant role in the subsequent case law. However, in relation to the purchase of a pair of spectacles, for which the reimbursement rules in Luxembourg provided for a flat rate, the Luxembourg Government had to concede that there could not be any effect on the financing or balance of the social security system.

- Next, the Court rejected the argument that the quality of treatment could be invoked on the ground of protection of human health under Article 36 TFEU in this context. Given the existence of harmonization and mutual recognition of professional education and training, and as the spectacles concerned were purchased on an ophthalmologist's prescription, the rules at issue could not be justified on this ground.[30]

In *Kohll* the Court similarly held that the requirement of prior authorization infringed the Article 56 TFEU freedom to provide services unless it was justified either by an overriding reason in the general interest, such as the possible risk of seriously undermining the financial balance of a social security system, or by the public health exception contained in Article 52 TFEU. **3.25**

As far as the quality of public health was concerned the Court held, as in *Decker*, that given the existence of coordination and harmonization Directives on the conditions for pursuing the medical professions, and on the mutual recognition of diplomas, the restrictions at issue could not be justified by the need to protect the quality of medical services. It thus linked the freedom to provide services to mutual recognition guarantees established in the context of the freedom of establishment. **3.26**

Hence, the Court held that the public health exception could be invoked only if the restriction involved served the objective of maintaining a balanced medical and hospital service open to all, or in so far as the maintenance of treatment capacity or medical competence on national territory is essential for the public health, and even the survival of, the population. However in *Kohll* it had not been shown that the authorization requirement was necessary or indispensable to these ends, eg for the maintenance of an essential treatment facility or medical service on national territory.[31] **3.27**

As all defences were rejected the authorization requirements were consequently held to be illegal in both cases, and reimbursement at the level of the Member State of affiliation to the social security system was therefore mandatory. In the context **3.28**

[30] Case C-120/95 *Decker*, supra n 19, paras 41 ff. With reference to Council Dir 92/51/EEC on a second general system for the recognition of professional education and training to supplement Dir 89/48/EEC [1992] OJ L209/25; Commission Dir 95/43/EC of 20 July 1995 to Council Dir 92/51/EEC on a second general system for the recognition of professional education and training to supplement Dir 89/48/EEC [1995] OJ L184/21.

[31] Case C-158/96 *Kohll*, supra n 19, paras 51–52. With reference to Case 72/83 *Campus Oil Ltd v Ministry for Industry and Energy* [1984] ECR 2727.

of this finding it is notable that the Court did not address the legality of the authorization requirement in Regulation 1408/71, Article 22. (This issue was raised by Advocate General Tesauro but not concluded on.)[32] A number of Member States intervened in *Kohll* and *Decker* and the rulings in these cases were widely regarded as important straight from the outset. However, widespread doubts remained as to whether they applied to Member States that operated systems other than reimbursement (that is to benefits in kind and NHS systems) as well as concerning their relevance to hospital care, as opposed to outpatient care and medical devices.

Smits* and *Peerbooms

3.29 In the *Smits and Peerbooms*[33] case of July 2001, three key problems were addressed: the applicability of free movement to hospital services in general and to benefit in kind systems in particular, and the legality of prior authorization systems as such. At issue was the prior authorization system for treatment abroad that formed part of the (since then reformed) 'benefits in kind' scheme in the Netherlands, where those persons who were subject to the social insurance scheme paid a nominal fee to a public health insurance provider (also funded by employers' contributions, and by State funds) who arranged for health care to be provided to them free of charge by contracted providers (which were almost exclusively located in the Netherlands). The authorization scheme for treatment abroad required first, that the treatment in question was considered 'normal' treatment in national professional circles, and second that it was held 'necessary' in the sense that adequate treatment would not be available without undue delay nationally. Ms Geraets-Smits had sought clinical treatment for Parkinson's disease in Germany; Mr Peerbooms had undergone clinical neurological (coma) treatment in Austria. In both cases prior authorization had been refused. The questions addressed to the ECJ in this context were whether having an authorization system in general, and more specifically whether the criteria on which this system relied, constituted barriers to free movement—and if so, whether overriding reasons in the general interest might apply to justify such a scheme.

Remuneration

3.30 Repeating its position in *Kohll*, the Court started out by stating that notwithstanding the power of the Member States to arrange their own social security schemes they must abide by EU law when doing so. Next, it addressed the argument raised (as in *Vanbraekel* see below) by a number of intervening Member States that hospital services did not constitute an economic activity in the sense of Article 50 EC (Article 57 TFEU) 'particularly when they are provided in kind and free of charge

[32] P Cabral, supra n 19, pp 392–3.

[33] Case C-157/99 *B.S.M. Geraets-Smits v Stichting Ziekenfonds VGZ and H.T.M. Peerbooms v Stichting CZ Groep Zorgverzekeringen (Smits and Peerbooms)* [2001] ECR I-5473. Annotation VG Hatzopoulos, supra n 23.

under the relevant sickness insurance scheme' (that is to say the benefits in kind scheme prevailing in the Netherlands). Advocate General Ruiz Jarabo-Colomer took the same position, in relation to benefit in kind systems in general. Because as a result he did not distinguish between hospital services and outpatient services his Opinion had no bearing on one of the key outcomes of this case: the justification for prior authorization requirements for hospital services. He based his argument on *Humbel* (1988),[34] following a complicated analysis distinguishing the Dutch system from the rule on third party payment qualifying as consideration in the case of *Bond van Adverteerders* (1988), finding that the payments involved were only indirectly based on the services performed and resembled those in NHSs.[35] The arguments raised in this context focused on the absence of remuneration and/or of a profit motive in a benefit in kind system, and on the fact that the parties concerned do not determine the nature of the service provided nor the price paid, as these are set in the context of a social security system.

The Court rejected all these arguments. First it repeated the position taken in *Kohll* that medical activities fall within the scope of Article 57 TFEU and then extended it by stating that 'there [is] no need to distinguish in that regard between care provided in a hospital environment and care provided outside such an environment'.[36] It had done the same in *Vanbraekel* (2001) without providing further reasoning on this point (and in the context of Regulation 1408/71; see paras 3.55–3.58 and 5.29–5.40).[37] After repeating that the fact that the rules at issue were social security rules did not exclude application of Articles 56 and 57 TFEU it tackled the benefit in kind issues. It immediately cut short the argument by pointing not to the nature of the underlying system in the Member State of affiliation, but to those transactions that had actually taken place between the patients in the case at hand, and the medical establishments in the Member States where the treatment was provided, in exchange for direct payment: clearly remuneration had been involved at this level. The benefits in kind nature of the system of the Member State of affiliation could not change this fact. **3.31**

In addition, the Court rejected the argument that Article 57 TFEU did not apply to benefit in kind systems as such, based on the fact that direct payments are in any event not required for Article 57 TFEU to apply, and given that the payments in fact made for hospital services by sickness insurance funds in the Netherlands (albeit at a flat rate) did indeed ('unquestionably') constitute consideration for these services and remuneration of the receiving hospitals which were consequently **3.32**

[34] Case 263/86 *Belgium v René Humbel and Marie-Thérèse Edel* [1988] ECR 5365.

[35] Case C-157/99 *Smits and Peerbooms*, Opinion of AG Ruiz-Jarabo Colomer, supra n 33, paras 26–33; Case 352/85 *Bond van Adverteerders and others v The Netherlands* [1988] ECR 2085.

[36] Case C-157/99 *Smits and Peerbooms*, supra n 33, para 53.

[37] Case C-368/98 *Abdon Vanbraekel* et al *v Alliance nationale des mutualités chrétiennes (Vanbraekel)* [2001] ECR I-5363, para 41.

engaged in economic activities. In sum, the Court engaged in a comprehensive refutation.

Restrictions and justifications

3.33 Next the ECJ considered the question of whether a restriction of the freedom to provide services was involved. It quickly established that both the requirement of 'normal' treatment and 'medical necessity' were likely to limit the granting of authorization, which constituted a restriction when compared to national treatment for which no authorization was required at all.[38] The Netherlands government claimed that authorization was not required where the sickness insurance funds had concluded prior agreements with hospitals in other Member States—just as they had with Dutch hospitals. The Court noted that it had received no information to this effect from the referring court, but found this was not likely to have much impact outside some border areas and therefore had little bearing on the case. That is: even if the claims of the Netherlands government were true there was discrimination in effect if not in a formal sense. Hence a barrier to the freedom to provide services was involved which could only be justified by overriding public interest considerations. This meant that first the overriding reasons should be shown, and then the safeguard measures invoked should be justified as necessary and proportionate in that light.

3.34 Citing *Kohll* (and like in *Vanbraekel*, see below) the Court again raised the three possible defences:

- The possible risk of seriously undermining a social security system's financial balance as an overriding reason in the general interest.
- The objective of maintaining a balanced medical and hospital service open to all in the context of the public health derogation under Article 52 TFEU.
- Likewise, under Article 52 TFEU restrictions, where the maintenance of treatment capacity or medical competence on national territory is essential for the public health, and even the survival of, the population.

In each case, the defence remained subject to the rules at issue actually being justifiable in the light of such overriding reasons and proportional to these ends. Of these three justifications the first was the primary one, as was also the case in subsequent cases.

3.35 In its assessment of the first question the Court focused on the need for planning as the key distinguishing characteristic for hospital services (compared against medical services provided in the surgeries of medical practitioners or at the patients' home). In this context it identified first, the need to ensure permanent access to

[38] Case C-157/99 *Smits and Peerbooms*, supra n 33, paras 65–66.

quality hospital services, and, second, the need to control costs and prevent wastage as a result of overcapacity. Importantly, the Court recognized:

> (...) that the hospital sector generates considerable costs and must satisfy increasing needs, while the financial resources which may be available for health care are not unlimited, whatever the mode of funding applied.[39]

And it held:

> (...) if insured persons were at liberty, regardless of the circumstances, to use the services of hospitals with which their sickness insurance fund had no contractual arrangements, whether they were situated in the Netherlands or in another Member State, all the planning which goes into the contractual system in an effort to guarantee a rationalised, stable, balanced and accessible supply of hospital services would be jeopardised at a stroke.[40]

The Court thus showed itself sensitive to the concerns of the Member State in terms of cost control and planning. The planning exception would eventually become the key exception in the services context.

Hospital treatment versus non-hospital (outpatient) treatment

Based on this reasoning, which for the first time put flesh on the bones of the exceptions, the Court found a prior authorization requirement for the assumption of costs of hospital treatment provided in another Member State both necessary and reasonable. Only after making a general statement to this effect did the Court relate this finding to the specifics of the sickness insurance system in the Netherlands with its system of contractual arrangements between hospitals and sickness insurance funds and all the planning effort required 'to guarantee a rationalised, stable, balanced and accessible supply of hospital services'.[41] Although the remainder of the judgment did not explicitly deal with non-hospital services, hereby a fundamental distinction was made between hospital services and non-hospital services that had first been proposed by Advocate General Tesauro in his Opinion on the *Kohll* and *Decker* cases,[42] which has remained key in all subsequent developments. **3.36**

Concerning the proportionality of the authorization scheme and its key conditions the Court held (in line with standing case law on prior authorization schemes in relation to the effectiveness of EU law)[43] that procedural guarantees are required which provide for requests to be dealt with objectively and impartially within reasonable time and subject to judicial control. **3.37**

---

[39] ibid, para 79.

[40] ibid, para 81.

[41] ibid, paras 80–81.

[42] Case C-158/96 *Kohll* and Case C-120/95 *Decker*, Opinion of AG Tesauro, supra n 28, paras 59–60.

[43] Case C-157/99 *Smits and Peerbooms*, supra n 33, para 90. With reference inter alia to Case C-205/99 *Asociación Profesional de Empresas Navieras de Líneas Regulares (Analir)* et al *v Administración General del Estado* [2001] ECR I-1271.

3.38 The condition that the treatment be 'normal' must be based on standards of international medical science. As regards the condition that the treatment must be 'necessary', authorization may be refused 'only if the same or equally effective treatment can be obtained without undue delay', which 'undue delay' is to be determined 'with regard to all the circumstances of the specific case and take due account not only of the patient's medical condition at the time when the authorization is sought but also of his past record'.[44] This is reminiscent of Article 22(2) of Regulation 1408/71 which provides that authorization may not be refused to a consumer 'where he cannot be given such treatment within the time normally necessary for obtaining the treatment in question in the Member State of residence taking account of his current state of health and the probable course of the disease'. In subsequent case law the same undue delay criterion was applied under Regulation 1408/71 (now Regulation 883/204) as under Article 56 TFEU.[45]

3.39 Concerning the condition of the necessity of treatment the ECJ noted:

> Such a condition can allow an adequate, balanced and permanent supply of high-quality hospital treatment to be maintained on the national territory and the financial stability of the sickness insurance system to be assured.[46]

And:

> Were large numbers of insured persons to decide to be treated in other Member States even when the hospitals having agreements with their sickness insurance funds offer adequate identical or equivalent treatment, the consequent outflow of patients would be liable to put at risk the very principle of having agreements with hospitals and, consequently, undermine all the planning and rationalisation carried out in this vital sector in an effort to avoid the phenomena of hospital overcapacity, imbalance in the supply of hospital medical care and logistical and financial wastage.[47]

In this manner the Court demonstrated that, far from focusing solely on the market freedoms, it had an open eye for the needs of the Member States in the management of their social security systems.

3.40 In *Smits and Peerbooms* therefore the Court clarified the earlier case law on several key points. On the one hand it confirmed the applicability of the freedom to provide services in the context of benefit in kind systems and to hospital services generally. On the other hand it found that, subject to the abovementioned conditions, a prior authorization requirement for hospital treatment could be justified. Moreover it was willing to accept the principle invoked by the Member States as sufficient justification, without requiring actual proof of the impact of patient mobility.

---

[44] Case C-157/99 *Smits and Peerbooms*, supra n 33, paras 103–4.

[45] cf Case C-56/01 *Patricia Inizan v Caisse primaire d'assurance maladie des Hauts-de-Seine (Inizan)* [2003] ECR I-12403, para 46.

[46] Case C-157/99 *Smits and Peerbooms*, supra n 33, para 105.

[47] ibid, supra n 33, para 106.

Müller-Fauré

The *Müller-Fauré and van Riet* case of May 2003[48] both confirmed and extended this case law in relation to benefits in kind systems and hospital care, and distinguished it in relation to non-hospital care. At issue were dental treatment received in Germany by Ms Müller-Fauré, and hospital and non-hospital treatment received in Belgium by Ms van Riet; both were Dutch nationals. In the case of Ms van Riet, who was suffering from wrist pain that required a surgical examination and then corrective surgery, authorization for treatment had been refused because the treatment concerned was available in the Netherlands, albeit following much longer waiting times. **3.41**

As in *Smits and Peerbooms* the question of prior authorization for non-contracted treatment was raised. This time the main questions addressed to the Court were, first, whether the essential characteristics of the benefits in kind system for sickness insurance in the Netherlands amounted to an overriding reason that might justify a derogation from Article 56 TFEU, and, second, what in the authorization context is meant by 'without undue delay', especially whether that condition must be assessed on a strictly medical basis, regardless of the waiting time for the treatment sought. An issue not raised by the referring court but in the arguments submitted to the ECJ concerned the existence of waiting lists as such, due to the availability of limited resources which were cited as requiring limits on the benefits provided and strict prioritization of their provision. **3.42**

The Court quickly confirmed its findings from *Smits and Peerbooms* that medical activities are services and that the fact that the applicable rules are social security rules does not place them outside the scope for the freedom to provide services. Likewise an authorization requirement that would deter or even prevent the use of services provided in other Member States constituted a barrier prohibited by Article 56 TFEU. The Court then examined whether this restriction might be justified by: **3.43**

- the protection of public health inasmuch as the system of agreements between health insurers and health care providers is intended to ensure that there are high-quality, balanced medical and hospital services open to all;
- the financial balance of the social security system; and
- the essential characteristics of the sickness insurance system in the Netherlands, which provides benefits in kind.

In other words it departed from its practice so far by now examining only one exception based on Article 57 TFEU, and two (possible) overriding reasons of public interest.

[48] Case C-385/99 *V.G. Müller-Fauré v Onderlinge Waarborgmaatschappij OZ Zorgverzekeringen UA and E.E.M. van Riet v Onderlinge Waarborgmaatschappij ZAO Zorgverzekeringen* [2003] ECR I-4509; M Flear, 'Case C-385/99 V.G. Müller-Fauré v. Onderlinge Waarborgmaatschappij O.Z. Zorgverzekeringen U.A. and E.E.M. van Riet v. Onderlinge Waarborgmaatschappij Z.A.O. Zorgverzekeringen' [2004] *Common Market Law Review* 209; AP van der Mei, supra n 24.

3.44 On the first of these justifications, it concluded no relevant evidence had been adduced, and that in any event it was closely linked to the second justification concerning the financial balance of the social security system. When examining this second ground it started out by stating, for the first time, that because it is self-evident that the cost of an individual treatment can never have a significant impact on the financing of a social security system, a comprehensive approach must instead be adopted.[49] In previous cases the Court had applied an opposite logic: that individual cases by definition did not have a (significant) impact as they would anyway have had to be reimbursed if the treatment had been provided in the Member State of affiliation, and that their effects could therefore be ignored.[50]

3.45 Therefore its willingness to look at overall effects formed a significant shift toward recognising the concerns of the Member States. In this context the Court made an explicit and fundamental distinction between hospital services where the financial balance might be at stake and non-hospital services where this was not the case (although acknowledging this might sometimes prove difficult to do):[51]

> In particular, certain services provided in a hospital environment but also capable of being provided by a practitioner in his surgery or in a health centre could for that reason be placed on the same footing as non-hospital services.[52]

Hospital services

3.46 Reaching back to *Smits and Peerbooms* the Court found that to enable the planning required to ensure accessibility, as well as to control costs and prevent wastage, a prior authorization requirement appeared both necessary and reasonable.

3.47 Next it examined the requirements of necessity and proportionality of the conditions attached to the grant of an authorization, after restating the general requirements for a general authorization scheme as also stated in *Smits and Peerbooms*. The focus here was on the necessity of the treatment, understood under the Dutch legislation as a function of the question whether the appropriate medical treatment was available nationally 'without undue delay'. The Court extended the rule established in *Smits and Peerbooms* that in making this assessment the national authorities must:

> (…) have regard to all the circumstances of each specific case and (…) take due account not only of the patient's medical condition at the time when authorisation is sought but also of his past record,

[49] Case C-385/99 *Müller-Fauré*, supra n 48, para 74.

[50] cf concerning hospital services Case C-368/98 *Vanbraekel*, supra n 37, para 52; non-hospital services Case C-158/96 *Kohll*, supra n 19, para 42; medical aids Case C-120/95 *Decker*, supra n 19, para 40.

[51] Case C-385/99 *Müller-Fauré*, supra n 48, para 75.

[52] ibid; cf M Flear, supra n 48, pp 223–6.

by adding (instead of 'but also of his past record'):

> (...) and where appropriate, of the degree of pain or the nature of the patient's disability which might, for example, make it impossible or extremely difficult for him to carry out a professional activity, but also of his medical history.[53]

By including these criteria it became clear that the Court was moving beyond a simple statement on the right to reimbursement for cross-border services to a more substantive evaluation designed to balance, on the one hand, the collective interest represented by the Member State to planning and financial control over social security services, and on the other the need for the health condition of the individual patient, including the impact on their job prospects, and the degree of pain involved. In other words at the same time as the Court accepted, in principle, public interest justifications, it defined under which conditions a patient's right to cross-border treatment based on the freedom to provide services overrides even legitimate public interest justifications based on a substantive understanding of the individual health issues involved. **3.48**

After recalling its reasoning in *Smits and Peerbooms* on the link between the condition concerning the necessity of treatment, and the supply of hospital treatment and financial stability of the sickness insurance system which might be threatened if an outflow of patients would lead to overcapacity, imbalance in supply and wastage, it then added: **3.49**

> However, a refusal to grant prior authorization which is based not on fear of wastage resulting from hospital overcapacity but solely on the ground that there are waiting lists on national territory for the hospital treatment concerned, without account being taken of the specific circumstances attaching to the patient's medical condition, cannot amount to a properly justified restriction on freedom to provide services. It is not clear from the arguments submitted to the Court that such waiting times are necessary, apart from considerations of a purely economic nature which cannot as such justify a restriction on the fundamental principle of freedom to provide services, for the purpose of safeguarding the protection of public health. On the contrary, a waiting time which is too long or abnormal would be more likely to restrict access to balanced, high-quality hospital care.[54]

In other words rationing, in particular by means of waiting times that went beyond rationalizing the usage of the system to avoid overcapacity and led to denial of treatment (a fine line to draw in many cases), was not accepted. Although the individual Member States still decide on the scope of the national social security coverage, waiting lists caused by under-capacity jeopardize public health and are not tolerated. The Court thus lost no time qualifying the broad understanding of the systemic needs of the Member States that it had first offered in *Smits and Peerbooms*, **3.50**

[53] Case C-157/99 *Smits and Peerbooms*, supra n 33, para 104; Case C-385/99 *Müller-Fauré*, supra n 48, para 90.

[54] Case C-385/99 *Müller-Fauré*, supra n 48, para 92.

indicating it would 'tip the scale' in the patients' interest where justified by their individual health status.[55]

Non-hospital services

3.51 As regards non-hospital medical services the Court confirmed *Kohll* in finding there was no evidence that the absence of a prior authorization requirement would have a significant impact on the social security system in the Netherlands, adding that:

> (...) care is generally provided near to the place where the patient resides, in a cultural environment which is familiar to him and which allows him to build up a relationship of trust with the doctor treating him. If emergencies are disregarded, the most obvious cases of patients travelling abroad are in border areas or where specific conditions are to be treated.[56]

In the latter cases agreements would tend to exist. Finally, because the reimbursement would in any event be limited to that which would apply for the same treatment in the Member State of affiliation the expenses involved would be the same and could not threaten the financial balance of the national social security system. Prior authorization could thus not be required for outpatient services.

Benefits in kind as overriding interest

3.52 Finally the Court addressed the question whether the essential characteristics of the Netherlands sickness insurance scheme merited being considered as an overriding reason of public interest. As a preliminary observation it noted first that the power of the Member States to organize their social security systems is not undermined by the fact that achieving the freedoms guaranteed by the Treaty would require making some adjustments to these systems—such as had been required by Regulation 1408/71.[57] Next it spelled out that 'a medical service does not cease to be a provision of services because it is paid for by a national health service or by a system providing benefits in kind', and that it is the prior authorization requirement which constitutes the barrier to the freedom to provide services, irrespective of the payment system in the Member State of affiliation.[58] The Court concluded:

> There is thus no need, from the perspective of freedom to provide services, to draw a distinction by reference to whether the patient pays the costs incurred and subsequently applies for reimbursement thereof or whether the sickness fund or the national budget pays the provider directly.

---

55 AP van der Mei, supra n 24, p 66.
56 Case C-385/99 *Müller-Fauré*, supra n 48, para 96.
57 ibid, para 102.
58 ibid, para 103.

Some commentators have interpreted these references to funding from the national budget as shots across the bow of the British NHS.[59]

Based on this reasoning the Court raised three arguments: 3.53

- that Member States with a benefits in kind system (or an NHS) already had to establish reimbursement mechanisms for treatment based on Article 22 of Regulation 1408/71;
- that in any event the level of reimbursement was limited to that provided by the sickness insurance scheme of the Member State of affiliation; and
- that nothing prevented a Member State with a benefits in kind system from fixing the reimbursement level for treatment in another Member State (where none existed in their own) provided these were based on objective, non-discriminatory and transparent criteria.

The Court therefore confirmed *Smits and Peerbooms* in stating that a benefits in kind system was not exempt from Article 56 TFEU, explicitly dismissing the claim that an 'overriding reason' might exist in this case.

Watts

In the celebrated *Watts*[60] case of May 2006, the Court for the first time extended its case law to an NHS system. Ms Watts, a UK national, had undergone hip replacement surgery in France after repeatedly being denied authorization for treatment abroad based on Article 22 of Regulation 1408/71 on the ground that the waiting time involved for treatment by the NHS involved no 'undue delay' (although the UK consultant responsible for her referral had acknowledged both that Ms Watts was in constant pain from the outset and a subsequent deterioration in her condition). The referring court submitted a large number of questions which revolved around the possibility to distinguish the NHS system and its various features from the earlier case law of the ECJ on the applicability of free provision of services and Article 22 of Regulation 1408/71, and the relevance in this context of budgetary constraints. 3.54

Undue delay and Article 22 of Regulation 1408/71

Citing *Vanbraekel*, the Court held that rights to reimbursement based on Article 22 of Regulation 1408/71 and under Article 56 TFEU could coexist. It then explicitly aligned the two parallel systems by confirming that the criterion 'within the time normally necessary for obtaining the treatment in question' in Article 22 was the same as that used to define the term 'undue delay' in the context of 3.55

[59] M Flear, supra n 48, pp 221–2.

[60] Case C-372/04 *Watts*, supra n 12. Annotation M Cousins, 'Patient Mobility and National Health Systems' [2007] Legal Issues of Economic Integration 183; G Davies, 'The effect of Mrs Watts' trip to France on the National Health Service' [2007] King's Law Journal 158.

Article 56 TFEU.[61] Some commentators have been critical of the Court's creation of two parallel regimes, noting that *Watts* could have been solved by 'a broad interpretation of Article 22 of Regulation 1408/71 as the implementation of the right to free movement under the Treaty.'[62] Arguably this bridge had already been burned in *Kohll* when the Court first embraced the notion of two parallel regimes.

3.56 The Court then set out to discuss the conditions under which this criterion was satisfied. In this context it first recalled its ruling in *Müller-Fauré* that the existence of waiting lists could not be decisive.[63] However in contrast to the more critical approach to rationing in *Müller-Fauré* which had appeared to suggest that only measures to avoid overcapacity and 'wastage' were relevant, the Court also held that given constantly rising demand for hospital treatment (as a function of technical developments and rising life expectancy) and 'necessarily' limited supply due to budget constraints, it could not be denied that waiting lists might be needed to manage supply and set priorities 'on the basis of the available resources and capacities'.[64] As funding was by definition finite, the principle of rationing was therefore accepted. Next, the existence of waiting lists, and their legitimate use, was balanced with the rights of patients as follows.

3.57 According to the Court:

> (…) in order to be entitled to refuse the authorisation referred to in Article 22(1)(c) of that regulation on the ground of waiting time, the competent institution must however establish that the waiting time, arising from objectives relating to the planning and management of the supply of hospital care pursued by the national authorities on the basis of generally predetermined clinical priorities, within which the hospital treatment required by the patient's state of health may be obtained in an establishment forming part of the national system in question, does not exceed the period which is acceptable in the light of an objective medical assessment of the clinical needs of the person concerned in the light of his medical condition and the history and probable course of his illness, the degree of pain he is in and/or the nature of his disability at the time when the authorisation is sought.[65]

In this context the Court also referred to the change made by Article 20 of Regulation 883/2004 replacing the relevant text of Article 22 of Regulation 1408/71 'within the time normally necessary for obtaining the treatment in question in the Member State of residence' with 'within a time-limit which is medically justifiable'.

3.58 If the resulting waiting time is a medically acceptable one set in a manner that takes account of developments in the health of the patient this would mean an authorization under Article 22 of Regulation 1408/71 could legitimately be refused to avoid

[61] Case C-372/04 *Watts*, supra n 12, paras 60ff. Substantively it thus confirmed Case C-56/01 *Inizan*, supra n 45, paras 45–46.

[62] M Cousins, supra n 60, p 192.

[63] Case C-385/99 *Müller-Fauré*, supra n 48, para 92.

[64] Case C-372/04 *Watts*, supra n 12, para 67.

[65] ibid, para 68.

such patient migration as might put at risk planning and rationalization in the hospital sector. Remarkably therefore—and unlike its earlier approach in *Inizan* (see para 3.67)—the Court thus made application of the authorization system under Regulation 1408/71 conditional on an overriding reason of general interest.[66] By adopting this standard of medically accepted waiting time the Court thus balanced the interest of national authorities in containing the outflow of patients with the individual patients' interests in speedier treatment. Adopting the medical acceptability standard also made the position of those who opposed patient mobility at all costs untenable.

Patients' rights under Article 56 TFEU

Confirming the earlier finding in *Müller-Fauré* the Court held that Article 56 TFEU applied in the case of hospital treatment in another Member State, regardless of the way in which the national system in the Member State of affiliation operates. It therefore found it unnecessary to determine whether the NHS itself provided a service in the sense of Article 56 TFEU. Because prior authorization was not required for NHS treatment, imposing it as a precondition for treatment in other Member States constituted an obstacle to the freedom to provide services. **3.59**

Next it examined possible justifications for such a restriction. The Court focused on the planning needs for hospital care in order to guarantee accessibility and to control costs, from which point of view (as found earlier in *Smits and Peerbooms* and *Müller-Fauré*) a prior authorization system appeared necessary and reasonable. **3.60**

However the conditions for said authorization would have to be justified in the light of the overriding considerations involved and be proportionate. In the first place the Court repeated the procedural requirements of decisions that must be based on transparent objective and non-discriminatory criteria and open to judicial review that could be based inter alia on independent expert advice. The UK manifestly failed to meet this condition as no criteria for refusing or granting authorization had been spelled out at all. Second, the Court recalled in slightly different wording the abovementioned criteria with regard to the use of waiting lists that it had previously set out in relation to authorizations based on Article 22 of Regulation 1408/71 in the same case: **3.61**

> A refusal to grant prior authorisation cannot be based merely on the existence of waiting lists intended to enable the supply of hospital care to be planned and managed on the basis of predetermined general clinical priorities, without carrying out an objective medical assessment of the patient's medical condition, the history and probable course of his illness, the degree of pain he is in and/or the nature of his disability at the time when the request for authorisation was made or renewed.

[66] ibid, paras 70–71. cf Case C-56/01 *Inizan*, supra n 45, paras 21ff.

> Where the delay arising from such waiting lists appears to exceed an acceptable time having regard to an objective medical assessment of the abovementioned circumstances, the competent institution may not refuse the authorisation sought on the grounds of the existence of those waiting lists, an alleged distortion of the normal order of priorities linked to the relative urgency of the cases to be treated, the fact that the hospital treatment provided under the national system in question is free of charge, the obligation to make available specific funds to reimburse the cost of treatment to be provided in another Member State and/or a comparison between the cost of that treatment and that of equivalent treatment in the competent Member State.[67]

With the above statement it addressed explicitly as unacceptable the various reasons brought forward to elevate planning above the needs of individual patients (eg the existence of waiting lists, the fact the health care provided was free of charge, etc). Instead the Court required an objective medical assessment on an individual basis—affirming the existence in EU law of patients' rights even in an NHS context.

Calculation of costs

3.62 The first difficulty concerning the calculation of costs, as regards Article 56 TFEU, was that there was no natural comparing point for reimbursement at the level in the Member State of affiliation, because in a (tax-funded) NHS system hospital treatment is free of charge. The second difficulty, as regards Article 22 of Regulation 1408/71, was that Member States of treatment might provide for reimbursement in full, or in part. This made the rule on the relationship between Article 56 TFEU and the Regulation 1408/71 regimes that was set out in *Vanbraekel*—which provided for reimbursement of the difference between the levels between the Member State of affiliation and the Member State of treatment—difficult to apply.

3.63 In a densely worded paragraph the Court ruled that in an NHS setting Article 56 TFEU required that treatment that was (or should have been) authorized must be reimbursed based on the objectively quantified costs of equivalent treatment[68] in that NHS system, but only up to the amount of the costs actually charged to the patient in the Member State of treatment. The notion of the need to establish a basis for reimbursement using objective, non-discriminatory and transparent criteria was first raised in *Müller-Fauré*.[69] The requirement set in *Watts* however goes further as it is cost-based. This means that NHS systems that are based upon different funding principles will now have to establish the costs of individual (types of) procedure, which may have important side-effects in highlighting choices that had so far remained implicit, as well as (presumably) differences in efficiency.[70] In other words where equivalent treatment by an NHS costs less (unless Regulation 1408/71 applies

[67] Case C-372/04 *Watts*, supra n 12, para 123.
[68] Case C-372/04 *Watts*, supra n 12, para 143.
[69] Case C-385/99 *Müller-Fauré*, supra n 48, para 107.
[70] G Davies, supra n 60, pp 164–5.

and the Member State of treatment provides for full reimbursement), this can lead to out-of-pocket expenses for patients, and it can never lead to reimbursements that are higher than the actual costs incurred. Covering ancillary costs such as travel and accommodation was considered to be required by Article 56 TFEU, but not by Article 22 of Regulation 1408/71, only in those cases where they would be covered as part of treatment in the Member State of affiliation, and not otherwise.[71]

Budgetary constraints

Finally, the Court addressed the provocative question whether, in the light of Article 168(7) TFEU, Article 56 TFEU or Article 22 of Regulation 1408/71 could force Member States to fund hospital treatment without reference to budgetary constraints. The relevant part of this sector-specific subsidiarity provision reads: 'Community action in the field of public health shall fully respect the responsibilities of the Member States for the organisation and delivery of health services and medical care.' According to the Court: **3.64**

> (…) the requirements arising from Article 49 EC [Article 56 TFEU] and Article 22 of Regulation No 1408/71 are not to be interpreted as imposing on the Member States an obligation to reimburse the cost of hospital treatment in other Member States without reference to any budgetary consideration but, on the contrary, are based on the need to balance the objective of the free movement of patients against overriding national objectives relating to management of the available hospital capacity, control of health expenditure and financial balance of social security systems.[72]

With reference to its earlier findings in *Müller-Fauré*, the ECJ briefly recalled that the Member States' responsibilities regarding health care did not exclude the need to make adjustments to social security systems where required by other Treaty provisions such as Article 56 TFEU. Hence it concluded there was no conflict with Article 152(5) EC (now Article 168(7) TFEU). With this the patient mobility case law had been extended to all Beveridge as well as Bismarck systems—that is to say across the EU as a whole.

E. Secondary and More Recent Cases

Apart from the cases that were discussed in detail above, the Court has handed down a larger number of less well known rulings that may nevertheless be useful inter alia to determine the scope of free movement in relation to Article 20 of Regulation 883/2004. With the significant exception of two recent infringement cases against Spain and France these cases confirm a strict approach to Article 56 **3.65**

[71] Case C-372/04 *Watts*, supra n 12, para 142; citing Case C-8/02 *Ludwig Leichtle v Bundesanstalt für Arbeit* [2004] ECR I-2641, paras 41ff.

[72] Case C-372/04 *Watts*, supra n 12, para 145.

TFEU, filling in the blanks as it were, that were left by the major cases discussed above. They will be surveyed briefly here.

Vanbraekel

3.66 In *Vanbraekel* (2001) the ECJ decided that where prior authorization had been granted based on Regulation 1408/71, but where a difference existed between the level of compensation in the Member State of treatment and the Member State of affiliation which was to the disadvantage of the patient, this difference would have to be compensated.[73] In this case it was also decided that intramural services fell within the scope of Article 56 TFEU.

Inizan

3.67 In *Inizan* (2003) the ECJ addressed the question whether Article 22 of Regulation 1408/71 itself might constitute a barrier to trade.[74] Notably the Court emphasized that Article 22 had created a new right to reimbursement which had not existed previously and therefore promoted the free movement of insured persons between the Member States as well as the provision of cross-border medical services. Hence there was a priori no question of a restriction. In addition the Court confirmed the parallel application of Article 56 TFEU and Article 22 of Regulation 1408/71.

Leichtle

3.68 In the *Leichtle* case (2004) the Court held that breaking off payments in the course of a procedure concerning reimbursements was a restriction of the freedom to receive services in Article 56 TFEU.[75] A refusal of authorization for the use of a health spa in another Member State could not be based exclusively on grounds of costs. Whether the use of a limited list of predominantly national health spas was discriminatory was left to the referring judge to decide.

Bosch

3.69 The *Bosch* case (2004) concerned the practice of the company sickness fund of Bosch to reimburse in full all costs for cross-border health care up to 200 DM, which was contested by the German insurance regulator.[76] As it had done in *Vanbraekel* the Court held that the applicability of the regime of Regulation 1408/71 did not exclude a more generous treatment in the Member State of affiliation.

[73] Case C-368/98 *Vanbraekel*, supra n 37.
[74] Case C-56/01 *Inizan*, supra n 46.
[75] Case C-8/02 *Leichtle*, supra n 71.
[76] Case C-193/03 *Betriebskrankenkasse der Robert Bosch GmbH v Germany* [2004] ECR I-9911.

Moreover the arrangement provided for full reimbursement (at least up to 200 DM) and hence met the requirements of the Regulation.

Keller

The *Keller* case (2005) concerned the scope of Article 22 of Regulation 1408/71.[77] Keller had obtained prior permission in Spain for a treatment in another Member State (Germany), but was referred to Switzerland for a superior treatment. The Court ruled that it was indeed up to the Member State of treatment to decide on the possible necessity of such a step without further intervention by the Member State of affiliation. The costs of treatment in a third country are met by the Member State of treatment and must subsequently be reimbursed by the Member State of affiliation if they are covered by its scheme of health insurance and/or provision. It should be noted that the Member State of treatment decides whether further treatment in the third country is covered by the scope of the benefits it provides for, and the Member State of affiliation determines whether the treatment provided is reimbursed or not. 3.70

Herrera

The litigation in *Herrera* (2006) focused on the reimbursement of travel and subsistence costs relating to health care received abroad.[78] The ECJ established that Article 22 of Regulation 1408/71 did not provide for such a right, but (as was the case in *Watts*) such a right did exist based on Article 56 TFEU provided that equivalent costs would have been reimbursed for a treatment in the Member State of affiliation. Otherwise the absence of reimbursement for such costs would obstruct free movement. (The referring court also asked whether discrimination between public and private providers in terms of reimbursement was allowed within Spain. The ECJ carefully avoided addressing this difficult question.) 3.71

Stamatelaki

Stamatelaki (2007) regarded the reimbursement of costs incurred abroad for private care, which was explicitly excluded by the relevant Greek legislation.[79] The ECJ considered this prohibition as an infringement of the proportionality requirement, because less restrictive criteria in combination with a prior authorization requirement could have achieved the same objective (to protect the financial balance of the social security system). 3.72

[77] Case C-145/03 *Heirs of Annette Keller v Instituto Nacional de la Seguridad Social (INSS) and Instituto Nacional de Gestión Sanitaria (Ingesa)* [2005] ECR I-2529.

[78] Case C-466/04 *Manuel Acereda Herrera v Servicio Cántabro de Salud* [2006] ECR I-5341.

[79] Case C-444/05 *Aikaterini Stamatelaki v NPDD Organismos Asfaliseos Eleftheron Epangelmation (Stamatelaki)* [2007] ECR I-3185.

Chamier-Glisczinski

3.73 In the *Chamier-Glisczinski* case (2009) the contested issue was whether, based on Regulation 1408/71, a German insured person could derive a right to long term care to which there was no entitlement in Austria, the Member State of residence (and prospective treatment), from the entitlements in the Member State of affiliation, or whether they could do so based on free movement of persons and/or services.[80] Concerning Regulation 1408/71 the ECJ held that even when no rights could be derived from the rules in the Member State of treatment, the Regulation did not exclude that the Member State of affiliation would grant a right to receive the relevant treatment. As regards the relationship between free movement and citizenship (Article 21 TFEU) the Court held, significantly, that in the absence of a harmonization requirement this did not preclude differences in social security coverage and therefore no new rights could be derived.

Commission v Spain

3.74 The infringement case of *Commission v Spain* (2010) concerned the question whether, in line with the *Vanbraekel* case, the Spanish authorities would be obligated to reimburse the difference between the reimbursement based on Regulation 1408/71 for emergency hospital treatment during a temporary stay in another Member State (France) and the reimbursement that would have been provided in the Member State of affiliation (Spain).[81] Hence the parallel application of the Regulation and the freedom to receive services in Article 56 TFEU was at issue. In this case the Court for the first time drew a fundamental distinction between planned hospital care on the one hand and 'unscheduled treatment' on the other (with reference to the increasing mobility of EU citizens, especially due to tourism or education, which could otherwise cause problems).[82] The Court found that in the latter case free movement does not require cost neutrality for each form of unscheduled treatment. The effects of the resulting differences in costs are 'too uncertain and indirect' to be capable of leading to a restriction of free movement. In other words: the reimbursement of the difference between the costs based on Regulation 1408/71 and the reimbursement based on Article 56 TFEU is not required for emergency treatment because the latter provision is not at issue. The Court thus distinguished from *Vanbraekel* which had not differentiated between different types of care.

3.75 The *Commission v Spain* case, which was decided by the Grand Chamber, appears to form an important new departure in the Court's case law on the freedom to

[80] Case C-208/07 *Petra von Chamier-Glisczinski v Deutsche Angestellten-Krankenkasse* [2009] ECR I-6095.

[81] Case C-211/08 *Commission v Spain (Hospital care)* [2010] ECR I-5267.

[82] ibid, para 76.

provide and receive services. The system of Regulation 1408/71 is presented as a form of risk equalization because cases which require additional reimbursement are compensated by other cases where the amount due is less that that due for national treatment. This system would be jeopardized if supplementary payments become the norm in case the coverage in the Member State of treatment is lower than that in the Member State of affiliation.[83]

Elchinov

The *Elchinov* case (2010) concerned the refusal by the Bulgarian authorities to reimburse an eye operation in Germany of which it was uncertain whether it was covered by the care that was insured in Bulgaria.[84] The Court determined that for medical care which cannot be provided in the Member State of residence of the insured person, prior authorization cannot be refused if (i) the national rules defines types of treatment which may be reimbursed and which correspond to the type of treatment at issue, and (ii) the insured person cannot receive an alternative equally effective treatment without undue delay. This requires reference to research based on objective and non-discriminatory criteria, taking into account all relevant medical and available scientific data. In addition this case confirms the ruling in *Vanbraekel* that in the system of Article 22 of Regulation 1408/71 requires application of the reimbursement regime that is most beneficial to the insured person.[85] **3.76**

Commission v France (extramural treatment)

In *Commission v France* (2010) the question was addressed whether a requirement of prior authorization could be imposed for the reimbursement of certain planned extramural treatment in another Member State which required the use of major medical equipment.[86] (The example used was positron emission tomography, used in the detection and treatment of cancer.) The Commission held that this possibility had already been excluded in earlier cases such as *Kohll* and *Müller-Fauré*: its position was that there was a clear distinction between intramural and extramural care on this point.[87] The Court however saw this as a justified restriction in the sense of an overriding reason of general interest in planning which could affect the financing of costly major medical equipment in the event that patients were to consume the relevant care abroad. In this sense therefore intramural care is to be treated similarly to extramural care. Moreover this judgment introduces quite an important new cost-based justification that sets limits on what negative integration can achieve. **3.77**

[83] ibid, paras 77–79.

[84] Case C-173/09 *Georgi Ivanov Elchinov v Natsionalna zdravnoosiguritelna kasa* [2010] judgment of 5 October 2010 (nyr).

[85] Case C-368/98 *Vanbraekel*, supra n 37.

[86] Case C-512/08 *Commission v France (extramural treatment)* [2010] judgment of 5 October 2010 (nyr).

[87] Case C-158/96 *Kohll*, supra n 19; Case C-385/99 *Müller-Fauré*, supra n 48.

This approach has meanwhile been codified in the Patients' Rights Directive—thereby setting the same limit in the context of (therefore partial) harmonization, or positive integration.[88]

Commission v Portugal (extramural treatment)

3.78 In the more recent *Commission v Portugal* case (2011) the Commission challenged the Portuguese system of not providing for any possibility for reimbursement of extramural treatment in another Member State unless it is highly specialized and not available in Portugal, even for treatment that does use major or costly medical equipment.[89] The Court held that this policy constituted a barrier to trade in services, which was not objectively justified, neither by a possible threat to the financial balance of the social security system, nor by the benefits in kind nature of the domestic Portuguese health care system. Accordingly, this case complements *Commission v France*, discussed immediately above.

F. Conclusion

3.79 This chapter has reviewed the case law in which the ECJ has developed a new set of tools—in the form of a parallel regime for patient mobility based on the freedom to provide services of Article 56 TFEU, alongside the pre-existing rules based on the free movement of workers provided by Regulation 1408/71, now Regulation 883/2004. The Court has successively determined that restitution based insurance systems,[90] benefits in kind based insurance systems,[91] and national health services systems[92] were obliged to enable the reimbursement of cross-border health care.

3.80 At the risk of some simplification, this case law can be summed up as follows.[93] The scope of social security coverage as such is determined by the Member State of affiliation alone and therefore not at issue. Nor is the right of individual patients to seek treatment abroad and pay for it themselves at stake: they are free to do so. Instead the focus of both the Article 56 TFEU 'parallel' regime and that of Regulation 883/2004 is on the conditions for the reimbursement of treatment abroad, when a patient is in principle entitled to the treatment involved in her or his Member State of affiliation.

[88] Dir 2011/24/EU, supra n 9, Art 8(2)(a)(ii).

[89] Case C 255/09 *Commission v Portugal (extramural treatment)* [2011] judgment of 27 October 2011 (nyr).

[90] Case C-158/96 *Kohll*, supra n 19; Case C-120/95 *Decker*, supra n 19.

[91] Case C-157/99 *Smits and Peerbooms*, supra n 33; Case C-385/99 *Müller-Fauré*, supra n 48.

[92] Case C-372/04 *Watts*, supra n 12.

[93] cf TK Hervey, 'The current legal framework on the right to seek healthcare abroad in the European Union' [2007] *Cambridge Yearbook of European Legal Studies* 261.

- When Article 56 TFEU is relied on, reimbursement is at the level of domestic treatment in the Member State of affiliation; and based on Regulation 883/2004, reimbursement is at the level of the Member State of treatment. Where the latter is lower than the former, the difference may be claimed based under Article 56 TFEU.[94]
- More complicated is the question whether prior authorization may be required. Based on Regulation 883/2004 prior authorization of treatment abroad is always required as a condition for reimbursement. Based on Article 56 TFEU, prior authorization (which is in principle a barrier to the freedom to provide services) may be required for hospital services. This is considered justified to safeguard the financial balance of the national social security system of the Member States and planning in the hospital sector.
- So far the Court has never required evidence before allowing this justification—albeit that in the context of preliminary rulings this may be due to the factual assessments being left to the referring national courts. Over time it has come to accept that prior authorization may be justified provided that material and procedural due process guarantees are respected concerning the objective and proportionate nature of the authorization process, notably fleshing out the concept of 'undue delay' by requiring due regard to the individual circumstances of each patient. These requirements are similar if not identical for the Article 56 TFEU setting and that of Regulation 883/2004.

In this manner the ECJ has balanced the public interest justifications invoked by **3.81** the Member States with the rights of individual patients based on free movement. At the same time as the Court has accepted public interest justifications potentially restricting a patient's right to cross-border treatment based on the freedom to provide services, it has defined conditions when patients' rights override even such public interest justifications based on a substantive understanding of the individual health issues involved. With few exceptions, in the infringement cases *Commission v Spain* and *Commission v France* (both 2010),[95] the Court has come down against restrictive national rules. The result of this balancing has been a significant increase in negative integration—the removal of market barriers.

The leading development concerning patient mobility meanwhile is in the area of **3.82** secondary law, with the adoption of the Patients' Rights Directive that entered into force on March 29th 2011.[96] This development appears to fit squarely within the dynamics of negative integration striking down national rules, and in turn fostering positive, or policy, integration by means of setting common norms in harmonization legislation. The preferred form for this is the Directive.

---

94 cf Case C-368/98 *Vanbraekel*, supra n 37.

95 Case C-211/08 *Commission v Spain*, supra n 81; Case C-512/08 *Commission v France*, supra n 86.

96 Dir 2011/24/EU, supra n 10.

3.83 It remains to be seen whether the degree of harmonization now achieved leaves room for further case law in this area that is based directly on the principles of freedom of services. For the time being however the momentum seems to have shifted from the sphere of primary law to that of secondary law—a development that can be seen as a sea-change in the application of EU law to health care and will be discussed in Chapter 5 (general) and Chapter 6 (health care specific). Before turning to that subject we will examine the more contentious issue of the application of the Treaty principle of freedom of establishment in health care in Chapter 4.

4

THE PRIMARY LAW OF THE INTERNAL MARKET: ESTABLISHMENT, GOODS, AND CAPITAL

A. Introduction

In Chapter 3 we have looked at the general legal characteristics of the four market freedoms of the internal market and we considered in detail the most important strand of case law with relation to access to health care systems: that of services. The application of the three other fundamental freedoms—establishment, goods, and capital—has so far been less developed in relation to health care provision in general. The free movement of goods in the pharmaceuticals sector, including borderline products, is a notable exception and indeed a considerable body of case law on this subject, to which numerous specialized studies are devoted, has evolved. The main principles, which have been of particular importance to market building, to cementing the internal market for medicines, are summarized in section C of this chapter. With regard to the freedom of establishment, as this chapter will explore, an important body of case law is emerging and the contours of how the EU toolbox can be applied to ensure market access for suppliers of health care are becoming clearer. Nevertheless as long as the Member States retain the right to determine the basic organizational parameters of their health care 4.01

systems, and in particular to determine whether health care is a profit or not-for-profit activity, and to closely regulate reimbursement, the concept of market entry in the sense of setting up competing health care facilities may prove untenable from an economic as well as a legal perspective.

4.02 As we will show in sections B and D, the more extensive definition of a restriction on market access now embraced in the ECJ's case law on the freedom of establishment and the freedom of capital may potentially impact upon the organization and regulation of national health care systems, especially if these systems have been opened up to a degree of competition or liberalization at national level. These cases will be discussed below, where they are analysed inter alia in relation to the parallels with and differences from the services case law. This allows for a degree of comparison of the practical effectiveness of the different instruments in the EU legal toolbox. This chapter also underlines the dynamic nature of the toolbox. Important developments in the case law could increase the reach of the toolbox over time.

B. Establishment

4.03 Although their national regulatory regimes differ widely, like any other market, health care markets in the EU are ultimately shaped by the interaction between the forces of demand and supply. At the same time demand and supply are relevant variables in terms of the EU legal regime, although so far not in equal measure. The advances made in the application of EU law on free movement to patients' rights (as discussed above), which enable patients' demand for cross-border access to various health care services (and goods) to be realized (also discussed above), are by now well documented.[1]

4.04 The case law which reflects the bearing of EU law on the supply side—in other words on the organization and delivery of health care and related intramural services—is so far much less studied.[2]

[1] cf eg G Davies, 'The effect of Mrs Watts' trip to France on the National Health Service' [2007] *King's Law Journal* 158; J van de Gronden, 'Cross-border healthcare in the EU and the organization of the national health systems of the Member States: The dynamics resulting from the European Court of Justice's free movement and competition law' [2009] *Wisconsin International Law Journal* 705; VG Hatzopoulos, 'Killing national health and insurance systems but healing patients? The European market for healthcare services after the judgments of the ECJ in *Vanbraekel* and Peerbooms' [2002] *Common Market Law Review* 683; TK Hervey, 'The current legal framework on the right to seek healthcare abroad in the European Union' [2007] *Cambridge Yearbook of European Legal Studies* 261.

[2] A noteworthy exception is K Stöger, 'The freedom of establishment and the market access of hospital operators' [2006] *European Business Law Review* 1545. cf earlier EI Kaldellis, 'Freedom of establishment versus freedom to provide services: an evaluation of the case – law developments in the area of indistinctly applicable rules' [2001] *Legal Issues of European Integration* 23. More recently L Hancher and W Sauter, 'One step beyond? From *Sodemare* to *Docmorris*: The EU's freedom of establishment case law concerning healthcare' [2010] *Common Market Law Review* 117.

- First, the right of health service providers to offer their services in competition with those provided in the patient's home Member State by establishing themselves has not been comprehensively analysed.
- Second, the possibilities for private investment in quasi-public or quasi-privatized hospitals or clinics, and to offer patients competitive health care, remain to be considered in more detail.
- Third, the question arises whether national governments can continue not only to organize health care provision along public or non-profit lines, but also, to favour such providers with preferential access to public funding.

The first of these three issues is the primary focus here, although the other two more complex issues are also touched upon. The starting point is that the Treaty rules on freedom of establishment are now generally interpreted as guaranteeing market access to all forms of transnational activity, including health care.[3] Thus, the interpretation of the freedom of establishment has developed, from the principle of national treatment, to a dual criterion of measures affecting access to the market and/or effects-based discrimination. (The argument is clearly reviewed by the Opinion of AG Tizzano in *CaixaBank* (2004). He sets out how this is the same logic as that in the context of free movement in *Keck and Mithouard* (1993).[4]) **4.05**

The relevance of this development in the recent case law is all the greater because, as a matter of EU law, Member States are not obliged to liberalize their health care sectors, although once these have been liberalized, turning back the clock becomes difficult.[5] In the *German hospital pharmacies* (2008) case the ECJ explicitly embraced this 'liberalization breeds liberalization' thesis by stating that: **4.06**

> (...) although the Community rules on the free movement of goods do not require that it should be possible for all hospitals situated in Member States to obtain supplies of medicinal products from external pharmacies, when a Member State provides for such a possibility, it opens that activity to the market and is accordingly bound by Community rules.[6]

This approach is similar to that in the Commission's state aid framework for services of general economic interest (SGEI) which provides that where services are already **4.07**

[3] cf in relation to establishment: Case C-442/02 *CaixaBank France v Ministère de l'Économie, des Finances et de l'Industrie (CaixaBank)* [2004] ECR I-8961; Joined Cases C-94/04 and C-202/04 *Federico Cipolla v Rosaria Fazari, née Portolese (C-94/04) and Stefano Macrino and Claudia Capoparte v Roberto Meloni (C-202/04) (Cipolla)* [2006] ECR I-11421.

[4] Case C-442/02 *CaixaBank*, Opinion of AG Tizzano, supra n 3. Joined Cases C-267 and C-268/91 *Criminal proceedings against Bernard Keck and Daniel Mithouard (Keck and Mithouard)* [1993] ECR I-6097.

[5] Case C-174/04 *Commission v Italy (voting rights)* [2005] ECR I-4933; C-503/99 *Commission v Belgium* [2002] ECR I-4809; Case E-2/06 *EFTA Surveillance Authority v Norway (waterfalls)* [2007] OJ C301/18.

[6] Case C-141/07 *Commission v Germany (hospital pharmacies)* [2008] ECR I-6935, para 41.

being provided, or can be provided, by undertakings in accordance with the rules of the market, and under conditions such as price and access to the service that are consistent with the public interest, these can no longer be defined as SGEI.[7]

4.08 At the same time, as recent studies have observed, an important outcome of the lack of clarity concerning the impact of EU law on national health policies is the emergence of a leading, if controversial, role for the ECJ in this policy field.[8] This role becomes all the more prominent in systems which mix market and solidarity-based health care provision and/or public and private financing. That involves not only conscious attempts at liberalization, but also public systems which tolerate the emergence of parallel private initiatives in an attempt to meet pent up demand. One example where the two are compatible is provided by the risk equalization systems for health insurance such as have been introduced in Ireland and the Netherlands. Risk equalization was examined in detail in *BUPA* (2008) (see Chapter 9).[9]

4.09 Unlike the freedom to provide services in the context of the development of patients' rights, recent case law concerning the supply side has not yet been discussed systematically. However, we believe this latest jurisprudence will become increasingly important to the course of health care liberalization and regulation of markets across the EU.

4.10 In this context one line of recent case law, notably represented by *Hartlauer* (2008), which concerned restrictions imposed under Austrian law on the setting up of outpatient dental clinics, suggests that where national measures are subjected to a consistency standard as part of the proportionality test the scope for market access is (or could be) broadened.[10] On the other hand, not just the 'notorious' *Sodemare* (1997) case but also more contemporary cases such as *DocMorris* (2009), on ownership rules for German pharmacies, show the ECJ is prepared to uphold obvious restrictions based on the argument that the profit motive is inherently suspect in

---

[7] Communication from the Commission, on the application of the European Union State aid rules to compensation granted for the provision of services of general economic interest [2012] OJ C8/4; Commission Decision of 20 December on the application of Article 106(2) of the Treaty on the Functioning of the European Union to State aid in the form of public service compensation granted to certain undertakings entrusted with the operation of services of general economic interest [2012] OJ L7/3; Communication from the Commission, European Union framework for State aid in the form of public service compensation (2011) [2012] OJ C8/15.

[8] TK Hervey and JV McHale, *Health Law and the European Union* (Cambridge: Cambridge University Press, 2004); E Mossialos et al (eds), *Health Systems Governance in Europe: the Role of Law and Policy* (Cambridge: Cambridge University Press, 2010).

[9] Case T-289/03 *British United Provident Association Ltd (BUPA)* et al *v Commission (BUPA)* [2008] ECR II-81. On solidarity more generally see: C Newdick, 'Citizenship, free movement and health care: Cementing individual rights by corroding social solidarity' [2006] *Common Market Law Review* 1645; T Prosser, 'Regulation and social solidarity' [2006] *Journal of Law and Society* 364.

[10] Case C-169/07 *Hartlauer Handelsgesellschaft mbH v Wiener Landesregierund and Oberösterreichischer Landesregierung (Hartlauer)* [2009] ECR I-1721.

health markets.[11] It is therefore valid to inquire what, if anything, has changed? Meanwhile in the abovementioned *German hospital pharmacies* case the 'unity and balance' of the system was found to warrant similarly obvious restrictions. In view of these mixed signals a more thorough analysis of the role of the ECJ concerning the freedom of establishment in the context of health care is necessary.

In particular it is useful to inquire why the ECJ has been prepared to support patient mobility and the right to freedom of choice in the health care sector but has been reluctant to embrace the freedom of health care providers to compete across borders to widen that choice. At the level of justification, the protection of public health and the rights of Member States to determine the level of protection is frequently endorsed by the EU courts; but does this mean that while it should remain uncontroverted that Member States have the right to regulate the quality of health care and its delivery, that it must necessarily follow that they should also have wide if not unlimited discretion to organize the means of delivery as well? The recent case law is instructive in this respect. **4.11**

The current legal situation

This section examines the division of competences between the European and national levels to set out how the various Treaty rules can impact on health care provision. **4.12**

Subsidiarity in health care

As Article 168 TFEU reminds us, in principle the Member States are sovereign in matters of health. This sector-specific emphasis of the subsidiarity principle appears to leave little scope for harmonization, and its application is in line with the settled case-law of the ECJ according to which EU law does not detract from the power of the Member States to organize their social security systems.[12] **4.13**

As the ECJ recently recalled in *DocMorris* (2009)—a case concerning the application of Article 43 EC (Article 49 TFEU) to Austrian legislation on the setting up and operation of outpatient dental clinics: **4.14**

> (...) it is for the Member States to determine the level of protection which they may wish to afford to public health and the way in which that level is to be achieved.

---

[11] Case C-70/95 *Sodemare SA, Anni Azzurri Holding SpA and Anni Azzurri Rezzato Srl v Regione Lombardia (Sodemare)* [1997] ECR I-3395; Joined Cases C-171/07 and C-172/07 *Apothekerkammer des Saarlandes* et al *v Deutscher Apothekerverband and Helga Neumann-Siewert v Saarland (DocMorris)* [2009] ECR I-4171.

[12] Case 238/82 *Duphar BV* et al *v The Netherlands (Duphar)* [1984] ECR 523, para 16; Joined Cases C-159/91 and C-160/91 *Christian Poucet v Assurances Générales de France and Caisse Mutuelle Régionale du Languedoc-Roussillon (Poucet)* [1993] I-637, para 6; Case C-70/95 *Sodemare*, supra n 11, para 27; Case C-158/96 *Raymond Kohll v Union des caisses de maladie (Kohll)* [1998] ECR I-1931, para 17.

> Since the level may vary from one Member State to another, Member States must be allowed discretion.[13]

4.15 Similarly, in considering the scope for derogation from the rules on free movement in general, the ECJ refuses to read across jurisdictions to require Member States to follow their neighbours. Hence it stated in relation to the legality of restrictions imposed under Belgian law on optical testing in the *Mac Quen* (2001) case:

> (…) the fact that one Member State imposes less strict rules than another Member State does not mean that the latter's rules are disproportionate and hence incompatible with Community law.[14]

4.16 The ECJ has repeated that in the absence of harmonization (that is, positive integration through secondary legislation), 'Member States must be allowed a margin of appreciation', to determine not just the level of protection but to some extent the means by which this achieved.[15] Yet this wording suggests a slightly less permissive approach than one based on 'discretion'; and it does not necessarily give a free hand when it comes to the organization of health care delivery. As will become clear from the more detailed discussion of the case law below, the Member States are in any event allowed to determine the pace of liberalization (or indeed the absence thereof), as long as they do so in a consistent and systematic manner.[16]

4.17 Although the organization of health care delivery is primarily a matter for the individual Member States, the sector is nonetheless subject to the Treaty rules on free movement and on competition, including the freedom of establishment.[17] As a result of the gradual encroachment of these rules into national systems, it has become strikingly apparent that national health care systems—and their organization—are not immune from EU law. Fifteen years on from the landmark *Decker* and *Kohll* (1997) cases,[18] the legal landscape has changed considerably on the demand side, with some hesitant and cautious shifts on the supply side, as explained below.

---

[13] Joined Cases C-171/07 and C-172/07 *DocMorris*, supra n 11, para 19; with reference to Case C-322/01 *Deutscher Apothekerverband eV v 0800 DocMorris NV, Jacques Waterval (Deutscher Apothekerverband)* [2003] ECR I-14887, para 103; as well as Case C-141/07 *Hospital pharmacies*, supra n 6; and Case C-169/07 *Hartlauer*, supra n 10, para 30. For an earlier formulation cf Case C-271/92 *Laboratoire de Prothèses Oculaires v Union Nationale des Syndicats d'Opticiens de France* et al *(LPO)* [1993] ECR I-2899, para 10; Joined Cases C-1/90 and C-176/90 *Aragonesa de Publicidad Exterior SA and Publivía SAE v Departamento de Sanidad y Seguridad Social de la Generalitat de Cataluña* [1991] ECR I-4151, para 16.

[14] Case C-108/96 *Criminal proceedings against Dennis Mac Quen* et al *(Mac Quen)* [2001] ECR I-837, para 33. With reference to Case C-384/93 *Alpine Investments* [1995] ECR I-1141, para 51; and Case C-3/95 *Reisebüro Broede* [1996] ECR I-6511, para 42.

[15] Case C-110/05 *Commission v Italy (motorcycle trailers)* [2009] ECR I-519, para 65.

[16] cf Case C-500/06 *Corporación Dermoestética SA v To Me Group Advertising Media (Dermoestética)* [2008] ECR I-0785, para 39; Case C-169/07 *Hartlauer*, supra n 10, para 63.

[17] The freedom of movement of workers will not be dealt with in this book.

[18] Case C-120/95 *Nicolas Decker v Caisse de maladie des employés privés (Decker)* [1998] ECR I-1831; Case C-158/96 *Kohll*, supra n 12.

The market freedoms

4.18 As we have seen in Chapter 3, Articles 56 and 57 TFEU apply to freedom of services, allowing the patient to move to the provider or the provider to the patient, on a temporary basis. Consequently, either way the health provider remains subject to the regulatory system of the Member State where it is established (the 'home' Member State). A host Member State is not allowed to impose further restrictions on the service provider as this would impose a double regulatory burden.[19] What we will discuss here is that if a health care provider wishes to move to another Member State on a more permanent basis, it can invoke Article 49 TFEU on the right to freedom of establishment. If they are normally provided for by remuneration then such services fall under the scope of the free movement rules, although this does not require direct payments in benefits in kind and national health service (NHS) systems.[20] The ECJ has also formulated the essence of Article 49 TFEU as 'the actual pursuit of an economic activity through a fixed establishment in another Member State for an indefinite period' in *Factortame II* (1991).[21] This provision has considerable scope to impact on national regulatory regimes. As we shall illustrate, the concept of establishment is broad and can range from starting up a biomedical laboratory to setting up a business as an optician, a pharmacy, or a hospital facility. The test is whether there is a stable and continuous participation in the economic life of the Member States in question.[22] Article 54 TFEU—which holds that companies and firms formed in accordance with the law of a Member State shall receive national treatment in (other) Member States—is often applied in parallel.

The recent case law on freedom of establishment in health care

4.19 This section focuses on the application of the rules on freedom of establishment in greater detail. As we have indicated above, the ECJ's rulings in *German hospital pharmacies* (2008), *Hartlauer* (2009) and *DocMorris* (2009)[23] suggest that the contours of the application of these rules to the supply side of the health care market are emerging and deserve closer analysis.[24]

4.20 Some two dozen cases where the freedom of establishment has been invoked in the context of health care provision have so far reached the ECJ. Of these, a number

[19] cf Case C-496/01 *Commission v France (laboratories)* [2004] ECR I-2351.

[20] cf Case C-157/99 *B.S.M. Geraets-Smits v Stichting Ziekenfonds VGZ and H.T.M. Peerbooms v Stichting CZ Groep Zorgverzekeringen) (Smits and Peerbooms)* [2001] ECR I-5473; Case C-372/04 *The Queen, on the application of Yvonne Watts v Bedford Primary Care Trust and Secretary of State for Health (Watts)* [2006] ECR I-4325.

[21] Case C-221/89 *R. v Secretary of State for Transport, ex parte Factortame (Factortame II)* [1991] ECR I-3905, para 20. Thus cited in E Barnard, *The substantive law of the EU: The four freedoms* (2nd edn, Oxford: Oxford University Press, 2007) 308.

[22] Case C-70/95 *Sodemare*, supra n 11, para 24.

[23] Case C-141/07 *Hospital pharmacies*, supra n 6; Case C-169/07 *Hartlauer*, supra n 10; Joined Cases C-171/07 and C-172/07 *DocMorris*, supra n 11.

[24] cf L Hancher and W Sauter, supra n 2.

primarily concern the harmonization of professional qualifications and are of lesser interest for the development of the interpretation of the freedom of establishment in health care.[25] However a couple of early cases are of note where the 'single practice rule' for doctors in France (in 1986) and respectively for both doctors and dentists in Luxembourg (in 1992) were struck down without much ado by the ECJ.[26] 'Continuity of care' was not held to merit a blanket prohibition and in particular the Luxembourg legislation was internally inconsistent (a theme that would subsequently reappear in the *Dermoestética* (2008) case on the prohibition of television advertisements for medical treatments).[27] A comparable case outside the context of harmonization, but centred on a requirement to take experience acquired in other Member States into account, is *Commission v Germany* (2007) (a case concerning psychotherapists).[28] Other cases primarily concern the freedom to provide services and/or free movement of goods and will be discussed under that heading.

4.21 First we will discuss the results in the main cases from *Sodemare* to *DocMorris* separately before analysing the conceptual developments in the case law.

Sodemare

4.22 The first substantive case on the freedom of establishment was handed down in *Sodemare* (1997).[29] In this case a private undertaking operating nursing homes contested the rejection of its request to be contracted for the provision of social security services of a health care nature by the Lombardy region in Italy.

4.23 Importantly, whereas Sodemare was legally required to provide certain health care services 'for elderly patients living independently' it was not entitled to obtain public reimbursement for these services.[30] Consequently, users were subject to higher charges when seeking services from for-profit providers such as Sodemare as opposed to publicly-funded providers, and Sodemare was in fact required to cross-subsidize between its various activities in order to comply with its public service duties—resulting in a situation where it had very low occupancy rates even in a context where waiting lists existed for the services concerned.[31]

[25] Eg Case C-319/92 *Salomone Haim v Kassenzahnärztliche Vereinigung Nordrhein (Haim I)* [1994] I-425; Case C-154/93 *Abdullah Tawil-Albertini v Ministre des Affaires Sociales* [1994] ECR I-451; Case C-277/93 *Commission v Spain (stomatology)* [1994] I-5515; Case C-424/97 *Salomone Haim v Kassenzahnärztliche Vereinigung Nordrhein (Haim II)* [2000] ECR I-5123; Case C-35/02 *Landeszahnärztekammer Hessen v Markus Vogel* [2003] ECR I-12229.

[26] Case 96/85 *Commission v France* [1986] ECR 1475; Case C-351/90 *Commission v Luxembourg* [1992] I-3945.

[27] Case C-500/06 *Dermoestética*, supra n 16, para 39.

[28] Case C-456/05 *Commission v Germany (psychotherapists)* [2007] ECR I-10517.

[29] Case C-70/95 *Sodemare*, supra n 11.

[30] ibid, at para 12 and again at para 16, question 5(d).

[31] Case C-70/95 *Sodemare*, supra n 11, Opinion of AG Fennelly, para 9.

The legality of the not-for-profit condition

The ECJ held, firstly, that the freedom of establishment was involved as Sodemare was 'involved on a stable and continuous basis in the economic life of Italy'. Next, when examining the non-profit condition it recalled that EU law does not detract from the powers of the Member States to organize their social security systems.[32] The ECJ's reasoning progressed in three steps: **4.24**

- It set out that the Italian system of social welfare was based on the principle of solidarity. As summarized by the Court, according to the Italian government the non-profit condition was required because: 'The choices made in terms of organization and provision of assistance by non-profit-making private operators are not influenced by the need to derive profit from the provision of services so as to enable them to pursue social aims as a matter of priority.'
- Next it stated: 'In that regard, it must be stated that, as Community law stands at present, a Member State may, in the exercise of the powers it retains to organize its social security system, consider that a social welfare system of the kind at issue in this case necessarily implies, with a view to attaining its objectives, that the admission of private operators to that system as providers of social welfare services is to be made subject to the condition that they are non-profit-making.'
- Moreover the Court held that being refused public service contracts did not place profit-making companies from other Member States in a less advantageous situation than profit-making firms in the Member States of establishment.[33]

Consequently, the ECJ went against the view of its Advocate General and concluded that the Italian ban on for-profit participation did not infringe Articles 49 and 54 TFEU, that is to say it did not restrict the freedom of establishment. Hence there was no need to invoke an exception. A notable feature of this judgment is that the fact that for-profit firms were blocked from reimbursement but were nevertheless expected to fulfil universal service obligations was not discussed. The fact that it was evidently more difficult for undertakings from other Member States—which must almost by definition be for-profit in order to attract funding—to enter the Italian system than for Italian undertakings (both for-profit and not for-profit) was flatly denied with little by way of reasoning. By highlighting that its decision should be seen in the context of 'the present state of Community law' the Court appears to have signalled that only the adoption of harmonization legislation could cause it to apply a stricter test to national measures in this area. **4.25**

The ECJ's assumption that a not-for-profit status enables operators to pursue social services as a matter of priority is perhaps naive (although this line of reasoning is **4.26**

[32] With reference to Case 238/82 *Duphar*, supra n 12, para 16; Joined Cases C-159/91 and C-160/91 *Poucet*, supra n 12, para 6.
[33] Case C-70/95 *Sodemare*, supra n 11, paras 31–33.

also confirmed in recent gambling cases).[34] Its approach may be based on the implicit idea that it is all very well to have a market mechanism for less essential purposes, but where issues of social importance are at stake other orderings that somehow produce superior results (which are conveniently not measured but achieved by definition) deserve priority. Of these alternative orderings there are essentially two: public, solidarity-based and/or non-profit making on the one hand, and private, based on self-regulation (sometimes also called corporatism), on the other hand. As we will see, when asked to choose between the market and these other two alternatives the ECJ so far invariably picks the latter.

Mac Quen

4.27 The *Mac Quen* (2001) case concerns charges of unlawful practice of medicine in Belgium brought against the employees of an optician's firm upon the complaint of the Belgian ophthalmologists' association.[35] (The contested practices included testing for hypertension of the eye, examining the state of the retina, examining the field of vision, and biomicroscopic examinations.) This question was not regulated by the existing harmonization legislation on the mutual recognition of diplomas, nor was the profession of ophthalmologist subject to other specific EU legislation. In principle, nationals of other Member States were subject to the same restrictions on the freedom of establishment as Belgian nationals—but the fact that they must comply with these conditions was regarded as an indication that establishment was restricted. (In other words, the fact that establishment was regulated in itself already triggered Articles 49 and 56 TFEU.)

Four-part test

4.28 In this case the ECJ applied the four-part test derived from the *Gebhard* (1995) case, that in order to be compatible with Articles 49 and 56 TFEU the measures concerned must be (1) non-discriminatory; (2) justified by imperative requirements in the general interest; (3) suitable to attain their objective; and (4) necessary to do so.[36] This approach is well in line with current ideas about the meaning of non-discriminatory barriers that focus on market access: market access is often seen as the driving force behind the theory of 'non-discriminatory' barriers to

[34] eg Joined Cases C-447/08 and C-448/08 *Criminal proceedings against Otto Sjöberg (C-447/08) and Anders Gerdin (C-448/08)* [2010] judgment of 8 July 2010 (nyr).

[35] Case C-108/96 *Mac Quen*, supra n 14.

[36] Case C-108/96 *Mac Quen*, supra n 14, para 25; citing Case C-55/94 *Reinhard Gebhard v Consiglio dell'Ordine degli Avvocati e Procuratori di Milano (Gebhard)* [1995] ECR I-4165, para 37; Case C-19/92 *Kraus v Land Baden-Wuerttemberg* [1993] ECR I-1663, para 32; Case C-243/01 *Criminal proceedings against Piergiorgio Gambelli* et al [2003] ECR I-13031, paras 64 and 65.

free movement.[37] Discrimination was not found to exist. Moreover, according to the Court, if a Member State chose to reserve particular treatments to a category of professionals holding specific qualifications then this may be regarded as an appropriate means by which to ensure attainment of a high level of protection.[38]

It is difficult to agree with this view on several counts. In the first place it may well be that such prohibitions fall more heavily on parties from other Member States. Second, it is clear that the rule at issue does not regulate whether particular functions are performed to an objective standard, but just who performs them. Third, given the lower barrier of approaching an optometrist (eg no waiting lists) the types of screening performed by them might well be beneficial for public health. **4.29**

Proportionality

As regards proportionality the ECJ set out its approach in three key statements: **4.30**

- It recalled: '(...) that the fact that one Member State imposes less strict rules than another Member State does not mean that the latter's rules are disproportionate and hence incompatible with Community law.'[39]
- Also it held: '(T)he mere fact that a Member State has chosen a system of protection different from that adopted by another Member State cannot affect the appraisal of the need for and the proportionality of the provisions adopted.'[40]
- Finally, the Court held that the assessment of the risk to public health may change: 'An assessment of this kind is liable to change with the passage of time, particularly as a sign of technical and scientific progress.'[41]

With this guidance, the matter was referred back to the national court. Substantially the same reasoning was followed in *Deutsche Paracelsus Schulen* (2002), where the ECJ found in favour of Austrian legislation blocking the training of lay medical practitioners that was legal in Germany (as was lay medical practice).[42]

---

[37] cf E Spaventa, 'From Gebhard to Carpenter: towards a (non-)economic European Constitution' [2004] *Common Market Law Review* 743; citing S Weatherill, 'After *Keck*: some thoughts on how to clarify the clarification' [1996] *Common Market Law Review* 885; C Barnard, 'Fitting the remaining pieces into the goods and persons jigsaw?' [2001] *European Law Review* 35; M Poiares Maduro, 'Harmony and dissonance in free movement' in M Andenas and W-H Roth (eds), *Services and Free Movement in EU Law* (Oxford: Oxford University Press, 2002) 41.

[38] For an earlier case cf Case C-61/89 *Criminal proceedings against Marc Gaston Bouchoucha* [1990] ECR I-3551.

[39] Case C-108/96 *Mac Quen*; With reference to Case C-384/93 *Alpine Investments BV v Minster van Financiën* [1995] ECR I-1141, para 51; Case C-3/95 *Reisebüro Broede v Gerd Sandker* [1996] ECR I-6511, para 42.

[40] ibid, para 34; with reference to Case C-67/98 *Questore di Verona v Diego Zenatti* [1999] ECR I-7289, para 34.

[41] ibid, para 36.

[42] Case C-294/00 *Deutsche Paracelsus Schulen für Naturheilverfahren GmbH v Kurt Gräbner (Paracelsus Schulen)* [2002] ECR I-6515.

4.31 Relating to the 'time heals all wounds' logic, in *Mac Quen* the Court referred to a German judgment where the contested treatments had been allowed. While in the absence of harmonization it is logical that Member States may differ in the degree of protection they accord public health, to suggest that technical and scientific progress occurs more or less independently in each Member State seems odd. At the same time this approach raises doubts about the rationality of the ban—which could have been addressed in the judgment.

4.32 The apparent assertion, that the fact that differing restrictions exist in different Member States—often in pursuit of the same goals—is irrelevant to their proportionality, seems mistaken. It is not contested here that it is up to the Member States to decide the level of health protection they wish to provide. The restrictions they impose have to be proportionate in that national setting and differences in treatment do not automatically entail a violation of the proportionality principle. However this need not exclude reading across experiences from other jurisdictions: if a less restrictive means is shown to be effective in attaining the same or even a higher level of protection would this not be relevant? If, instead, the point is that no less restrictive means test will ever be applied but only a 'not manifestly disproportionate' test this should be spelled out. However, this is an inherent limitation to negative integration that is not particular to health care. Moreover, once positive integration—secondary harmonization legislation—exists the least restrictive means test should apply. This distinction is not currently made systematically.

Greek opticians

4.33 In the *Greek opticians* (2005) case the European Commission charged Greece with infringement of Article 49 TFEU by means of a requirement that only authorized opticians could hold optician's shops, providing a minimum of 50 per cent of the capital, and participating in a maximum of two shops (provided both were in the name of separate authorized opticians).[43] The Commission held that the objective of protecting the public health could equally well have been obtained by requiring the presence of qualified, salaried opticians or associates in each optician's shop (as well as by the rules for civil liability and requiring professional indemnity insurance), the restriction was found to go beyond what was necessary: hence, to be disproportionate. The ECJ thus applied a less restrictive means test. As a consequence Greece was found to be in breach of Articles 49 and 54 TFEU. Although this case did not seem remarkable at the time it demonstrates a level of assertiveness the ECJ has rarely displayed since then; generally taking a permissive attitude to comparable restrictions—notably in *German hospital pharmacies* (2008) and *DocMorris* (2009).

[43] Case C-140/03 *Commission v Greece (opticians)* [2005] ECR I-3177.

German psychotherapists

The Commission had brought this 2007 case against Germany for infringement of Article 49 TFEU because when establishing a maximum number of psychotherapists per region, based on regional needs, it had declined to take previous professional activities outside Germany into account in establishing protected rights (in the context of a transitional arrangements).[44] **4.34**

Restrictions

The ECJ examined whether a restriction on the freedom of establishment existed in this case where experience acquired under the statutory sickness scheme of another Member State was not taken into account. It recalled that: **4.35**

> (…) a law, even if applicable to all, which makes entitlement to a right subject to a condition of residence in a region of a Member State, and thereby favours nationals of that Member State over nationals of other Member States, runs counter to the principle of non-discrimination.[45]

Established rights and limiting numbers irrespective of need

However, the ECJ held that an established right such as retaining clients constituted an overriding ground of public interest. This seems surprising—it would have been more appropriate to examine the reasons for restricting the supply of psychotherapists. Giving vested interests the role of an overriding ground of public interest does not appear a promising approach—it enables entrenchment of the status quo without further reasoning. And more importantly: where is the public interest involved? Moreover, the Court held that the German provisions: **4.36**

> (…) must be regarded as appropriate to preserving the established rights of those persons while limiting the number of psychotherapists practising under the German statutory sickness insurance scheme, independently of need.[46]

In view of the patient mobility case law on 'undue delay' in the context of the freedom to provide and receive services (reviewed in Chapter 3) it is not clear what could be the justifiable objective of a scheme limiting the availability of health care provision that failed to take into account patients needs. Finally, however, Germany failed the proportionality test, as it had not established that taking a less harsh measure would have satisfied its objectives while avoiding the abovementioned discrimination. It should be noted in this context that in infringement cases the burden of proof is on the Member States. **4.37**

[44] Case C-456/05 *Commission v Germany (psychotherapists)* [2007] ER I-10517.
[45] ibid, para 56; with reference to Case C-274/96 *Bickel and Franz* [1998] ECR I-7637, para 26.
[46] ibid, para 64.

Corporación Dermoestética

4.38 At issue in this 2008 case was the Italian prohibition on advertisements for medical treatments on national television, whereas such advertisements were allowed on regional and local stations.[47] In principle, Member States are allowed to impose stricter prohibitions on advertising than those laid down in the relevant harmonization legislation;[48] however, such rules are liable to make it more difficult for economic operators to gain access to the Italian market—as well as restricting the freedom to provide services.

4.39 Because national advertising was prohibited yet regional and local broadcasting were allowed: 'such rules exhibit an *inconsistency* which the Italian Government has not attempted to justify and cannot therefore properly attain the public health objective which they seek to pursue.'[49] Hence the Italian legislation was held to be inappropriate for justifying an exception to Articles 49 and 56 TFEU.

4.40 It should be noted that the criterion of 'consistency' that is developed here is an important one, which reappears in the *Hartlauer* (2009) case (as well as, there, 'applied in a systematic manner') that is discussed below. It appears to form the basis for a contextual proportionality test that is prepared to accept given policy objectives on their own merits but requires them to be pursued in a coherent and logically defensible way, that is to say not at cross purposes.

Hartlauer

4.41 This 2009 case concerns the refusal of regional governments in Austria to give the Hartlauer Corporation permission to set up and operate independent outpatient dental clinics in the regions of Vienna and Oberösterreich.[50] According to the relevant national legislation, authorization of a health institution required taking into account representatives of vested interests (established dentists) who were already contracted by sickness funds in determining whether there was a need. To provide context it should be added the relevant legislation further defines who was eligible to practice together as a group practice, which was not subject to a prior examination of need, and also that Austria had both a benefits in kind insurance and a reimbursement system of health insurance (the latter at a maximum of 80 per cent of the costs incurred).

[47] Case C-500/06 *Dermoestética*, supra n 16.

[48] Council Dir 89/552/EEC of 3 October 1989 on the coordination of certain provisions laid down by Law, Regulation or Administrative Action in Member States concerning the pursuit of television broadcasting activities [1989] OJ L298/23, Art 14(1).

[49] Case C-500/06 *Dermoestética*, supra n 16, para 39 (emphasis added).

[50] Case C-169/07 *Hartlauer*, supra n 10.

Reasoning for the refusal

Hartlauer was refused access on the ground that its establishment 'would not have the effect of substantially accelerating, intensifying or improving the provision of dental medical care' so 'there was *no need* for the institution'.[51] In the case of Vienna, the analysis was based on the ratio between the number of inhabitants and the number of dental practitioners, in the case of Oberösterreich it was based on an examination of waiting times. **4.42**

This assessment by the Austrian authorities is worth noting because if private parties are prepared to invest it seems evident that there is a service to be provided (as they would scarcely do so otherwise). The only other explanation might be that supply-induced-demand may occur. This is the argument that health care providers are likely to create their own demand: for example after a hospital purchases an expensive MRI scanning machine the number of cases where it is used may well be determined by the need to pay off the machine instead of exclusively by objective patient needs. This argument is often invoked by public authorities seeking to contain health care costs. **4.43**

Restriction of establishment

The ECJ held that since the level of protection of public health may vary from one Member State to the other, Member States must be allowed discretion.[52] However it also pointed out that in the case under consideration permission was required to set up an establishment regardless of whether a contract would be concluded to provide benefits in kind. (That is, also if Hartlauer wished to operate purely on the basis of restitution.) **4.44**

Hereby the requirement of prior permission (authorization) deprived Hartlauer from access to the market for dental care in Austria altogether, which formed a restriction of the freedom of establishment. **4.45**

The public health exception

Austria, in its defence, in fact raised the supply-induced-demand argument, oddly, alongside the argument that an uncontrolled expansion of services would have harmful economic consequences for incumbents who were apparently not able to induce demand. This does not appear logical especially in view of the 80 per cent reimbursement rate that would tend to put brakes on demand by requiring co-payments (out-of pocket expenses for patients)—and given there was no obligation to extend the benefit in kind system to Hartlauer's clinics. **4.46**

---

[51] ibid, para 18, (emphasis added).

[52] ibid, para 30; citing Case C-141/07 *Hospital pharmacies*, supra n 6, para 51.

4.47 The ECJ proceeded to evaluate the defence of the protection of public health, which in its view involves:

(1) a balanced high-quality medical or hospital service open to all—which involves the maintenance of treatment capacity or medical competence on national territory; and
(2) the objective of preventing the risk of serious harm to the financial balance of the social security system, which involves planning intended to control costs and to prevent wastage of 'financial, technical and human resources'.[53]

4.48 The Court then examined the possible need for planning, taking into account that 'it is permissible for a Member State to organize medical care in such a way that it gives priority to a system of benefits in kind'.[54] However it was not satisfied that the Austrian legislation was appropriate.

4.49 First, there was a clear form of discrimination because group practices were allowed to be established without any form of prior authorization whereas they offered the same services as outpatient clinics. Moreover they were likely to give rise to the same objections, if these were to be taken seriously. Hence the Court held:

> In those circumstances it must be concluded that the national legislation at issue (…) does not pursue the stated objectives in a consistent and systematic manner.[55]

It should be noted that this develops the consistency criterion as used in the Italian *Dermoestética* case and forms a counterpoint to the 'unity and balance of the system' in the *German hospital pharmacies* case as well (the latter a free movement of goods case that will be discussed below, all three of these cases having been decided in 2008).

4.50 Second, recalling its general case law on appropriate procedural guarantees, that was also invoked in the patients' rights context, the ECJ established that prior authorization schemes must be based on objective, non-discriminatory criteria known in advance, in such a way as to adequately circumscribe the exercise of national authorities' discretion.[56] On this count it found that no pre-existing criteria were in place and that the assessment was made, in part, based on the responses by potential direct competitors. For obvious reasons this fell short of minimum standards of procedural fairness.

[53] ibid, para 47; citing Case C-372/04 *Watts*, supra n 20, paras 103–4.
[54] ibid, para 53.
[55] ibid, para 63.
[56] ibid, para 63; citing Case C-205/99 *Asociasción Profesional de Empresas Navieras de Líneas Regulares (Analir)* et al *v Administración General del Estado* [2001] ECR I-1271, paras 37–38; Case C-385/99 *V.G. Müller-Fauré v Onderlinge Waarborgmaatschappij OZ Zorgverzekeringen UA and E.E.M. van Riet v Onderlinge Waarborgmaatschappij ZAO Zorgverzekeringen* [2003] ECR I-4509, paras 84–85.

Conclusion

Consequently the ECJ concluded that the system of prior authorization in place was not appropriate for ensuring the objective of protecting public health and the legislation in point was precluded by Articles 49 and 54 TFEU. By focusing on consistency, requiring a systematic approach, and procedural guarantees, the Court applied a process oriented test concerning proportionality. This makes it possible to use EU law to pick apart systems that fail in terms of their internal logic (or are forced to compromise with pressures for change they can no longer contain), opening up the road to market entry, in other words new establishment. **4.51**

DocMorris

In this case a rule in the German law on pharmacies ('Apothekengezetz') that all pharmacies must not only be run but also owned by an independent pharmacist was at issue (in 2009).[57] This requirement was examined by the full Court of Justice from the perspective of freedom of establishment in Articles 49 and 54 TFEU. The German federal government claimed the contested law was justified by the protection of public health. The regional government of Saarland, DocMorris, and the Commission claimed the restriction was neither suitable nor necessary to attain this objective. There was thus a split between the national and the regional levels of government in Germany on this issue. **4.52**

Under the terms of the contested license to operate a branch pharmacy that had been provided by the Saarland government, DocMorris (established in the Netherlands) was already required to recruit a pharmacist to manage its pharmacy personally and under his responsibility. At issue therefore was primarily the ownership requirement under German law. **4.53**

The ECJ first recalled that EU law does not detract from the power of the Member States to organize their social security systems, although they must in doing so respect EU law, in particular the Treaty provisions on free movement. It also stated that it is for the Member States to determine the level of health protection they wish and that for that reason, they must be allowed discretion. **4.54**

Restriction on the freedom of establishment

Next, the ECJ established that a restriction on self employment by means of a prior authorization requirement and reserving the activity concerned to certain economic operators by definition constitutes a restriction of free movement. Hence it examined whether this might be justified by an overriding reason in the general interest. **4.55**

[57] Joined Cases C-171/07 and C-172/07 *DocMorris*, supra n 11.

Non-discrimination and capable of justification

4.56 The ECJ quickly established that the legislation at issue applied without discrimination (the first condition) and was covered by the protection of public health (the second condition):

> More specifically, restrictions on those freedoms of movement may be justified by the objective of ensuring that the provision of medicinal products to the public is reliable and of good quality.[58]

Appropriateness

4.57 Next the ECJ looked at whether it was appropriate to exclude non-pharmacists from ownership. In doing so it distinguished pharmaceuticals from other goods stating that: (i) unnecessary or incorrect consumption of medicinal products could cause serious harm to health; and (ii) over-consumption or incorrect use of medication could lead to the waste of financial resources.

4.58 In this context, the ECJ held:

> (…) it must be accepted that Member States may require that medicinal products be supplied by pharmacists enjoying genuine professional independence. They may also take measures which are capable of eliminating or reducing a risk that that independence will be prejudiced because such prejudice would be liable to affect the degree to which the provision of medicinal products to the public is reliable and of good quality.[59]

4.59 As an aside, it might be remarked that this appears a quixotic view in a world where industry promotional campaigns heavily target 'independent' pharmacists. Moreover entrants have every incentive not to cause serious harm to health or waste financial resources as their business would otherwise surely fail. It is also of note that no proof was supplied that the national system in fact delivers better (or for that matter any particular) results. Next, the Court pursued the theme of professional independence:

> It is undeniable that an operator having the status of pharmacist pursues, like other persons, the objective of making a profit. However, as a pharmacist by profession, he is presumed to operate the pharmacy not with a purely economic objective, but also from a professional viewpoint.[60]

4.60 It also held that for pharmacist-owners 'the making of a profit is tempered' whereas it is not for pharmacists who are employed. According to the ECJ, non-pharmacists by definition do not provide the same safeguards. On the facts of the case this is odd, because DocMorris had been licensed precisely to own a pharmacy operated by a pharmacist—just not owned by him. It could just as well be argued that being

[58] ibid, para 28; with reference to Case C-322/01 *Deutscher Apothekerverband*, supra n 13, para 106.
[59] ibid, para 35.
[60] ibid, para 37.

freed from the burden of financial responsibility better enabled this pharmacist to live up to deontological standards. Moreover it is not clear why adequate alternative safeguards could not be in place even in the absence of an owner/pharmacist on the premises.

Significantly, the ECJ explicitly pointed out the analogy with social welfare services in *Sodemare* to the effect that: **4.61**

> (...) unlike the case of a pharmacy operated by a pharmacist, the operation of a pharmacy by a non-pharmacist may represent a risk to public health, in particular to the reliability and quality of the supply of medicinal products at retail level, because the pursuit of profit in the course of such operation does not involve moderating factors such as those (...) which characterise the activity of pharmacists (see by analogy, with regard to the provision of social welfare services Case C-70/95 *Sodemare and Others* [1997] ECR I-3395, paragraph 32).[61]

The ECJ then also listed some of the practices which pharmacists who were not themselves owners might, in its eyes, be guilty: (i) manufacturers or wholesalers might encourage them to promote the medicinal products which they produce or market themselves; (ii) they might be encouraged to sell off medicinal products which it is no longer profitable to keep in stock. **4.62**

The arguments of DocMorris and the Commission that the public interest objective was pursued in an inconsistent manner (eg in view of the rule that a single pharmacist could own and operate as many as three pharmacies, and that hospitals were allowed to employ in-house pharmacists) were rejected. Here too, the ECJ vented implicit accusations: **4.63**

> (...) having regard to the fact that those hospitals provide medical care, there are no grounds for assuming that they would have an interest in making a profit to the detriment of the patients for whom the medicinal products of the pharmacies which they house are intended.[62]

This observation suggests that other parties would have an interest in making profits to their patients' detriment. In our view that makes no business sense because they would lose their customers, at least as long as alternative providers of the services concerned existed, which is why markets are normally trusted to be self-correcting in this respect (albeit within the confines of competition law in cases of dominance abuse).

Necessity

Finally the ECJ examined the fourth element, that of necessity. It rejected the possibility of relying on an employed pharmacist operating the premises: **4.64**

> (...) there is a risk that legislative rules designed to ensure the professional independence of pharmacists would not be observed in practice, given that the interest of a

[61] ibid, para 39.
[62] ibid, para 48.

> non-pharmacist in making a profit would not be tempered in a manner equivalent to that of self-employed pharmacists and that the fact that pharmacists, when employees, work under an operator could make it difficult for them to oppose instructions given by him.[63]

Consequently the Court found the measure necessary. It distinguished this case from the *Greek opticians* (2005) case because the potential harm to health and waste of financial resources in the case of medicinal products was much greater (than in the case of opticians).

4.65 Protecting entrenched professional interests is a potentially counterproductive way of guaranteeing the public interest. Nowhere in the ruling is there any suggestion that such schemes should be judged not just based on their claims or good intentions, but on the merits; that is in terms of specific obligations and verifiable performance measures. Moreover the notion of the pharmacist directly employed by the pharmaceutical industry is a red herring: this was not the business model DocMorris proposed to use.

4.66 It should be recognized however that the *DocMorris* case is not a complete return to the *Sodemare* approach. Instead of ruling that no breach of Article 49 TFEU existed here a justification was necessary and the *Gebhard* test is applied (see para 4.28). This can be seen as a first step toward testing the rationality and consistency of the public policy in question: one step beyond. A more in-depth analysis of this case law is presented below after a short description of two more recent cases.

Blanco Pérez en Chao Gómez

4.67 *Blanco Pérez en Chao Gómez* (2010) concerned the Spanish system for spatial distribution of pharmacies based on a licensing regime with criteria for population density and the minimum distance between pharmacies.[64] The ECJ applied a strict proportionality test and took the view that this restriction was justified because it acted in an overriding reason of public interest—the provision of a safe and high quality supply of medication to the public—in a suitable (or, coherent and systematic) and necessary manner. It held that the suggestion by the applicants and the Commission that pharmacists should be free to establish themselves in regions where the minimum level of pharmacies had already been reached failed to achieve the objective of the regime because at the same time too few pharmacists might be established elsewhere. It should be noted however that the award of additional points in the selection procedure to pharmacists who had obtained their professional experience in Spain was found to be discriminatory and in breach of the freedom of establishment.

[63] ibid, para 54.
[64] Joined Cases C-570/07 and C-571/07 *Blanco Pérez and Chao Gómez* [2010] ECR I-4629.

Commission v France (laboratories)

In this 2010 case,[65] the French requirement that capped the participation of non-professional biologists in bio-medical analysis laboratories at 25 per cent was at stake.[66] The ECJ had to choose between two precedents—that of the *Greek opticians* (para 4.33) where such restraints were held not justified—and that in *Italian pharmacies* (discussed below under freedom of capital at para 4.117) where the nature of the products involved had been found to justify public ownership restrictions. Because the risks to public health involved in operating bio-medical laboratories were thought to be similar to those in dispensing pharmaceuticals, the guarantees held inherent in the profession of biologist were thought key (even in the absence of any specific standard or set of deontological rules). Hence limiting ownership to this profession was found suitable, necessary, and proportionate (see paras 4.52–4.66 and 4.81–4.85 (*DocMorris*); para 4.117 (*Italian pharmacies*)). Note by contrast however that in the same year the Commission found the industry association of these French laboratories guilty of infringing the cartel prohibition of Article 101(1) TFEU by means of price fixing and foreclosure, and fined them.[67] Clearly the corporatist arrangements involved were not innocuous. **4.68**

Analysis

In this section we take a closer look at the trends that emerge from the case law discussed above. **4.69**

Toward non-discriminatory restrictions

In its early case law applying Article 49 TFEU to health care the ECJ displayed a cautious if not conservative approach. Notably in *Sodemare*,[68] it departed from the Advocate General's Opinion. It held that it was justified for a Luxembourg based for-profit undertaking to be denied public funding to run homes for the elderly in Italy. This ruling was based on the theory that the relevant legislation reserving participation in the state social welfare system to non-profit operators did not discriminate because undertakings from other Member States were not in a worse situation than domestic for-profit undertakings (which were likewise excluded). Yet if the only way to enter a market is to adopt the prevailing non-profit form of organization this creates an obvious disincentive. Entrants typically require outside investment, funds which they cannot hope to raise on a non-profit basis as investors **4.70**

[65] Case C-89/09 *Commission v France (laboratories)* [2010] judgment of 16 December 2010 (nyr).

[66] cf below Case C-141/07 *Hospital pharmacies*, supra n 6, under the free movement of goods; and Case C-531/06 *Commission v Italy (pharmacies)* [2009] ECR I-4103, under free movement of capital.

[67] *ONP* (Case 29510) [2010] C(2010) 8952 final, Commission Decision of 8 December 2010 based on Article 101 TFEU. <http://ec.europa.eu/competition/antitrust/cases/dec_docs/39510/39510_1203_3.pdf> accessed 23 February 2012.

[68] Case C-70/95 *Sodemare*, supra n 11.

who can choose between alternative investments will demand dividends—and at the same time, a guarantee that the investment will be viable and that they will be efficient providers.

4.71 In the subsequent decade the ECJ gradually departed from this narrow approach. This move is in line with the general trend in the free movement case law which, already by the mid-1990s, saw the Court condemning a wide range of national measures liable to hinder, or make less attractive, the exercise of fundamental freedoms guaranteed by the TFEU, and made these measures subject to justification. In contrast to Article 56 TFEU on services, which can be used to challenge double regulation, Article 49 TFEU on establishment can be relied upon to challenge the very existence of regulatory measures as barriers, even if they lack any specific cross-border element.

4.72 This trend in the health care establishment case law implies a departure from, if not a reversal of, *Sodemare*. It suggests that Member States may no longer a priori have a wide margin of discretion to distinguish between profit and non-profit providers. Instead they will have to justify even non-discriminatory restrictions to the freedom of establishment which must be both necessary to fulfil a public interest objective and proportionate to this objective.

4.73 This analysis appears consistent with the recent services case law on gambling in *Sjöberg and Erdin* (2010).[69] Here a Swedish interdiction of advertising for-profit gambling operations was found acceptable under the freedom to provide services based on a public interest justification. (At the same time exclusive rights were found potentially compatible provided that they were enforced in a non-discriminatory manner.) Similarly in *Commission v Italy* (2009) the ECJ found an obligation to offer third party liability insurance constituted a barrier as it interfered with the business model of insurers from other Member States.[70] However this was found to be necessary and appropriate with regard to the social objective pursued—the availability of such insurance throughout the national territory. The apparent articulation in this case of a rule that different and/or innovative business models are in principle not to be interfered with where they are to the benefit of the national status quo is potentially significant to the health care sector, even if recent cases like *Commission v France* (*laboratories*), above, (where it was not applied) make clear that it is too early to signal a definite trend in this direction.

[69] Joined Cases C-447/08 and C-448/08 *Sjöberg and Gerdin*, supra n 34. cf Case C-42/07 *Liga Portuguesa de Futebol Profissional and Bwin International Ltd v Departamento de Jogos da Santa Casa da Misericórdia de Lisboa* [2009] ECR I-7633.

[70] Case C-518/06 *Commission v Italy* [2009] ECR I-3491. Similar: Case *C-384/93 Alpine Investments BV v Minister van Financiën* [1995] ECR I-1141. cf D Chalmers, G Davies and G Monti, *European Union Law* (2nd edn, Cambridge, Cambridge University Press 2010), 795–97.

Proportionality—a cautious approach to justifying market access barriers?

In summary it is possible to conclude, first, that the ECJ now readily finds breaches of the freedom of establishment in the health care sector, and second, that it will generally examine whether non-discriminatory regulatory entry barriers can be exempted based on the four part *Gebhard* test. In order to be compatible with Articles 49 and 56 TFEU such barriers must be (1) non-discriminatory; (2) justified by imperative requirements in the general interest; (3) suitable to attain their objective; and (4) necessary to do so.[71] In the context of this test the criteria of appropriateness (proportionality) and necessity are key. Here a strict ('least restrictive means') test is sometimes applied, as in *Greek opticians*, and in *German Psychotherapists*,[72] as well as in *Hartlauer*. In all three cases the national rules at issue related to the organization of the delivery of the service at issue. In all three cases the ECJ held that the objectives of protecting public health (while justifiable) could be achieved by other means. **4.74**

Yet in its *Mac Quen* (2001) ruling the Court made three notable statements on proportionality in the context of the application of the free movement rules to the health sector.[73] It recalled that (i) different degrees of strictness of national regulation were compatible with EU law, and that (ii) systems would not be compared between Member States to establish necessity and proportionality.[74] It also stated (iii) that views on risk to public health were liable to change over time to reflect technical and scientific progress.[75] Substantially the same reasoning was followed in *Deutsche Paracelsus Schulen* (2002), where the ECJ found in favour of Austrian legislation blocking the training of lay medical practitioners which was legal in Germany (as was lay medical practice).[76] **4.75**

As was mentioned above the existence of differing types of restrictions in different Member States should not be disqualified as irrelevant in terms of proportionality. Evidently it remains up to the Member States to decide the level of *health protection* they wish to provide for their citizens and the *restrictions* they impose have to be proportionate in that specific context. Nevertheless there can be benefits involved in reading across experiences from other jurisdictions. For instance if a less restrictive means is shown to be effective in attaining the same or even a higher level of protection this should be at least relevant to the proportionality test, even if it is not necessarily conclusive. **4.76**

[71] Case C-70/95 *Sodemare*, supra n 11, para 25; citing Case C-55/94 *Gebhard*, supra n 36 para 37; Case C-19/92 *Kraus*, supra n 36, para 32; Case C-243/01 *Criminal proceedings against Piergiorgio Gambelli* et al [2003] ECR I-13031, paras 64–65.

[72] Case C-456/05 *Commisson v Germany*, supra n 44.

[73] Case C-108/96 *Mac Quen*, supra n 14.

[74] ibid, para 33; with reference to Case C-384/93 *Alpine Investments*, supra n 39, para 51; Case C-3/95 *Reisebüro Broede*, supra n 39, para 42.

[75] ibid, para 36.

[76] Case C-294/00 *Paracelsus Schulen*, supra n 42.

Appropriateness and necessity

4.77 As discussed in the *Greek Opticians* (2005) case, the Commission challenged a Greek measure imposing a requirement that (inter alia) only authorized opticians could own and operate optician's shops as an infringement of Article 43 EC (Article 49 TFEU).[77] The ECJ used a least restrictive means test and it clearly recognized that a particular form of organization was not necessarily the only way to deliver the necessary level of protection of the consumer. By contrast in *Commission v France (laboratories)* (2010) the nature of the health care involved was held to entail greater risks to the consumer and therefore ownership restrictions were necessary—as it had held for pharmacies in the 2008 goods case that will be discussed below (see *German hospital pharmacies* at paras 4.108–4.111).

4.78 As was set out in more detail above, *Hartlauer* (2009), concerned a reference from the Austrian administrative court relating to the refusal of regional governments in Austria to give the Hartlauer Corporation permission to set up and operate independent outpatient dental clinics in the regions of Vienna and Oberösterreich.[78] The ECJ found that there was a clear form of discrimination because group practices were allowed to be established without any form of prior authorization whereas they offered the same services as outpatient clinics. Moreover they were likely to give rise to the same objections, if these were to be taken seriously.

4.79 The ECJ developed the 'consistency' criterion that was first used in the Italian *Dermoestética* case and forms a counterpoint to the 'unity and balance of the system' in the *German hospital pharmacies* case as well (both decided in 2008). In *Dermoestética* national advertising for medical treatments was prohibited yet regional and local broadcasting was allowed, showing an inconsistency which could not be justified.

4.80 The resulting consistency requirement allows entrants to contest protectionist regulation with internal contradictions. But in other cases the Court declines to submit national regulation to a stricter test of appropriateness in the context of *Gebhard*, as recently confirmed, for example, in *German Hospital pharmacies* as well as *Italian pharmacists* and *DocMorris*. In these cases the application of the public interest exception was not seriously examined on its merits. No accountability to public standards is required nor is evidence of any kind in terms of actual results. Nor is an economic analysis (such as in a cost versus benefits sense) performed: instead unsubstantiated claims are put forward that entrants driven by the profit motive are liable to exploit their consumers and even damage their health while depleting health care financing in the process.

---

[77] Case C-140/03 *Commission v Greece (opticians)* [2005] ECR I-3177.

[78] Case C-169/07 *Hartlauer*, supra n 10. cf Case C-531/06 *Commission v Italy (Italian pharmacists)* [2009] ECR I-4103.

Towards a more nuanced approach in DocMorris?

In its *DocMorris* (2009) ruling the ECJ looked at whether it was appropriate to exclude non-pharmacists from ownership of a pharmacy. In doing so it distinguished pharmaceuticals from other goods stating that: unnecessary or incorrect consumption of medicinal products could cause serious harm to health; and over-consumption of incorrect use of medication could lead to the waste of financial resources. These risks could be averted by pharmacists enjoying genuine professional independence, not by employees. **4.81**

It also held that for pharmacist-owners 'the making of a profit is tempered' whereas it is not for pharmacists who are employed. According to the ECJ, non-pharmacists by definition do not provide the same safeguards. On the facts of the case this is odd, because DocMorris had been licensed precisely to own a pharmacy operated by a pharmacist—just not owned by him. It could just as well be argued that being freed from the burden of financial responsibility better enabled this pharmacist to live up to deontological standards. Moreover it is not clear why adequate alternative safeguards could not replace the presence of an owner/pharmacist on the premises. **4.82**

Significantly and as in the *Italian pharmacies* case (goods, see para 4.117),[79] the ECJ explicitly pointed out the analogy with social welfare services in *Sodemare*.[80] The Court then also listed some of the practices of which pharmacists who were not themselves owners might, in its eyes, be guilty: manufacturers or wholesalers might encourage them to promote the medicinal products which they produce or market themselves; and/or they might be encouraged to sell off medicinal products which it is no longer profitable to keep in stock. **4.83**

The arguments of DocMorris and the Commission that the public interest objective was pursued in an inconsistent manner (as a single pharmacist could own and operate as many as three pharmacies, and because hospitals were allowed to employ in-house pharmacists) were rejected. Here the Court stated that there were 'no grounds for assuming that the pharmacists would have an interest in making a profit to the detriment of the patients for whom the medicinal products of the pharmacies which they house are intended'.[81] Finally the Court rejected the possibility of relying on an employed pharmacist operating the premises: because they would be unable to temper the profit making interest of the operator under which they worked.[82] **4.84**

Consequently the Court found the measure necessary. As it would do in *Commission v France* (bio-medical laboratories, 2010), it distinguished *DocMorris* from the 2005 *Greek Opticians* case because the potential harm to health and risk of waste of **4.85**

[79] Case C-531/06 *Italian pharmacists*, supra n 78, para 63.
[80] Joined Cases C-171/07 and C-172/07 *DocMorris*, supra n 11, para 39.
[81] ibid, para 48.
[82] ibid, para 54.

financial resources in the case of medicinal products was much greater (than in the case of opticians).[83]

Patient mobility versus establishment

4.86 It is also evident that the ECJ's approach to patient mobility in its extensive jurisprudence on this matter[84] diverges from that concerning freedom of establishment in health care. Although in both lines of cases broadly the same types of 'public interest' exceptions are invoked, in the patient mobility cases these are trumped by procedural and material guarantees designed to protect the individual patient (or, individual patients' rights and the right of choice). A similar logic does not exist in the establishment context, when freedom of market access and inevitably competition are at stake. There appears to be limited appreciation or scope for the possibility that the freedom of establishment can stimulate efficient market entry, spreading best practices throughout the EU, and hence potential health care improvements which could also be to the benefit of patients and patients' choice.

Financial versus regulatory issues

4.87 To date, the ruling in *Sodemare* is one of the few establishment cases touching on reimbursement while the majority of the remaining cases deal with health standards. The main exception is *Hartlauer* where the ECJ considered the threats of supply-induced-demand (even although the pharmacists' cases implicitly touch on this too) to the coherence of the system. In *Hartlauer* the Court took a strict line and found no threat to the coherence of the system at issue. In those cases where it decides primarily on the public interest to maintain health standards it often does so by reference to the services of practitioners belonging to a specific medical profession, or to self-regulation by such professions (sometimes called corporatism). Regrettably, the ECJ tends to confine its analysis to the necessity and appropriateness of such formal qualifications, as opposed to going on to examine their wider effects on the supply or organizational side of health provision.

C. Goods

4.88 The Treaty's fundamental protection of the free movement of goods has been of considerable importance in guaranteeing the access of medicines, medical devices, and related products to national markets. As we shall see in Chapter 5, a raft of

[83] Case C-140/03 *Opticians*, supra n 77.

[84] On services case law see W Sauter, 'The Proposed Patient Mobility Directive and the Reform of Cross-Border Healthcare in the EU' [2008] TILEC Discussion Paper No 2008–034 <http://ssrn.com/abstract=1277110> accessed 23 February 2012; on free movement of services, goods and establishment see L Hancher and W Sauter, 'One Foot in the Grave or One Step Beyond? From Sodemare to DocMorris: The EU's Freedom of Establishment Case Law Concerning Healthcare' [2009] TILEC Discussion Paper No 2009–28 <http://ssrn.com/abstract=1429315> accessed 23 February 2012.

secondary legislation governs the process of marketing authorization for most of these types of products so that Member States are no longer entitled to impose barriers to trade through national legislation in order to protect public health. Secondary legislation does not lead to centralized authorization procedures for all products and national controls remain legitimate. Furthermore, important aspects of pharmaceutical regulation, including price and profit control, are subject to only a very minimal degree of harmonization.[85] Finally, the impact of intellectual property rights on dividing territories into distinct national markets cannot be ignored. Article 34 TFEU which prohibits measures which have an equivalent effect to restrictions on import, remains of key importance. Each of these topics is the subject of a considerable body of case law and attendant commentary[86] and we will confine ourselves to a few salient remarks on the nature and scope of Article 34 TFEU.

Pharmaceuticals

In the paragraphs below we will first deal with the pharmaceuticals sector before moving on to free movement of goods in a broader sense. We will look at parallel imports, the role of intellectual property rights, as well as price and profit regulation and restrictions on reimbursement. **4.89**

Parallel imports

Parallel trade refers to the act of importing a product from one country to another and placing the products outside the distribution channels authorized by the product manufacturer. It is usually a response to price (and currency) divergence across markets. The importing Member State may benefit from parallel imports of pharmaceuticals as it can lead to lower prices for health care funds and insurers, but at the same time it is entitled to check that the parallel product is equivalent to the product marketed through the authorized distribution channels. **4.90**

In accordance with the principle of mutual recognition, developed by the ECJ in the *De Peijper* (1976) pharmaceuticals case, the importing Member State should accept controls carried out in the Member State of origin and is not entitled to require the product to undergo extensive testing to establish its safety, efficacy, and quality.[87] **4.91**

[85] Council Dir 89/105/EEC of 21 December 1988 relating to the transparency of measures regulating the prices of medicinal products for human use and their inclusion in the scope of national health insurance systems [1989] OJ L40/8.

[86] L Hancher, 'The pharmaceutical market; Competition and free movement actively seeking compromises' in M McKee, E Mossialos and R Baeten (eds), *The Impact of EU Law on Health Systems* (Brussels: P.E.I-Peter Lang, 2002) 235.

[87] Case 104/75 *Adriaan de Peijper, Managing Director of Centrafarm BV* [1976] ECR 613.

Intellectual property rights

4.92 Medicines are usually protected by intellectual property rights (IPR), including patents, trademarks, and copyrights. The exercise of these rights by their holders has been subjected to Article 34 TFEU on numerous occasions, so that while the courts have recognized the existence of IPR rights as validly conferred by national law, and as protected by the exception of Article 36 TFEU, the exercise of those rights must not constitute a barrier to their free circulation. This is known as the doctrine of exhaustion.[88] This doctrine, as first laid down by the ECJ in 1971 in the *Deutsche Grammophon* case, prevents the intellectual property (IP) owner from using its IP right to stop the parallel trade of goods 'placed on the market by him or with his consent in another Member State'.[89] The ECJ reached this conclusion by considering Article 34 TFEU in the light of what was then Article 3(g) EC which required instituting a system that ensured competition was not distorted,[90] and stressing that if the IP owner could stop the distribution of goods in the internal market:

> (...) on the sole ground that such distribution did not take place on national territory such a prohibition, which would legitimize the isolation of national markets, [this] would be repugnant to the essential purposes of the Treaty, which is to unite national markets into a single market.[91]

4.93 This principle was subsequently applied to patents for pharmaceuticals in the *Centrafarm v Sterling Drug* (1974) case, and to trademarks in *Centrafarm v Winthorp* (1974) in the same year and later in *Centrafarm v American Home Products* (1978),[92] as well as to attempts to invoke copyright or trademark rights to prevent re-packaging of products in a series of cases from the 1990s onwards.[93] IPR rights are exhausted, and parallel trade cannot be prevented if the product is lawfully

[88] An important exception is the 'Specific Mechanism' enabling the IPR holder to enforce its right against parallel trade from the new MS—see Annex IV of the Act of Accession [2003] OJ L236/797; Annex V, Ch I of the Protocol of the Accession Treaty for Romania and Bulgaria [2005] OJ L157/103.

[89] Case 78/70 *Deutsche Grammophon Gesellschaft mbH v Metro-SB-Großmärkte GmbH & Co. KG* [1971] ECR 487, para 6.

[90] Now Protocol 27 of the Consolidated versions of the Treaty on European Union and the Treaty on the Functioning of the European Union [2010] OJ C83/309.

[91] Case 78/70 *Deutsche Grammophon*, supra 89, para 12.

[92] Case 15/74 *Centrafarm BV and Adriaan de Peijper v Sterling Drug Inc* [1974] 1147; Case 16/74 *Centrafarm BV and Adriaan de Peijper v Winthrop BV* [1974] 1183; Case 3/78 *Centrafarm BV v American Home Products Corporation* [1978] 1823.

[93] Joined Cases C-427/93, C-429/93 and C-436/93 *Bristol-Myers Squibb v Paranova A/S (C-427/93) and C. H. Boehringer Sohn, Boehringer Ingelheim KG and Boehringer Ingelheim A/S v Paranova A/S (C-429/93) and Bayer Aktiengesellschaft and Bayer Danmark A/S v Paranova A/S (C-436/93)* [1996] ECR I-3457; Case C-232/94 *MPA Pharma GmbH v Rhône-Poulenc Pharma GmbH* [1996] ECR I-3671; Joined Cases C-71/94, C-72/94 and C-73/94 *Eurim-Pharm Arzneimittel GmbH v Beiersdorf AG (C-71/94), Boehringer Ingelheim KG (C-72/94) and Farmitalia Carlo Erba GmbH (C-73/94)* [1996] ECR I-3603.

marketed in another Member State by the IPR holder, a licensee, or by a person legally or economically dependent on the IPR holder.[94]

The ECJ subsequently confirmed and refined the exhaustion principle in a series of cases involving pharmaceutical products. The principle has subsequently been incorporated into secondary legislation aimed at harmonizing IP rights throughout Europe. Blocking, by means of agreements between producers of pharmaceutical products and consumers, has been found to infringe the cartel prohibition of Article 101 TFEU, a finding which has been refined with respect to the necessary consent to collusion by the contracting parties.[95] **4.94**

Price and profit regulation

Member States are entitled to control their health budgets, of which pharmaceutical expenditure is an important part. In doing so however they should not discriminate against imported products. The ECJ has been less strict in its application of Article 34 TFEU to pricing regulation in general: the mere existence of price regulation does not constitute a barrier to trade. It is necessary for the party invoking Article 34 TFEU to show that the regulation involved discriminates against imports, for example by not allowing for costs incurred outside the Member State to be included in the price calculation methodology. Similarly, price freezes may be contrary to Article 34 TFEU if importers cannot recoup their costs. Profit regulation can also fall foul of Article 34 TFEU for the same reasons. **4.95**

Thus in cases such as *Commission v Italy* and *Commission v Belgium* the ECJ upheld the legality of national price and profit regulation as the Commission had failed to prove that imported products were in fact discriminated against by either national regime.[96] **4.96**

Restrictions on reimbursement

If an imported product is not included in a 'positive list' or features in a 'negative list' for reimbursement by health care funds as a result of a state measure, then it is effectively excluded from the national market in question. In *Roussel* (1983) and *Duphar* (1984) the ECJ balanced the free movement rights of the pharmaceutical undertakings involved against the interest of the Member States to control the **4.97**

---

94 Joined Cases C-267/95 and C-268/95 *Merck & Co. Inc., Merck Sharp & Dohme Ltd and Merck Sharp & Dohme International Services BV v Primecrown Ltd, Ketan Himatlal Mehta, Bharat Himatlal Mehta and Necessity Supplies Ltd and Beecham Group plc v Europharm of Worthing Ltd* [1996] ECR I-6285.

95 Case C-277/87 *Sandoz prodotti farmaceutici SpA v Commission of the European Communities* [1990] ECR I-45; Joined Cases C-2/01 P and C-3/01 *P Bundesverband der Arzneimittel-Importeure eV and Commission of the European Communities v Bayer AG* [2004] ECR I-23.

96 Case 56/87 *Commission v Italy* [1988] ECR 2919; Case C-249/88 *Commission v Belgium* [1991] ECR I-1275.

prices of pharmaceuticals in order to contain health care costs.[97] In *Duphar* the Court held that the fact that, at that time, not consumers but social security institutions covered the costs of pharmaceuticals was justification for a national scheme aiming to control costs provided that it was non-discriminatory, based upon objective criteria without reference to the origin of the producers.

Free movement beyond pharmaceuticals

4.98 We now move on to free movement of goods more broadly speaking.

Marketing and selling arrangements

4.99 For reasons of consumer protection and the protection of public health, products are often marketed through certain outlets, albeit that with the exception of prescription only products, there is no further secondary legislation governing the marketing phase to patients/consumers, although advertising of prescription products is subject to a total ban in accordance with EC Directive 2001/83/EC.[98] This leaves substantial scope for Member States to adopt widely diverging policies in this respect so that in some Member States infant milk formula can be bought around the clock in supermarkets, while in others these products are only available from pharmacies. The growth of internet pharmacies as well as 'inset' pharmacy counters in supermarkets has challenged traditional national pharmacists' monopolies. The rules on free movement have been invoked to spearhead the challenge.

4.100 Since the *Keck* (1993) case the freedom of movement for goods has the special characteristic that certain restrictions are not seen as barriers to trade that must be removed but as acceptable selling arrangements that fall outside the scope of EU law.[99] In *Keck* the ECJ determined that restrictions that are not related to the nature of the product but to the way in which it is marketed, or selling arrangements, fall outside the prohibition:

> (...) so long as those provisions apply to all relevant traders operating within the national territory and so long as they affect in the same manner, in law and in fact, the marketing of domestic products and of those from other Member States.[100]

4.101 This requires that such selling arrangements do not affect the nature of the product (such as weight, size, and/or composition), but only the conditions under which it can be traded (such as a prohibition of loss-leading sales, no Sunday trading, and/or limiting the sales of certain goods to pharmacies). Also they must be

[97] Case 181/82 *Roussel Laboratoria BV and others v The Netherlands* [1983] ECR 3849; Case 238/82 *Duphar BV and others v The Netherlands* [1984] ECR 523.

[98] Dir 2001/83/EC of the European Parliament and of the Council of 6 November 2001 on the Community Code relating to Medicinal Products for Human Use, as amended [2004] OJ L311/67.

[99] Joined Cases C-267/91 and C-268/91 *Criminal proceedings against Bernard Keck and Daniel Mithouard* [1993] ECR I-6097.

[100] ibid, para 16.

non-discriminatory—both formally and in fact. So far this rule has had limited impact in the health care area as restrictions on selling through particular channels, such as pharmacies, can often be justified on consumer or health protection grounds. The main two 'selling arrangements' cases concerning health care are briefly discussed below.

Hünermund

4.102 In Hünermund (1993) the ECJ held that the prohibition, by a publicly backed professional association of pharmacists, from advertising quasi-pharmaceutical products outside the pharmacy fell outside the scope of Article 34 TFEU under the *Keck* rule, provided the rules involved were non-discriminatory, that is both by origin and by the effect that they would have on the marketing of non-domestic products.[101]

Commission v Greece

4.103 *Commission v Greece* (1995) concerned the Greek prohibition on the marketing of infant milk formula other than by pharmacies. This was regarded as no more than a selling arrangement as it identified the points of sale for distribution. Moreover it applied without distinction according to the origin of the products in question. Because Greece, in any event, did not produce infant milk formula there could be no question of privileging domestic production.[102]

4.104 Next we will briefly discuss the goods cases that are closer in substance to the establishment cases that were discussed above.

Schumacher

4.105 The *Schumacher* (1989) case was decided before the existence of the celebrated *Kohll* and *Decker* case law. It concerned a German prohibition on the import of pharmaceuticals for personal use, in this case from France, while the contested drug was available prescription free in both Member States concerned.[103] The ECJ considered this to be a restriction of the free movement of goods that could not be saved by an appeal to the exception for public health. It ruled that the general German prohibition was disproportionate and that moreover the existing degree of harmonization and mutual recognition legislation concerning the delivery from a French pharmacy guaranteed a comparable level of protection to that of a German pharmacy.

Decker

4.106 The *Decker* (1998) case has already been discussed in Chapter 3 under the freedom to provide services heading, as it was decided in tandem with the services case

[101] Case C-292/92 *Ruth Hünermund* et al *v Landesapothekerkammer Baden-Württemberg* [1993] ECR I-6787.
[102] Case C-391/92 *Commission v Greece (Infant formula)* [1995] ECR I-1621.
[103] Case 215/87 *Heinz Schumacher v Hauptzollamt Frankfurt am Main-Ost* [1989] ECR 617.

Kohll.[104] In this case the Court held that a prior authorization requirement for the purchase of a pair of spectacles in another Member State was discriminatory and could not be justified based on overriding reasons of general interest. This was because reimbursement was limited to a fixed amount so the financial balance of the social security system in Luxembourg would not be at risk.

Deutscher Apothekerverband

4.107 *Deutscher Apothekerverband* (2003) concerned the German prohibition of sales and advertisements for the sales by mail order or Internet of medication for which the distribution was reserved to pharmacies.[105] Because these marketing and selling arrangements formed a restriction, especially on market entrants from other Member States (in this case the Dutch company 0800 DocMorris NV), it was seen as a case of discrimination and the *Keck* exception for selling arrangements did not apply.[106] The ECJ held that stricter national rules with respect to prescription drugs could benefit from an appeal to the public health exception in Article 36 TFEU. For non-prescription (over the counter) drugs, however, supervision in the Member State of origin was considered adequate, and hence the German rule was held to form an infringement in this respect.

German hospital pharmacies

4.108 *German hospital pharmacies* (2008) involved the German requirement that the pharmacist providing medication to hospitals had to be able to be on the scene forthwith.[107] On the one hand the ECJ held that a Member State which liberalized the provision of medication to hospitals, as Germany had done, should logically provide access in accordance with EU law. On the other hand the ECJ accepted that the German restrictions, which aimed to guarantee that a single pharmacist would not only be responsible for providing the medication but would also always be in the vicinity, guaranteed:

> (…) that all the elements of the system for the supply of medicinal products to hospitals in Germany are equivalent and mutually compatible, and thereby guarantee the unity and balance of that system.[108]

4.109 Thus in *German hospital pharmacies* the Court, without much by way of reasoning, held that the contested legal provisions which made it impossible for German hospitals to be supplied by pharmacies outside Germany were justified because the unity and balance of the system for the supply of medicinal products in Germany had to be ensured. Consequently, the Court held the German system 'clearly' does

[104] Case C-120/95 *Decker*, supra n 18.
[105] Case C-322/01 *Deutscher Apothekerverband*, supra n 13.
[106] Joined Cases C-267/91 and C-268/91 *Keck*, supra n 100.
[107] Case C-141/07 *Hospital pharmacies*, supra n 6.
[108] ibid, para 56.

not go beyond what is necessary. In addition, it pointed out that the system proposed by the Commission (with separate supplying and monitoring pharmacies) would be financially wasteful. The ECJ then went on to emphasize first, the need for planning the hospital system, and secondly, avoiding financial waste.[109]

Superficially, the 'unity and balance' of the system may appear something akin to the 'consistency' criterion in *Dermoestética* and *Hartlauer*, or the financial balance of the medical systems in the earlier patient mobility cases, and a reasonable enough standard. However, it is by no means evident why the process of contracting for medicines through *in situ* pharmacists by individual hospitals should be seen as forming part of a system that required coherence and balance: the hospitals concerned do not depend on each other in a relevant manner in this context, financially or otherwise. For the same reason, planning was in no way affected—nor was any evidence presented that in Germany planning of hospitals' spatial or geographical distribution is relevant to the case (or for that matter actually takes place). In other words: there simply is no system here that requires unity and balance. **4.110**

On a more positive reading this judgment could be seen as allowing a Member State to plan a gradual reorganization (eg to move former internal services to an external setting) without the risk of having that controlled transformation threatened by the free movement rules and the 'barbarians at the gate'. At the same time the ECJ gave little credence to the Commission attempts to demonstrate that public health objectives need not have been put at risk if the requirement that the pharmacist should be local had been eliminated, and that other measures were realistically possible and would not have imposed unnecessary costs on the system. The ruling therefore appears to be based on the implicit assumption that if a system of organization of certain health care activities is inextricably linked with a certain standard or level of protection, then any further analysis of the different components of that system can be avoided by assuming a need for unity and balance. **4.111**

Ker-Optika Bt

The *Ker-Optika Bt* (2010) case concerned a Hungarian prohibition on the distribution (selling and supplying) of contact lenses via the Internet.[110] Here the electronic commerce directive[111] was held to apply alongside the provisions of Articles 34 and 36 TFEU. Because the requirement that contact lenses be sold only in specialized **4.112**

[109] Referring to Case C-157/99 *Smits and Peerbooms*, supra n 20; Case C-385/99 V.G. *Müller-Fauré v Onderlinge Waarborgmaatschappij OZ Zorgverzekeringen UA and E.E.M. van Riet v Onderlinge Waarborgmaatschappij ZAO Zorgverzekeringen (Müller-Fauré)* [2003] ECR I-4509; Case C-372/04 *Watts*, supra n 20.

[110] Case C-108/09 *Ker-Optika Bt v ÀNTSZ Dél-dunántúli Regionális Intézete* [2010] judgment of 2 December 2010 (nyr).

[111] Dir 2000/31/EC of the European Parliament and of the Council of 8 June 2000 on certain legal aspects of information society services, in particular electronic commerce, in the Internal Market [2000] OJ L178/1.

shops was held to have an indirectly discriminatory effect, the *Keck* exception for selling arrangements did not apply. This was because the ban deprived traders from other Member States of a particularly effective means of selling their products and therefore significantly impeded market access. As regards the appeal to the public health exception, this was not held justified because the measure concerned was not proportional in the sense that it was not necessary and the need could have been met by 'measures which subject to certain restrictions only the first supply of lenses and which require the economic operators concerned to make available a qualified optician to the customer'.[112] Hence an infringement of EU law was established.

Evaluation

4.113 The case law on Article 34 TFEU has been of fundamental importance to the promotion and protection of parallel trade in pharmaceuticals, and the ECJ has been prepared to place priority on the proper functioning of the internal market at the expense of the rights of IPR holders. With regard to the residual freedom of Member States to invoke the public health exception in Article 36 TFEU, or to rely on the 'overriding requirements of public policy', the Court has where possible relied on the doctrine of mutual recognition to avoid unnecessary duplication of national controls. With regard to pricing and reimbursement the case law seeks to strike a balance between the legitimate national interest to maintain or impose budgetary controls without erecting barriers to free movement of goods. The case law on marketing however is broadly in line with the case law on free movement of services. We observe on the one hand cases based on individual rights such as *Decker*, which reflect the services case law, and on the other cases concerning goods that revolve around obscure 'systemic' risks such as we have seen in the establishment case law like in *German hospital pharmacies*. An important difference is the relevance of the selling arrangements rule which holds exclusively for goods. Apart from that it is relevant that secondary legislation exists for medical devices which will be dealt with in Chapter 6. First however we will briefly cover the freedom of capital.

D. Capital

4.114 The freedom of capital is the last of the four freedoms and it has been a latecomer in fulfilling a role as an essential pillar of the internal market following the amendments to what was then Article 73b EC by the Treaty of Maastricht. Article 63 TFEU prohibits all restrictions on the movement of capital not only by between Member States but also, and uniquely, between the latter and third countries. The ECJ has confirmed that this Article is now subject to the same principles of

[112] Case C-108/09 *Ker-Optika Bt*, supra n 110, para 74.

interpretation as the other freedoms. It has recognized that both Article 63 TFEU and the important 1988 Capital Directive[113] are directly effective. Moreover the concept of restriction is broadly interpreted. The exceptions provided for in Article 65 TFEU are interpreted narrowly and cannot be invoked for purely economic considerations. This has been confirmed in a long series of cases relating to privatization of key strategic sectors, where the Member State sought to maintain some form of supervision in the public interest through a 'golden share' mechanism.[114] As with the other freedoms, the ECJ has emphasized that the concept of restriction goes beyond the mere elimination of discrimination and extends to any rule that affects the position of a person acquiring a shareholding in a firm and as such is liable to be deterred from making an investment. A Member State cannot rely on public policy grounds to justify certain critical decisions such as significant investments and mergers.

Article 63 TFEU is also of considerable relevance to national tax restrictions including restrictions in relation to third countries, to such an extent that the Member States have fought back and have inserted a new exception in the Treaty of Lisbon.[115] In the meantime, at least as far as tax restrictions are concerned, the ECJ has moved towards an exclusive approach in respect of the application of the freedoms, so that the rules on establishment or services often take precedence over those concerning capital. **4.115**

It follows that Article 63 TFEU is of relevance to regulatory restrictions against investing in the health care sector.[116] For the time being, such restrictions certainly exist in numerous Member States and in a practical sense the restrictions on the freedom of establishment all concern restrictions on the free movement of capital as well; this is because in general terms it is likely that market entry across national borders will require investments—and create investment opportunities. In this context the fear of the profit motive repeatedly displayed by the ECJ should be contrasted by the opportunities for enhanced efficiency and shaking up entrenched vested interests that is likely to leave a margin for improvement and allows both public and private returns. **4.116**

[113] Council Dir 88/361/EEC of 24 June 1988 for the implementation of Article 67 of the Treaty [1988] OJ L178/5.

[114] eg Case C-483/99 *Commission v France* [2002] ECR I-4781; Joined Cases C-282/04 and C-283/04 *Commission v The Netherlands* [2006] ECR I-9141; Case C-112/05 *Commission v Germany* [2007] ECR I-8995; Case C-543/08 *Commission v Portugal* [2010] judgment of 11 November 2010 (nyr).

[115] Art 65(1)(a) and (b) TFEU.

[116] cf Case C-567/07 *Minister voor Wonen, Wijken en Integratie v Woningstichting Sint Servatius* [2009] ECR I-9021, concerning a prior authorization requirement for housing cooperatives investing across borders.

Italian pharmacies

4.117 So far *Italian pharmacies* (2009) is the main example of a case where this connection was made explicitly.[117] In this case the ECJ found a restriction of the freedom of capital, as well as of establishment, in Italian legislation that, first, reserved the operation of private pharmacies to pharmacists, firms, or operating companies composed entirely of pharmacists, and second, that banned distribution undertakings from acquiring a stake in companies operating municipal pharmacies. Next however (as already discussed above), with reference to *Sodemare* (which involved a prohibition on for-profit activities),[118] the restrictions involved were accepted based on overriding reasons of general interest. This ruling is similar to that in *German hospital pharmacies* (2008) summarized under free movement of goods.[119] A similar 2010 case that was discussed above under the freedom of establishment concerned the cap of 25 per cent on holdings in bio-medical analysis laboratories by non-professional biologists in France.[120] In neither of the latter two cases was free movement of capital invoked.

E. Conclusion

4.118 The overview of the recent EU case law on freedom of establishment in the health care sector indicates that despite its broad interpretation of Article 49 TFEU to incorporate non-discriminatory measures, the ECJ remains reluctant to tackle the complexities of national health systems. The rulings in the handful of goods cases (outside the pharmaceutical sector) and capital cases available so far underscore this observation. As *Hartlauer* confirms, the ECJ may be more intrepid where the Member State itself has already elected for a mixed system—as in one way or another many are compelled to do by the increasing demands on health care. Nevertheless much of the ECJ's case law suggests that the Court suspects that, by nature, market access solutions are not to be trusted in health care matters due to the inherently corrupting effect of the profit motive. If this stance solidifies it would certainly be a profoundly problematic position for it to adopt in an EU which is, after all, based on the principle of an internal market (if not the principle of free and open markets).

4.119 However, as the *BUPA* case on risk equalization between competing private insurers (that will be discussed in Chapter 9) shows, the European Courts may be open to validating—although not itself imposing—market-based solutions in health care that are explicitly designed to incorporate solidarity. This category that is likely

[117] Case C-531/06 *Italian pharmacists*, supra n 79.
[118] Case C-70/95 *Sodemare*, supra n 11.
[119] Case C-141/07 *Hospital pharmacies*, supra n 6.
[120] Case C-89/09 *Commission v France (laboratories)*, supra n 65.

to grow in importance since the Lisbon Treaty was adopted with its panoply of goals, values, and principles.[121] Meanwhile, the German Constitutional Court recently cited *Sodemare* to justify the claim in its Lisbon Judgment that the essential locus of decision making power on this count remains national, and social exceptions to the market freedoms continue to exist in the form of imperative reasons of general interest.[122] With regard to the application of the free movement of goods rules more generally, the courts had initially tried rather to limit their potential application to challenge a myriad of national regulatory rules which serve imperative interests by distinguishing between selling or marketing arrangements and rules relating to product characteristics. Nevertheless as section C has highlighted, this case law is also complex and evolving so that many national rules imposing point of sale restrictions can also be caught by Article 34 TFEU.

At the same time, it is generally acknowledged that compared to the comparatively simple command and control systems of public provision, markets in general and perhaps health markets in particular need more regulation as a framework for efficient transactions (to reduce transaction costs); thus liberalization breeds regulation. The need for rules is therefore likely to be inescapable in systems that are in transition and in search of a balance between solidarity, social cohesion, and efficiency. What is at issue is the nature of these rules. Above all what is required is a clearer definition of the public interest as a basis for strictly proportionate regulatory intervention. **4.120**

At present, in the absence of harmonization, the ECJ appears to leave it entirely up to the national courts and national authorities to strike this balance. While this cautious approach may be understandable given the sensitivities involved, it should not be overlooked that in practice this primarily means protecting vested national interests—not least among them incumbent health care providers. In this respect it is illustrative how many of the cases discussed here resulted from challenges lodged by professional organizations keen to defend the status quo. **4.121**

What could give? There appear to be at least three possibilities, which are not mutually exclusive. **4.122**

- First, the current tentative steps towards harmonization may herald future improvement. The Patients' Rights Directive will lead to the development of costing principles for hospital services, and standards relating to the right to an informed choice (including on quality and performance in terms of outcomes)

[121] Case T-289/03 *BUPA*, supra n 9; Treaty of Lisbon amending the Treaty on European Union and the Treaty establishing the European Community, signed at Lisbon, 13 December 2007 [2007] OJ C306/1.

[122] BVerfG, 2BvE 2/08 *Gauweiler v Treaty of Lisbon*, Judgment of 30 June 2009, paras 1–421, at para 398; Case C-70/95 *Sodemare*, supra n 11; alongside a similar reference to inter alia Case C-385/99 *Müller-Fauré*, supra n 110.

that will highlight relative performance and inefficiencies across the EU. This could increase pressures for change—including market entry. Further harmonization could result. Such changes however are time consuming.

- Second, in our view, the case law on establishment has evolved sufficiently to request that the Commission provides an 'interpretative communication' on the application of the Treaty rules to the health sector, this would be in the interest of consistency and predictability.[123]
- Third, on the economic side, in the meantime, a more robust approach to testing the assumptions put forward on both sides of the debate would be a significant advance for all concerned, but most importantly, for patients.

4.123 When assessing the ECJ's recent record on the application of the fundamental freedoms to the health sector, and in particular in relation to establishment, we should not forget that only a decade ago, in *Sodemare* the ECJ found no infringement of Article 49 TFEU at all, but by 2009, in *DocMorris*, a public health defence was required even for non-discriminatory measures, involving a proportionality test based on consistency and rationality. This should be seen as a significant advance.

4.124 If the proportionality test is refined to embrace a consistency standard, underpinned by a more robust economic analysis, this could pave the way to substantial improvements in guaranteeing the application of the free movement rules in the health sector. This need not challenge Member States' authority over the standard of health protection at all. At most it could open up debate on the organization of health care services delivery, while potentially improving health outcomes. Finally, it might well serve to introduce a more objective approach to defining the public interest and to ensure a more robust examination of the various interests involved.

[123] cf Commission Communication on the consequences of the Court's judgment in *Cassis de Dijon* [1980] OJ C256; Commission Communication of cross border services [1993] OJ C334; Commission interpretative communication on concessions under Community law [2000] OJ C121/02. For an analysis of the value of such texts cf BMP Smulders, 'Institutional aspects of European Commission guidance in the area of antitrust law' [2009] *Competition Policy International* 25.

5

GENERAL SECONDARY LEGISLATION AND HEALTH CARE

A. Introduction

5.01 In this chapter we will deal with the main areas of secondary legislation that are of general (or horizontal) application; that is to say legislation which is not specifically aimed at health care, but that does significantly influence the health care sector because it is applicable to health care alongside other sectors. Chapter 6 will cover the sector-specific (vertical) secondary law that is adopted to deal with health care in particular. Chapter 7 will deal with the latest health care specific legislation that, as will be explained in more detail in that chapter, is more consumer-oriented.

5.02 As was set out in Chapter 2 on the EU toolbox, the EU disposes of different types of legal instruments. Most important is the Regulation, which is directly binding in all its aspects and does not need to be transposed into national law, and then the Directive, which is binding with respect to its results only but normally requires transposition into national law in order to become fully effective. We should also bear in mind the doctrine of direct effect when transposition occurs too late or imperfectly, and the related doctrine of consistent interpretation, which requires provisions of national law to be interpreted in line with the wording of EU law as much as possible. In these situations, EU Directives may have effects or trigger liability—and create rights for citizens—without intercession by the Member State. Directives are the instrument of choice for the completion of the internal market because they are result-oriented on substance while allowing the Member States flexibility on the means employed to reach their ends.

5.03 All of these secondary rules share the characteristic that they generally involve positive or policy integration: new common rules are introduced, by way of contrast to the direct application of the Treaty freedoms where national rules which are at odds with EU law are struck down. As we have seen in the previous chapters, negative integration works by striking down national barriers (often in the form of national regulation) based on the internal market freedoms on goods, persons (including establishment), services, and capital. Here the common objective is to promote integration by means of common norms where specific rules are necessary to coordinate the different national settings, and to guarantee the desired degree of protection of the interests involved.

5.04 General secondary EU law that is of major relevance to health care is related to patient mobility and has so far been restricted to the Services Directive, the Non-Life Insurance Directives, and social security legislation in the context of free movement for workers. As we also explain in section E of this chapter, the Directives on Public Procurement have an important impact on the purchase of goods, services, and works by health authorities; while in section F of this chapter, we examine the major, if unexpected, consequences of the Working Time Directive on employment conditions for health care professionals.

B. The Services Directive

5.05 The initial strategy of the European Commission concerning legislation on patient mobility was to include health services in the Services Directive that was presented as a key step in completing the internal market.[1] Although this approach was possibly already out of step with the mood of the times when it was proposed, the internal market was then still seen by many as a platform popular enough to carry the added weight of this particular liberalization proposal. Thus Article 23 (that is, a single article) of the original proposal for the Services Directive in March 2004

[1] Dir 2006/123/EC of the European Parliament and of the Council of 12 December 2006 on services in the internal market [2006] OJ L376/36.

codified the case law on free movement in health care.[2] However while the Commission's elaboration in several supporting documents on Article 23 was exhaustive on the need for a codification on patients' rights, it failed to explain—at least to the satisfaction of the EU legislature—why this should be done in the context of the Services Directive. The main argument used by the Commission was that patient mobility was a key citizens' right and therefore required inclusion in the section of the Services Directive that was dedicated to strengthening the rights of European citizens as recipients of services.[3]

The inclusion of health services was in fact strongly resisted both by the European Parliament and the Council from the outset and became one of the reasons why the Services Directive eventually seemed in danger of foundering completely. Thus the European Council of March 2005 already indicated that the proposed Services Directive was not acceptable as it stood.[4] In its April 2005 Report on patient mobility and health care developments, the European Parliament objected strongly to inclusion of health care in the proposed Services Directive, although it did call for the Commission to act on a wide range of issues related to patient mobility and wider cooperation between health systems. At this stage the European Parliament did not call for new legislation but for Commission Guidelines and a 'Charter' on patients' rights.[5] The amendments to the Services Directive that were proposed in the November 2005 report by the internal market and consumer protection committee of the European Parliament also included deletion of Article 23.[6] Alongside a number of other significant exceptions such as for various social services as well as services of general economic interest (SGEI) the Commission subsequently removed this Article from its amended proposal of April 2006 in order to forestall failure of the Services Directive as a whole.[7] As a result, health services are now completely excluded from the scope of the Services Directive as it was finally **5.06**

[2] Commission Proposal for a Directive of the European Parliament and of the Council on services in the internal market [SEC(2004) 21] COM (2004) 2 final.

[3] Proposal for a Directive on services in the Internal Market—Explanatory note on the activities covered by the proposal, 25.06.2004 and Explanatory note from the Commission Services on the provisions of the proposed Directive on services in the Internal Market relating to the assumption of healthcare costs, 16.07.2004, both found on the DG Market site dedicated to the Services Directive and its background <http://ec.europa.eu/internal_market/services/services-dir/proposal_en.htm> accessed 23 February 2012.

[4] Council of the European Union, European Council Brussels—22 and 23 March 2005—Presidency conclusions No 7619/1/05 REV1, para 22.

[5] European Parliament Committee on the Environment, Public Health and Food Safety, *Report on patient mobility and healthcare developments in the European Union* (Rapporteur: John Bowis) (A6-0129/2005) (dated 29 April 2005).

[6] European Parliament Committee on the Internal Market and Consumer Protection, *Report on the proposal for a directive of the European Parliament and of the Council on services in the internal market* (Rapporteur: Evelyne Gebhardt) (A6-0409/2005) (dated 15 December 2005).

[7] Commission, Amended proposal for a Directive of the European Parliament and of the Council on services in the internal market COM (2006) 160 final.

adopted in December 2006, which is made explicit by its Article 2(2)(f).[8] This Article excludes:

> (...) healthcare services whether or not they are provided via healthcare facilities, and regardless of the ways in which they are organized and financed at national level or whether they are public or private.

By way of explanation Recital 22 of the Preamble states:

> The exclusion of health services from the scope of this Directive should cover healthcare and pharmaceutical services provided by health professionals to patients to assess, maintain or restore their state of health where those activities are reserved to a regulated health profession in the Member State in which the services are provided.

Recital 23 of the Preamble reads:

> This Directive does not affect the reimbursement of health care provided in a Member State other than that in which the recipient of the care is resident. This issue has been addressed by the Court of Justice on numerous occasions, and the Court has recognised patients' rights. It is important to address this issue in another Community legal instrument in order to achieve greater legal certainty and clarity to the extent that this issue is not already addressed in Council Regulation (EEC) No 1408/71 of 14 June 1971 on the application of social security schemes to employed persons, to self-employed persons and to members of their families moving within the Community.

5.07 According to the Commission's own subsequent analysis the approach of including patient mobility in the Services Directive was unacceptable to the EU legislature because it failed to take into account the technical complexity, sensitivity to public opinion, and major support from public funds involved in health care.[9] Remarkably enough, as will be discussed in Chapter 7, this culminated in support for a specific legal instrument. Paradoxically the result—the Patients' Rights Directive, eventually adopted in 2011—goes much further than the single Article in the Services Directive that was eliminated with such fracas. Moreover the question remains to what extent health care was effectively excepted. According to Recital 22 of the Preamble the exception only applies to care provided to patients and, by implication, not to the provision of other services between, by, and to, health care providers. For example, a hospital contracting with consultants or other providers of health care services would arguably be covered by the Directive; so would a provider of health insurance.

C. The Non-Life Insurance Directives

5.08 Over time the EU has adopted four Directives that are relevant to non-life insurance activities. The most important of these in general terms is the 1992 Third

[8] Dir 2006/123/EC, supra n 1.

[9] Commission Communication, Proposal for a Directive of the European Parliament and of the Council on the application of patients' rights in cross-border healthcare presented by the Commission, COM (2008) 414 final, Explanatory Memorandum, para 1.

Non-Life Insurance Directive,[10] and the most recent is the 2009 Solvency II Directive.[11] They serve to ensure the functioning of the internal market in non-life insurance, including health insurance, especially to secure the freedom of establishment. The relevant mechanisms are home country control, notably a single system for authorization and financial supervision by the Member State which is the seat of the head office. The Third Non-Life Insurance Directive determines that once a Member State allows private insurance of a particular type of risk, it accepts that any insurer who is admitted to the insurance branch anywhere in the EU is entitled to cover this risk based on the freedom to provide services and/or the freedom of establishment.[12] The Third Non-Life Insurance Directive also provided for the harmonization of solvency requirements, which is now spelt out in detail in the abovementioned Solvency II Directive.[13] (The latter are not discussed here as they are too technical and specific for our present purposes.) Member States are not allowed to set additional requirements, such as imposing regulation of prices and coverage.

At paras 5.10–5.23 we will primarily discuss whether the relevant regimes are applicable, instead of the more generic respective rules such as those on home country control, authorization and supervision themselves, which would require a degree of detail for which space is not available. In this context it is important that the Directives contain three relevant exceptions to its standard regime which is based on the premise that Member States may not interfere in setting rates of conditions. These are: **5.09**

- the social security exception in Article 2(1)(d) of the First Non-Life Insurance Directive;
- the general good exception in Article 28 of the Third Non-Life Insurance Directive; and
- the health insurance exception in Article 54 of the last mentioned Directive.

Each of these exceptions is now discussed briefly, followed by a look at Article 206 of the Solvency II Directive which deals with private health insurance as an alternative to social security. Finally we will turn to the question of which activities insurances undertakings may pursue.

[10] Council Dir 92/49/EEC of 18 June 1992 on the coordination of laws, regulations and administrative provisions relating to direct insurance other than life assurance and amending Directives 73/239/EEC and 88/357/EEC (Third Non-Life Insurance Directive) [1992] OJ L228/1. cf S Thomson and E Mossialos, 'Private health insurance and the internal market' in E Mossialos et al (eds), *Health Systems Governance in the Europe: the role of European Union Law and Policy* (Cambridge: Cambridge University Press 2010) 427–28.

[11] Dir 2009/138/EC of the European Parliament and of the Council of 25 November 2009 on the taking-up and pursuit of the business of Insurance and Reinsurance (Solvency II) [2009] OJ L335/1. See section 5 on health insurance in Annex III.

[12] Council Dir 92/49/EEC, supra n 10.

[13] S Thomson and E Mossialos, supra n 10, p 427.

The social security exception

5.10 Article 2(1)(d) of the First Non-Life Insurance Directive provides for an exception for 'insurance forming part of a statutory system of social security'.[14] It remains unclear under what conditions an insurer is covered by this exception. In Case C-206/98 *Commission v Belgium* (2000) the ECJ holds that Directive 92/49 EC is 'applicable to insurance forming part of a statutory scheme of social security offered by insurance undertakings at their own risk'. Apart from suggesting that risk taking is the key element this begs the question what are 'insurance undertakings'.[15]

5.11 This question has not so far been answered by the ECJ although the so-called 'Bolkestein letter' of 2003 (issued by then Commissioner Bolkestein responsible for the internal market and dealt with at paras 5.18–5.23 under the health insurance exception) has provided an answer.[16] However both the status of the letter as well as the accuracy of some of the views stated there remain open to doubt. Some of the literature cites the cases of *Garcia* (1996) and *Commission v France* (2000) in support of a three-pronged test whereby only insurance undertakings operating at their own risk, following insurance techniques, and on the basis of contractual relationships governed by private law are covered by the Directives.[17] However we have not found a solid basis for this view in the cases cited, nor for a similar statement in the Bolkestein letter (see further below).

5.12 Our proposed solution is finding that if the entity concerned is both (i) an undertaking providing (insurance) services in a market; and (ii) is doing so at its own risk (consistent with *Commission v Belgium*) then regardless of whether it forms part of a statutory scheme or is governed by public law it would be covered by the Non-Life Insurance Directives. Otherwise merely choosing a public law regime would simply remove even competitive insurance schemes from the scope of the Directives on purely formal grounds.

5.13 In this context the ruling in *Freskot* (2003) is relevant where the ECJ held that the scope of the definition of a service in the context of the First Non-Life Insurance Directive and of Articles 56 and 57 TFEU is the same: the concept of consideration is key, as is the question of who decides on the levels of the rates concerned. However the ECJ, in *Freskot*, also states that if markets for insurable natural risks are

[14] First Council Dir 73/239/EEC of 24 July 1973 on the coordination of laws, regulations and administrative provisions relating to the taking-up and pursuit of the business of direct insurance other than life assurance [1973] OJ L228/3.

[15] Case C-206/98 *Commission v Belgium (accidents at work insurance)* [2000] ECR I-3509, para 44.

[16] Letter from then Commissioner Bolkestein (internal market) to Hans Hoogervorst, Dutch Minister for Health of 25 November 2003, subject: Dutch health insurance system, CAB/PvB/D(03)0848.

[17] S Thomson and E Mossialos, supra n 10, p 427; citing Case C-238/94 *José García* et al *v Mutuelle de Prévoyance Sociale d'Aquitaine* et al [1996] ECR I-1673 and Case C-296/98 *Commission v France* [2000] ECR I-3025.

concerned, that are subject to compulsory insurance in a particular Member State, then undertakings established in other Member States may nevertheless challenge the legality (and proportionality) of the restrictions involved under the freedom to provide services.[18]

The 'general good' exceptions

Article 28 of the Third Non-Life Insurance Directive provides that insurance contracts shall be freely concluded unless there is a conflict with legal provisions protecting the general good. That is: **5.14**

> The Member State in which a risk is situated shall not prevent a policyholder from concluding a contract with an insurance undertaking authorized under the conditions of Article 6 of Directive 73/239/EEC, as long as that does not conflict with legal provisions protecting the general good in the Member State in which the risk is situated.

This general good criterion is also incorporated in Article 54(1) of the Directive that relates specifically to health insurance. Elucidating both provisions is a Commission Communication published in the year 2000.[19] **5.15**

The general good is not defined in EU law. Accordingly the categories that the general good may cover are in principle not limited and may be determined at national level. The abovementioned Commission's Communication states that relying on the general good exception requires that the measures concerned must:[20] **5.16**

(i) operate within an area that is not already harmonized;
(ii) pursue an objective of the general good;
(iii) be non-discriminatory;
(iv) be objectively necessary; and
(v) proportionate to the objective concerned;
(vi) in addition it is necessary that the general good objective is not already safeguarded by rules set in the Member State of establishment.[21]

The absence of harmonization is key. This means that because the health insurance exception is specifically harmonized in Article 54 of the Third Non-Life Insurance Directive we may assume that as a consequence it is in principle no longer possible to invoke, in addition or in the alternative, the general good exception in Article 28 thereof, with regard to health insurance. However the general good conditions **5.17**

---

[18] Case C-355/00 *Freskot AE v Elliniko Dimosio* [2003] ECR I-5263, paras 56–60, 63.

[19] Commission Interpretative Communication, Freedom to provide services and the general good in the Insurance sector [2000] OJ C43/5.

[20] This is in line with standard case law: eg for services Case C-76/90 *Manfred Säger v Dennemeyer & Co. Ltd* [1991] ECR I-4221; for establishment, Case C-55/94 *Reinhard Gebhard v Consiglio dell'Ordine degli Avvocati e Procuratori di Milano (Gebhard)* [1995] ECR I-4165.

[21] Interpretative Communication on the general good, supra n 19, pp 16–17.

listed above apply equally under Article 54 of the Directive where the general good criterion was incorporated too, albeit in this case restricted to health insurance (an example of the specific rule trumping the general rule).

The health insurance exception

5.18 Article 54 of the Third Non-Life Insurance Directive provides an exception to the principle of non-intervention in the setting of insurance premiums and conditions.[22] It regards insurance agreements that 'may serve as a partial or complete alternative to health cover provided by the statutory social security scheme'. This means that it should be seen as an exception that covers alternative and not supplementary or complementary types of health insurance.[23] (However as we will see in Chapter 9 in *BUPA* (2008), supplementary insurance was found to be covered by a service of general economic interest (SGEI), calling into question the abovementioned distinction.)

5.19 At the time it was adopted, Article 54 was tailor-made for a number of Member States operating private health insurance systems as (partial) substitute for public schemes: Ireland; the Netherlands; and Germany. The permissible conditions listed in Article 54(2) and in Recital 24 of the Directive closely match the conditions in place in these Member States. The question is whether over time this arrangement will slowly turn into a straitjacket as new modes of regulation develop that were not envisaged at the time of drafting; however, at least the clarification of this provision in 2003 by the so-called 'Bolkestein letter', concerning the reforms of the Dutch health care system, shows that the room for intervention at national level may be considerable.

5.20 The Bolkestein letter stated that the Dutch regime, characterized by open enrolment, mandatory coverage, uniform rates (at a level freely determined by the insurer), and a risk equalization fund, could be justified under Article 54 of the Third Non-Life Insurance Directive as these principles appeared necessary to ensure the legitimate objective of the Dutch government. The legitimate objective in this context was to guarantee health care as a basic social right. Hence all residents were to have access to health insurance guaranteeing a basis package of essential care for an acceptable premium. However the letter stressed that the measures concerned must be limited to what was objectively necessary.[24] In addition it suggested that

[22] This Article is materially identical to Art 206 of the Solvency II Dir 2009/138/EC, supra n 11. See Annex III.

[23] Case T-289/03 *British United Provident Association Ltd (BUPA)* et al *v Commission* [2008] ECR II-81.

[24] For a diverging view see F Paolucci, A den Exter and W van de Ven, 'Solidarity in competitive health insurance markets: analysing the relevant EC legal framework' [2006] *Health Economics, Policy and Law* 107–26.

the risk insurance scheme might need to be considered under the state aid rules (see Chapter 9 on state aid).

It is worth noting that the letter does not recoup the six general conditions of the general good that Article 54(2) already listed. Nor does it state that given prior harmonization the permissible deviations from the general rules of the Directive found in Article 54(2) are exhaustive so the general good is unable to accommodate further variations at Member State level. Instead an assessment is made that relies on criteria that are set out in Recital 24 of the Preamble to the Directive: open enrolment, rating on a uniform basis according to the type of policy and lifetime cover, and to participate in loss compensation schemes: **5.21**

> Whereas to this end some Member States have adopted specific legal provisions; whereas, to protect the general good, it is possible to adopt or maintain such legal provisions in so far as they do not unduly restrict the right of establishment or the freedom to provide services, it being understood that such provisions must apply in an identical manner whatever the home Member State of the undertaking may be; whereas these legal provisions may differ in nature according to the conditions in each Member State; whereas these measures may provide for open enrolment, rating on a uniform basis according to the type of policy and lifetime cover; whereas that objective may also be achieved by requiring undertakings offering private health cover or health cover taken out on a voluntary basis to offer standard policies in line with the cover provided by statutory social security schemes at a premium rate at or below a prescribed maximum and to participate in loss compensation schemes; whereas, as a further possibility, it may be required that the technical basis of private health cover or health cover taken out on a voluntary basis be similar to that of life assurance.

In EU law generally the Recitals of a Directive are only of interpretative value and do not form separate legal provisions that can be relied on. The approach in the Dutch case was perhaps also based on the theory that the (limited) degree of harmonization achieved allows for the abovementioned additional exceptions. This suggests the remaining scope for general good exemptions under Article 54 of the Third Non-Life Insurance Directive at present is wide or even completely open-ended, constrained only by the proportionality test involved. Judicial clarification of this issue would be welcome. **5.22**

The Bolkestein letter also details what it states is the line set out by the case law of the ECJ, according to which: **5.23**

> (...) insurance activities forming part of a statutory system of social security fall under the scope of the Insurance Directives when they are conducted by insurance undertakings at their own risk following insurance techniques and on the basis of contractual relationships governed by private law.

The legal form expressly stated in the Directives themselves, again according to the letter, is immaterial as long as these three conditions are met. However this is not by any means an uncontested definition of what determines the scope of the Third Non-Life Insurance Directive. The status of the Bolkestein letter is no more than that of informal Commission guidance in a particular case.

Private health insurance and acceptable constraints

5.24 The Recitals to the Solvency II Directive set out clearly the status of private health insurance in the context of public norms with regard to the risks to be insured. This is detailed further in Article 206 of the Solvency II Directive on private health insurance as an alternative to social security. Here it is stated that such private schemes may be subject to general good conditions and prior public scrutiny as well as the requirement that they are operated on an actuarial basis similar to life insurance provided that certain conditions are met. These conditions mainly concern the actuarial nature of the scheme as well as (inter alia) the right to carry over benefits to other providers.

5.25 Jointly, these rules show that whereas private health insurance is generally caught by the Non-Life Insurance Directives, at the same time public interest exceptions remain available that provide considerable scope for maintaining a regulatory framework for such insurance.

Line of business restrictions

5.26 The Non-Life Insurance Directives apparently place line of business restrictions upon insurance undertakings that are relevant, for example, to health care insurers that want to participate in the activities of health care providers (also called vertical integration). Article 8(1) of the First Non-Life Insurance Directive provides:[25]

> The home Member State shall require every insurance undertaking for which authorization is sought to: (...) (b) limit its objects to the business of insurance and operations arising directly there from, to the exclusion of all other commercial business.

However on the other hand Article 18(1) of the same Directive states:

> Member States shall not prescribe any rules as to the choice of the assets that need not be used as cover for the technical provisions referred to in Article 15.

5.27 The case law of the ECJ makes clear that the first provision should be read as a limiting clause that refers to the level of the solvency requirements when carrying out its own business, not to the right to hold stakes in non-insurance undertakings:

> (...) the purpose of the prohibition preventing insurance undertakings from carrying on commercial business other than insurance business, laid down in the amended Article 8(1)(b) of Directives 73/239 and 79/267, is in particular to protect the interests of insured persons against the risks which the exercise of such business could entail for the solvency of those undertakings. It follows that the aforesaid provision

[25] First Council Dir 73/239/EEC, supra n 14; last amended by Council Dir 2006/101/EC of 20 November 2006 adapting Directives 73/239/EEC, 74/557/EEC and 2002/83/EC in the field of freedom to provide services, by reason of the accession of Bulgaria and Romania [2006] OJ L363/238.

> does not prevent insurance undertakings from holding shares in public limited companies carrying on commercial business other than insurance business and to the assets of which the financial risks are confined.[26]

Similarly, in the health insurance case *ABBOI* (2000) where mutual benefit societies were engaged both in health insurance and (other) commercial activities, the ECJ held that:

> (…) Article 8(1)(b) of Directive 73/239 does not preclude mutual benefit societies engaged in insurance business from participating, within the limits of their respective free assets, in a body with legal personality and legal autonomy which is involved in commercial business – such as an association of mutual benefit societies – provided that the financial risks inherent in such business attach only to the assets possessed by that body.[27]

In summary, it should be possible for a health insurer to belong to the same group as say a health care provider such as a hospital or a chain of pharmacies provided that at all times the solvency requirements for its insurance activities are met. Turning this around, and given that the ECJ in the abovementioned cases established the direct effect of said provisions (both Article 18(1) and Article 8(1)(b) of the Directive), health insurers may invoke the right to do so, for example against public measures designed to block vertical integration.[28] **5.28**

D. The Coordination of Social Security Regulation

The need to coordinate social security systems far predates the Patients' Rights Directive and indeed the case law on patient rights, going back to Council Regulation 3 of 1958.[29] These rules were set out in a manner that was close to their form in Regulation 1408/71 (which was replaced by Regulation 883/2004 on 1 May 2010), which was also to play an important role in the free movement case law of the ECJ.[30] The basis of this legislation is that which now forms Article 48 TFEU on the measures that are necessary to provide for the freedom of movement for workers as set out in Article 45 TFEU. **5.29**

[26] Case C-241/97 *Försäkringsaktiebolaget Skandia (publ)* [1999] ECR I-1879, para 47.

[27] Case C-109/99 *Association basco-béarnaise des opticiens indépendants v Préfet des Pyrénées-Atlantiques (ABBOI)* [2000] ECR I-7247, para 64.

[28] cf EHM Loozen, EJ Schut and M Varkevisser, 'Verticale integratie tussen zorgverzekeraars en zorgaanbieders' [2010] Markt en Mededinging 5.

[29] Council Reg No 3 on social security for migrant workers [1958] JO 30/561, 597.

[30] Reg (EEC) No 1408/71 of the Council of 14 June 1971 on the application of social security schemes to employed persons and their families moving within the Community [1971] OJ L149/2; last amended by Reg (EC) No 1992/2006 of the European Parliament and of the Council of 18 December 2006 [2006] OJ L392/1 (Regulation 1408/71). It replaced Council Reg No 3 on social security for migrant workers [1958] JO 30/561, 597. On 1 May 2010 Reg 1408/71 was replaced by Reg (EC) 883/2004 of the European Parliament and of the Council of 29 April 2004 on the coordination of social security systems [2004] OJ L166/1.

5.30 This necessity follows from giving effect to the freedom of movement of workers in a situation that was characterized by detailed and very different social security systems in the various Member States, leading to a fragmentation of these rules and rights that applied in a particular case.[31] The objective of these Regulations was not harmonization of social security standards as such. Instead they merely pursue coordination in relation to the place where rights to benefits are acquired, the aggregation of time periods relevant to acquiring rights to benefits, and the payment of such benefits. This is necessary to determine the rights of workers under the different national schemes.[32] Remarkably enough, legally-resident third country nationals (whose numbers in many Member States equal or exceed the number of EU migrant workers for whom Regulation 1408/71 was originally designed) have only been covered since the adoption of Regulation 859/2003.[33] According to Article 90 of Regulation 883/2004 its predecessor Regulation 1408/71 will remain in force for the purposes of Regulation 859/2003 until the latter is itself repealed or modified. This is because the scope of the general Regulation 883/2004 as set out in its Article 2 does not cover third country nationals, whereas Regulation 859/2003 was designed to extend social security coverage to them.

5.31 Just like its predecessor (and in fact like the 2011 Patients' Rights Directive), Regulation 883/2004 strictly respects the right of the Member State to determine the extent and scope of its national social security benefits, provided these are applied in a non-discriminatory manner to workers from other Member States.[34] For the present discussion it is relevant that this may involve enjoying health care in a Member State other than that where the worker is insured (the Member State of affiliation), and the reimbursement of this treatment by the insurance system with which he is affiliated. Article 20 of Regulation 883/2004 requires the worker to obtain prior authorization for (non-emergency) care from the competent body in his Member State of affiliation. There is thus no unconditional EU law based right to patient mobility involved here: in other words an element of home country control prevails.

5.32 This arrangement already existed well before the free movement case law of the ECJ in relation to health care that was discussed in Chapter 3 emerged, resulting in two related, but parallel, reimbursement systems.

[31] F Pennings, *European Social Security Law* (5th edn, Antwerp: Intersentia, 2010).

[32] cf Case 21/87 *Felix Borowitz v Bundesversicherungsanstalt für Angestellte* [1988] ECR 3715, para 23 (and the references provided there); Case 100/78 *Claudino Rossi v Caisse de compensation pour allocations familiales des régions de Charleroi et Namur* [1979] ECR 831, para 13.

[33] Council Reg (EC) No 859/2003 of 14 May 2003 extending the provisions of Reg (EEC) No 1408/71 and Reg (EEC) No 574/72 to legally resident nationals of third countries who are not already covered by those provisions solely on the ground of their nationality [2003] OJ L124/1.

[34] cf F Pennings, 'Inclusion and exclusion of persons and benefits in the new co-ordination Regulation' in M Dougan and E Spaventa (eds), *Social Welfare and EU Law* (Oxford: Hart Publishing, 2005).

However it is not necessary to make use of the right to free movement in order to invoke Regulation 883/2004.[35] Most importantly in the present context, with regard to the right to medical treatment, this is clearly shown by the fact that Regulation 883/2004 covers not only the right to emergency care, or the right to care when residing abroad but in particular also the right to obtain treatment in another Member State, provided the conditions set in Article 20 of the Regulation are met (formerly Article 22 of Regulation 1408/71). This right has been extended further from time to time, beyond just those nationals of EU Member States who have at any time worked or resided in another Member State.[36] Thus, since 1995, it applies to all persons who are nationals of a Member State and who are insured under the legislation of a Member State (and their family members residing with them),[37] and since May 2003 to legally-resident nationals of third countries.[38] **5.33**

Article 19 of Regulation 883/2004 provides an absolute right to emergency medical care in another Member State, and Article 20, subject to prior authorization, a therefore qualified general right to medical care in another Member State (the Member State of treatment). It is this latter type of care, elective or planned care, which is relevant here. According to Article 20(2) (or Article 22(2) as it stood in marginally different wording in Regulation 1408/71 at the time of the *Kohll* judgment), this authorization may not be refused: **5.34**

> (...) where the treatment in question is among the benefits provided for by the legislation in the Member State where the person concerned resides and where he cannot be given such treatment within a time-limit which is medically justifiable, taking into account his current state of health and the probable course of his illness.

However, as the beginning of this quotation clearly shows, it depends on the scope of the social security legislation in the Member State of affiliation whether a treatment is covered by this provision in the first place. Regulation 883/2004 does therefore not harmonize the level of social security benefits extended which were always and continue to be determined exclusively at national level. Article 20 provides for two alternative types of benefit: either benefits in kind (that is treatment) **5.35**

---

[35] Case C-2/89 *Bestuur van de Sociale Verzekeringsbank v M.G.J. Kits van Heyningen* [1990] ECR I-1755.

[36] Dir 2004/38/EC of the European Parliament and of the Council of 29 April 2004 on the right of citizens of the Union and their family members to move and reside freely within the territory of the Member States amending Reg (EEC) No 1612/68 and repealing Dir 64/221/EEC, 68/360/EEC, 72/194/EEC, 73/148/EEC, 75/34/EEC, 75/35/EEC, 90/364/EEC, 90/365/EEC and 93/96/EEC [2004] OJ L158/77.

[37] According to Art 22a, inserted by Council Reg (EC) No 3095/95 of 22 December 1995 amending Reg (EEC) No 1408/71 on the application of social security schemes to employed persons, to self-employed persons and to members of their families moving within the Community, Reg (EEC) No 574/72 fixing the procedure for implementing Reg (EEC) No 1408/71, Reg (EEC) No 1247/92 amending Reg (EEC) No 1408/71 and Reg (EEC) No 1945/93 amending Reg (EEC) No 1247/92 [1995] OJ L335/1.

[38] Council Reg 859/2003, supra n 33.

in the Member State of treatment, with compensation paid by the Member State of affiliation directly to the Member State of treatment based on Article 35 of Regulation 883/2004, or direct reimbursement at the level in force in the Member State of treatment by the Member State of affiliation of the patient in the event he or she had paid the relevant costs on their own account. It is primarily this latter situation that has given rise to litigation in the context of the patient mobility case law, along with the conditions of the prior authorization requirement. Finally it is important to note that the levels of reimbursement applicable in the Member State of treatment under the Article 20 regime may be below the actual costs that patients have to meet, especially in Member States of treatment with significant co-payments (that is out-of-pocket expenses for patients).

5.36 In this manner Regulation 1408/71 provided, for almost 30 years, not just the basic framework but the only framework for patient mobility in the EU which has continued its existence as Regulation 883/2004. As discussed in Chapter 3 this primacy has changed over the course of the past decade as the result of the patient mobility case law that concerns both the applicability of Article 56 TFEU and the scope of Regulation 883/2004, establishing not just parallel but converging regimes between the two. It is not intended here to provide a complete overview of the health care cases that involved Regulation 883/2004 or its predecessor 1408/71. Many of them have already been dealt with in the discussion of the services case law above. Just three more are mentioned here.

Van der Duin

5.37 *Van der Duin* (2003) concerned a Dutch citizen, entitled to Dutch pension benefits, who was a resident in France but wished to receive medical treatment in the Netherlands.[39] In this case it turned out that Article 22 of Regulation 1408/71 was applicable (prior authorization requirement) and that the responsible authority in the Member State of residence had to decide whether treatment in another Member State was allowed, including in the Member State responsible for paying pension, and that it (the Member State of residence) would have to meet the costs of the treatment concerned.

Chamier-Glisczinski

5.38 In *Chamier-Glisczinski* (2009) the issue at stake was whether a German-insured person who resided in Austria could use Regulation 1408/71 to derive a right to long term care that was not covered in the Member State of residence from the applicable Regulation in the Member State of affiliation, or whether this was possible

[39] Case C-156/01 *R.P. van der Duin v Onderlinge Waarborgmaatschappij ANOZ Zorgverzekeringen UA and Onderlinge Waarborgmaatschappij ANOZ Zorgverzekeringen UA v T.W. van Wegberg-van Brederode* [2003] ECR I-7045.

based on the free movement of persons or freedom of services.[40] Concerning Regulation 1408/71 the ECJ held that if the Member State of residence did not confer certain rights, this did not exclude the possibility that the Member State of affiliation would nevertheless award such rights. As regards free movement it held that this did not exclude differences in social security legislation and hence no rights—including citizenship-based rights—could be derived from this freedom in the present context.

Van Delft

Most recently, *Van Delft* (2010) dealt with the conflict between the Dutch authority for health insurance and a number of pensioners of Dutch nationality who had moved to other EU Member States and wished to retain their own private insurance and refused to accede to the new Dutch health insurance system.[41] The pensioners invoked not only Regulation 1408/71 but also Articles 21 and 45 TFEU concerning the right to travel to and to stay in other Member States for citizens, and respectively the free movement of workers. In relation to Regulation 1408/71 the ECJ concluded that this provides a coherent system of conflict rules which excludes free choice of the applicable regime by the individuals concerned. Free movement of workers did not apply as the pensioners had not worked abroad. However the ECJ held that possibly (for the national court to determine) there had been discrimination between persons resident in the Netherlands and abroad with regard to the degree of continuity of the insurance coverage that was ensured when the new insurance system was introduced. If so, this would amount to a violation of the citizenship rights of the plaintiffs. **5.39**

For a more complete discussion we refer to the specialized literature with respect to the complex area of EU social security law and its increasing interaction with EU citizenship.[42] **5.40**

E. Public Procurement

Introduction

The European rules on public procurement require that public contracts must be awarded in accordance with strict requirements regarding publicity, transparency, and non-discrimination, in order to ensure that public procurement is open to EU-wide competition and that suppliers in any Member State are given an equal **5.41**

[40] Case C-208/07 *Petra von Chamier-Glisczinski v Deutsche Angestellten-Krankenkasse* [2009] ECR I-6095.

[41] Case C-345/09 *J.A. van Delft* et al *v College van zorgverzekeringen* [2010] judgment of 14 October 2010 (nyr).

[42] F Pennings, supra n 31.

opportunity to bid for, and win, public contracts. 'Contracting entities', such as health authorities, may be required to follow the relevant, specific, and often, technical procedures when they contract to purchase works, as well as services, above a certain value.

5.42 The primary aim of the EU procurement regime is to open up the services market to competition and thus prevent national authorities from favouring local suppliers. Public procurement is a purchasing method that promotes competition between potential providers. On the one hand participants may expect a fair chance of landing a contract while on the other hand those awarding the contract not only obtain savings but also ensure procedural guarantees are respected that will limit the risk of the award being legally contested. The logic involved is that because the contracting authorities are not undertakings and are therefore not disciplined by their competitors, nor by the EU competition rules, they need to be controlled at least as concerns their purchasing behaviour.

5.43 Nevertheless, the value represented by the procurement activities of the public sector is significant not only in terms of money spent, or quite simply 'buyer power', but also in terms of the power to influence how and what services are available on the market and under what conditions.[43] Procuring authorities may seek to pursue both primary (economic) and secondary (such as promoting wider social goals or technological innovation) objectives through their procurement policies. At the same time, Recital 6 of the Public Procurement Directive states that 'nothing in this Directive should prevent the imposition or enforcement of measures necessary to protect public health provided that these measures are in conformity with [TFEU]'.[44]

5.44 The pursuit of both primary and secondary objectives has to comply with the EU regime if the various conditions for the application of that regime are to be met.[45] The substantive rules are contained in Directive 2004/18. This consolidated Public Procurement Directive replaces three separate Directives covering, respectively—supplies contracts, works contracts, and services contracts. The Public

[43] cf K Lundvall, H Ballebye Okholm, M Marcusson, S Jespersen and M Birkeland, 'Can Public Procurement spur innovations in healthcare' (*Copenhagen Economics*, 2009) <www.vinnova.se> accessed 23 February 2012; V Hatzopolous and H Stergious, 'Public procurement law and healthcare: from theory to practice' in J van de Gronden, E Szyszczak, U Neergaard and M Krajewski (eds), *Healthcare and EU Law. Legal Issues of Services of General Interest* (The Hague: TMC AsserPress/Springer Verlag, 2011); V Hatzopoulos, 'Public procurement and state aid in national healthcare systems' in E Mossialos et al (eds), *Health Systems Governance in Europe: The Role of European Union Law and Policy* (Cambridge: Cambridge University Press, 2010).

[44] Dir 2004/18/EC of the European Parliament and of the Council of 31 March 2004 on the coordination of procedures for the award of public works contracts, public supply contracts and public service contracts [2004] OJ L134/114. Cf P Trepte, *Public Procurement in the EU: A Practitioner's Guide* (2nd edn, Oxford: Oxford University Press, 2007).

[45] ibid.

Procurement Directive is in turn based on the Treaty principles of free movement,[46] and if a contracting authority intends to invoke public health reasons for rejecting a tender it must follow the appropriate procedures as provided in relevant secondary legislation.

Below we will look at the different regimes provided by the Public Procurement Directive, the scope of the Directive and the definition of contracting authority, the relevant obligations, and the remedies available under the Procurement Remedies Directive.[47] **5.45**

The importance of the type of organization concerned

To what extent do the European rules on procurement affect the provision of health care in the Member States? This question is not easy to answer in a categorical manner, as much depends on the organization of the health sector in question, and as underlined in previous chapters, this may vary substantially from one Member State to another. The application of the procurement rules is also dependent on whether national health services are organized on the basis of collective solidarity with most functions being carried out by public sector authorities. Private sector provision will generally escape the rigours of the procurement regime, but is subject to competition law as described in Chapter 8. As a rule of thumb, (provided it is a health care service) the nature of the service that is being procured is less important that the status of the entity procuring that service as a 'contracting authority'. **5.46**

The case law

An overview of ambulance and/or health care transport services shows that the outcomes are not always predictable. In the *Tögel* (1998) case,[48] for example, the ECJ held that the award of ambulance transport services contracts should be made in accordance with the former Services Directive 92/50[49] (now the Procurement Directive 18/2004). Likewise, in the *Commission v Italy* (2007) case concerning ambulance services, the Court found that the obligation to abide by the public procurement rules applied even if the intention of the authority was to award the contract to a non-profit organization such as the Red Cross, using volunteers.[50] In the earlier German ambulance case *Glöckner* (2001) however, the ECJ had ruled **5.47**

---

[46] Dir 2004/18/EC, supra n 44, Recital 2. See also Case C-507/03 *Commission v Ireland (An Post)* [2007] ECR I-9777, para 77.

[47] Council Dir 89/665/EEC of 21 December 1989 on the coordination of the laws, regulations and administrative provisions relating to the application of review procedures to the award of public supply and public works contracts [1989] OJ L395/33.

[48] Case C-76/97 *Walter Tögel v Niederösterreichische Gebietskrankenkasse* [1998] ECR I-5357.

[49] Council Dir 92/50/EEC of 18 June 1992 relating to the coordination of procedures for the award of public service contracts [1992] OJ L209/1 (replaced by the Procurement Dir 2004/18/EC, supra n 44).

[50] Case C-119/06 *Commission v Italy* [2007] ECR I-168.

that ambulance contracts could be awarded on the basis of a prior authorization, without a tendering procedure.[51] This was so because the services in question constituted a service of general economic interest (SGEI) and other transport services served to finance the former. (This is interesting because subsequently public procurement has become a preferred method of assigning SGEI in the state aid context—see Chapter 9.) In *Commission v Ireland* (2007), the Court held that there was no contractual relationship between the health authority and Dublin City Council, which provided the ambulance services, each one being empowered by law to provide emergency ambulance services.[52] Finally, in *Commission v Italy* (2007) the ECJ also allowed the government to pursue its own system of contract awards without a public tender.[53]

Some complications

5.48 Given this lack of clarity, at least on the surface of these cases, it is necessary to examine the EU procurement regime in more detail. It should be kept in mind however there are a number of complications:

- First, the procurement regime is enacted in a series of Directives and national implementing legislation may extend the scope of the relevant obligations on the national contracting entities.
- Furthermore, the EU courts have fashioned a number of general procurement 'principles' derived from the Treaty rules on free movement of goods and services, and applied them to certain contracts which are not subject to the specific procurement rules set down in the Directives.[54]
- To complicate matters further, in 2006 the Commission published an Interpretative Communication on the application of the general principles of EU law to the award of contracts which do not fall within the scope of the Directives (due to their low value) or that do not attract the full procedural obligations, such as contracts for certain services set out in an Annex to Directive 2004/18 (often referred to as 'non-priority' or 'Annex II Part B' services, which includes health care services). The Communication sets out the basic standards of transparency and impartiality that must apply to the advertising, award, and review of such contracts.[55] The Communication in fact codifies the case law of the EU courts on the application of the free movement rules to the award of contracts or licences and concessions not covered by the EU procurement regime as such. This is the

[51] Case C-475/99 *Firma Ambulanz Glöckner v Landkreis Südwestpfalz* [2001] ECR I-8089.

[52] Case C-532/03 *Commission v Ireland* [2007] ECR I-11353.

[53] Case C-119/06 *Commission v Italy* [2007] ECR I-168.

[54] Case C-324/98 *Teleaustria Verlags GmbH and Telefonadress GmbH v Telekom Austria AG, joined party: Herold Business Data AG* [2000] ECR I-10745.

[55] Commission Interpretative Communication on the Community law applicable to contract awards not or not fully subject to the provisions of the Public Procurement Directives [2006] OJ C179/2. The legality of this communication was challenged by Germany in Case T-258/06 *Germany v Commission* [2010] ECR II-2027.

reason why the General Court in 2008 rejected as inadmissible a claim by Germany that the Communication had exceeded the scope of the Public Procurement Directives and was therefore an illegal assumption of state powers.[56] Furthermore, the Treaty rules on free movement override secondary legislation and so these rules, as interpreted by the Court must be followed even if they are stricter than the 'mild regime' for Annex II Part B services.

In the following sections we will consider first the types of health services to which the procurement regime may apply. We will then turn to the definition of 'contracting authorities'. A short description of the procedures for selecting and awarding tenders is then provided. We then turn to the recently published proposals to revise the EU procurement rules.[57] In the final section we focus on the Remedies Directive. **5.49**

The scope of Directive 2004/18—when do the Procurement Directives apply?

Health is covered—in principle, as all services are covered—with certain explicit exceptions. The contract must involve the purchase of goods, or services, or works above certain thresholds. The Directive does not define public services as such. Currently the threshold for the award of service contracts is set at €125,000 for government departments and €193,000 for regional or local authorities in relation to Annex II Part A services.[58] If these thresholds are not met, however, but the contracting entity is an emanation of the state then, based on the relevant case law of the ECJ, it must still abide by the so-called 'procurement principles'—that is its contracts must be awarded in accordance with the basic principles of transparency, publicity, and non-discrimination, as discussed below. **5.50**

Service concessions

Service concessions are expressly excluded from the Directive, in accordance with its Article 1(4). A service concession is defined as: 'a contract of the same type as a public service contract except for the fact that the consideration for the provision of the services consists either solely in the right to exploit the service or in this right together with payment.' The dividing line between a public services contract which is covered by the Directive if the relevant thresholds are met, and a services concession, which is not, is not easy to draw. It may be noted that the relevance of the distinction between a public services contract and a services concession will **5.51**

[56] Case T-258/06 *Germany v Commission* [2010] ECR II-2027.

[57] Proposal for a Directive of the European Parliament and of the Council on public procurement, COM (2011) 896 final, 20 December 2011.

[58] New thresholds entered into force on 1 January 2010 based on Commission Reg (EC) No 1177/2009 of 30 November 2009 amending Dir 2004/17/EC, 2004/18/EC and 2009/81/EC of the European Parliament and of the Council in respect of their application thresholds for the procedures for the award of contracts [2009] OJ L314/64.

diminish if the Commission's recent proposal to introduce a new Directive on service concessions is adopted.[59]

5.52 In the *Bavarian Red Cross* (2011) case the municipal authorities terminated a number of rescue service contracts and concluded contracts for the transport of patients to a number of organizations, including the Bavarian Red Cross, without putting those contracts out to tender. The absence of the tender procedure was challenged before the German regional courts and resulted in a reference to the ECJ. The Court held that the question of whether the contracts were to be classified as a service concession or a public service contract must be considered exclusively in the light of EU law as opposed to the various regional legal principles. The Court held that the method of remuneration was one of the determining factors for the classification of a service concession. In this particular case the provider of the rescue services did not receive payment from the contracting authority which awarded the contract but from usage fees which it was entitled to obtain, under national law, from the social security institutions from which the insured persons received rescue services. The fact that the amounts of the fees were not determined by the provider by agreement with the social security institutions, which also have the status of a contracting authority, did not affect that finding. The ECJ held that it was nevertheless of key importance to establish who bears the risk of operating the service in question, so that as long as the operator runs an operating risk, even a very limited one by reason of the fact that the amount of usage fees in question depends on annual negotiations with third parties such as social security institutions, and where it is not assured full coverage of the costs of managing its activities, then the contract must be classified as a service concession.[60]

5.53 Even for contracts which are subject to the Directives, the application of the procurement principles to the health sector has been limited given that contracts for Annex II Part B services, which include health services, are largely excluded from the full public procurement regime. Whilst tenders in the sector remain subject to general EU principles, which require tenders to provide services to the relevant contracting authorities to be provided in accordance with principles of transparency, non-discrimination, and equal treatment, which requires adherence to the Directives' rules on non-discriminatory technical specifications (Article 23), the extent to which these principles are observed in practice tends to vary across the Member States. Some Member States have chosen to subject the Annex II Part B services to a more onerous national procurement regime. It should be noted, however that in its recent Green Paper on the modernization of EU procurement policy, the Commission has consulted on whether to abolish the lighter touch procurement regime for Annex II Part B services and apply the standard regime to all

[59] Proposal COM (2011) 896 final, supra n 57.

[60] Case C-274/09 *Privater Rettungsdienst und Krankentransport Stadler* [2011] judgment of 10 March 2011 (nyr).

service contracts instead. At the time of writing of this book it has not yet concluded on new policies or concrete proposals on this point.

5.54 As stated, health services are currently enumerated in category 25 of Annex II Part B, also known as Part B or non-priority services. The main (sub-) categories of health services included here are listed in the Common Procurement Vocabulary (CPV) 2008. The CPV was adopted by Regulation 213/2008 and consists of the main vocabulary for defining the subject matter of the contract.[61] These services are considered to offer less potential for cross-border competition. However they remain subject to the general principles of the TFEU.[62] In the abovementioned *Tögel* (1998) case, concerning ambulances with on-board medical personnel, the ECJ held that a single activity can be made up of several types of services each of which will be classified separately as priority and non-priority services.[63] If the value of the former exceeds the latter, then the entire service offering will be considered as priority services. There is no obligation to separate out priority and non-priority services and award separate contracts,[64] but care must also be taken that any splitting up of the services in question into priority and non-priority does not appear to have been contrived to avoid the relevant threshold provisions of the Directive. Similarly, services should not be packaged in a way that leads to artificial grouping together of contracts to avoid the full application of the Directives.[65]

5.55 If the service in question is included in Annex II Part B, and none of the exceptions provided for in Articles 17 (service concessions) or 18 (service contracts awarded on the basis of exclusive rights) apply, then it is necessary to consider whether the light procurement regime (Article 23) applies to the particular transaction at hand. Land transactions and 'in-house' transactions (see paras 5.68–5.70) are by no means the only exemptions from the full force of the EU public procurement regime, but exemptions are difficult to invoke successfully. For example, and at least prior to the recent financial crisis, resort to the 'extreme urgency' exemption was most unlikely to succeed, as illustrated by two cases in the medical devices sector discussed below.

Commission v Greece (medical devices)

5.56 In this case (2009)[66] the ECJ held that contracting authorities, which have issued an invitation to tender for the supply of medical devices (hospital supplies) bearing

[61] Commission Reg (EC) No 213/2008 of 28 November 2007 amending Reg (EC) No 2195/2002 of the European Parliament and of the Council on the Common Procurement Vocabulary (CPV) and Dir 2004/17/EC and 2004/18/EC of the European Parliament and of the Council on public procurement procedures, as regards the revision of the CPV [2008] OJ L74/1.

[62] See Case C-234/03 *Contse SA, Vivisol Srl and Oxigen Salud SA v Instituto Nacional de Gestión Sanitaria (Ingesa), formerly Instituto Nacional de la Salud (Insalud)* [2005] ECR I-9315.

[63] Case C-76/97 *Tögel*, supra n 48.

[64] Case C-411/00 *Felix Swoboda GmbH v Österreichische Nationalbank* [2002] ECR I-10567.

[65] cf P Trepte, supra n 44.

[66] Case C-489/06 *Commission v Greece* [2009] ECR I-1797.

the CE marking, cannot reject, on grounds of protection of public health, the tender in respect of such products, directly and without following the safeguard procedure provided for in the Council Directive on medical devices.[67] If a contracting authority considers that the tender in respect of medical devices bearing the CE marking may compromise public health, it is required to inform the competent authority with a view to setting that safeguard procedure in motion. In that context, a practice of the contracting authorities of rejecting tenders in respect of medical devices bearing the CE certification marking amounts to a failure on the part of a Member State to fulfil its obligations under the EU procurement regime.

5.57 The Court ruled that Greece had failed to fulfil its obligations under EU rules on common safety standards for products as well as on public procurement by rejecting offers from suppliers of medical equipment bearing the CE marking. The European Commission subsequently referred Greece back to the ECJ because of its failure to apply EU rules on public procurement as regards contracts for supplies of medical equipment to hospitals. In the Commission's view, Greece continues to infringe EU law and has not complied with the Court's judgment.

Medipac-Kazantzidis

5.58 *Medipac-Kazantzidis* (2007) was an earlier health care procurement case involving Greece that likewise concerned public hospital purchases of medical devices bearing the CE marking.[68] However in this case an exception to the procurement rules was found justified. The ECJ acknowledged that the suspension of a tendering procedure for the supply of medical devices may lead to delays liable to give rise to problems with running a large hospital and considered that a situation of urgency. Hence the hospital was entitled to take interim measures required to enable it to procure medical devices. However the hospital had to demonstrate that there was a situation of urgency justifying the derogation from the principle of free movement of goods.[69]

The definition of a public contract

5.59 This brings us to the relevant definitions. Public contracts are (i) contracts; (ii) for pecuniary interest; and (iii) concluded in writing between one or more economic operators and one or more contracting authorities, according to Article 1(2)(a) of Directive 2004/18. If one of these three constitutive elements is absent, there is no public service contract. The Directive does not however define 'consideration' but two 2007 cases in the field of health care procurement regarding ambulance services (already mentioned above) have provided some clarification.

---

[67] Council Dir 93/42/EEC of 14 June 1993 concerning medical devices [1993] OJ L169/1, Arts 8 and 18.

[68] Case C-6/05 *Medipac-Kazantzidis AE v Venizeleio-Pananeio (P.E.S.Y. KRITIS)* [2007] ECR I-4557.

[69] ibid, paras 60–62.

- In *Commission v Italy* (2007) the ECJ considered whether services carried out by non-profit associations such as the Red Cross fell within the scope of the Directive given that the providers only received a reimbursement for their fixed costs.[70] The Court held that the services were rendered on behalf of, and paid for, by a contracting authority by virtue of a contract.
- In *Commission v Ireland* (2007) the ECJ dismissed the Commission's claims that a contract existed between the health authority and Dublin City Council.[71] The Court held that the mere existence of funding arrangements between two public bodies did not imply that the provision of services constituted a contract.

A more recent noteworthy case regarding the definition of public contracts is *Mehiläinen Oy* (2010).[72] This case concerned an agreement between a municipality and an independent private company for the establishment of a joint undertaking, belonging to them in equal shares, to which their respective occupational health and wellbeing activities were transferred, and by which the municipality and the private company committed themselves to acquiring from the new joint undertaking, occupational health and wellbeing services for their own employees. The ECJ held that: **5.60**

> Directive 2004/18/EC must be interpreted as meaning that (...) the award by the contracting authority of the contract relating to the services for its own staff, the value of which exceeds the threshold laid down by that directive, and which is severable from the contract establishing the [joint venture] company, must be made in accordance with the provisions of that directive applicable to the services in Annex II B thereof.[73]

Hence contracts such as the one concluded in this outsourcing joint venture remain squarely covered by the procurement rules, even if the agreements setting up the joint venture as such do not. **5.61**

Contracting entities

As we have seen the scope of the Public Procurement Directive is defined by contracts, as discussed above, concluded by contracting entities that are public authorities or parties assimilated to that status. Hence the entities covered by the Directive fall into two categories: (i) public authorities and associations formed by one or several of such authorities; and (ii) bodies governed by public law and associations formed by one or several of such bodies. **5.62**

---

[70] Case C-119/06 *Commission v Italy*, supra n 52, paras 47–50

[71] Case C-532/03 *Commission v Ireland*, supra n 52, para 42

[72] Case C-215/09 *Mehiläinen Oy and Terveystalo Healthcare Oy v Oulun kaupunk* [2010] judgment of 22 December 2010 (nyr).

[73] ibid, para 47.

5.63 This latter category is subject to three cumulative criteria:[74]

- the organization must be established for the purpose of meeting needs in the general interest which do not have an industrial or commercial criterion;
- the body must have legal personality; and
- the entity must be either financed or supervised by another public authority.

All health care entities which are part of the State (central, regional, or local) are public authorities in the sense of category (i) above and are subject to the Directive; Annex IV provides a non-exhaustive list of central government authorities. Annex III provides a non-exhaustive list of 'bodies governed by public law' in the sense of category (ii).[75] In cases such as the abovementioned *Commission v Ireland* and *Commission v Italy* (ambulance services), classic 'public health authorities' were involved. However even if a health care entity is not included in Annex III, it could still be subject to the Directive as a 'body governed by public law'.

5.64 As a rule of thumb, entities performing economic activities are subject to the competition rules as discussed in Chapter 8, whereas entities that are not performing such activities are subject to the procurement regime. However an undertaking such as a hospital may perform both types of activities—eg self-employed doctors are undertakings whereas doctors employed by the hospital meeting the three criteria listed above are not.[76] Insurance funds may be subject to the procurement rules if organized on the basis of solidarity.[77]

The ECJ has recently applied the three criteria to determine whether an entity active in the field of health care is a 'body governed by public law'.

Oymanns

5.65 In this 2009 German case, the first two conditions (a general interest need and legal personality) were fulfilled, but the extent to which the sickness insurance fund was financed or supervised by the State was unclear.[78] The Court underlined that (emphases added):

> (...) financing of a statutory sickness insurance scheme (...), which is brought into being by a measure of the State, is, in practice, guaranteed by the public authorities and is secured by methods of collection which fall under the provisions of public law,

[74] cf Case C-44/96 *Mannesmann Anlagenbau Austria AG* et al *v Strohal Rotationsdruck GesmbH* [1998] ECR I-73.

[75] Case C-532/03 *Commission v Ireland*, supra n 52; Case C-119/06 *Commission v Italy*, supra n 50.

[76] Joined Cases C-180/98 to C-184/98 *Pavel Pavlov* et al *v Stichting Pensioenfonds Medische Specialisten* [2000] ECR I-6451.

[77] Case C-205/03 P *Federación Española de Empresas de Tecnología Sanitaria (FENIN) v Commission* [2006] ECR I-6295.

[78] Case C-300/07 *Hans & Christophorus Oymanns GbR, Orthopädie Schuhtechnik v AOK Rheinland/Hamburg* [2009] ECR I-4779.

> satisfies the condition of being financed, *for the most part*, by the State for the purposes of the application of the Community rules on the awarding of public contracts.[79]

Moreover:

> (...) there is financing, *for the most part*, by the State when the activities of statutory sickness insurance funds are chiefly financed by contributions payable by members, which are imposed, calculated and collected according to rules of public law such as those in the main proceedings. Such sickness insurance funds are to be regarded as bodies governed by public law and therefore as contracting authorities.[80]

The ECJ concluded that these payments between the funds and their members did not involve contractual consideration because both membership and contributions were mandated by law. Hence this amounts to a situation where there is financing 'for the most part' by the State. It is worth noting that in this case the funds are expressly listed in Annex III. The Commission observed before the Court that the lists are intended only to ensure transparency but are not conclusive. Hence there is a need for further analysis by the Court. **5.66**

So far therefore the case law to date does not provide definitive guidance, given the emphasis placed in *Oymanns* on financing 'for the most part' to bring the German sickness funds within the scope of the Directive. This leaves open the question of whether hospitals or clinics who receive financial support as well as private contributions could be exposed to the procurement regime. Each case will turn on its own specific facts. As a general rule, undertakings in the sense of the competition and state aid rules are not contracting authorities and vice versa. This is logical because undertakings are already disciplined by competition and/or the competition and state aid rules. **5.67**

In-house contracting

The public procurement regime does not apply when an authority decides to provide services in-house, as in the Irish ambulance services case. Moreover, the regime does not apply even when there is a contract but that is between the authority and its wholly-owned company. This is referred to as the *Teckal* exemption, based on the decision of the ECJ in *Teckal*[81] and the subject matter of a series of subsequent ECJ cases decided in 1999, including most recently *Auroux*,[82] *Asemfo*,[83] *Apermc*,[84] **5.68**

[79] ibid, para 57.
[80] ibid, para 59.
[81] Case C-107/98 *Teckal Srl v Comune di Viano and Azienda Gas-Acqua Consorziale (AGAC) di Reggio Emilia* [1999] ECR1-8121.
[82] Case C-220/05 *Jean Auroux* et al *v Commune de Roanne (Auroux)* [2007] ECR I-385.
[83] Case C-295/05 *Asociación Nacional de Empresas Forestales (Asemfo) v Transformación Agraria SA (Tragsa) and Administración del Estado (Apermc)* [2007] ECR I-2999.
[84] Case C-220/06 *Asociación Profesional de Empresas de Reparto y Manipulado de Correspondencia v Administración General del Estado* [2007] ECR I-12175.

and *Commission v Italy*.[85] There are two conditions both of which must be satisfied in order for the *Teckal* exemption to apply, both of which are interpreted strictly. First, the authority must exercise a control over the company which is similar to that which it exercises over its own departments. There must not be even minority participation—actual or prospective—by a private undertaking. There must be no independence with regard to decision making. The authority must retain decisive influence over both strategic objectives and significant decisions. Secondly, the company must carry out the essential part of its activities with the controlling authority.

5.69 However, the ruling of the ECJ in the *Coditel Brabant* (2008) case is seen to provide more flexibility.[86] The delegation of public interest tasks to a body set up in cooperation with other local authorities, without any private sector involvement, should in principle be considered as not needing to be the subject of a call for competitive tenders. The mere fact that a body operates on a commercial basis and is in competition with private sector providers is not a relevant factor for the purposes of the *Teckal* exemption. An important characteristic of true local authority cooperation consists of the equality of decision making and without dominant control being exercised by one of the local authority partners. Both conditions are capable of being satisfied in the case of a multiplicity of authorities.[87]

5.70 If this were not permitted, local authorities wishing to cooperate with one another would have to outsource the provision of these services to third party market operators, which would amount to forced privatization, by means of the application of the public procurement rules, of the services they provide. The latter services may be in the public interest. Should the first *Teckal* condition be construed in this way, it would mean giving undue weight to competition aims at the expense of the proper local authority autonomy.

The obligations on contracting entities if the rules apply

5.71 When awarding contracts covered by Annex II Part A, awarding authorities must follow one of three principal procedures, summarized below. The contracting authority must apply objective pre-qualification criteria to select candidates. The list of criteria supplied in the Directive is exhaustive. The contract should be awarded either on the basis of the lowest price or more usually, the most economically advantageous offer, which is the best value for money. The award criteria, which may

[85] Case C-337/05 *Commission v Italy* [2008] ECR I-2173.

[86] Case C-324/07 *Coditel Brabant SA v Commune d'Uccle and Région de Bruxelles-Capitale* [2008] ECR I-8457.

[87] See Case C-220/05 *Auroux*, supra n 82, at para 63; Case C-295/05 *Asemfo*, supra n 83, at paras 57, 62, 65 and 67; Case C-220/06 *Apermc*, supra n 84, at paras 52–54, 58 and 62; as well as earlier cases especially Case C-340/04 *Carbotermo SpA and Consorzio Alisei v Comune di Busto Arsizio and AGESP SpA* [2006] ECR I-4137, at para 37 (first condition) and para 60 (second condition).

include factors such as technical merit, time for completion or delivery, and price, must be published in advance. Technical specifications which discriminate against certain suppliers cannot be used.[88]

- *Open procedure:* under this procedure, all interested parties may submit tenders. This procedure is most suited to contracts for the procurement of non-specialist goods (such as stationery) particularly where the contract award criterion is the lowest price only.
- *Restricted procedure:* here only those suppliers invited by the authority may submit tenders. Once tenders have been submitted, post-tender negotiations are generally not permitted (although clarification of tenders is permissible). Although the dividing line between negotiation and mere clarification is not clear cut, it would appear that discussions on fundamental aspects, such as price, are ruled out.
- *Negotiated procedure:* this is a flexible procedure which allows contracting authorities to consult contractors or suppliers about its choices and negotiates the terms of the contract with one or more of them. In cases where prior overall pricing is not possible, the competitive negotiated procedure may be followed. A notice that is placed in the Official Journal calls interested parties to come forward and the authority then chooses a short list of parties with whom it would negotiate.

The basic procedural requirement under all these procedures is that the awarding authority advertises the contract in the Official Journal 'S' series and in addition, the authority must follow various other detailed procedural obligations, including allowing a given minimum number of days for interested parties to respond to the notice. The relevant time limits may be varied if urgency renders them impracticable (Article 38(8) of Directive 2004/18). In December 2008 the Commission announced that the exceptional nature of the current economic situation following the global financial crisis, can give rise to a presumption of urgency in progressing with major public works so that the relevant time limits for the use of the restricted procedure can be substantially reduced. **5.72**

Alternative procedures

In addition to these three basic procedures, the Public Procurement Directive 2004/18 introduced a fourth procedure for 'particularly complex contracts' where the contracting authority is not objectively able to define the technical means to satisfy its needs or it is not objectively able to identify in advance the legal and/or financial make-up of a project. The *competitive dialogue procedure* may be used where the use of the open or restricted procedure would not allow the award of **5.73**

[88] See generally, P Trepte, supra n 44.

the contract. This allows for greater flexibility to discuss its contractual needs with potential bidders. Having advertised and then selected a short list of candidates, it may then open a dialogue to discuss all aspects of the contract.

5.74 A further variation provided in the Directive relates to *framework agreements*, lasting no more than four years, between one or more contracting authorities and one or more economic operators, to establish the terms governing contracts to be awarded during a given period, in particular with regard to price and where appropriate, quantity. The normal procedures must be used to conclude the framework agreement but specific contracts under that framework agreement can then be awarded directly.

The proposed reforms

5.75 On 20 December 2011 the Commission issued a proposal to revise the existing procurement Directives. The current rules are considered to give rise to uncertainty and lack flexibility. The proposals provide for a simplified, more flexible, user-friendly approach. Importantly for the health sector, the distinction between Annex II Part A and Part B services would be abolished. Health and social service contracts with a value higher than €500,000 will be subject to a specific regime and contract notices for the award of health and social services contracts above this threshold must be published in the Official Journal of the European Union (OJEU). This special regime could include a wide variety of contracts, for example for clinical services, education, and training. However such contracts will not be subject to the full procurement regime, but only to the basic procurement principles of transparency and equal treatment as discussed above. Thus the contracting authorities may take into account the need to ensure quality, continuity, accessibility, availability and comprehensiveness of the services, the specific needs of different categories of users, the involvement and empowerment of users, and innovation.

5.76 All other tendering by a health authority which meets the definition of a contracting entity or authority, as discussed above, will be subject to the full force of the final Directive, when adopted. Thus services such as legal and accountancy services or catering services will be subject to the full regime. The choice of procurement procedure will revolve around two basic forms: the open and the restricted procedures, but the intention is to allow the negotiated procedure and the competitive dialogue to be used more easily than at present. In addition Member States may allow contracting authorities to make use of a new procedure for the procurement of innovation—so-called innovation partnerships.

5.77 Furthermore the proposal provides that contracts can either be awarded using either 'the lowest cost' or 'the most economically advantageous tender' criterion. The proposal therefore introduces the possibility to award decisions on life-cycle costs of products, services, or works to be purchased, covering all stages of the production of the good, service, or work in question; from raw material acquisition or generation of resources until final disposal. The costs may include not only direct monetary expenses but also external environmental costs if these can be monetized and verified.

Importantly for the health sector, the proposed Directive also clarifies when contractual relationships between public bodies would not be subject to the Directive. Building upon the case law of the ECJ as discussed above, the proposal excludes agreements between public bodies to jointly carry out their public service tasks in the public interest. Contracts awarded by a contracting authority to another public body on which it exerts control, and which carries out at least 90 per cent of its activities for the controlling authority, are also excluded from the procurement rules. 5.78

Remedies

The substantive procurement rules are backed up by a Directive dealing specifically with remedies.[89] The Procurement Remedies Directive 89/655 requires Member States to ensure that effective remedies and means of enforcement are made available to suppliers who believe they have been harmed by an infringement of the substantive procurement rules. This Directive is directly effective so that even if a Member State has failed to correctly implement it, redress should still be possible. The Commission published proposed amendments to the Procurement Remedies Directive in 2007 and these reforms, now incorporated into Directive 2007/66 had to be implemented by December 2009.[90] In particular the Directive requires that interim measures are available from national courts or tribunals, in order to obtain an interim suspension order suspending the award procedure in question. An award contract cannot be set aside once the resulting contract has been entered into, however. 5.79

The 1989 Directive also stipulated that national courts or tribunals must be given the power to make orders setting aside unlawful decisions or acts and for the amendment of contract documents. Member States are entitled to stipulate that such set aside and amendment orders can only be requested prior to the date on which the contract in question is entered into. It should be noted however that the ECJ has confirmed that national rules should allow that the decision to award the contract can be reviewed and set aside prior to its conclusion. This essentially means that where the national rules do not allow for the contract to be set aside after it has been 5.80

[89] Council Dir 89/665/EEC, supra n 47.

[90] Dir 2007/66/EC of the European Parliament and of the Council of 11 December 2007 amending Council Dir 89/665/EEC and 92/13/EEC with regard to improving the effectiveness of review procedures concerning the award of public contracts [2009] OJ L335/31.

concluded there should be some form of announcement or time delay between award and conclusion of the contract, so as to allow time for challenge.[91]

5.81 The 2007 Directive now incorporates these principles into its substantive rules—a 10 day calendar period must expire between the date of award and the conclusion of the contract. Finally the Directive requires that a remedy in damages must be available to a claimant including the costs incurred in preparing the bid as well as the loss of the profit which would have been derived from the contract.[92] To date there appear to have been few successful actions for damages. An unsuccessful claimant can also bring a complaint to the Commission who in turn can initiate an infringement procedure against the Member State concerned.

5.82 The proposed revisions to the current Directives would introduce new governance rules, and Member States could be required to designate a single authority responsible for monitoring, implementing, and controlling procurement. Contracting authorities would be obliged to submit information on all contracts for supplies and services above €1 million to this body, which will then scrutinize the contracts.

General principles of EU law and the interpretative communication

5.83 According to the case law of the ECJ the general principles of non-discrimination and equal treatment, transparency, proportionality, and mutual recognition, even apply to contract awards that are not, or not fully, subject to the provisions of the Public Procurement Directives.[93] In these cases the relevant distinction is whether or not contracting authorities are involved.

5.84 The Commission's 2006 interpretative communication on this matter—which is partly based on the transparency case law of the ECJ—concerns the advertising and award of the contract as well as judicial protection:

> That obligation of transparency which is imposed on the contracting authority consists in ensuring, for the benefit of any potential tenderer, a degree of advertising sufficient to enable the services market to be opened up to competition and the impartiality of procurement procedures to be reviewed.[94]

The rules set out in the communication also apply to contract awards below the turnover threshold of the Public Procurement Directive (€193,000 as mentioned

---

[91] Case C-81/98 *Alcatel Austria AG* et al, *Siemens AG Österreich and Sag-Schrack Anlagentechnik AG v Bundesministerium für Wissenschaft und Verkehr* [1999] ECR I-7671.

[92] See Case C-348/10 *Norma-A SIA and Dekom SIA v Latgales plānošanas reģions (Latvian transport case)* [2011] judgment of 10 November 2011 (nyr)—Dir 2007/66/EC has no retroactive effect.

[93] Case C-324/98 *Telaustria*, supra n 54; Case C-231/03 *Consorzio Aziende Metano (Coname) v Comune di Cingia de' Botti* [2005] ECR I-7287; Case C-458/03 *Parking Brixen GmbH v Gemeinde Brixen and Stadtwerke Brixen AG* [2005] ECR I-8585. cf Communication on contract awards, supra n 55.

[94] Case C-324/98 *Telaustria*, supra n 54, para 62.

above) as well as to awards above the thresholds to which only the mild regime applies:

> (...) although certain contracts are excluded from the scope of the Community directives in the field of public procurement, the contracting authorities which conclude them are nevertheless bound to comply with the fundamental rules of the Treaty.[95]

Hence contracts such as service concessions, concluded by providers of health care services who qualify as contracting authorities, are also subject to the rules in the interpretative communication that expresses the core of the abovementioned general principles of EU law. In this context a key requirement is to ensure that interested parties from other Member States can also take notice of the contract award and participate in it. For instance, qualifications and diplomas from other Member States must be recognized as equivalent and the timeframe for reaction needs to be long enough for reactions from other Member States. If the proposed revisions to the EU procurement regime are adopted, these general principles will continue to apply to all contracts for health and social services above the €500,000 threshold, albeit that the contract notices and award notices for these contracts would have to be published in the OJEU. **5.85**

Conclusion

In summary, health care services are currently subject to a relatively mild regime meaning that mainly transparency and non-discrimination requirements apply. Nevertheless the relevance of the procurement rules to the health care sector has increased over recent years given the ECJ's broad interpretation of the application of the rules to mixed funding as well as the transparency case law and the interpretation by the Commission thereof. Given the degree of technical legal detail this subject involves, contracting health care authorities may well require specialist advice. **5.86**

F. The European Working Time Directive

As we have already noted in the introductory chapter, Article 153 TFEU gives the EU power to adopt directives in various employment fields, including health and safety at work and working conditions. These Directives apply to all sectors, with few exceptions. Health care professionals who satisfy the status of employee or worker are treated in the same way as any other worker. This has not been without problems as the troubled history of the implementation of the European Working **5.87**

[95] Communication on contract awards, supra n 55, para 1.2; Case C-59/00 *Bent Mousten Vestergaard v Spøttrup Boligselskab* [2001] ECR I-9505, para 20.

Time Directive (EWTD) of 2003 (replacing an earlier 1993 Directive), has illustrated.[96]

5.88 Working time is also an area which has seen considerable judicial activity, with a series of judgments from the ECJ expanding the scope of the Directive, still referred to by the Court as a minimum harmonization measure, yet with major consequences for the health sector. In particular, rulings by the ECJ have stated that any employee who is working on call at a hospital or health centre should have their entire shift counted as working time, even if only a fraction of it is actually spent working. These rulings also mean that employees must take compensatory rest to make up for any unplanned overtime as soon as the period of work ends, rather than at a later time, such as the next day. These decisions have created specific problems for services that require adequate 24-hour staffing. The EWTD thus provides a useful example of how EU legislation that is not specifically directed at the health sector can have a profound impact upon it. This is at least in part because the ECJ's interpretation of key concepts has resulted in legislation which is quite different in its scope to that envisaged by the Member States at the time the original directive was enacted.

5.89 The EWTD has proved challenging for health care services such as accident and emergency services which operate on a 24-hour basis. Not only has it imposed a large administrative burden on health care organizations, it has also impacted on staffing levels and costs as well as the time available for patient care and for training the new generation of doctors. The implementation of the Directive has been far from 'plain sailing' and it has brought with it problems for the way care is planned and provided. In the United Kingdom, for example, it is possible for individual staff to opt out of the 48-hour week in order to work longer hours—but entire departments or groups of staff cannot do so collectively.

5.90 The ECJ's rulings have in turn prompted a process to amend the current Directive, but so far a political compromise has proved elusive. The legislative process involves the so-called 'social partners' (representing employers' and employees' organizations) who can negotiate at European level and conclude agreements which can in turn amend EU legislation under certain conditions. The current modified proposal, now under discussion between the social partners, updates key aspects of the Directive: the definition of on-call time, the reference periods for calculating the 48-hour maximum working week, and the opt-out from the 48-hour week. The mechanics of this legislative process are beyond the scope of the present volume

[96] Dir 2003/88/EC of the European Parliament and of the Council of 4 November 2003 concerning certain aspects of the organisation of working time [2003] OJ L299/9; replacing Council Dir 93/104/EC of 23 November 1993 concerning certain aspects of the organisation of working time [1993] OJ L307/18 (as amended by Dir 2000/34/EC of the European Parliament and of the Council [2000] OJ L195/41).

however. Instead, the following sections will examine the basic provisions of the ETWD and the key court cases.

The scope of the Directive

Directive 2003/88, the EWTD,[97] is intended to require a minimum degree of harmonization of working time. In the recent case of *Fuß* (2010) the ECJ states that: 5.91

> (...) it must be pointed out that the purpose of Directive 2003/88 is to lay down minimum requirements intended to improve the living and working conditions of workers through approximation of national rules concerning, in particular, the duration of working time. That harmonisation at EU level in relation to the organisation of working time is intended to guarantee better protection of the safety and health of workers by ensuring that they are entitled to minimum rest periods – particularly daily and weekly – and adequate breaks and by providing for a ceiling on the average duration of the working week (see, inter alia, *Pfeiffer and Others*, paragraph 76, and *Fuß*, paragraph 32).[98]

The original Directive was introduced to adopt minimum standards—in other words to create a 'floor of rights' while allowing Member States the right to legislate for higher protection where they chose to do so.[99]

The EWTD has been described as 'striking' for its complexity, its lack of clarity, and its attempt at both rigidity and flexibility.[100] The rigidity is said to lie in its choice of 48 hours as the maximum working week (Article 6(b)), eleven hours per 24 hour period as daily rest (Article 3), and a maximum of 8 hours per 24 hour period as night work (Article 8(a)). The lack of clarity lies in the complexity of calculating the reference periods over which the average working time and rest times are to be calculated and definitions of key terms such as 'working time' (Article 2(1)). Flexibility is also demonstrated by the possibilities for derogations and delayed implementation (Article 17). The Directive limits the average working hours per week to 48 hours, but allows Member States to opt out from that provision. Below we discuss the case law relative to these categories. 5.92

---

[97] Dir 2003/88/EC, supra n 96.

[98] Case C-429/09 *Günter Fuß v Stadt Halle* [2010] judgment of 25 November 2010 (nyr), para 33.

[99] The original legal basis for the 1993 Dir was unsuccessfully challenged by the UK in Case C-84/94 *United Kingdom v EU Council* [1996] ECR I-5755. The Court held that: 'where the principal aim of the measure is the protection of health and safety, Art 118A EC (now Art 153(4) TFEU) must be used, albeit that such a measure may have ancillary effects on the establishment and functioning of the internal market' (para 22).

[100] C Barnard, 'EU 'Social' Policy: From Employment Law to Labour Market Reform' in P Craig and G De Burca (eds), The Evolution of EU Law (Oxford: OUP, 2011).

Simap

5.93 The Directive defines 'working time' as the period a worker is working at his/her employer's disposal and carrying out his or her duties (Article 2(1)). Many employers in the health sector had assumed that time spent awaiting emergency calls but not actually working, was excluded from the calculation of working time. In *Simap* (2000), which stemmed from a referral from the Court of Appeal of Valencia in a case involving Spanish doctors in hospitals working in teams, without any time restrictions, the ECJ ruled that on-call duty by doctors must count as working time when they are present at the facility but also when they are on call at home if they are actually working.[101] The classification of working hours can be applied when the employee performs a service for the employer or is situated on the premises of the employer and is at the employer's disposal. In the *Dellas* (2005) case, the ECJ held that the classification as working time within the meaning of the Directive cannot depend on the intensity of the employee's work but follows solely from his obligation to be at his employer's disposal. Hence national legislation providing for a system of equivalence with a weighting mechanism for workers in social and medico-social establishments was not permissible.[102]

Jaeger

5.94 In *Jaeger*[103] (2003) the ECJ was required to clarify whether on-call duty hours in an emergency department were to be considered working time. The relevant German law distinguished between 'readiness for work', 'on-call service', and 'stand by', so that only the first category would constitute actual work that was eligible for payment while the other two constituted resting time, as no professional tasks were preformed. The Court held that Dr Jaeger's on-call hours at the Kiel municipal hospital had to be considered as working time, regardless of whether he was resting or treating patients. Furthermore the time spent asleep or otherwise inactive could not count towards the rest periods because the employee 'must be able to remove himself from the working environment, to enable him to relax and dispel the fatigue caused by the performance of these duties'. The relevant German provisions which classified the employee's hours of inactivity during the on call period as rest periods, and that provided compensation only for that time in which the employee actually worked were incompatible with the Directive (see para 75 of the judgment in *Jaeger*). Derogations were not permitted in this case as Article 17(1) only extends to specified Articles of the Directive and not to its Article 2 on the definition of

---

[101] Case C-303/98 *Sindicato de Médicos de Asistencia Pública (Simap) v Conselleria de Sanidad y Consumo de la Generalidad Valenciana (Simap)* [2000] ECR I-7963.

[102] Case C-14/04 *Abdelkader Dellas and Others v Premier ministre and Ministre des Affaires sociales, du Travail et de la Solidarité* [2005] ECR I-10253.

[103] Case C-151/02 *Landeshauptstadt Kiel v Norbert Jaeger* [2003] ECR I-8389.

working time. Hence the German classification of 'readiness for work', 'on call', and 'stand-by' became obsolete.

Derogations from certain of the minimum requirements laid down in the Directive do remain possible, subject to the conditions set out in Article 17. Such derogations must be set out in laws, regulations, administrative provisions, or collective agreements, and provide compensatory rest ensuring at least the same degree of protection. Derogations from the rest requirements (Article 8), and the reference periods (Article 16) are explicitly allowed where the services must be provided continually (Article 17(3)(c)(i)). For doctors in training there is a specific transitional period before the full implementation of the '48 hour week' requirement which takes the specific nature of activities of doctors in training into account (Recital 7 to the Directive). Although the transitional period for implementation of the Directive was intended to expire in 2009, a Member State can still request the Commission to grant a further delay of three years, but must justify the application. **5.95**

Pfeiffer

Although rulings such as *Jaeger* resulted in more states taking advantage of the individual opt-out from the EWTD,[104] as discussed in Chapter 2 the *Pfeiffer* (2004) case[105] has further limited the scope of the derogation allowing Member States to allow individual workers to opt out of the 48 hour limit. In *Pfeiffer* the ECJ, in accordance with its judgment in the *Jaeger* case, held that the calculation of the maximum period of daily and weekly working time, on-call duty time had to be taken into account. Individual consent to opt out must be given freely and expressly and it is not sufficient for the employment contract to refer to a collective agreement permitting an extension of the working week. **5.96**

As the Court recognized in the *Dellas* (2005) case, where national law fixes a ceiling more favourable to workers, in particular for the maximum weekly working time, the relevant thresholds for ascertaining whether the protective rules laid down by that Directive are complied with are exclusively those set out in the Directive.[106] **5.97**

However, Directive 2003/88 does not contain any provision regarding the sanctions applicable where the minimum requirements laid down by it are infringed, for example regarding the duration of working time. Recent court rulings have now begun to fill this gap in what the ECJ itself still recognizes to be a measure of minimum harmonization. **5.98**

[104] A number of Member States have used this individual opt-out clause (Art 17(5) EWTD) for health workers, but the United Kingdom has enabled all workers to do so.

[105] Joined Cases C-397/01 to C-403/01 *Bernhard Pfeiffer (C-397/01)* et al *v Deutsches Rotes Kreuz, Kreisverband Waldshut eV* [2004] ECR I-8835.

[106] Case C-14/04 *Abdelkader Dellas and Others v Premier ministre and Ministre des Affaires sociales, du Travail et de la Solidarité* [2005] ECR I-10253.

State liability for non-implementation of the EWTD: the Fuß *case*

5.99 As discussed in Chapter 2, the doctrine of state liability has been developed as a remedy of last resort where Member States have failed to implement a directive but where the doctrines of indirect effect and consistent interpretation fail to provide a remedy in national law. The requirements developed in the state liability case law are that: (i) the provision in question must be intended to confer rights on individuals; (ii) the breach must be sufficiently serious; and (iii) there must be a causal link between the damage sustained by the injured parties and the breach of the obligation resting on the state. In its recent ruling in *Fuß* (2010)[107], the ECJ recalled that:

> (…) in accordance with settled case-law, the principle of State liability for loss or damage caused to individuals as a result of breaches of EU law for which the State can be held responsible is inherent in the system of the treaties on which the European Union is based.[108]

5.100 Article 6(b) of Directive 2003/88, in so far as it imposes on Member States a maximum limit for the average working week from which every worker must benefit, because it is a minimum requirement, was deemed to constitute a rule of EU social law of particular importance: 'the scope of which may not be subject to any conditions or restrictions whatsoever and which confers on individuals rights upon which they are entitled to rely directly before the national courts.'[109] Hence an infringement of Article 6(b) will be sufficiently serious where the decision concerned was made in manifest breach of the case law of the ECJ in the matter.

5.101 In this case, the plaintiff, Mr Fuß was obliged, under German law, to work an average of 54 hours per week, including 24-hour shifts made up of a period of time on active service and a period on stand-by, even after the ECJ had already delivered judgment in *Simap* and in *Jaeger*. The Court ruled that, 'since the failure to comply with the requirements of Article 6(b) occurred in obvious disregard of the Court's case-law, it must be regarded as a sufficiently serious breach of EU law'. It was for the referring court to establish whether, as seemed to be apparent from the documents before the Court, there was a direct causal link between the breach of Article 6(b) and the loss or damage suffered by Mr Fuß, resulting from the lost rest periods which he would have enjoyed had the maximum weekly working time provided for by the provision been respected.

---

[107] Case C-429/09 *Fuß*, supra n 98.

[108] ibid, para 45, citing Joined Cases C-6/90 and C-9/90 *Andrea Francovich and Danila Bonifaci* et al *v Italy* [1991] ECR I-5357, para 35; Joined Cases C-46/93 and C-48/93 *Brasserie du Pêcheur SA v Germany and The Queen v Secretary of State for Transport, ex parte: Factortame Ltd* et al [1996] ECR I-1029, para 31; and Case C-118/08 *Transportes Urbanos y Servicios Generales* [2010] ECR I-635, para 29.

[109] Joined Cases C-46/93 and C-48/93 *Brasserie du Pêcheur and Factortame*, supra n 108, para 57; Case C-118/00 *Gervais Larsy v Institut national d'assurances sociales pour travailleurs indépendants (INASTI)* [2001] ECR I-5063, para 44; and Case C-224/01 *Gerhard Köbler v Austria* [2003] ECR I-10239, para 56.

Finally, the ECJ held that in accordance with the case-law, reparation for such damage caused to an individual should be ensured by a public-law body, such as Stadt Halle or the Land Saxony-Anhalt, where that damage was caused by domestic measures taken by that body in breach of EU law. Moreover, EU law also does not preclude a public law body, in addition to the Member State itself, from being liable to make reparation for loss or damage caused to individuals as a result of such measures.[110] **5.102**

Review

Given the adverse reactions from health sectors throughout the EU to the *Simap* and *Jaeger* cases, many Member States called for a review of the Directive. The Directive itself contains two provisions allowing for their review prior to the expiry of a seven-year period, calculated from the deadline for transposition by the Member States that is prior to 23 November 2003. These provisions concern the derogations from the reference period for the application of Article 6 (maximum working week) and the option of not applying Article 6 if the worker agrees to carry out such work (the opt-out). **5.103**

The European Commission had first presented its proposal for a revised Directive in May 2004.[111] On 17 December 2009 the European Parliament rejected the Commission's proposal and voted to abolish national opt-outs to the Working Time Directive and enforce an EU-wide maximum working week of 48 hours. The Parliament's position also stipulated that any period of on-call time, including inactive time, must count as working time; a stalemate ensued. The proposed Directive was then referred to a conciliation committee of Council and Parliament, but for the first time in EU legislative history, following its introduction in the Amsterdam Treaty, the conciliation process did indeed fail. Hence the Directive of 2003 remains in force, and this has left Member State exposed to continuing challenges to their national legislation—and indeed damages actions—in a flood of cases referred to the ECJ. **5.104**

G. Conclusion

In our review of the Services Directive, the Non-Life Insurance Directives, the Coordination of Social Security Regulation, Public Procurement Directives, and the Working Time Directive we have discussed the main, horizontal instruments of **5.105**

[110] Case C-424/97 *Salomone Haim v Kassenzahnärztliche Vereinigung Nordrhein* [2000] ECR I-5123, paras 31–32.

[111] Commission Communication concerning the re-exam of Directive 93/104/EC concerning certain aspects of the organization of working time, COM (2003) 843 final. This document aimed to consult the European Parliament and the Council, but also the European Economic and Social Committee, the Committee of the Regions and the social partners, on a possible revision of the text. With regard to the European social partners, this communication was to be considered as the first phase of consultation pursuant to Art 154(2) of the Treaty.

secondary law that are of particular relevance to health care, and have a considerable impact at national level. This is the case even where—in the example of the Services Directive—the original objective had been to exclude health care. In other cases the impact of the horizontal rules concerned is so severe—as is the case with the Working Time Directive—that a bespoke regime for health care might seem in order. As we have shown throughout this chapter, the case law of the ECJ has greatly expanded the scope of these Directives. The importance of the doctrines of direct effect and consistent interpretation are evident here. Member States have been required to adapt their national regimes even if they have not been willing to implement the Directives in full.

5.106 The Court has also relied on the underlying primary TFEU principles to impose onerous obligations even in situations where the directives in question do not apply. In this way the ECJ has fashioned a set of 'procurement principles' which can apply to public health care purchasing not caught by the Directives. If the proposed revisions to the EU procurement regime are adopted, the health care sector will enjoy a more tailored regime within the Directive for the purchase of health and social services but will be otherwise subject to the full force of the EU procurement rules in respect of all other purchases over the specified thresholds. This latter type of expenditure typically amounts to around 30 per cent of a hospital's operating costs.

5.107 As we have seen in Chapters 3 and 4 on primary law, the interaction between the freedom to provide and receive services with the Coordination of Social Security Regulation has been especially important for the emergence of the new but separate regime of the Patients' Rights Directive that will be discussed in the next chapter. In Chapter 6 we will also seek to explain why a new sector-specific (or: vertical) regime was introduced, rather than bringing the existing horizontal system in line with the prevailing views.

6

HEALTH CARE SPECIFIC SECONDARY LEGISLATION

A. Introduction

In the previous chapters, concerning the internal market, we have first dealt with the directly applicable Treaty rules, and then with the secondary rules that are of general application across sectors (or horizontal), and which therefore include health care. In this chapter we turn to the secondary rules (notably Regulations and Directives) that directly concern health care. These can also be described as health care specific (sectoral, or vertical) rules. **6.01**

It is often thought that there is little sector-specific EU law relating to health care; however this depends on which sector it is compared with. Health care clearly does not have a 'common market organization' such as agriculture and fisheries or transport; at the same time some important common rules do exist—more so than with regard to the other 'social' sectors of the economy such as pensions, social security, or education, at least so far. **6.02**

The health care specific EU legislation that is examined in this chapter is especially relevant to the supply side of the internal market, and is rooted in the free movement principles and concerns mutual recognition of professional **6.03** qualifications,[1] pharmaceuticals,[2] and medical devices.[3] In addition there are now new sector-specific rules on patients' rights and access to information on pharmaceuticals and we deal with these measures separately in Chapter 7 because they represent a significant new development towards a focus on the demand side—the rights of consumers and patients. These two Directives, although linked to the internal market concept, build on other Treaty objectives, including social cohesion. As will emerge from this chapter and the following Chapter 7, the regulatory techniques employed to pursue these different Treaty objectives often diverge—not least because different trade-offs are at stake. This involves the Member States' sovereign rights to ensure high levels of protection versus internal market prerogatives, as well as social cohesion. Could the need to address information asymmetries in order to enable consumers to derive the maximum benefit from the internal market trump national concerns to contain health care costs or to protect incumbent providers?

6.04 The regulatory techniques, such as mutual recognition, that are applied to health care in the sector specific rules discussed in this chapter are not of course themselves health care specific. Rather they represent the different alternatives to full harmonization that, as explained in Chapter 1, the EU has developed over time to promote the internal market objective on the one hand while accommodating national

[1] The key text in this area is now Dir 2005/36/EC of the European Parliament and of the Council of 7 September 2005 on the recognition of professional qualifications [2005] OJ L255/22 (last amended by Commission Reg (EC) No 1430/2007 [2007] OJ L320/3) which covers inter alia specialized and general doctors as well as nurses, dental practitioners and pharmacists. Dir 2005/36/EC replaced a number of harmonization and mutual recognition directives for the individual health professions that dated back to the mid-1970s.

[2] eg Council Dir 89/105/EEC of 21 December 1988 relating to the transparency of measures regulating the pricing of medicinal products for human use and their inclusion within the scope of national health insurance systems [1989] OJ L40/8; Dir 2001/20/EC of the European Parliament and of the Council of 4 April 2001 on the approximation of the laws, regulations and administrative provisions of the Member States relating to the implementation of good clinical practice in the conduct of clinical trials on medicinal products for human use [2001] OJ L121/34; Dir 2001/83/EC of the European Parliament and of the Council of 6 November 2001 on the Community code relating to medicinal products for human use [2001] OJ L311/67 (last amended by Dir 2008/29/EC of the European Parliament and of the Council [2008] OJ L81/51); Reg (EC) No 726/2004 of the European Parliament and of the Council of 31 March 2004 laying down Community procedures for the authorisation and supervision of medicinal products for human and veterinary use and establishing a European Medicines Agency [2004] OJ L136/1. Cf L Hancher, 'The Pharmaceuticals market: Competition and free movement actively seeking compromises' in M McKee, E Mossialos and R Baeten (eds), *The Impact of EU Law on Healthcare Systems* (Brussels: P.I.E.-Peter Lang, 2002), 235–75.

[3] eg Council Dir 90/385/EEC of 20 June 1990 on the approximation of the laws of the Member States relating to active implantable medical devices [1990] OJ L189/17; Council Dir 93/42/EEC of 14 June 1993 concerning medical devices [1993] OJ L169/1; Dir 98/79/EC of the European Parliament and of the Council of 27 October 1998 on *in vitro* diagnostic medical devices [1998] OJ L331/1; Dir 2007/47/EC of the European Parliament and of the Council of 5 September 2007 amending Council Dir 90/385/EEC on the approximation of the laws of the Member States relating to active implantable medical devices, Council Dir 93/42/EEC concerning medical devices and Dir 98/8/EC concerning the placing of biocidal products on the market [2007] OJ L247/21. cf C Altenstetter, 'Regulation of medical devices in the EU' in M McKee, E Mossialos and R Baeten (eds), supra n 2, pp 277–303.

differences and national sensitivities in the sector on the other. As we shall explain below, the realization of internal market objectives is by no means the only goal of the EU institutions. Health now plays an important role in the Europe 2020 agenda. In its Communication of 29 June 2011, 'A budget for Europe 2020', the Commission has stressed that:

> (...) promoting good health is an integral part of the smart and inclusive growth objectives for Europe 2020. Keeping people healthy and active for longer has a positive impact on productivity and competitiveness. Innovation in health care helps take up the challenge of sustainability in the sector in the context of demographic change.

Also, action to reduce inequalities in health is deemed important to achieve 'inclusive growth'.[4]

The overall issue to keep in mind in this context is to what extent we see common techniques emerging, and to what extent these affect the regulation of the health care sector at a national level in new ways. **6.05**

B. The Mutual Recognition of Medical Professional Qualifications

The relevance of mutual recognition

As we have seen in previous chapters, the secondary EU law related to patient mobility was initially limited to social security legislation aimed at the freedom of movement for workers. Nevertheless, there is a further body of secondary legislation that is relevant to health care at large. Apart from the secondary rules for goods (medical devices and pharmaceutical products),that will be discussed in sections C and D of this Chapter, these rules in large part concern the mutual recognition of qualifications for the medical professions.[5] This is not surprising as Article 53(2) TFEU itself contains a provision encouraging the removal of restrictions in this area: **6.06**

> In the case of the medical and allied and pharmaceutical professions, the progressive abolition of restrictions shall be dependent upon coordination of the conditions for their exercise in the various Member States.

Because this is a specialized topic that cannot be done justice in the context of the present volume the discussion will be limited to a number of general points.

---

[4] Proposal for a Regulation of the European Parliament and of the Council on establishing a Health for Growth Programme, the third multi-annual programme of EU action in the field of health for the period 2014-2020 (Brussels, 9 November 2011), COM(2011) 709 final.

[5] The key text in this area is Dir 2005/36/EC of the European Parliament and of the Council of 7 September 2005 on the recognition of professional qualifications [2005] OJ L255/22. cf M Peeters, M McKee and S Merkur, 'EU law and health professionals' in E Mossialos et al (eds), *Health Systems Governance in Europe: The Role of European Law and Policy* (Cambridge: Cambridge University Press 2010) 589; and T Hervey and J McHale, *Health Law and the European Union* (Cambridge: Cambridge University Press, 2004) 58.

6.07 Mutual recognition means that if the individual involved meets the standards for entry into a profession in one Member State then their professional qualifications will be recognized in the other Member States without additional requirements. The advantage of this technique is that as long as the Member States can agree on harmonizing the minimum set of essential requirements that must be met, variations between Member States need not be ironed out by means of laborious negotiations and lengthy legislative procedures in order to make free movement of (in the case currently under discussion) services and establishment of health care professionals possible. Mutual recognition is a regulatory technique associated with the so-called '1992 programme' and the '1987 Single Act' designed to complete the internal market by means of 'smart' regulation.

6.08 From the 1970s onwards, initially a system of specialized Directives for all different medical professions (medical specialists and general practitioners, nurses responsible for general care, dental practitioners, veterinary surgeons, midwives, and pharmacists) was introduced. In 2005 all these were consolidated into a single Directive on the recognition of professional qualifications.[6] Under its terms, health professionals benefit from the automatic recognition of their qualifications, on the basis of harmonized minimum training requirements. These rules are now under reconsideration by the Commission (see paras 6.14–6.17).[7]

The mutual recognition case law

6.09 The mutual recognition rules have required adjustments to national rules in a number of cases, such as that concerning the Italian requirement that all dentists should also be qualified as general practitioners (medical doctors).[8] Apart from this, part of the case law relating to the freedom of establishment concerns problems in relation to mutual recognition of professional qualifications.

6.10 The principle that the quality of doctors in the different Member States must be regarded as equivalent was asserted by the ECJ in the cases *Kohll* and *Decker* (1998), which we have already cited repeatedly.[9] In *Kohll* the Court stated:

> It follows [from the EU rules in this area] that doctors and dentists established in other Member States must be afforded all guarantees equivalent to those accorded to

[6] ibid; O Odudu, 'Are state owned healthcare providers that are funded by general taxation undertakings subject to competition law?' [2011] *European Competition Law Review* 231.

[7] European Commission, Evaluation of the professional qualifications Directive 2005/36/EC, Brussels, 5 July 2011; Green paper, Modernising the Professional Qualifications Directive, COM(2011) 367 final.

[8] Case C-202/99 *Commission v Italy (dentists)* [2001] ECR I-9319.

[9] Case C-158/96 *Raymond Kohll v Union des caisses de maladie (Kohll)* [1998] ECR I-1931, paras 47–49; and Case C-120/95 *Nicolas Decker v Caisse de maladie des employés privés (Decker)* [1998] ECR I-1831, paras 42–43; with reference to Case C-215/87 *Heinz Schumacher v Hauptzollamt Frankfurt am Main-Ost (Schumacher)* [1989] ECR 617, para 20; Case C-62/90 *Commission v Genrmany (Imports of pharmaceuticals)* [1992] ECR I-2575, para 18.

doctors and dentists established on national territory, for the purposes of freedom to provide services.[10]

Consequently the Treaty exceptions with regard to health care in Articles 52 and 62 TFEU were not held applicable in *Kohll* and unqualified mutual recognition was demanded. This position was repeated inter alia in 2007 when the Court ruled that the Greek authorities could not invoke the quality of private clinics in other Member States as a reason to refuse reimbursement of treatment there in *Stamatelaki* (2007).[11] 6.11

The case law often concerns the recognition of professional qualifications which have been acquired in third countries and are recognized by the original Member State of residence but not by a second Member State once residence is taken up there: there is no EU law rule that requires unconditional recognition of such third country professional qualifications just because they have been honoured by another Member State. However, in cases such as *Haim I*, *Tawil-Albertini* (both in 1994) and *Hocsman* (2000) the ECJ clearly indicated that the professional experience and qualifications obtained in third countries must be taken into account.[12] In this manner it effectively provided a sector-specific interpretation of the general rule that had been established with regard to professional training and experience in *Vlassopoulou* (1991).[13] In *Tennah-Durez* (2003) the ECJ ruled that for general recognition it is decisive where the diploma was awarded (Belgium in this case), not where (part of) the professional training had taken place (Algeria in this case).[14] In *Haim II* (2000) an exception to mutual recognition was made for the language skills that may be required for a doctor. However the Court noted that the dentist concerned might have a limited knowledge of German but could serve an important linguistic minority in Germany as he spoke Turkish.[15] 6.12

What has been discussed here only applies with respect to formal qualifications. The remaining restrictions with relation to medical professions and mutual recognition coincide with the restrictions on the freedom of establishment that have 6.13

[10] Case C-158/96 *Kohll*, supra n 9, para 48.

[11] Case C-444/05 *Aikaterini Stamatelaki v NPDD Organismos Asfaliseos Eleftheron Epangelmation (OAEE)(Stamatelaki)* [2007] ECR I-3185, paras 36–37.

[12] Case C-319/92 *Salomone Haim v Kassenzahnärztliche Vereinigung Nordrhein (Haim I)* [1994] ECR I-425; Case C-154/93 *Abdullah Tawil-Albertini v Ministre des Affaires Sociales* [1994] ECR I-451; Case C-238/98 *Hugo Fernando Hocsman v Ministre de l'Emploi et de la Solidarité* [2000] ECR I-6623.

[13] Case C-340/89 *Irène Vlassopoulou v Ministerium für Justiz, Bundes- und Europaangelegenheiten Baden-Württemberg* [1991] ECR I-2357.

[14] Case C-110/01 *Malika Tennah-Durez v Conseil national de l'ordre des médecins* [2003] ECR I-6239.

[15] Case C-424/97 *Salomone Haim v Kassenzahnärztliche Vereinigung Nordrhein (Haim II)* [2000] ECR I-5123.

already been discussed in Chapter 4.[16] In the establishment context Member States may continue to insist on national prerogatives such as non-profit requirements or ownership restrictions even at the expense of internal market objectives.

The new proposals

6.14 In June 2011 the European Commission published a Green Paper on modernising the Professional Qualifications Directive,[17] followed in December 2011 by a proposal for a revised Directive.[18] Among the proposed general changes are the introduction of an (electronic) European professional card that should facilitate checking credentials and an enhanced use of the internal market information system (IMI), a secure on-line information system for the exchange of data between authorities in different Member States. As regards the medical professions, a system of automatic mutual recognition based on minimum training requirements is already in place that makes medical education across the EU comparable. However an issue raised in the evaluation exercise concerns the lack of transparency on the contents of training programmes for diplomas issued in the health sector. Refinements of this system are proposed.

6.15 The proposed Directive would seek to bar practitioners banned from practice in any Member State from seeking employment elsewhere based on a mutual warning system. In addition, as before, proof of language skills may be required, but only after the relevant qualification has been recognized and only where reasonable and necessary—that is it should not form a means of excluding professionals from the labour market.

6.16 Learning requirements are to reflect the need for life-long learning in the health professions. The proposed Directives will introduce European Credit Transfer and Accumulation System (ECTS) credits as a (non-binding) measuring system for educational qualifications. Basic medical training will have to consist at least five years (instead of now six) comprising 5,500 hours of university education and access to nurses' and midwives' training must require completing 12 years (now only ten) of general education. Both basic dentist training requirements, at five years of university (or equivalent) training, and pharmacists, training requirements at five years of university, remain the same. Finally, the case law on partial access to

[16] Such as the German quota system for psychotherapists. cf Case C-456/05 *Commission v Germany (Psycho therapists)* [2007] ECR I-10517.

[17] EU Commission, Green Paper: Modernising the professional qualifications Directive (Brussels, 22 June 2011), COM(2011) 367 final.

[18] Proposal for a Directive of the European Parliament and of the Council amending Directive 2005/36/EC on the recognition of professional qualifications and Regulation on administrative cooperation through the Internal Market Information System (Brussels, 19 December 2011), COM(2011) 883 final. cf NHS European office, Mobility of health professionals across Europe, Briefing February 2012, issue 8. <http://www.nhsconfed.org/Publications/briefings/Pages/Mobility-across-Europe.aspx> accessed 24 February 2012.

exercise some but not all of a profession's activities (where not all requirements for full practice are met) will be codified.[19]

6.17 It is important to note that these are so far just proposals, which are not uncontested. For instance some Member States will want more equivalents to university training or minimum general education to be recognized and there has been criticism of the European professional card as a cumbersome change that would not add much value to what would already be available from the IMI database. The new rules are likely to be amended in the legislative process (under the ordinary legislative procedure or 'co-decision') before they are adopted by the European Parliament and Council.

C. The Rules on Pharmaceutical Products

6.18 Like medical devices, pharmaceutical products are goods and, as such, one of the oldest areas of focus for creating a functioning internal market without barriers to trade concerning health care. At the same time pharmaceuticals involve health risks and considerable costs to the authorities of the Member States, while representing a knowledge-intensive and lucrative area of manufacturing. All of these aspects must be managed. Hence, on the one hand, pharmaceuticals are regulated by the EU in order to protect consumers and to promote an effective functioning of the internal market but, on the other hand, they are also the subject of national and European industrial policy.[20] Obviously there is tension between these various objectives. In this context, conditions for admission to the market and intellectual property rights (IPR) play an important role, just like the continuous discussion on parallel imports (arbitrage between Member States with high prices and those with lower prices) which may help to reduce prices but where the bulk of the benefits is enjoyed by the arbitrageurs themselves. Meanwhile there is the ongoing struggle between branded pharmaceuticals and generic drugs that are based on the same active ingredient. The rules with respect to pharmaceuticals are too extensive to be dealt with here other than in a cursory manner. Pricing for pharmaceuticals is dealt with in some more detail below, as this topic provides a useful insight into how a minimum harmonization measure has been interpreted by the courts, while Chapter 7 looks at the topic of the emergence of consumer rights to information in

[19] cf Case C-330/03 *Colegio de Ingenieros de Caminos, Canales y Puertos v Administración del Estado* [2006] ECR I-801.

[20] eg Council Dir 89/105/EEC of 21 December 1988 relating to the transparency of measures regulating the prices of medicinal products for human use and their inclusion in the scope of national health insurance systems [1989] OJ L40/8; Dir 2001/20/EC of the European Parliament and of the Council of 4 April 2001 on the approximation of the laws, regulations and administrative provisions of the Member States relating to the implementation of good clinical practice in the conduct of clinical trials on medicinal products for human use [2001] OJ L121/34.

the sensitive field of pharmaceuticals advertising. Readers with a specific interest in pharmaceuticals regulation are however referred to the specialized literature.[21]

6.19 There are two procedures for admitting pharmaceutical products to the market, a centralized procedure and a decentralized one, which builds upon the principle of mutual recognition.[22] The centralized procedure is coordinated by the European Medicines Agency (EMEA), while the decentralized procedure is based on a request for admission in a single Member State, which next relies on mutual recognition for admission in other Member States. For biotechnology, new chemical entities, and other highly innovative products, the centralized procedure is obligatory.

Intellectual property

6.20 The intellectual property in pharmaceuticals in the EU is protected by patents (20 years) and by a supplementary patent certificate, plus marketing and data-exclusivity, in order to prolong the effective term of patent protection. This is done in compensation for the lengthy approvals procedure which eats into the term of the patent before patented pharmaceuticals make it into the market. Producers of generic products may only market their products eight years after the regulatory approval of the original product, followed by two years during which the data-exclusivity and the marketing-exclusivity apply.[23] Meanwhile, the *AstraZeneca* (2010) case has shown that pharmaceutical companies can make strategic use of these different forms of protection and the various terms of their expiration in order to frustrate market entry for the particular active ingredient by producers of generic drugs.[24] In this case the General Court upheld the Commission's intervention, based on the abuse of dominance provision in Article 102 TFEU, against the abuse of rights and procedures by AstraZeneca.

Pharmaceuticals pricing

6.21 Because pharmaceutical products are goods, based on cases such as *Decker* (1998) and *Duphar* (1984) the overriding reason of public interest of protecting the

[21] cf L Hancher, 'The Pharmaceuticals market: Competition and free movement actively seeking compromises', in M McKee, E Mossialos and R Baeten (eds), supra n 2, 235; L Hancher, 'The EU pharmaceuticals market: parameters and pathways' in E Mossialos et al (eds), *Health Systems Governance in Europe: The Role of European Law and Policy* (Cambridge: Cambridge University Press, 2010) 635; T Hervey and J McHale, supra n 5, Chapter 8, p 282.

[22] Reg (EC) No 726/2004 of the European Parliament and of the Council of 31 March 2004 laying down Community procedures for the authorisation and supervision of medicinal products for human and veterinary use and establishing a European Medicines Agency [2004] OJ L136/1.

[23] L Hancher, supra n 21, pp 651–2.

[24] Case T-321/05 *AstraZeneca AB and AstraZeneca PLC v Commission* [2010] judgment of 1 July 2010 (nyr). This case was an appeal against *AstraZeneca* (Case COMP/A.37.507/F3) Commission Decision 2006/857/EC [2006] OJ L332/24, relating to a proceeding under Art 82 of the EC Treaty and Art 54 of the EEA Agreement. (See the discussion below in Ch 8.)

financial balance of the social security system is applicable,[25] which includes having recourse to price controls. Pricing policy with respect to pharmaceuticals is still largely in hands of the Member States, although EU transparency requirements do exist based on Directive 89/105/EEC.[26] This requires the competent authorities to provide an annual list of the products for which prices have been fixed as well as any approved price increases. In the event that the competent authorities decide not to allow a pharmaceutical product to be marketed at the price proposed by the requesting party they must motivate this decision based on objective and verifiable criteria. In the event that prices are frozen the need to do so must be reconsidered at least once annually.

There are a number of recent cases concerning the transparency of price setting with regard to pharmaceuticals and possible limits on the powers of the Member States to freeze prices based on the abovementioned Directive that will be discussed below.[27] **6.22**

Thus in *AIM* (2010) the ECJ has stated that: 'Directive 89/105 has as its underlying principle the idea of minimum interference in the organisation by Member States of their domestic social security policies.'[28] The *AIM* ruling demonstrates that the freedom of the Member States to design their social security systems is still dominant,[29] although the actions of the Member States must be in accordance with procedural and substantive rules of due process and must be based on objective and verifiable facts. It should also be possible to request an individual exception to a general pricing measure by means of a reasoned decision. Is up to the individual Member States if, when deciding on the possible need to free the prices of pharmaceuticals, they take into account 'pharmaceutical expenditure alone, health expenditure overall or even other types of relevant expenditure'.[30] The issue of pricing regulation is discussed in more detail below. **6.23**

Pricing issues

Prices of pharmaceuticals diverge widely throughout the EU not just as a matter of relative purchasing power but also due to widespread governmental intervention in these prices, largely aiming to control health care expenditure. This has led to phenomena such as the pharmaceutical companies blocking parallel imports in order **6.24**

---

[25] Case C-120/95 *Decker*, supra n 9, paras 39–40.

[26] Dir 89/105/EEG, supra n 2.

[27] ibid, concerning its Art 4.

[28] Joined Cases C-471/07 en C-472/07 *Association générale de l'industrie du médicament (AGIM) ASBL* et al *and Sanofi-Aventis Belgium SA v Belgium* [2010] ECR I-113, para 16. cf Joined Cases C-352/07 to C-356/07, C-365/07 to C-367/07 and C-400/07 *A. Menarini Industrie Farmaceutiche Riunite Srl* et al [2009] ECR I-2495.

[29] Citing Case C-238/82 *Duphar BV* et al *v Netherlands (Duphar)* [1984] ECR 523, para 16; Case C-245/03 *Merck, Sharp & Dohme BV v Belgium* [2005] ECR I-637, para 28.

[30] cf Joined Cases C-352/07 to C-356/07, C-365/07 to C-367/07 and C-400/07 *Menarini*, supra n 28, paras 48, 54 en 61; and Joined Cases C-471/07 en C-472/07 *AVGI*, supra n 28, para 23.

to avoid low prices imposed in one Member State spilling over into other health care markets. It is clear that pricing interventions by the Member States distort the internal market. However it is accepted by the ECJ as the Member States retain sovereignty over the manner in which they design their social policy regimes in this regard. As the Court stated in *Duphar* (1984) in relation to a so-called 'negative list' of preparations that would not be reimbursed in the Netherlands:

> [...] it must be recognised that Community law does not detract from the powers of Member States to organise their social security systems and to adopt, in particular, provisions intended to govern the consumption of pharmaceutical preparations in order to promote the financial stability of their healthcare insurance schemes.[31]

It should come as no surprise then that any meaningful harmonization of pricing for pharmaceutical products has been an elusive target for the EU.

6.25 However there is one measure of EU legislation in place in this field, the Price Transparency Directive of 1989,[32] which is presently in the process of being re-examined for review and renewal. We will first look at this Directive, then at the relevant case law, and finally, briefly, at the proposals for review.

The Price Transparency Directive

6.26 The Directive starts from the assumption that disparities in the 'national measures of an economic nature' on the marketing of medicinal products (that is various price controls) may negatively affect the functioning of the internal market in medicinal products. It then sets out requirements for such measures which are intended to ensure that they do not constitute barriers to trade: if price controls abide by the rules set out in the Directive they are compatible with the internal market.

6.27 At the same time the Directive does not affect the policy rationale of the national measures concerned: its primary aim is to increase transparency and objectivity in national procedures relating to price and profit controls. Moreover, if the process of setting prices and profit caps becomes more transparent, interested parties can establish whether EU law is respected, in particular whether the processes favour domestic production over imports of pharmaceuticals.[33]

6.28 Hence the Price Transparency Directive contains basic procedural guarantees to ensure objectivity in decision making on pharmaceutical prices. Decisions have to be taken within 90 days (which can be extended by a further 90 days if additional information must be gathered) from an application and must contain a statement

---

[31] Case 238/82 *Duphar BV* et al *v The Netherlands* [1984] ECR 523.

[32] Council Dir 89/105/EEC of 21 December 1988, relating to the transparency of measures regulating the pricing of medicinal products for human use and their inclusion in the scope of national health insurance systems [1989] OJ L40/8. cf C Schoonderbeek and J Lisman, 'EU member states and the Transparency Directive', in *PLC Cross-border Life Sciences Handbook 2009*, pp 33–8.

[33] L Hancher, supra n 21.

of reasons based on objective and verifiable criteria. In addition, applicants must be informed on the remedies available against a decision and, based on the case law (discussed below), this must involve access to judicial review. The Directive covers the various methodologies for price controls on pharmaceuticals that are prevalent in the Member States:

- prior approval requirements, with rules on the timeframe and annual publication requirement of approved price increases;
- price freezes, which are to be reviewed at least once a year based on the prevailing macro-economic conditions;
- systems of direct or indirect profitability controls (profit skimming above a set limit), requiring transparency on the accounting methods used;
- positive lists of products that will be reimbursed, with further procedural guarantees; and
- negative lists of products that will not be reimbursed, with comparable additional procedural guarantees.

Finally, the Directive establishes a consultative committee of Member States' representatives that advises the Commission and the Member States on matters regarding the Directive. The Price Transparency Directive has not once been amended despite being in existence for over 20 years. It has however been the subject of significant case law that is summarized below. **6.29**

The case law on pharmaceuticals pricing

Commission v Austria

This 2001 case concerned the Austrian practice of maintaining a register for pharmaceuticals of which the cost would be automatically reimbursed (with exceptions or additions, such as branded medication specifically prescribed on medical grounds), instead of a 'positive list' as under Article 6 of the Price Transparency Directive.[34] The ECJ ruled that the sole determining factor was that the inclusion of a medicinal product on the register normally meant that its cost would be automatically be borne by the national social security scheme. Hence the rules of Article 6 applied. The Court also ruled that the general EU law principle of the requirement of judicial review of administrative decisions meant there was a general requirement for judicial review under the Directive. The Austrian review by independent experts fell short of this. **6.30**

Commission v Finland

Here (in 2003) the scope of Article 6 of the Directive was again at issue in relation to the Finnish practice of having a separate second list for medicinal products with **6.31**

[34] Case C-424/99 *Commission v Austria* [2001] ECR I-9285.

a higher than standard cover to which the conditions set out in the Directive were not applied.[35] The ECJ found this to be at odds with the requirement to allow verification of the application of objective criteria and non-discrimination. It also held that any national measure with regard to controlling prices for medicinal products for human use was caught by the Directive. Implementing a dual procedure that exempted higher cover from the rules of the Price Transparency Directive was therefore found to be in breach of the Directive.

Merck, Sharp & Dohme BV v Belgium

6.32 At issue in this case from 2005 were the implications of a refusal to include medicinal products on a positive list under Article 6 of the Price Transparency Directive that had been quashed in a judicial review by a Belgian court.[36] The undertakings concerned pleaded in favour of an automatic entry on the list of products covered by the insurance system as the 90 day time limit for a further administrative decision had been exceeded. The ECJ however pointed out that because the Directive expressly covered automatic consequences in its Articles 2(1) and 3(1), and not in the case of its Article 6, this meant automatic entry on the list was not available as a remedy under the Directive. Instead, it was up to the Member State to determine the effects of exceeding the time limit while respecting equivalence with comparable national situations and not obstructing the realization of EU law rights.

Glaxosmithkline SA v Belgium

6.33 This case, which was decided on the same day as the abovementioned one, also concerned time limits under the Directive.[37] Again the ECJ stated that it was a matter of national law to deal with the consequences of judicial annulment of a decision by a Member State under Article 6 of the Price Transparency Directive. However the Court also ruled that effective judicial protection under EU law meant a new decision under Article 6 would have to be taken within a set time limit and in any event not more than the 90 days originally provided by the Directive.

Pohl-Boskamp

6.34 This German case was decided in 2006.[38] The ECJ ruled that a Member State could not exclude non-prescription drugs from the benefits of the national health system, while allowing exceptions to this rule to be decided upon without respecting the procedural requirements of Article 6 of the Price Transparency Directive; a dual system, one respecting the Directive and one not, was not acceptable.

---

[35] Case C-229/00 *Commission v Finland* [2003] ECR I-5727.

[36] Case C-245/03 *Merck, Sharp & Dohme BV v Belgium* [2005] ECR I-637.

[37] Case C-296/03 *GlaxoSmithKline SA v Belgium* [2005] ECR I-669.

[38] Case C-317/05 *G. Pohl-Boskamp GmbH & Co. KG v Gemeinsamer Bundesausschuss* [2006] ECR I-10611.

Menarini

6.35 Arguably the most far-reaching case on the Price Transparency Directive is *Menarini* (2009).[39] In this case the ECJ held that the general Article 1 of the Directive and its Article 4 on price freezes meant that the Member States could adopt general measures reducing the prices of all or some categories of pharmaceuticals—even in the absence of a prior price freeze. (The only explicit mention of price decreases in the Directive is found in Article 4(1) on price freezes.) This is because: (i) such national measures reducing prices are national measures to control the prices within the meaning of Article 1(1) of the Directive (which does not spell out any particular form of price control but just sets out general principles for any decision on price); and (ii) the underlying principle of the Directive is that of minimum interference in the organization of the domestic social security policies of the Member States. This ruling significantly increases the scope for Member States to intervene in the sector.

The 2010 review

6.36 As mentioned the Directive has not been amended in over 20 years, which may seem unusual for such legislation. Numerous past attempts to update the Directive have failed, however. The Commission has meanwhile launched a consultation concerning a possible update that lasted through the spring of 2011.[40] One of the options that it has tabled is a thorough review of the Directive to establish a more modern set of binding rules to reflect the growing complexity of reimbursement and pricing controls at national level. In addition the scope of the Directive could be extended to cover medical devices alongside pharmaceuticals. It should be noted that industry representative bodies are not in favour of reviewing the Directive. This is because they fear that the clock might be turned back on a piece of legislation that has served them well in terms of imposing objective decisions and judicial review. Instead they would prefer more extensive soft law guidance on issues like providing information on diseases and relevant treatments and comparing different drugs for their effectiveness.[41] On 12 March 2012 the Commission proposed to adopt a new Directice repealing Directive 89/105/EEC.

[39] Joined Cases C-352/07 to C-356/07, C-365/07 to C-367/07 and C-400/07 *A. Menarini Industrie Farmaceutiche Riunite Srl and Others v Ministero della Salute and Agenzia Italiana del Farmaco (AIFA)* [2009] ECR I-2495.

[40] See <http://ec.europa.eu/enterprise/sectors/healthcare/public-consultation/index_en.htm#h2-9> accessed 24 February 2012.

[41] 'Pharma urges EU not to revise Transparency Directive' (*Pharma Times Online*, 26 May 2011) <http://www.pharmatimes.com> accessed 24 February 2012.

D. The Rules on Medical Devices

Introduction

6.37 Medical devices are an increasingly important health care sector due to their impact on health and the increasingly large expenditure on such devices.[42] Because the regulation of the sector is not widely known, and due to its growing economic and social importance, we examine the current regulatory techniques deployed and some of the legal issues to which this type of approach gives rise. The number of different types of medical devices on the market is currently estimated to be over 200,000 in Europe[43]and about 80,000 in the United Kingdom alone.[44]

6.38 Products ranging from spectacles to sophisticated diagnostic imaging equipment are currently subject to the EU medical devices legislation which comprises of a series of Directives. As explained in Chapter 2, Directives allow the Member States to introduce some flexibility into their national legal orders providing they ensure the aims of the directives are realized. A particular legal feature of medical devices control at EU level is the reliance on non-binding guidelines. Commission guidance is considered to be the definitive statement of a medical device manufacturer's obligations in certain areas, as will be explained below. A further feature of the sector is the reliance on the so-called 'new approach' to harmonization of the technical requirements or specifications for medical devices (discussed in a separate section below). Given the vast array of products and product types with highly technical requirements, it is extremely difficult to adopt product-specific norms or standards.

6.39 Finally, medical devices are often also subject to certain horizontal regulation, including the Directive concerning Restriction on Hazardous Substances (RoHS)[45] and the Regulation concerning Registration, Evaluation, Authorisation and Restriction of Chemicals (REACH)[46] which in turn govern certain types of

---

[42] C Altenstetter, 'Regulation of Medical Devices in the EU' in M McKee, E Mossialos and R Baeten (eds), *The Impact of EU Law on Healthcare Systems* (Brussels: P.E.I.-Peter Lang, 2003); C Altenstetter, and G Permanand, 'The EU regulation of medical devices and pharmaceuticals in comparative perspective' [2007] Review of Policy Research, 385–405.

[43] AG Fraser et al, 'Clinical evaluation of cardiovascular devices – principles, problems and proposals for European regulatory reform' [2011] EUR Heart Journal, 1673–86.

[44] 'How medical devices are regulated in the UK' [2010] *Drugs Ther Bull*, 48, 82–84.

[45] Dir 2011/65/EU of the European Parliament and of the Council of 8 June 2011 on the restriction of the use of certain hazardous substances in electrical and electronic equipment [2011] OJ L174/88.

[46] Reg (EC) No 1907/2006 of the European Parliament and of the Council of 18 December 2006 concerning the Registration, Evaluation, Authorisation and Restriction of Chemicals (REACH), establishing a European Chemicals Agency, amending Dir 1999/45/EC and repealing Council Reg (EEC) No 793/93 and Commission Reg (EC) No 1488/94 as well as Council Dir 76/769/EEC and Commission Dirs 91/155/EEC, 93/67/EEC, 93/105/EC and 2000/21/EC [2006] OJ L396/1.

processes or chemical substances used in specific types of medical devices. The EU's RoHS Directive covering electronic devices will also cover medical devices and aims to improve collection and recycling rates of electronic devices across the EU, as well as to cut down on illegal exporting of electronic waste products from the EU. Medical devices and in vitro diagnostic (IVD) products had previously been exempted from the RoHS, but that exemption will not be extended except for active implants. As such, medical devices and monitoring and control instruments will have three years to comply with RoHS following the Directive's adoption; IVD products will have five years to comply.

Where certain aspects of the marketing of a medical device are not covered by the sector specific Directives, such as advertising to the public, this does not mean that this particular activity is immune from EU law. It may in fact be subject to a series of EU measures governing the product marketing methods in general, as we shall explore further below. **6.40**

The focus in this section is on those elements of the current regime that distinguish medical devices regulation from other forms of health care product regulation at EU level. This contrast regards in particular the regulation of pharmaceuticals, which are subject to an all-inclusive, tailor-made sector specific regime characterized by strong centralization of control at EU level at all stages from clinical development to marketing. **6.41**

The internal market context

The historical trajectory of medical device regulation is deeply embedded in the internal market-building project that took off in the mid-1980s and that galvanized around the Single European Act and flexibilization of EU rules. Rules relating to the safety and performance of medical devices were harmonized in the 1990s with the adoption of the Active Implantable Medical Devices Directive of 1990,[47] followed by a 1993 Directive on Medical Devices[48] and finally the In Vitro Diagnostic Medical Devices Directive of 1998.[49] Medical device vigilance was first mandated in 2007 by a modifying Directive amending the previous medical device Directives, and introducing new essential requirements and recommendations concerning **6.42**

[47] Council Dir 90/385/EEC of 20 June 1990 on the approximation of the laws of the Member States relating to active implantable medical devices [1990] OJ L189/17.

[48] Council Dir 93/42/EEC of 14 June 1993 concerning medical devices [1993] OJ L169/1.

[49] Council Dir 98/79/EC of 27 October 1998 on *in vitro* diagnostic medical devices [1998] OJ L331/1.

clinical evaluation and vigilance.[50] Next it was required in 2009 by an amendment concerning common technological specifications for IVD devices.[51]

6.43 The relevant stakeholders have pursued a political and legal strategy for establishing an EU wide legislative regulatory framework for medical devices that has remained separate from the older and established pharmaceutical regime. French opposition to the application of the EU approach on 'CE marking' from 1990 to 1998, and the political debates over setting up a European agency on medical devices separate from the European Medicines Agency are illustrative of this strategy.

6.44 As the use and complexity of diagnostic and therapeutic devices is increasing (particularly in cardiovascular medicine) and expenditure on devices contributes significantly to the escalating cost of health care in the EU, the European Commission announced, in 2008, a fundamental revision or 'recast' of the Medical Device Directives. This is designed to clarify and strengthen the current legal framework in order to reflect technological advances and the changing patterns of medical practice as well as increasing concern in relation to clinical problems relating to the failure of medical devices.[52] Drafting of this legislation is carried out in the first instance by the Cosmetics and Medical Devices Unit established since 2010 within the Commission's Directorate General for Health and Consumer Affairs (DG Sanco). Previously this unit had been part of DG Enterprise. The European approach diverges markedly from that applied in the USA where the evaluation and approval of medical devices is the responsibility of a centralized regulatory agency, the Food and Drug Administration.

6.45 The 2011 Council Conclusions on innovation in the medical device sector emphasize the balance to be struck between the widely differing policy goals in this sector—ranging from industrial policy and innovation to patient safety and public health.[53]

The Directives on medical devices

6.46 What are medical devices? In EU law, a medical device is *not* an organ, not a prescription drug, not a transplant, not a human tissue-engineered product, not a blood product, nor cosmetics. A medical device is everything else that is used in

---

[50] Dir 2007/47/EC of 5 September 2007 amending Council Dir 90/385/EEC on the approximation of the laws of the Member States relating to active implantable medical devices, Council Dir 93/42/EEC concerning medical devices and Dir 98/8/EC concerning the placing of biocidal products on the market [2007] OJ L247/21.

[51] Commission Decision 2009/886/EC of 27 November 2009 amending Decision 2002/364/EC on common technical specifications for *in vitro* diagnostic medical devices [2009] OJ L318/2.

[52] European Commission Roadmap: Proposal for a Directive concerning medical devices (recast) [2008] <http://ec.europa.eu/governance/impact/planned_ia/roadmaps_2012_en.htm#SANCO> accessed 24 February 2012.

[53] Council conclusions on innovation in the medical device sector [2011] OJ C202/7.

clinical practice, research, laboratory testing, and patient care. This means a massive number of heterogeneous products are covered.[54] EU regulation of medical devices has, from its initiation, proceeded on the basis of classifying medical devices by risk categories and has followed the so-called 'New Approach' to product standardization discussed at paras 6.49–6.53. Devices are assigned to four groups according to risk and these relate to different levels of testing and evidence that are required before they can be approved for marketing.

Fifteen years after its first involvement in three medical device-specific directives discussed below—the Active Implantable Medical Devices Directive of 1990, the Medical Devices Directive of 1993 and the In Vitro Devices Directive of 1998—in 2005 the Commission proposed new draft rules to replace the earlier measures as well as a new proposal for a fourth Directive to support cell or tissue-based therapies.[55] The objective of drafting these four Directives and other rules was to enhance EU-wide regulatory capacity at the same time as avoiding the rise of divergent national approaches. The draft fourth Directive aimed to create a stand-alone 'single, integrated and tailored European regulatory framework' for advanced therapies (all gene-, cell-, or tissue-based therapies), thus completing a regulatory framework specific to medical devices. A single integrated framework has however not been adopted so far. As noted, a less ambitious amending and updating Directive to the three existing Directives was adopted in 2007.[56] **6.47**

In 2008 the Commission consulted stakeholders on the revision or 'recast' of the current legal framework,[57] and issued a summary report in late 2008.[58] Following a second public consultation launched in June 2010, the Commission is currently proposing a number of amendments to simplify this complex and fragmented area of legislation which is fraught with national variation. It also aims to ensure a more equal level of protection of public health and to keep the European industry competitive by aligning the EU regime with the global market, and has published roadmap of the trajectory it intends to pursue.[59] In order to understand the present **6.48**

[54] Dir 98/79/EC of the European Parliament and of the Council of 27 October 1998 on *in vitro* diagnostic medical devices [1998] OJ L331/1.

[55] Proposal for a Dir of the European Parliament and of the Council amending Council Dirs 90/385/EEC and 93/42/EEC and Dir 98/8/EC of the European Parliament and the Council as regards the review of the medical device directives (SEC(2005)1742—COD 2005/0263) COM/2005/0681 final.

[56] Dir 2007/47/EC of the European Parliament and of the Council of 5 September 2007 amending Council Dir 90/385/EEC on the approximation of the laws of the Member States relating to active implantable medical devices, Council Dir 93/42/EEC concerning medical devices and Dir 98/8/EC concerning the placing of biocidal products on the market [2007] OJ L247/21.

[57] <http://ec.europa.eu/health/medical-devices/files/recast_docs_2008/public_consultation_en.pdf> accessed 24 February 2012.

[58] <http://ec.europa.eu/health/medical-devices/files/recast_docs_2008/responses/responses_public_consultation_recast_en.pdf> accessed 24 February 2012.

[59] <http://ec.europa.eu/governance/impact/planned_ia/docs/2008_sanco_081_medical_devices_en.pdf> accessed 16 August 2011.

legal framework and to anticipate proposed reforms it is necessary to appreciate the so-called 'New Approach' and the related system of CE marking.

The 'New Approach' and the CE mark

6.49 The traditional way of harmonizing product standards is carried out by legislation that obliges certain product types produced in EU to have the same technical specifications. This approach to harmonization of rules consists of often very highly detailed legislation for each product category. Such harmonization is also called full or maximum harmonization. This harmonization approach is for instance used in the sectoral legislation for cars. The traditional approach to harmonization is not suitable for all product sectors and certainly does not produce results quickly. This is why, in 1985, the 'New Approach' to technical harmonization and standards was adopted by the European Council. This approach fitted in well with the internal market project of the time, with reliance on more flexible ways of regulation and mutual recognition. The New Approach is a regulatory technique whereby product legislation is restricted to the requirements necessary to protect the public goals of health and safety.

6.50 In accordance with the New Approach, legislation sets out certain essential requirements with which products must comply in order to benefit from free movement within the EU. In order to minimize administrative burdens, the approach presupposed that pre-market review and approval by regulators would be replaced by a variety of conformity assessment techniques, carried out by the manufacturer or by a third-party assessor of conformity. The design, manufacture, and release of all products must conform to appropriate quality assurance standards.

Origins of the New Approach and CE mark

6.51 The first attempt to define the New Approach dates back to a 1985 Council Resolution on the New Approach.[60] This provided that any New Approach legislation would be limited to defining key essential requirements and detailed technical specifications would be set out in harmonized EU standards. Compliance with standards was not however mandatory as this could hinder innovation. Manufacturers had the choice not to apply harmonized standards or other technical solutions, but compliance with harmonized standards would realise a presumption of conformity with the essential requirements and therefore free movement across the EU. The final component of the New Approach consists of a safeguard procedure whereby Member States could prevent or restrict the marketing of non-conforming products, or address shortcomings in the harmonized standards. A 1989 Council Resolution on the 'global approach' to conformity

[60] Council Resolution of 7 May 1985 on a new approach to technical harmonization and standards [1985] OJ C136/1. cf J Pelkmans, 'The New Approach to Technical Harmonization and Standardization' [1987] Journal of Common Market Studies, 249–69.

assessment further refined the New Approach and created the concept of the 'CE' (that is a conformity mark), which manufacturers could apply to their products once they had demonstrated conformity with the essential requirements.[61] Where possible, manufacturers were to have a degree of flexibility to choose from a variety of modular conformity assessment procedures in order to allow them to adapt the procedures to their products and the stage of their development.

Legislation

Originally, two Decisions of 1990 and 1993 provided general guidelines and procedures for conformity assessment procedures.[62] These measures have now been superseded by a new Decision 756/2008 on CE marking, Regulation 764/2008 on national technical rules, and Regulation 756/2008 on accreditation and market surveillance.[63] The Regulations of 2008 set out rules on market surveillance, accreditation of notified bodies, and rules on the application of national technical requirements. The revised system introduces better rules on market surveillance to protect both consumers and professionals from unsafe products, including imports from third countries. It enhances the confidence in and quality of conformity assessments of products through reinforced and clearer rules on the requirements for notification of conformity assessment bodies (testing, certification, and inspection laboratories) including the increased use of accreditation. The conformity assessment procedures share certain common themes, including the possibility of the conformity assessment based on documentary checks, product type approval, or quality assurance systems. The procedures can be conducted either by the manufacturer (for lower risk products) or by third party conformity assessment bodies that have been licensed by the national regulator of the products (Notified Bodies). 6.52

The New Approach has nevertheless eventually produced a significant number of 'total harmonization' Directives, which as explained in Chapter 2, leave no further room for national legislation. In the context of the Medical Devices Directives, the 6.53

[61] Council Resolution of 21 December 1989 on a global approach to conformity assessment [1990] OJ C10/1.

[62] Council Decision 90/683/EEC of 13 December 1990 concerning the modules for the various phases of the conformity assessment procedures which are intended to be used in the technical harmonization directives [1990] OJ L380/13; 93/465/EEC: Council Decision of 22 July 1993 concerning the modules for the various phases of the conformity assessment procedures and the rules for the affixing and use of the CE conformity marking, which are intended to be used in the technical harmonization directives [1993] OJ L220/23.

[63] Decision No 768/2008/EC of the European Parliament and of the Council of 9 July 2008 on a common framework for the marketing of products, and repealing Council Decision 93/465/EEC [2008] OJ L218/82; Reg (EC) No 764/2008 of the European Parliament and of the Council of 9 July 2008 laying down procedures relating to the application of certain national technical rules to products lawfully marketed in another Member State and repealing Decision No 3052/95/EC [2008] OJ L218/21; Reg (EC) No 765/2008 of the European Parliament and of the Council of 9 July 2008 setting out the requirements for accreditation and market surveillance relating to the marketing of products and repealing Regulation (EEC) No 339/93 [2008] OJ L218/30.

role of definitions is key because manufacturers must be able to know which regime is applicable. This is not always evident and there are numerous 'borderline' issues that the Commission has attempted to resolve by issuing guidelines. Below we look at CE marking and labelling before turning to the role of Notified Bodies.

- *CE marking:* on completion of the conformity assessment procedure the manufacturer must affix the CE marking. The CE mark is mandatory by law and must be used for all medical devices. Each Directive sets out separate procedures regarding CE marking. The CE mark provides national market surveillance authorities with confirmation that the relevant medical device is marketable and fulfils the EU conformity provisions.
- *CE labelling:* the CE mark of conformity must appear at all times in a visible and legible form. Violations of the provisions regarding the fitting of a CE mark may be considered by national courts as a violation of rules on unfair trading practices and a national court may prohibit further distribution of the device until the fitting of the CE mark complies with the relevant Medical Devices Directive. The CE mark is not however a mark or seal of quality or safety, but an authoritative sign that the product has provided the relevant authorities with declaratory information that the product or device is marketable and fulfils the relevant conformity provisions.[64]

Notified Bodies

6.54 Notified Bodies are usually private commercial entities that are licensed by national medical device regulators to perform conformity assessments of medical devices. Notified Bodies must comply with various requirements laid down in the relevant annex of the relevant Directive (see for example Annex IX of the In Vitro Devices Directive), including the requirement to have appropriate staff to perform conformity assessments; furthermore these bodies should be impartial. In particular the body cannot consult in the development of a medical device and also perform the resulting conformity assessment, although an affiliated company may do this. Remuneration should not be linked to the number of conformity assessments performed. A criticism of the present regime is that in spite of the above-mentioned requirements the Notified Bodies are still not entirely independent from the manufacturers and conflicts of interest cannot be excluded.

6.55 In principle, manufacturers are free to choose any appropriately qualified Notified Body within the European Economic Area (EEA). Although there are limited safeguards to prevent an approach based on multiple notifications in order to find a Notified Body willing to issue a certificate of conformity; a criticism of the system is that Notified Bodies are anxious to retain customers. Thus suspicions of forum

[64] Commission staff working document, *Feasibility of a consumer safety mark and its possible relation to CE marking*, COM (2008) 3065.

shopping have arisen. A national regulatory authority may however withdraw the licence of a Notified Body if it fails to adhere to standards that national device regulators deem appropriate or acceptable. Obviously this latter judgement may vary from one country to another and the Directives and their Annexes provide little further guidance.

The Notified Body must review the technical file submitted by the manufacturer and assess the latter's quality management system, and evaluate any evidence submitted based on laboratory, animal and clinical studies. The manufacturer submits a sample of the device under review and the Notified Body may conduct direct testing, and inspect the manufacturer's production and quality control processes. If these tests are judged satisfactory then the Notified Body issues a certificate (valid for a maximum of five years, subject to renewal) and the manufacturer can affix the CE mark. **6.56**

The CE approval is binding throughout the EU. Thus a product notified to the appropriate bodies in France, for example, can be distributed throughout the EUwithout any further conformity assessment procedure. This in turn means that the scope for Member States to restrict the import and export of medical devices which have been certified as being in conformity with the requirements of the Directive is severely restricted. This is illustrated by two recent cases. **6.57**

Medipac In Case C-6/05 *Medipac-Kazantzidis* (2007) the Court ruled that, in so far as Directive 93/42 constitutes a harmonization measure adopted pursuant to what is now Article 114 TFEU it: **6.58**

> [...] is intended to promote the free movement of medical devices which have been certified as being in compliance with that Directive, precisely by replacing the various measures which have been taken in this field in the Member States, and which may amount to an obstacle to that free movement.[65]

Kemikalieinspektionen In Case C-288/08 *Kemikalieinspektionen v Nordiska Dental AB* (2010) the ECJ went on to hold: **6.59**

> Article 4(1) of Directive 93/42, which requires Member States not to create any obstacle to the placing on the market or the putting into service within their territory of medical devices bearing the 'CE' marking provided for in Article 17 thereof, must be interpreted as precluding the adoption by Member States of measures liable to constitute an obstacle to the free movement of medical devices bearing that marking, such as, for example, an export prohibition.

65 Case C-6/05 *Medipac-Kazantzidis AE v Venizeleio-Pananeio (P.E.S.Y. KRITIS)* [2007] ECR I-4557, para 51.

> [...] Article 8(1) of Directive 93/42 places Member States which have found there to be risks, linked to medical devices [...] under a duty to take all appropriate interim measures to withdraw those medical devices from the market, or to prohibit or restrict their being placed on the market or put into service. In those circumstances, the Member State concerned is required under that provision to notify the Commission immediately of the measures taken, indicating in particular the reasons for those measures.
>
> [...] where a Member State considers – in relation to a given product or group of products – that, in order to ensure protection of health and safety and/or to ensure that public health requirements are observed [...], the availability of such products should be prohibited, restricted or made subject to particular requirements, it may also take any necessary and justified transitional measures. The Member State concerned is then to inform the Commission and all the other Member States accordingly, giving the reasons for its decision.[66]

6.60 Consequently even under the New Approach there are considerable restraints imposed upon the discretion of the Member States in accordance with the presumption of free movement under the banner of the CE marking.

The Directives and related instruments

6.61 In this section we will consider the individual Directives in greater detail and examine their main objectives and shortcomings. The implementation of these measures is accompanied by a considerable body of soft law. Two aspects are crucial in this respect. First, the manufacturer must identify which of the Directives is applicable to the product in question, and second, it must select the appropriate risk category.

The Medical Devices Directive

6.62 Directive 93/42 defines a medical device as:

> (...) any instrument, apparatus, appliance, software, material or other article, whether used alone or in combination, including the software intended by its manufacturer to be used specifically for diagnostic and/or therapeutic purposes and necessary for its proper application, intended by the manufacturer to be used for human beings for the purpose of:
>
> - diagnosis, prevention, monitoring, treatment or alleviation of disease,
> - diagnosis, monitoring, treatment, alleviation of or compensation for an injury or handicap,
> - investigation, replacement or modification of the anatomy or of a physiological process,
> - control of conception,
> - and which does not achieve its principal intended action in or on the human body by pharmacological, immunological or metabolic means, but which may be assisted in its function by such means.[67]

[66] Case C-288/08 *Kemikalieinspektionen v Nordiska Dental AB* [2009] ECR I-11031, paras 21, 24 and 25.

[67] Dir 93/42, supra n 48, Art 1(2)a.

In Vitro Devices Directive—medical devices

In Vitro Devices Directive medical devices are a sub-set of medical devices. The In Vitro Devices Directive 98/79 defines an In Vitro Devices Directive medical device as: 6.63

> (...) any medical device which is a reagent, reagent product, calibrator, control material, kit, instrument, apparatus, equipment or system intended by the manufacturer to be used *in vitro* for the examination of specimens, including blood and tissue donations, derived from the human body solely or principally for the purpose of providing information:
> - concerning a physiological or pathological state, or
> - concerning a congenital abnormality, or
> - to determine the safety and compatibility with potential recipients, or
> - to monitor therapeutic measures.

Borderline issues

These two definitions are not entirely watertight and raise a number of borderline issues in relation to both medicines and other classes of health care products as well as to other consumer products that may or may not have a laboratory or diagnostic purpose. The Medical Devices Directive expressly excludes medicinal products as defined in Directive 2001/83 from its scope. It is clear from the wording of both the Medical Devices Directive and the In Vitro Devices Directive that the intention of the manufacturer drives the classification. Second, and unlike a medicinal product, a medical device does not achieve its principal intended action in or on the body by pharmacological means. The Medical Devices Directive was amended in 2007 so that its Article 1.5(c) clarifies the definition of the device in that Directive to emphasize that the product's principal mode of action is determinative, while Article 2(2) of the Medicines Directive 2001/83 regulating the marketing of pharmaceutical products also provides that in the event of doubt, the definition of a medical product will trump the definition of any other product in any other EU legislation, thus placing the emphasis on a higher degree of consumer protection: 6.64

> In cases of doubt, where, taking into account all its characteristics, a product may fall within the definition of a 'medicinal product' and within the definition of a product covered by other Community legislation the provisions of this Directive shall apply.

The In Vitro Devices Directive also raises a number of issues, in particular the borderline between *in vitro* devices and analytical or research products with no medical purpose. In this latter category fall two broad classes of products (a) products for the detection of physiological or pathological states or harmful pathogens, and (b) general laboratory products. Devices such as breathalysers for example do not have a medical purpose. 6.65

In Vitro Devices Directive accessories

6.66 The Directive defines an 'accessory' as 'an article which, whilst not being an in vitro diagnostic medical device, is intended specifically by its manufacturer to be used together with a device to enable that device to be used in accordance with its intended purpose'. In Vitro Devices Directive medical device accessories are deemed to be In Vitro Devices Directive medical devices in their own right and are subject to the appropriate conformity assessment and CE marking rules. Classification of certain devices can be problematic such as devices incorporating both specimen collection and analytical functions. For example a device for vacuum suction of saliva with an integral receptacle containing a human immunodeficiency virus (HIV) agent will be an In Vitro Devices Directive medical device. By contrast a blood glucose monitoring system providing a continuous supply of the patient's specimen for in vitro analysis will be a medical device because there is no 'dissociation' of the specimen from the patient.

6.67 Where medicinal products are sold together with an In Vitro Devices Directive medical device necessary to use the medicine appropriately, it may be assumed that the product must comply with the Directive 2001/83 and that the In Vitro Devices Directive medical device component need not be separately CE marked. However the Commission has indicated that the In Vitro Devices Directive medical device component should be CE marked.[68] Internal control and calibration materials for use in conjunction with In Vitro Devices Directive medical devices are normally In Vitro Devices Directive devices in themselves, except where they are internationally certified as reference material or material for external quality assurance.

6.68 The In Vitro Devices Directive rules apply when a manufacturer wishes to place a medical device on the EU market or put the device into service, for example on its own premises. This also includes any use of an IVD device for diagnostic purposes involving human samples. The term 'making available' is wide and includes any transfer of a product whether for commercial purposes or free of charge. Importantly, the term applies to the offer to transfer the product in its commercial distribution chain with a view to transfer to either a distributor or user. The In Vitro Devices Directive does not contain specific provisions governing advertising and promotion, but the wide definition of placing on the market may render pre-market promotion to be in breach of the applicable rules. Products displayed at trade fairs or exhibitions need not however be CE marked provided that the devices are not used on specimens taken from participants and that a visible sign clearly indicates that the devices cannot be marketed or put into service until they have been brought into compliance with the requirements of the In Vitro Devices Directive.

[68] See MEDDEV, 2.14/1 rev1, January 2004 <http://ec.europa.eu/consumers/sectors/medical-devices/files/meddev/2_14_ivd_borderline_issue_jan2004_en.pdf> (last accessed 18 June 2012).

Active implantable medical devices (AIMD)

This category is governed by a separate Directive 90/385.[69] Article 1(2)b determines that an 'active medical device' means any medical device relying for its functioning on a source of electrical energy or any source of power other than that directly generated by the body or gravity. Active implantable device means any active medical device that is intended to be totally or partially introduced, surgically or medically, into the human body or by medical intervention into a natural orifice, and that is intended to remain after the procedure, for example, a cardiac pacemaker. As with medical devices in general, Article 2 provides that Member States must take all necessary steps to ensure that active implantable medical devices may be placed on the market and put into service only if they do not compromise the safety and health of patients users and, if applicable, other persons when properly implanted, maintained and used in accordance with their intended purposes. **6.69**

Essential marketing requirements

A distinctive feature of medical devices regulation is the reliance on self-assessment in the pre-marketing and marketing stages. By way of illustration we explain this process in relation to the Active Implantable Medical Devices and the In Vitro Devices Directives. **6.70**

- *Active Implantable Medical Devices Directive:* active implantable medical devices must satisfy the essential requirements set out in Annex 1 of Directive 90/385, with account being taken of the intended purpose of the devices concerned. Such devices must be designed and manufactured in such a way that when implanted under the conditions and for the purposes specified by the manufacturer, their use does not compromise the clinical conditions and safety of patients or, as appropriate, other persons during the lifetime of the device anticipated by the manufacturer, where the device is subject to stresses that may occur under normal conditions of use. Devices must also bear a code by which they and their manufacturer can be unequivocally identified with regard to the type of device and year of manufacturer. When a device or its accessories bear instructions required for the operation of the device or indicate operating or adjustment parameters by means of a visual system, such information must be understandable to the users/patient.[70]
- *In Vitro Devices Directive:* an In Vitro Directive medical device can only be put into service or put on the market if the device conforms with the applicable essential requirements, as listed in Annex I to the In Vitro Devices Directive. The essential requirements also provide details of the labelling requirements for In Vitro Directive medical devices and general information that must accompany these products. The requirements are very broad and general albeit that more

[69] Dir 90/385, supra n 47.
[70] See further Annex I to the Directive.

detailed and specific requirements relate to devices that may emit hazardous, visible and/or invisible radiation for example.

6.71 Manufacturers may choose to apply harmonized standards to the design and quality assurance processes for their products, or may choose to demonstrate conformity through other means. European harmonized standards are developed by European standard bodies such as CEN (the European Committee for Standardisation) and CENELEC (the European Committee for Electrotechnical Standardisation) and are published in the Official Journal of the European Union (OJEU).

Risk classification

6.72 A manufacturer must first classify the device in accordance with certain pre-defined risk categories set out in the relevant Directive. The manufacturer must ensure that the device meets the essential requirements for that risk category by following the appropriate conformity assessment for that device and if appropriate it must seek notified body input. For low-risk devices (such as stethoscopes) little evaluation is required and the manufacturer is allowed to self-declare conformity with the essential requirements, affix a CE mark, and register its product with the competent Notifying Body.

6.73 By way of illustration, there are four categories of In Vitro Directive medical devices that are classified in order of increasing perceived risks:

- General In Vitro Directive medical devices, that is all such devices other than those listed in Annex II for self testing;
- In Vitro Directive devices for self-testing, excluding self-test devices covered by Annex II;
- In Vitro Directive devices listed in Annex II, List B including reagents and products for testing certain listed diseases as well as devices for self-testing blood sugar levels; and
- In Vitro Directive devices listed in Annex II, List A, including reagents and products for such diseases as hepatitis, HIV I and II.

6.74 The manufacturer must demonstrate safety and conformity with the legal requirements contained in the first annexes of the respective Directives. In this respect the manufacturer can refer to the relevant technical standards as developed by CEN or CENELEC. The clinical data used for the conformity assessment may be a critical evaluation of the relevant scientific literature currently available relating to the design characteristics, intended purpose, safety and performance of a device, when it is demonstrated to be equivalent to another device which already complies with relevant essential requirements and for which there are data. Alternatively, the manufacturer may present a critical evaluation of the results of all reported clinical investigations that have addressed residual safety concerns. For high risk products—that is products in Class III of the Medical Devices Directive or Annex II B of the

In Vitro Directive, including invasive or implantable devices such as pacemakers—the manufacturer must conduct human clinical investigations, but it is not compulsory that these take the form of observational or randomized clinical trials.

The role of soft law

In order for this complex and fragmented system to function, and in order to avoid significant national variation in its implementation, the Commission has produced a large number of non-binding guidelines to support national authorities in applying the EU legal framework.[71] These documents are highly technical in nature and focus on individual products. They are not as such, prescriptive or normative instruments. The guidelines on classification of borderline products, for example, specifically state that they: **6.75**

> (...) shall not 'prescribe' which regulatory framework applies or how the classification rules must be applied by national authorities. Rather, [the manual] shall serve as one out of many elements supporting the national competent authorities in their case-by-case decisions on individual products.[72]

At the same time the need for an effective procedure to ensure consistency and legal certainty with regard to borderline and classification cases throughout the EU was widely endorsed in the Commission's recent consultations on the reform of the current legal framework.[73] The majority of respondents suggested that empowering an expert committee to take decisions in this respect was the most appropriate way forward. A role for the EMEA was rejected, however. As regards the adoption of further harmonization measures, especially in relation to standardization, the majority of respondents to the Commission's public consultation on the reform of the regulatory framework reacted negatively to proposals for further harmonization, and considered the framing of voluntary (international) standards and/or the drawing up and regular updating of guidance as their preferred option over detailed specifications in a binding Community Act. **6.76**

Soft law 'interpretative' guidelines will therefore probably remain an important instrument to allow this complex system to function effectively, even if the current Directives are reformed. In this respect, soft law is not an alternative 'governance technique' or a substitute for European regulation. **6.77**

---

[71] These guidelines are available at <http://ec.europa.eu/health/medical-devices/documents/index_en.htm> accessed 24 February 2012.

[72] Manual On Borderline And Classification In The Community Regulatory Framework For Medical Devices, Version 1.10 (08-2011). <http://ec.europa.eu/health/medical-devices/files/wg_minutes_member_lists/borderline_manual_ol_en.pdf> accessed 24 February 2012.

[73] European Commission, Recast Of The Medical Devices Directives—Summary Of Responses To The Public Consultation (Entr/F/3/D(2008) 39582), Brussels, 5 December 2008.

Recent issues on the scope of the Directives

Weakness of clinical data requirements

6.78 A major criticism of the current EU legislative framework is the vague nature of the rules on clinical evaluation of medical devices. European guidance relates primarily to good clinical practices and the methodology of clinical trials and specify in detail how clinical studies of devices should be performed, but they do not deal with the more important question of when they are required nor is there clear guidance on the requisite standard of clinical performance. Current requirements relate to technical performance and safety and not to evidence of clinical efficacy. Specific criteria including standards applied by the Notified Bodies are not readily available, and essential requirements for the clinical evaluation of individual types of devices are not included in EU guidance.

6.79 Some stakeholders have expressed their concern that tighter regulation for clinical testing of devices before approval would stifle innovation and delay the availability of useful new devices. At the same time the typical product cycle of a medical device is much shorter than that for a pharmaceutical product. The clinical value of an implantable or diagnostic device may be influenced by the expertise of the operator. Classical clinical trials, as required in the pharmaceutical sector, may not always be possible or appropriate. Risk will be influenced by the population in which a device is used and so clinical indications must be considered when risk is being estimated. The extension of the present framework to include stricter controls on clinical evaluation is one of the most controversial aspects of the current debate on the direction of its future reform. While some stakeholders would prefer a considerable tightening of pre-marketing controls, others argue that post-marketing surveillance (PMS) should be the main instrument to ensure medical device safety.

Coverage

6.80 As noted, the In Vitro Devices Directive currently covers risk assessment, independent pre-market review, and requirements for labelling. However, there is disagreement between EU Member States about the scope of the Directive; that is, whether it covers all aspects of test performance or is limited to analytical performance of the test. Importantly, and by way of example, in some Member States, new genetic tests are routinely classified as low risk unless this classification is challenged. In fact, no new genetic tests have been added to the high-risk list (In Vitro Devices Directive, Annex II) since publication of the Directive itself in October 1998. This classification means that no independent evaluation of manufacturers' claims is required before a test comes to market, as these tests are consequently exempt from the requirement for independent pre-market review.

6.81 The UK's Human Genetics Commission, in its report 'More Genes Direct' of November 2007, noted the possibility of updating the Annexes of the In Vitro Devices Directive and requested that the national regulator, the Medicines and

Healthcare Products Agency (MHRA), continued to seek to ensure that the European Commission works proactively, rather than reactively, to update the Annexes. It therefore recommended that the risk classification of genetic tests covered by the In Vitro Devices Directive, but currently classified as low risk, should be reviewed.[74]

The In Vitro Devices Directive, and consequently the national regulator, is only concerned with devices used for medical purposes. The UK's MHRA claim that so-called 'lifestyle' tests are not clinical tests so would not be covered by the In Vitro Devices Directive. The term 'lifestyle test' lacks a precise definition but is sometimes used to describe tests such as nutrigenetic tests, where the intended use of the test is to provide lifestyle advice such as dietary guidance. The MHRA draws a distinction between these and what it deems 'tests for a medical purpose'.[75] The Human Genetics Commission questioned the MHRA's position and suggested that 'lifestyle' tests may be considered In Vitro Devices Directive devices if their purpose is to help in the prevention of disease. Moreover, a number of regulatory authorities have indicated they agree with the Human Genetics Commission.[76] Whilst some DNA tests, such as forensic and paternity tests, clearly fall outside the In Vitro Devices Directive, nutrigenetic tests, which are intended to improve health and prevent disease, and which often give risk predictions for common diseases such as cancer and heart disease, are considered In Vitro Devices Directive devices in many jurisdictions, but not in the EU.[77] **6.82**

The vigilance procedure

Where a Member State finds that medical devices correctly put into service and used in accordance with their intended purpose may compromise the health and safety of patients/users or, where applicable other persons, it shall take all appropriate measures to withdraw such devices from the market or prohibit or restrict their being placed on the market or their being put into service (for example, Article 7 of the Active Implantable Medical Devices). **6.83**

Incidents must be reported to the Commission and other Member States. There is however considerable divergence across the Member States in respect of vigilance procedures. Some countries have specified that Notified Bodies should participate **6.84**

---

[74] Human Genetics Commission, *More Genes Direct: A report on developments in the availability, marketing and regulation of genetic tests supplied directly to the public* (2007) para 3.9.

[75] Human Genetics Commission, supra n 73.

[76] The Director of FDA's Office of In Vitro Diagnostics was asked whether such tests were covered by FDA's regulations for medical devices, and answered in the affirmative (US Congress, 2006). In Australia the Therapeutic Goods Administration (TGA) has issued guidance on the issue (TGA, 2007).

[77] A Commission report issued in February 2011 concluded that there was a broad support among stakeholders for revision of the In Vitro Directive, adoption of a risk-based classification and keeping an exemption for 'in-house' testing.

in the PMS of medical devices in which case they receive reports of adverse incidents. If a device is to be removed from the market, the Notified Body should suspend its certificate. Coordination between competent authorities and Notified Bodies has been strengthened at European level through the creation of various groups and networks. In addition the European Databank on Medical Devices (Eudamed) was created in 1998 to allow Member States to strengthen surveillance by exchanging information about adverse events related to the use of medical devices. As from May 2011 reporting has become mandatory. Competent authorities will have rapid access to the database[78] but Eudamed is not open to the public.

6.85 A weakness of the present system is that PMS is the sole responsibility of the manufacturer and that the role of the regulatory bodies in following up or coordinating post-marketing surveillance studies is relatively weak. Data is not collected on a coordinated or uniform reporting basis and is not available to the public or indeed to the medical profession. There are no requirements for physicians to report incidents relating to defective medical devices. The reform of the current system of vigilance is also under consideration in the context of the 'recast' of the directives, as mentioned above.

Advertising of medical devices

6.86 The advertising or promotion of medical devices is not subject to a specific harmonized regime, such as the current and proposed regime for pharmaceutical products, discussed in Chapter 7. This is not however to say that this topic is left entirely to national regulation. Importantly, a number of general Directives aimed at preventing misleading or unfair advertising practices apply to medical devices. These include the Unfair Commercial Practices Directive 2005/29 EC[79] and the Misleading Comparative Advertising Directive 2006/114 EC.[80] Furthermore, the marketing of medical devices may be subject to general harmonizing Directives which may prevent a Member State from restricting sale to certain outlets.

6.87 In Case C-108/09 *(Hungarian contact lenses) Ker-Optica* (2008)[81] sold contact lenses via its Internet site (see also Chapter 4). By a decision of 29 August 2008, the competent authorities prohibited this activity, relying in particular on the provisions of a Ministry of Health Order, under which the only ways in which contact

---

[78] Commission Decision of 19 April 2010 on Eudamed, C(2010)2363 [2010] OJ L102/45.

[79] Dir 2005/29/EC of the European Parliament and of the Council of 11 May 2005 concerning unfair business-to-consumer commercial practices in the internal market and amending Council Dir 84/450/EEC, Dirs 97/7/EC, 98/27/EC and 2002/65/EC of the European Parliament and of the Council and Reg (EC) No 2006/2004 of the European Parliament and of the Council (Unfair Commercial Practices Directive) [2005] OJ L149/22.

[80] Dir 2006/114/EC of the European Parliament and of the Council of 12 December 2006 concerning misleading and comparative advertising [2006] OJ L376/21.

[81] Case C-108/09 *Ker-Optica (Hungarian contact lenses)* [2010] judgment of 2 December 2010 (nyr).

lenses can be sold are either in a shop which specializes in the sale of medical devices or by home delivery for final consumption. On a request for a preliminary ruling, the ECJ held that the Hungarian rules relating to the selling of contact lenses fell within the scope of Directive 2000/31/EC on electronic commerce,[82] since they concerned the act of selling such lenses via the Internet. Unhelpfully, national rules relating to the supply of such contact lenses are not covered by that Directive. However the Court ruled that Articles 34 and 36 TFEU, and Directive 2000/31, must be interpreted as precluding national legislation which authorizes the selling of contact lenses only in shops which specialize in medical devices because this is disproportionate to the public health concerns that were invoked.

Summary

The EU framework for medical devices regulation is undoubtedly complex given that it is contained in different Directives, and supplemented by various implementing decisions as well as interpretative documents. There is no single source, such as an official website which can be consulted to confirm how a particular medical device has been classified or to review the evidence on which it has been approved. Moreover the transposition of these Directives is subject to substantial national variation, and critics argue that there is no convincing reason why high risk devices should be regulated in a fragmented system in contrast to the uniform and essentially centralized system applied to pharmaceutical products. There are both striking regulatory gaps, as in the case of clinical evaluation, and confusing overlaps between the Directives, including borderline products, as well as disparate national practices on the classification of certain types of products for the purposes of the current EU framework. **6.88**

The regulation of medical devices appears to have been traditionally driven by internal market and related industrial policy objectives. Hence, even though the EU's Strategy on public health for 2008 to 2013, published as a White Paper in 2007, announced that new medical technologies must be evaluated properly, including for cost effectiveness and equity, and that health policy must be based on the best scientific evidence derived from relevant research, there are widespread doubts that the regulation of medical devices meets these lofty ambitions. **6.89**

Meanwhile the conclusions of the 3095th Council meeting on Health and Consumer Affairs—Health issues of June 2011[83] may suggest that there is now broad agreement on the proposed 'recast' of the current Directives. The new proposals **6.90**

[82] Dir 2000/31/EC of the European Parliament and of the Council of 8 June 2000 on certain legal aspects of information society services, in particular electronic commerce, in the Internal Market (Directive on electronic commerce) [2000] OJ L178/1.

[83] Press release 10986/11 of the 3095th Council meeting on Employment, Social Policy, Health and Consumer Affairs—Health issues (Luxembourg, 6 June 2011).

should include the following important recommendations which may go some way to remedy the regulatory gaps and weaknesses of the current system:

- The system of risk based classification should be improved (in particular for in vitro diagnostic medical devices and 'new products' as appropriate).
- Clinical data from pre-marketing studies and post-marketing experience (vigilance reports, post-marketing clinical follow-up, European registers) must be collected in a transparent way and to a greater extent in order to provide the clinical evidence which fulfils regulatory purposes and can, where appropriate, assist health technology assessment, whilst fully recognising and respecting national competences for the latter.
- The revised Directives, expected to be tabled in early 2012, should furthermore encourage better consideration of the needs of patients and health care professionals in the design process as well as the regulation of medical devices.

E. Conclusion

6.91 In this chapter we have considered various regulatory techniques which have been used primarily to promote the internal market dimension of products and services in health care. These range from universally applicable minimum standards and essential requirements backing up mutual recognition to soft law in the shape of formally non-binding guidelines. The scope left for freedom to organize health care matters at national level reduces in inverse proportion to the degree of harmonization achieved at EU level. Nevertheless as these instruments deal essentially with the free movement of products and services across the internal market, Member States still retain substantial discretion to regulate or otherwise steer the demand side—to limit patient access to these goods and services. As the section on pharmaceutical pricing has demonstrated, the courts have been strict in their enforcement of the 1989 Directive—but this measure harmonizes only procedures, not substance. At the same time the overview provided above leads to the observation that the secondary EU law concerning health care is far from systematic or complete in its coverage. Even the comparatively detailed and complex regime that has been established over time for medical devices leaves major lacunae.

6.92 This overall picture is perhaps not surprising given the subsidiarity clause found in Article 168(7) TFEU. The consequences are wide variations in the nature, method, and degree of EU level regulation. It is clear nonetheless that with medical devices and pharmaceuticals, health care *goods* have traditionally been more closely regulated at EU level than health care *services*. The creation of a single European market for potentially risky goods has required complex legislation and a high degree of harmonization in order to ensure that national regulatory disparities do not preclude trade. But it is also clear from our discussion of the various measures reviewed in this chapter that the internal market perspective if still a dominant one, is gradually giving ground to additional European objectives, including that of social protection and social cohesion.

As we will see in the next chapter a limited degree of EU regulation of access to cross border services has been achieved recently. There we will also examine legislation, currently in preparation, concerning access to information on prescription products. In both cases a demand-side or consumer-oriented dimension is becoming more explicit, where trade offs between different competing interests have to be made. What can and should consumers demand to benefit from the EU health care market, and from whom? This trend may be indicative of future directions in the EU law on health care. **6.93**

7

THE NEW EU HEALTH CARE LEGISLATION

A. Introduction

In the previous chapter we have looked in turn at the various vertical instruments of EU law, that is to say the rules specifically designed with respect to health care. This has allowed us to illustrate the different methods and techniques, such as mutual recognition, that exist in EU law to enable a balance between a common interest in integration and the public interests of the individual Member States. In a sense this sets out the status quo of EU law in respect to the supply side of health care provisions. **7.01**

In the current chapter we will now look at the 'new' EU health care legislation in the form of, first, the Patients' Rights Directive of 2011 and, second, the proposed changes to the legal framework for advertising of prescription pharmaceuticals. These two topics are dealt with in somewhat greater detail here than the secondary legislation discussed in the previous chapter, both because they are new and raise novel legal issues and also because we want to examine whether they have elements in common—notably, their being patient and/or consumer rights oriented—that may point to future trends in EU law on health care. **7.02**

B. The Patients' Rights Directive[1]

7.03 On 29 March 2011 the Patients' Rights Directive, codifying the patients' mobility case law of the ECJ, came into force. National rules have to be brought in compliance with this Directive by 25 October 2013. Given its central relevance to the development of EU law on health care its history will be traced in some more detail here before the contents of the Directive are discussed.[2]

Developments in Council and European Parliament

7.04 Following the removal of all references to health care from the Services Directive (2006/123/EC), institutional support began to emerge for specific Community legislation concerning patient mobility. At the Health Council of 1 June 2006, Ministers adopted Conclusions and a Statement of common values and principles in EU health systems which noted that the Commission had not just withdrawn Article 23 on health care from the proposed Services Directive but also intended to develop a Community framework providing legal certainty in this area.[3] The Council recognized the need to clarify the implications of the ECJ's case law on free movement and while underlining the importance of 'protecting the values and principles that underpin health systems in the EU' called for the Commission to take these into account when drafting specific proposals concerning health services.

7.05 This appears to have tied in with parallel developments in the European Parliament. In spite of its earlier resistance to legislation on health care and the freedom to provide services in this context (it had instead called for guidelines and various other softer forms of intervention in its April 2005 Report referred to above), the European Parliament soon came round to the need for a binding instrument. Thus in a Resolution on cross-border health care of March 2007, it called inter alia for codification, by introduction of a legislative framework, of the case law of the ECJ.[4] The European Parliament did so again in a subsequent Resolution evaluating the exclusion of health care from the Services Directive in May 2007, calling for an appropriate legal instrument.[5]

---

[1] Dir 2011/24/EU of the European Parliament and of the Council of 9 March 2011 on the application of patients' rights in cross-border healthcare [2011] OJ L88/45; W Sauter 'Harmonization in health care: The EU patients' rights directive' in B Cantillon, H Verschueren, and P Ploscar (eds), *Social Inclusion and Social Protection in the EU: Interactions between Law and Policy* (Antwerp: Intersentia, 2012), 105.

[2] COM(2008) 415 Final, Proposal for a Directive of the European Parliament and of the Council on the application of patients' rights in cross-border health care, 2 July 2008.

[3] Council Conclusions on common values and principles in European Union health systems [2006] OJ C146/1 (Statement in Annex).

[4] European Parliament Resolution of 23 May 2007 on the impact and consequences of the exclusion of health services from the Directive on services in the internal market (2006/2275(INI)), P6_TA(2007)0201.

[5] European Parliament Resolution of 15 March 2007 on Community action on the provision of cross-border healthcare, P6_TA(2007)0073.

The consultation

Parallel to these political developments the Commission carried out a consultation on Community action concerning health services that was launched in September 2006 and lasted until early 2008.[6] Given the background of failure of the Services Directive and because the abovementioned support from the European Parliament and the Council had not (fully) emerged yet, the Commission took a careful approach. In this consultation it aimed to collect information not just on patient mobility, which it estimated to affect less than one per cent of health care expenditure within the EU, but more broadly on health care issues where the Member States might welcome Community action. As such it focused on the need for legal certainty and on identifying areas where EU action might be complementary to that at national level. In fact patient mobility is only one of four possible types of cross-border health care. These are: cross-border provision of services, the use of services abroad (patient mobility), permanent establishment of health care providers in other Member States, and temporary mobility of health professionals.[7] **7.06**

Regarding legal certainty the Commission started from the premise that the ECJ's rulings were clear in and of themselves and that no preconditions could be attached to the exercise of patients' rights as recognized by the Court. Consequently, the main issues it raised for consultation concerned the need for clarifying procedures, for the identification of competent authorities and their responsibilities, a liability and compensation regime, and for a safeguard regime for the Member State of treatment. In addition the Commission wanted to know whether a binding legal instrument (Regulation or Directive) or, instead, a soft law form of guidance was preferred. As regards complementary action it identified mainly European networks of centres of reference (for specialization in eg rare diseases or complex treatments), management of innovation and sharing data and evidence for policy making. These were broadly the topics that were also within the scope of an existing group of high level officials of the Member States and that had been flagged by an earlier high level process of reflection (at ministerial level). They were thus well-established.[8] **7.07**

As regards the impact of patient mobility, the responses to the consultation again revealed a general lack of data but were not inconsistent with the Commission's prior estimate of one per cent of health care expenditure, and an upwards trend. Legal clarification was suggested in relation to the right to treatment abroad, on the **7.08**

[6] Commission Communication of 26 September 2006 on the Consultation regarding Community action on health services, SEC(2006)1195/4. The results were summarized in the Commission document, Summary report of the responses to the consultation regarding 'Community action on health services' (not dated, 2007). cf <http://ec.europa.eu/health/ph_overview/co_operation/mobility/patient_mobility_en.htm> accessed 24 February 2012.

[7] Commission Communication on the Consultation, supra n 5, p 5.

[8] ibid, p 9.

conditions for prior authorization, the definition of health services and hospital care (including a query from the UK government on whether the ECJ had in fact ruled there could be no justification for a prior authorization regime for non-hospital care, or whether it had not so far seen such a justification),[9] and of pricing for cross-border care. As might have been expected, it was widely held that responsibility for clinical supervision should rest with the Member State of treatment, and liability for harm and redress thereof with the provider of the treatment. More remarkably, in view of the fact that such a safeguard clause was subsequently introduced into the Patients' Rights Directive, the Commission reported no coherent requests for a safeguard procedure in the Member State of treatment—that is to avoid them being flooded with patients (although the fact this was not signalled may simply be consistent with the very low numbers so far involved). Equally remarkable was the apparent lack of responses concerning provider establishment.

7.09 Finally, concerning the legal instrument to be chosen with regard to patient mobility, the Commission reported a comparable level of support by those who preferred extending the existing Regulations on the coordination of social security systems, and those preferring a new Directive on patient mobility. In fact the Commission was already engaged in preparing a proposal for such a Directive during the course of the consultation, which proposal the Commission (having originally planned to adopt it in December 2007) eventually adopted on 2 July 2008.

Renewing the social agenda

7.10 The proposal for a Directive 'on the application of patients' rights in cross-border health care' as presented in July 2008 formed part of a raft of some 20 documents and proposals jointly billed as a renewed social agenda for 21st century Europe.[10] In contrast to the earlier attempt to embed patient mobility in the economic logic of the Services Directive, the connecting theme behind the July 2008 package was to complement the Lisbon growth strategy of the EU from a social perspective.

7.11 Another difference between the proposed Patients' Rights Directive and the failed earlier attempt to include a single Article on health care in the Services Directive is that the proposal was a full-fledged dedicated legal instrument purporting to provide a complete and coherent legal regime for all the issues involved.

[9] Summary Report, supra n 6, p 15.

[10] cf Commission Communication of 2 July 2008 on the Renewed social agenda: Opportunities, access and solidarity in 21st century Europe, COM(2008) 412 final; Commission press release IP/08/1070, Commission proposes renewed social agenda to empower and help people in 21st century Europe, Brussels, 2 July 2008; Commission memo MEMO/08/471, Renewed Social Agenda: The elements of the package, Brussels, 2 July 2008.

Impact assessment: quantifying the case for codification

The proposal was published with an Impact Assessment which the Commission used to motivate its choice between different policy options.[11] The Impact Assessment stated that over 12 months: four per cent of the EU population had received medical treatment in another Member State; that 70 per cent of the EU population believed such treatment would be reimbursed; and that over half the EU population was open to travelling to another EU Member State to receive treatment.[12] **7.12**

The Impact Assessment further stated that cross-border health care accounted for one per cent of public health care expenditure.[13] Hence, the overall impact of patient mobility in the EU is small, although its local impact may be much greater, for instance in border regions, smaller Member States, tourist areas, and in systems or for treatments involving high co-payments (out of pocket expenses for patients).[14] Overall, the Impact Assessment identified 'a rising trend for cross-border health care and significant potential demand from citizens to explore cross-border health care where it is quicker, better, cheaper or more convenient for them'.[15] The Impact Assessment showed that a dedicated Directive covering both hospital and non-hospital care would provide net benefits in relation to the costs involved, more specifically a positive balance of €179.6 million, with 780,000 additional patients (annually) receiving treatment, for the EU as a whole. **7.13**

There seems to be a contradiction at play here. The Commission struggled with the need to argue on the one hand, that something meaningful was happening which required EU legislation and, on the other hand, that the impact of this legislation on national social security regimes will be small enough that prior authorization requirements are unlikely to be justified. The Commission has not been successful in doing the latter: one of the main differences between the proposal and the Directive as adopted is that the latter leaves considerable room for appeals to overriding reasons of general interest based on an exception for planning that the ECJ had recognized in this context. This planning exception can even be invoked by the Member State of treatment to justify safeguard measures that had not been foreseen in the proposal. It is still an open question to what extent quantification will be required to demonstrate the necessity and proportionality requirements **7.14**

[11] supra n 2 (with an Explanatory Memorandum); Commission staff working document of 2 July 2008 accompanying document to the proposed patients' rights Directive: Impact Assessment, SEC(2008) 2163.

[12] Impact Assessment, supra n 11, pp 6–7; citing European Commission, *Cross-border health services in the EU, Analytical report for DG Sanco* (2007, Flash Eurobarometer series #210).

[13] That is approximately €9.7 billion. EU GDP is €12,149 billion of which some 7.6 per cent (€967 billion) is spent on public healthcare. Impact Assessment, supra n 11, p 9 (Eurostat figures 2006/2007).

[14] ibid.

[15] ibid, p 11.

with respect to the planning exception. So far however the ECJ has not required quantification.

The dynamics of 'old' and 'new' patient's rights

7.15 'Patients' rights', the key to the title chosen by the Commission for the proposal, refers to a concept that is much broader in scope than the reimbursement of cross-border medical treatment (the old patients' rights that the ECJ had developed in its case law).[16] In the Directive this broader concept is primarily linked to the common principles that are framed as obligations of the Member State of treatment. These include quality and safety standards, access to the information necessary for (or 'relevant to') informed choice (or transparency), the means to complain and obtain remedies (or accountability), compensation for harm, and privacy rights. These can, in effect, easily be rephrased as a set of new and potentially highly significant rights to cover all patients, not merely mobile ones. In this way 'old' patients' rights may be generating 'new' ones: both categories will be examined further below.

Legal basis and scope

Legal basis

7.16 In line with the proposal, the Directive as it was ultimately adopted is based on the harmonization provision of Article 114 TFEU. Surprisingly, the European Parliament and the Council have added Article 168 TFEU to this so the Directive also has a sector-specific basis in the Treaty. The use of Article 114 TFEU shows the Directive aims to secure the establishment and functioning of the internal market.[17] This is justified by the fact that although the ECJ judgments clarified patients' rights they have not proven sufficient in and of themselves to enable patients to avail themselves of these rights widely or in an effective manner. (Or: they have so far been frustrated by the Member States.)

7.17 Article 168 TFEU is added to reflect the common ambition of a high level of health protection. In this context, the Directive aims to form a framework that both provides clarity about the rights to reimbursement for health care provided in other Member States as well assuring that such cross-border health care is of high quality, safe, and efficient, which could not be done effectively by individual Member States. The Directive is the first piece of harmonization legislation in the area of health care: we may now expect any future such legislation to be based on Article 168 TFEU as well.

[16] cf the World Health Organization at <http://www.who.int/genomics/public/patientrights/en/> accessed 24 February 2012.

[17] On the relevant legal basis cf D Wyatt, 'Community competence to regulate medical services' in M Dougan and E Spavent (eds), *Social Welfare and EU Law* (Oxford: Hart Publishing, 2005), 131.

At the same time the Directive is required to respect not just the general subsidiarity provision in Article 5 TEU but also the provisions of Articles 6(a) and 2(5) TFEU and Article 168(7) TFEU, which provides a special subsidiarity clause with respect to the responsibility of the Member States for the organization and delivery of health care. As was already clarified by the ECJ in *Müller-Fauré* (2003) and *Watts* (2006) however, this provision does not mean that adjustments to national systems may not be required by other Treaty obligations, such as Article 56 TFEU on the freedom to provide and receive services.[18] **7.18**

The basic assumption however is that, in line with Article 168 TFEU, the Member States retain full responsibility for determining what medical services are covered by their national social security regimes and for the actual provision of health care.[19] Accordingly, Article 7(3) of the Patients' Rights Directive reads: **7.19**

> It is for the Member State of affiliation to determine, whether at a local, regional or national level, the health care for which an insured person is entitled to the assumption of costs and the level of assumption of those costs, regardless of where the health care is provided.

Finally, Article 168 TFEU is also relevant for the cooperation efforts of the Member States with relation to health care and/or public health, some of which are covered by the Directive (such as e-health and the other cooperation topics that will be addressed below). **7.20**

Scope

The scope of the Directive appears to cover all types of curative care without distinction in relation to their funding regime, hence it is not limited to health care in the sense of Article 168(7) TFEU, but also covers health care that is provided privately outside the public health setting: **7.21**

> Union action shall respect the responsibilities of the Member States for the definition of their health policy and for the organisation and delivery of health services and medical care. The responsibilities of the Member States shall include the management of health services and medical care and the allocation of the resources assigned to them (…).

The proposal had made this explicit in its definition of health care. Article 3(a) of the Directive now defines health care as follows:

> 'Healthcare' means health services provided by health professionals to patients to assess, maintain or restore their state of health, including the prescription, dispensation and provision of medicinal products and medical devices.

[18] Case C-385/99 *V.G. Müller-Fauré v Onderlinge Waarborgmaatschappij OZ Zorgverzekeringen UA and E.E.M. van Riet v Onderlinge Waarborgmaatschappij ZAO Zorgverzekeringen (Müller-Fauré)* [2003] ECR I-4509, para 102; Case C-372/04 *The Queen, on the application of Yvonne Watts v Bedford Primary Care Trust and Secretary of State for Health (Watts)* [2006] ECR I-4325, para 147.

[19] cf Preamble of the Dir, supra n 1, recitals 3a and 5a.

7.22 However the right to reimbursement—which is actually the core of the Directive—is linked to the position of the patient as an insured person covered by a social security system in line with Regulation 883/2004. Long term care and the donation or medical use of organs and blood, and public immunization schemes are not covered.

Parallel regimes based on Article 56 TFEU and Article 48 TFEU continued

The right to treatment

7.23 The EU will continue to have two parallel regimes for the authorization and/or reimbursement of cross-border health care: one is the existing regime for the coordination of social security based on Regulation 883/2004 (formerly Regulation 1408/71)[20] and thereby on Article 48 TFEU on free movement of workers; and the other is the new regime of the Directive, replacing that directly based on the freedom to provide and receive services in Article 56 TFEU which does not appear to have been implemented in most Member States with respect to cross-border health care.

7.24 The ECJ had effectively merged the two regimes as far as the right to treatment was concerned, based on the 'undue delay' criterion, first effectively in *Inizan* (2003). Here it was stated that determining undue delay requires:

> (...) hav[ing] regard to all the circumstances of each specific case and to take due account not only of the patient's medical condition at the time when authorisation is sought and, where appropriate, of the degree of pain or the nature of the patient's disability which might, for example, make it impossible or extremely difficult for him to carry out a professional activity, but also of his medical history.[21]

The two regimes were merged explicitly in *Watts* (2006):[22]

> (...) there is no reason which seriously justifies different interpretations depending on whether the context is Art. 22 of Regulation No 1408/71 or Art. 49 EC, since in both cases the question is (...) whether the hospital treatment required by the patient's medical condition can be provided on the territory of his Member State of residence within an acceptable time which ensures its usefulness and efficacy.

---

[20] Reg (EC) 883/2004 of the European Parliament and of the Council of 29 April 2004 on the coordination of social security systems, OJ 2004 L166/1; replacing Reg (EEC) No 1408/71 of the Council of 14 June 1971 on the application of social security schemes to employed persons and their families moving within the Community [1971] OJ L149/2.

[21] Case C-56/01 *Patricia Inizan v Caisse primaire d'assurance maladie des Hauts-de-Seine* [2003] ECR I-12403, para 46; with reference to Case C-157/99 *B.S.M. Geraets-Smits v Stichting Ziekenfonds VGZ and H.T.M. Peerbooms v Stichting CZ Groep Zorgverzekeringen (Smits and Peerbooms)* [2001] ECR I-5473, para 104; and Case C-385/99 *Müller-Fauré*, supra n 17, para 90.

[22] Case C-372/04 *Watts*, supra n 18, para 60.

Under the terms of the Directive its relationship with the Regulation will henceforth be determined by a clear priority rule and an exception to this rule, while responsibility for both is clearly assigned as well. This is because Article 8(3) of the Directive provides that in case of a request for prior authorization the Member State of affiliation will determine whether the conditions for the application of Regulation 883/2004 are met. If this is the case, the prior authorization is granted in accordance with the Regulation unless the patient himself requests otherwise—that is to say requests to obtain a prior authorization in accordance with the Directive instead. This appears to be a relatively straightforward system that leaves little room for misunderstandings and a distinct improvement over the proposal which left too many responsibilities on this count with the patient—especially with regard to determining whether 'undue delay' might be involved. This means that the earlier risk that the meaning of undue delay would come to diverge between the two legal instruments has also been addressed. **7.25**

Undue delay: a time-limit which is medically justifiable

The right to treatment without undue delay had not been properly addressed by the proposal because it was not used as a material norm for assessing the merits of the requests for prior authorization. On this issue therefore the Directive also provides a clear improvement over the proposal. **7.26**

The right to treatment without undue delay surfaces twice in the Directive: **7.27**

- Article 8(5) concerning health care that can be subject to a prior authorization requirement provides that such authorization may not be refused: (i) if the health care in question is among the benefits to which the insured person is entitled in the Member State of affiliation; and (ii) when this health care cannot be provided on its territory within a time-limit which is medically justifiable, based on an objective medical assessment of the patient's medical condition, the history and probable course of his illness, the degree of pain he is in and/or the nature of his disability at the time when the request for authorization was made or renewed. This means the central role for this important material norm, developed in the case law, is maintained by the Directive.
- Article 9(3) of the Directive provides that requests for prior authorization must be treated within reasonable time limits (as did the proposal) made public in advance, and that when considering a request for cross-border health care Member States shall take into account the specific medical condition and urgency and individual circumstances. In addition to this material norm, Article 9(4) sets out the procedural requirements developed in the case law such as the right to a reasoned decision on a case by case basis and subject to judicial review.

In this manner, undue delay was given an appropriate role, preventing divergence with the case law on this criterion as well as in relation to Regulation 883/2004. **7.28**

As a result the room to invoke the freedom to provide (or enjoy) services directly, without reference to the Directive, was reduced.

The right to reimbursement

7.29 The basis for reimbursement (at the level prevailing in the Member State of treatment for Regulation 883/2004 and at that of the Member State of affiliation for Article 56 TFEU, or now the Directive) will continue to differ under the two regimes. Whereas under Regulation 883/2004 the general rule is that patients do not have to meet the costs of treatment directly, under the regime of the Directive payment by the patient subject to subsequent reimbursement is the rule.

Would an amendment of the social security rules have sufficed?

7.30 These observations on the similarities and the differences between the two systems raise the question whether a separate Directive is in fact necessary and whether amending the social security coordination Regulation 883/04 would have sufficed instead. Perhaps this may partly be explained by the fact that two competing Directorates General of the Commission are involved here (SANCO, for the Directive, and EMPLOY for Regulation 883/2004). Another possible explanation is that given the time and effort that had been invested in the new social security coordination regulation the Commission was reluctant to reopen the negotiations to obtain a new health care section. The latter is all the more likely given the failure of the attempt to enter a health care paragraph in the context of the Services Directive.

7.31 In this context it is important to consider what type of dynamics the Directive is likely to entail that would not otherwise have occurred: in large measure this is likely to be determined by the new patients' rights and to a lesser extent by the cooperation provisions.

The framework for cross-border health care: the old patients' rights

7.32 We now move on to the codification of the ECJ's patient mobility case law.

Reimbursement of actual costs

7.33 The core of the codification of the obligations for the Member State of affiliation is formed by Article 7 on general principles for reimbursement of costs; Article 8 regarding prior authorization requirements; and Article 9 on the procedures concerned. Article 5 on the responsibilities of the Member State of affiliation provides an anchor for the various obligations, such as ensuring that the cost for cross-border health care is reimbursed in accordance with the Directive.

7.34 As a counterpoint to the obligations of the Member State of treatment set out in Article 4 of the Directive, its Article 7 sets out a number of obligations on the Member States of affiliation in relation to patients ('insured persons') travelling to other Member States for treatment that is covered by the benefits to which they are entitled in their Member State of affiliation. The most important of these obligations is that the Member States of affiliation must reimburse the actual costs for such treatment up to the level applicable to the same or similar treatment in the Member State of affiliation. However Member States are not blocked from going beyond their obligations under the Directive to provide supplementary reimbursement of treatments in other Member States.[23]

Member States of affiliation will also be required to have a transparent mechanism for the calculation of such costs, which must be based on objective, non-discriminatory criteria that are known in advance.[24] This seemingly self-evident requirement is likely to have far-reaching consequences, especially for benefits in kind and national health systems (NHS) that in most cases are likely to lack useful pre-existing cost information on which reimbursement can be based. Given the difficulties associated with the introduction of sound cost accounting principles, a common EU understanding of such principles may be required before long. **7.35**

Supplementary conditions

Article 7(7) of the Directive also provides for the possibility for the Member State of affiliation to impose additional conditions at national, regional, or local level upon insured persons who are requesting reimbursement of costs for cross-border health care (such as selection criteria and conditions of an administrative or regulatory nature), in the same way as it would if the health care were provided in its territory. However these conditions cannot be discriminatory or go beyond what can be justified based on the planning exception with respect to ensuring access to health care and/or controlling health care expenditure which is repeated at this point of the Directive (and which will be more fully addressed below). **7.36**

Non-hospital care: full liberalization

What the proposal had made explicit is regulated by omission in the Directive: patients are entitled to seek non-hospital care which is covered by their national social security regime in other Member States without prior authorization, and are entitled to reimbursement at the level as if the care had been provided in the Member State of affiliation. It is assumed therefore that this will, by definition, not undermine the financial equilibrium of social security systems. **7.37**

Although the categories of intramural and extramural care do not appear in the Directive—the distinction is now between health care that may or may not be **7.38**

[23] cf Case C-208/07 *Petra von Chamier-Glisczinski v Deutsche Angestellten-Krankenkasse* [2009] ECR I-6095.

[24] cf Case C-358/99 *Müller-Fauré*, supra n 18, para 107; Case C-372/04 *Watts*, supra n 18, para 143. cf G Davies, 'The effect of Mrs Watts' trip to France on the National Health Service' [2007] *King's Law Journal* 158, at 164–65.

subjected to a prior authorization requirement—the distinction between these two types of care remains sensitive. Apart from the question of whether an overnight stay is involved, which is easily answered (although it may be answered differently between different jurisdictions or health care providers), health care that can be subject to prior authorization requirements also concerns health care involving the use of highly specialized and cost-intensive infrastructure or medical equipment.[25] The Member States themselves determine which types of care are involved and notify these to the Commission.

Hospital care and specialized care: the end of prior authorization regimes?

7.39 For the most contested type of cross-border care, that which requires at least one overnight stay as well as specialized and cost-intensive care, the Directive allows the Member State of affiliation to introduce a prior authorization system. Hospital services and specialized care concern health care that requires an overnight stay (for one or more nights) and involves the use of highly specialized and costly medical infrastructure or equipment, or involves treatments that present a particular risk to the patient or the population at large. Article 8(2) reads as follows:

> Healthcare that may be subject to prior authorisation shall be limited to healthcare which:
> (a) is made subject to planning requirements relating to the object of ensuring sufficient and permanent access to a balanced range of high-quality treatment in the Member State concerned or to the wish to control costs and avoid, so far as possible, any waste of financial, technical and human resources and:
> (i) involves overnight hospital accommodation of the patient in question for at least one night; or
> (ii) requires use of highly specialised and cost-intensive medical infrastructure or medical equipment;
> (b) involves treatments presenting a particular risk for the patient or the population, or
> (c) is provided by a healthcare provider which, on a case-by-case basis, could raise serious and specific concerns relating to the quality or safety of the care with the exception of healthcare which is subject to Union legislation ensuring a minimum level of safety and quality throughout the Union.
> Member States shall notify the categories of healthcare referred to in point (a) to the Commission.

Moreover, a prior authorization system must be limited to what is necessary and proportionate, and may not constitute a means of arbitrary discrimination.

Contrasts between the proposal and the Directive

7.40 The proposal had set up something very different: the Member States would have had to provide actual evidence that the outflow of patients due to cross-border

[25] Case C-512/08 *Commission v France (extramural treatment)* [2010] judgment of 5 October 2010 (nyr).

hospital care *seriously* undermined their social security system or planning in the hospital sector. However, the Commission clearly believed these data did not exist and even proposed that the Directive should state so explicitly. Thus Recital 31 of the Preamble to the proposal read:

> The evidence available indicates that the application of free movement principles regarding use of healthcare in another Member State within the limits of the cover guaranteed by the statutory sickness insurance scheme of the Member State of affiliation will not undermine the health systems of the Member States or financial sustainability of their social security systems.

Likewise in its Explanatory Memorandum the Commission clearly states that based on its Impact Assessment:

> (...) there is no evidence to suggest that such care [hospital care] will undermine the financial sustainability of health and social security systems overall or the organization, planning and delivery of health services.[26]

And:

> The evidence available as set out in the impact assessment indicates that the application of free movement principles regarding use of healthcare in another Member State within the limits of the cover or the sickness insurance scheme of the Member State of affiliation will not undermine the health systems of the Member States or financial sustainability of their social security systems.[27]

That is to say the financial balance would not be undermined at all, let alone seriously.

The Directive itself requires only that prior authorization systems are not just based on planning requirements related to access and/or costs (the financial balance of the social security system is no longer cited as a separate overriding reason of general interest but is also subsumed by the planning exception), but also meet the requirement of necessity and proportionality. It seems that this is a much lighter burden of proof which also approximates the approach that the ECJ itself has followed so far more closely. A secondary, but not unimportant, aspect is that in this manner evidence of the underlying cost structure is also less likely to be required. The chance that Member States will prefer to forfeit the opportunity of introducing a prior authorization system in order to avoid having to justify their costs is likewise reduced; hence there is more room to introduce or maintain prior authorization systems under the Directive than there was under the proposal. **7.41**

Conditions

Conditions are imposed in three different places. In Article 8(2)(a) the prior authorization requirements for 'intramural care' are set out. Article 7(7) sets out **7.42**

[26] supra n 11, p 16.
[27] ibid, p 14.

conditions, criteria of eligibility, and regulatory and administrative formalities (such as the requirement to consult a general practitioner in order to obtain a referral for specialized care). Article 7(9) opens up the possibility of subjecting the rules on reimbursement themselves to limitations based on the planning exception related to access and cost control. In all three cases the planning exception is invoked, that is planning requirements relating to the object of ensuring sufficient and permanent access to a balanced range of high-quality treatment in the Member State of affiliation or to the wish to control costs and avoid, so far as possible, any waste of financial, technical, and human resources.

Safeguard measures

7.43 More remarkable is the fact that based on Article 4(3) of the Directive the same planning exception applies for safeguard measures imposed by the Member States of treatment. In this respect the Directive is both more detailed and more coherent than the original proposal, although it also means significantly increasing the scope of the overriding reason of general interest as formulated in the case law.

7.44 Finally, as was already mentioned, whereas the proposal required cross-border health care to 'seriously undermine' the financial balance and/or planning of health care in the Member State of affiliation before the exception could be invoked, the Directive itself only mentions the existence of an 'objective justification'. This means the requirements for a successful reference to the overriding reason of general interest have been relaxed considerably in relation to the proposal and in some respects the case law (that is to say in relation to safeguard measures as well as eligibility criteria and the reimbursement rules). Apart from the fact that the norm for the exception was relaxed it can now also be applied more widely. Compared to the proposal this provides the Member States additional possibilities to fence off their national health care markets.

Reasons to refuse prior authorization

7.45 Before discussing the new patients' rights, as well as cooperation, we will briefly cover another innovation in the Directive: the reasons for refusal. In line with the case law, paragraph 5 of Article 8 of the Directive sets out that where treatment cannot be provided without undue delay, prior authorization must always be granted. Paragraph 6 of Article 8 encapsulates the possible grounds for a refusal of a request for prior authorization, listing: an unacceptable patient (health) risk; a risk that the general public will be exposed with reasonable certainty to a substantial safety hazard; and health care to be provided by a health care provider that raises serious and specific concerns relating to the respect of standards and guidelines on quality of care and patient safety. This limitation of the grounds for refusal is appropriate given the broadened scope for requiring prior authorization which respectively raises barriers to cross-border health care based on planning exceptions.

Common principles for health care: the new patients' rights

Rights to accountability and transparency

Consistent with Article 168(7) TFEU, the Patients' Rights Directive starts by setting out the key principle that the Member State of treatment bears responsibility for the organization and delivery of health care. The main innovation in this respect is that its Article 4 the Directive sets out common principles for health care that can be seen as a new set of patients' rights. These correspond with the responsibilities of the Member States of treatment and are not based on the free movement case law of the ECJ. Instead, the principles are based on Council Conclusions of 2006 to the same effect,[28] which drew on the existing systems (or at least ambitions) of the Member States (the Council had resisted earlier proposals to define patients' rights at EU level).[29] Universality, access to high-quality care, equity, and solidarity are asserted as the guiding principles for Member States of treatment. **7.46**

In substance, the Directive mainly requires the Member States of treatment to provide quality and safety standards for health care based on dynamic international best practice standards (the application of which is monitored and enforced), and to ensure the right to the information necessary for an informed choice, to make complaints and guarantees of redress and remedies, to privacy, to equal treatment, and to non-discrimination. The right to an informed choice involves, in particular, information about availability, prices, and outcomes of health care. The Member State of treatment is obliged to provide for adequate systems of liability insurance. Finally, the Member States of treatment must also create national contact points where patients can access the information concerned. **7.47**

The duty to provide information, especially, appears to be of greater significance. It is worth noting that the relevant information to enable patient choice is so far hardly available at national level, let alone information relevant to patient choice that is comparable to information derived from other Member States.[30] Article 4 does include the proviso that Member States of treatment who already provide 'relevant information' to their inhabitants do not need to provide more extensive information for the benefit of patients from other Member States. In this context the meaning of the term 'relevant information' is significant: the proposal had required '*all* relevant information'. Should the information concerned facilitate making choices between treatments in different Member States or just between **7.48**

[28] Council Conclusions on common values and principles in European Union health systems [2006] OJ C146/1 (Statement in Annex).

[29] cf T Hervey, 'The legal basis of European Community public health policy' in M McKee, E Mossialos and R Baeten (eds), *The Impact of EU Law on Health Care Systems* (Brussels: PIE.-Peter Lang, 2002), 46–47.

[30] cf O Damman, 'Public reporting about healthcare users' experiences: the Consumer Quality Index' (PhD thesis Tilburg University, April 2010).

treatment options? At least the latter appears probable. The references to information concerning 'outcomes of the health care provided' have been purged from the Directive. The toughest category however—that of quality—has been retained. Hence even this limited obligation to provide information may yet provide the thin end of the wedge towards transparency-based reform.[31]

Universal applicability for the new patients' rights?

7.49 In the proposal, the scope of Article 4 was not clearly defined. The Council Conclusions on which the text was (and is) based were clearly of general application and the wording (referring to health care in general) likewise implied a general application. However the heading ('Member State of treatment') suggested norms that applied to patients from other Member States.

7.50 This is now changed in the Directive as adopted: both the heading and the wording of Article 4 now mention cross-border treatment explicitly. However because it is difficult to see how such fundamental norms of accountability and transparency could possibly be implemented solely for the benefit of patients from other Member States it is assumed here that they are universal rights that will apply to all patients, not just those moving across borders. This would involve a major step in terms of accountability to patients, and by health care providers.

Safeguards measures for Member States of treatment

7.51 Although the proposal enabled a derogation from free movement to the Member State of affiliation in the shape of prior authorization requirements, it foresaw none for the Member State of treatment. In this regard the Directive has introduced an important change: according to Article 4(3) of the Directive the same planning exception (concerning access to health care and/or cost control) that can be invoked by the Member State of affiliation is available to the Member State of treatment as well. The measures introduced in this respect must be made public in advance. This is an exception to the principle of non-discrimination with regard to nationality that applies to patients from other Member States more generally, including with respect to the prices charged for the health care provided. That such a possibility has been introduced is not illogical since Article 114(4) TFEU specifically opens the possibility of safeguard measures, and Article 114 TFEU was the legal basis chosen for the Patients' Rights Directive (alongside Article 168 TFEU).

7.52 Safeguard measures are relevant as in the absence of tariff rebalancing it may clearly happen that charges for treatment of patients from other Member States are out of line with actual costs but attractive to the health care provider in question (eg to fill empty beds). In such cases payment may cover only marginal costs rather than

[31] cf D Delnoij and W Sauter, 'Patient information under the EU patients' rights Directive' [2011] *European Journal of Public Health* 271–72; R Baeten and W Palm, 'The quality and safety paradox in the patients' rights Directive' [2011] *European Journal of Public Health* 271–74.

a share of fixed costs—putting pressure on public funding. On the one hand, such developments could well contribute to undermining the financial sustainability and coherence of the existing national social security systems—while on the other hand contributing to pressure toward much needed rationalization and rebalancing. Hence the impetus toward change as a result of the Patients' Rights Directive is likely to involve Member States in their role as Member States of treatment, not just as Member States of affiliation.

Cooperation

The Directive envelopes five types of cooperation that had previously been the subject of the intergovernmental Open Method of Coordination (OMC).[32] The five types are listed below: **7.53**

- Mutual assistance and cooperation: this regards all kinds of (including bilateral) cooperation including the information exchange between the national contact points that are to be established according to Article 4 of the Directive.
- Recognition of prescriptions issued in another Member State: if a medicinal product is authorized to be marketed on their territory then prescriptions issued for such a product in another Member State must be recognized and dispensed (this provision enables delegated rule making by the Commission).
- European reference networks: these are voluntary networks that aim to combat, in particular, rare diseases requiring highly specialized health care, and promote, eg the development of new diagnoses and treatments (this provision enables delegated rule making by the Commission as well).
- E-Health: this concerns electronic developments in health care and the work that is being done on developing the inter-operability between systems and the necessary minimum data set, with a view toward building a high level of trust and security.
- Cooperation on health technology assessment: this aims to avoid needless duplication of procedures and thereby to contribute to a faster and more effective assessment of the relevant technological developments.

Although not key in the harmonization setting of the Directive these elements are nevertheless important to the continued collaboration between the Member States in this field. By creating cross-border policy communities they may contribute to support for further integration of health care markets—possibly by spill-over, and including further harmonization.

[32] cf S Greer and B Vanhercke, 'The hard politics of soft law: the case of health' in E Mossialos et al, supra n 29, 186.

Further analysis

7.54 The development of the law on patient mobility appears to fit the mould of the typical interaction between positive and negative integration: first, national measures obstructing the freedom based on individual rights to provide and receive services (in this case) are struck down by the ECJ, and then, the need arises for re-regulation to fill the gap left, providing sufficient consensus for a more liberal EU regime to emerge. As a process this is noteworthy because it occurs in cases where, in the absence of negative integration, there would not have been support for common norms. This can be illustrated by a more detailed discussion of the following two topics: justifying prior authorization requirements; and the scope for change based on the new patients' rights.

Prior authorization requirements: liberalization by transparency?

7.55 As we have seen, the scope for invoking the planning exception has been increased in the Directive. However the necessity and proportionality of the measures involved—notably prior authorization requirements—remain to be shown by the Member State of affiliation. The practical difficulties of demonstrating the need for a prior authorization system are considerable. The proposal, with its exception based on the financial balance of the social security system, raised questions such as: how, in a sector where the cost of an individual treatment is not known, could it be plausibly argued that transferring such treatments abroad would jeopardize the financial balance of the system?; and, how could it be demonstrated that the financial balance of a social security system is threatened if basic measures of sound administration and business practice such as proper cost accounting and tariff rebalancing are lacking?

7.56 This problem may have been reduced when the proposal was watered down but did not disappear where the planning exception speaks of the wish to control costs and ways to avoid wasting resources. It may well be that in spite of the Member States' best efforts (in Council) to increase the scope of the planning exception its application may raise difficulties for them. The increasing requirement to provide comparable data on prices and quality and even costs (for instance, when required to motivate a reimbursement granted or requested) triggered by the old patients' rights may yet help shake up national health care markets.

New patients' rights: harmonization

7.57 Apart from harmonization of the standards for the prior authorization scheme, harmonization is to be found in the main innovation of the proposal in relation to the case law, which is formed by the obligations of Member States of treatment, or new patients' rights. These are likely to ensure the enduring impact of patient mobility on Member States both when sending patients abroad, and when receiving them. The obligations involved have their origins in Council Conclusions of 2006,[33] but under

[33] Council Conclusions, supra n 28.

the Directive are legally binding and justiciable. Moreover, the ensuing rights—especially to accountability and to transparency on availability, prices, and outcomes of health care—will accrue not just to mobile patients, but to all patients in each Member State. Arguably, this is the key element of positive integration to be introduced by the Directive. In summary, the addition of the 'new', broader patients' rights (to accountability and transparency) to the codification of the 'old' patients' rights to reimbursement could create momentum for broader change.

Potentially, we are therefore looking at a chain of events leading toward fundamental change. The links of this chain are the following: **7.58**

1. the creation of rights to reimbursement for treatment abroad in the patient mobility case law;
2. the creation of rights to a certain standard of treatment abroad by the Directive;
3. the extension of these rights to patients treated at home by the Directive; and
4. the leveraging of these rights to begin transforming national health care systems.

By choosing the legislative route on patient mobility the Commission took the calculated risk that in the course of the legislative process the relatively clear-cut and far-reaching case law of the ECJ based on Article 56 TFEU itself would be diluted. This may now have paid off because the Directive incorporates a number of elements designed to set in motion further changes in health care systems at national level—to a significant degree precisely based on patients' rights, which will in the longer term promote both greater efficiency and accountability.

At the same time the fact that the focus both of the recent case law and of the proposed Directive has been centred on the patient fits well with in a consumer (and/or citizen) oriented approach to European integration and is consistent with the social policy agenda that is being developed as a response to public scepticism about the benefits of the EU—just as it would be in line with a demand-based economic view. It is also consistent with most perspectives that accept the positive potential of a role for the EU in the socio-economic realm. **7.59**

Conclusion

The Patients' Rights Directive sets out a framework for cross-border health care in the EU. Old rights to reimbursement of costs are supplemented by new rights to transparency and accountability and are being combined with a formalization of OMC based cooperation. Benefits are not harmonized but the conditions for access to cross-border health care are to a significant extent. **7.60**

The main technical content of the Directive can be divided into three parts: **7.61**

- First, the Directive is based on the planning exception related to access and cost control. For the Member State of affiliation this concerns: (i) the system of prior authorization in Article 8(2); as well as, (ii) the other requirements that can be imposed in Article 7(7); (iii) the possibility to limit the application of the rules on reimbursement in Article 7(9). For the Member States of treatment the planning exception can be invoked for (iv) safeguard measures. (It is worth noting that options (ii) through (iv) did not appear in the original proposal.) The norm applied is whether recourse to this exception is objectively justified, necessary, and proportional. In line with the case law—but in contrast to the proposal—it does not appear necessary for the Member States to provide quantitative evidence (a burden of proof that would be difficult to meet given the likely scale of cost imbalances prevalent in the various health care systems).

- Second (and again in contrast to the proposal), the Directive is clearly based on the concept of undue delay, which appears in the limited set of grounds on the basis of which prior authorization may be refused in Article 8(6), and in the administrative requirements for this procedure (concerning time limits) in Article 9(3). In this manner the Directive is also more in line with Regulation 883/2004, as well as the relevant case law, than was the proposal.
- Third, and finally, other due process guarantees are imposed as well, such as the right to a decision on a case by case basis that is subject to judicial review in Article 9(3), and the (entirely new) limited list of grounds for refusal in Article 8(6) (discussed at para 7.45). This completes the material and procedural norms that had already been developed in the case law.

7.62 Based on these three elements the Directive forms a coherent system that for this reason alone already forms an improvement on the proposal. However, apart from leaving less room for uncertainty, it also leaves less room for secondary effects such as exposing the underlying costs of treatment. In summary, the Commission's proposal follows the familiar sequence whereby striking down barriers to the market freedoms breeds the need for elaborating rights and obligations in legislation that strikes a new balance between private freedoms and legitimate public interests. For health care this is no less than a watershed given the constitutional barriers that had been erected in the Lisbon Treaty against harmonization in this field and which have now been breached.

C. The Rules on Advertising of Pharmaceuticals

7.63 EU law currently prohibits direct-to-consumer advertising of medicinal products subject to prescription. This is because Article 88(1) of Directive 2001/83/EC[34]—the so-called Community code relating to medicinal products for human

[34] Dir 2001/83/EC of the European Parliament and of the Council of 6 November 2001 on the Community Code relating to Medicinal Products for Human Use, as amended [2004] OJ L311/67.

use—imposes an absolute ban on advertising of prescription products to the general public including 'any form of door-to-door information, canvassing activity, or inducement designed to promote the prescription, supply, sale or consumption of medicinal products'.[35] This Article has been deemed by the ECJ to amount to a complete harmonization. Article 86(2) of the same Directive identifies types of information which are not covered by this ban, but without providing for a harmonized framework on the contents and quality of non-promotional information, and Article 88(4) provides for certain exceptions from the ban, for example, for the conduct of advertising on vaccination campaigns. Article 94 regulates the advertising of medicinal products to health care professionals.

Because full harmonization is involved, Member States cannot diverge from these prohibitions in any way in their national legislation implementing Directive 2001/83/EC. However, although the Directive defines the concept of advertising, it does not regulate the provision of non-promotional information on medicines. This opens the door to conflicting views on what constitutes the borderline between advertising and provision of non-promotional information. Hence disparities arise across what ought to be a single market for pharmaceuticals, as well as cross-country inequalities in access to information. At the same time, in the absence of clear standards, information of varying quality can cross both EU internal and external borders via the media and Internet. **7.64**

Revision of the absolute ban on advertising has been repeatedly on the EU political agenda in the context of the debate on access to information for patients and the role of the pharmaceutical industry in providing information directly to consumers.[36] The Commission's response has been to table a legislative proposal[37] in the form of a Directive amending Articles 86–100 of Directive 2001/83/EC and a Regulation amending, inter alia, Article 20 of Regulation (EC) No 726/2004 on the authorization and supervision of medicinal products and inserting a new **7.65**

cf L Hancher and ME Földes, 'Push or Pull? – Information to Patients and European Law' [2011] *European Journal of Consumer Law* (forthcoming).

35 Art 86(1) of Dir 2001/83/EC, supra n 34.

36 R Baeten, 'EU pharmaceutical policies: direct-to-consumer advertising' in C Degryse (ed), *Social Developments in the European Union* (European Trade Union Institute, 2009) 173–200.

37 Commission of the European Communities, Proposal for a Directive of the European Parliament and of the Council amending, as regards information to the general public on medicinal products subject to medical prescription, Directive 2001/83/EC on the Community code relating to medicinal products for human use, COM(2008) 663 final; Commission of the European Communities, Proposal for a Regulation of the European Parliament and of the Council amending, as regards information to the general public on medicinal products subject to medical prescription, Regulation (EC) No 726/2004 laying down Community procedures for the authorization and supervision of medicinal products for human and veterinary use and establishing a European Medicines Agency, COM(2008) 662 final.

Title VIIIa on information to the general public on medicinal products subject to prescription.[38]

7.66 This proposal aims to meet the legitimate claims of patients who wish to have improved access to objective information while also giving the manufacturers of pharmaceutical products a clearer legal framework within which to provide that information. Although the European courts have examined the scope of the advertising ban in a number of recent cases, these rulings have so far not fully clarified the dividing line between non-promotional information and advertising. Hence there is a need for further legislation on this issue.

The European Commission proposal in the light of current EU law

Background

7.67 Advertising of prescription drugs has been banned under European Directives since the adoption of Council Directive 92/28/EEC on the advertising of medicinal products for human use.[39] Further to a 2008 public consultation the European Commission adopted a proposal to amend the current legal framework for this issue, which consists of Directive 2001/83/EC and Regulation No 726/2004/EC.[40] Arguing that the pharmaceutical industry can be a valuable source of non-promotional information on prescription medicines, the Commission proposed to increase the industry's role in direct-to-consumer information on its products. To increase legal clarity, it proposed to harmonize the rules on industry provision of non-promotional information.

7.68 In order to ensure that adequate safeguards are in place, the Commission's proposal aimed to define the type of information that may be disseminated by the industry, and to set forth quality standards defined at Community level, to be applied consistently to the information content and presentation. It would have restricted the dissemination channels to be used by the industry to Internet websites, health-related publications as defined by the national competent authorities, and written answers to information requests received from consumers. It prohibited dissemination by TV, web-TV, radio, and distribution of unsolicited materials to the public. Furthermore, it established an obligation for Member States to put in place effective monitoring mechanisms with specific rules for Internet-based dissemination of information. It envisaged clarifying the distinction between advertising and

[38] Reg (EC) No 726/2004 of the European Parliament and of the Council of 31 March 2004 laying down Community procedures for the authorization and supervision of medicinal products for human and veterinary use and establishing a European Medicines Agency [2004] OJ L136/1.

[39] See Art 3(1) of Dir 92/28/EEC of 31 March 1992 on the advertising of medicinal products for human use [1992] OJ L113/13. Dir 92/28/EEC was repealed by Dir 2001/83/EC (see supra n 37 for reference).

[40] supra n 37.

non-promotional information on prescription products while maintaining the ban on advertising for all classes of prescription products.

The Commission's proposal as tabled in 2010 takes Articles 114 and 168(4) TFEU as its legal base, and included a number of important amendments to the existing framework: **7.69**

- it extended the types of information that may be disseminated by the industry;
- it established a set of harmonized quality standards imposed on information content and presentation; and
- it established an obligation for Member States to ensure adequate and effective monitoring of information dissemination by the industry. The proposal to amend Regulation 726/2004/EC creates a responsibility for the European Medicines Agency to deliver opinions on certain types of information prior to dissemination; and
- ensured Member States would also be responsible for imposing—under an accelerated procedure—adequate and effective sanctions for non-compliance with the rules set forth in the proposal.

Before turning to the reception of the proposal by the European Parliament at its first reading, and the Commission's amended proposal, as adopted by it in October 2011, we will look briefly at the case law of the ECJ on Directive 2001/83/EC. **7.70**

Case law developments

The European courts have been asked on a number of occasions to rule on the scope of Article 88 and a number of related provisions in Title VIII, and to determine whether the Directive's prohibitions on advertising extend to various forms of promotional activities, including financial incentives by persons or bodies not associated with commercial interests. This case law exposes the weakness of the current definitions and it reveals that faced with borderline cases, the ECJ has erred on the side of caution. **7.71**

Gintec In *Gintec* (2007) the ECJ handed down a landmark judgment on the interpretation of Directive 2001/83/EC.[41] The controversial issue at stake was whether imposing stricter provisions of national law was in line with the Community code. The ECJ clearly stated that: **7.72**

> (...) Directive 2001/83 brought about complete harmonisation in the field of advertising of medicinal products and lists expressly the cases in which Member States are authorised to adopt provisions departing from the rules laid down by that directive.

Hence where the Directive does not expressly allow the Member States to deviate from its standards, they may not provide for stricter rules.

[41] Case C-374/05 *Gintec International Import-Export GmbH v Verband Sozialer Wettbewerb eV.* [2007] ECR I-9517.

7.73 *Damgaard* This 2009 case originated from a Danish court and involved the legality of information provided by a journalist on a particular treatment for gout that was available in Sweden, but not in Denmark.[42] The ECJ considered that the definition of 'advertising' in Directive 2001/83/EC emphasizes the purpose of the message, that is to say the promotion of the prescription, supply, sale, or consumption of medicinal products. It ruled that the dissemination by a third party of information about a medicinal product, including its therapeutic or prophylactic properties, may be regarded as advertising, even though the third party is acting on his own initiative and is completely independent from the manufacturer or the seller of the medicinal product. Therefore, for the purposes of the Directive, advertising appears to include any communication even from a third party independent of the producer of the product, regarding medicinal products, that may be liable to harm public health.

7.74 *ABPI* In the *ABPI* (2010) case the ECJ was asked to rule on the scope of Article 86(1) and Article 94(1) of Directive 2001/83/EC.[43] These provisions concerned advertising to the general public and a prohibition on financial inducements to health care providers respectively. In the context of a UK scheme to promote cost control, primary health care trusts and local health boards introduced schemes aimed at medical practices inducing them with financial incentives to prescribe to their patients either specific branded or generic medicine products. The industry association ABPI objected to this scheme. The ECJ ruled that its approach in *Damgaard* could not be applied in a case where public authorities need to disseminate information about a medicinal product. Similarly as regards financial inducements, the Court held that the prohibition cannot apply to national public health authorities, in particular, in so far as this concerns the rationalization of public expenditure. As health policy defined by a Member State does not pursue any commercial aim, a financial incentive that forms part of such a policy cannot be regarded as commercial promotion.

7.75 *Novo Nordisk* In this 2011 Estonian case the interpretation of Article 87(2) of Directive 2001/83 was at issue, which states that 'all parts of the advertising of a medicinal product must comply with the particulars listed in the summary of product characteristics'.[44] The main issue for the ECJ was to clarify whether advertising can provide information which is compatible with, but not included in the statement of product characteristics. According to the Court the primacy of public health protection over the freedom of speech, as well as the principle of proportionality, cannot justify limiting the prohibition only to advertising claims

[42] Case C-421/07 *Damgaard* [2009] ECR *I-2629.*

[43] Case C-62/09 *Association of the British Pharmaceutical Industry* v *Medicines and Healthcare Products Regulatory Agency* [2010] ECR I-3603.

[44] Case C-249/09 *Novo Nordisk AS v Ravimiamet* [2011] judgment of 5 May 2011 (nyr).

which contravene the statement of product characteristics. The Court also ruled that the prohibition on advertising claims which conflict with the summary of product characteristics extends to adverts for medicinal products directed at qualified health professionals as well as the general public. However it further held that information which should be (but is not yet) included in the statement of product characteristics might be included in such advertising. This ruling underlines the fundamental importance for companies to draw an appropriate distinction on a case-by-case basis between advertising and scientific information.

MSD v Merckle In *Damgaard* the ECJ had left open the issue of how to draw a distinction between the prohibited advertising of prescription products destined for the general public and the provision of lawful information on these products. In *MSD v Merckle* (2011) the ECJ ruled that the dissemination of information on prescription products on the manufacturer's website which consists solely of the faithful reproduction of the packaging and a literal reproduction of the statement of product characteristics and is not accompanied by any additional elements does not constitute dissemination for advertising purposes.[45] The information in question was only available according to the 'pull' system (patients seeking information). Had the information been rewritten or edited, this would have been classified as advertising, and as such, prohibited. **7.76**

The European Parliament Amendments

The European Parliament adopted some 78 amendments to the Commission's draft legislation on 24 November 2010. Its amendments essentially focused on the obligation of pharmaceutical companies to provide information to the general public, while further breaking down the content, the form, and the goals of such information. No mandatory obligations to make information available were included in the Commission's draft. The Parliament proposed a distinction between information that the industry must always make available to the general public—labelling, package leaflet and assessment report approved by competent authorities during the course of marketing authorization—and information that the industry may choose to make available (after approval by the competent authorities) such as information on environmental impact, prices, pack changes, instructions for use, pre-clinical tests, and clinical trials. **7.77**

Clearly there is a certain convergence between the approaches developed by the ECJ in the *MSD* case, by the Commission and the European Parliament. The case law does go some way to providing a workable set of criteria to distinguish information **7.78**

[45] Case C-316/09 *MSD Sharp & Dohme GmbH v Merckle GmbH* [2011] judgment of 5 May 2011 (nyr).

provision from advertising. Yet additional legislative safeguards remain necessary to ensure that the 'patient-pull' principle can be fully realized and guaranteed.

The Commission's amended proposal

7.79 In accordance with the European Parliament's proposed amendments, the Commission has now proposed a new text for Article 86 so that:

> (...) advertising of medicinal products shall include any form of information, canvassing activity or inducement designed to promote the prescription, supply, sale or consumption of medicinal products by the marketing authorization holder directly or indirectly through a third party acting on his behalf or following his instructions: it shall include in particular:
> (a) the advertising of medicinal products to the general public
> (b) advertising of medicinal products to persons qualified to prescribe or supply them,
> (c) visits by medical sales representative to persons qualified to prescribe medicinal products
> (d) the supply of samples
> (e) the provision of inducements to prescribe or supply medicinal products by gift etc
> (f) sponsorship of promotional meetings attended by persons qualified to prescribe supply medicinal products
> (g) sponsorship of scientific congresses attended by such persons.
>
> The following are not covered by this Title:
> (a) the labelling and the accompanying package leaflets
> (b) information relating to human health or diseases provided there is no reference even direct, to individual medicinal products and information to investors and employees.[46]

7.80 A new Article 100b regulates the information which must be available to the general public and includes the most recent summary of the product characteristics as approved by the competent authorities; the most recent labelling and package leaflet as so approved; and the most recent publicly accessible version of the assessment report as drawn up by those authorities. Information which may be provided includes information on the disposal and collection system, information on prices, information for use of the product, and on the pre-clinical tests and clinical trials, and any other types of information as approved by the competent authorities that are relevant to support the proper use of the product in question.

7.81 This information must be objective, verifiable, up to date, reliable and unbiased, and must be patient-oriented to adequately meet the needs and expectations of patients. It must clearly state the source of the information and must not contradict

[46] Amended proposal for a Directive of the European Parliament and of the Council Amending Directive 2001/83/EC, as regards information to the general public on medicinal products subject to medical prescription and as regards pharmacovigilance, COM (2011) 633 final.

the summary of product characteristics, labelling and package leaflet as approved by the competent authorities. Comparisons between medicinal products are not allowed (see Article 100b).

Monitoring of information after it has been made available is to be assured in accordance with Article 100g. As a general principle, information which has not been approved before as part of the marketing authorization procedures needs to be verified by competent authorities prior to it being made available. Contrary to the original Commission proposal, Member States may not opt for voluntary control through self-regulation or co-regulation unless the system of pre-control is already implemented in existing mechanisms adopted prior to 31 December 2008. In particular, information provided over the Internet must be monitored by the appropriate national authorities in accordance with Article 100h. Printed material would only be made available if specifically requested by members of the public. However those Member States with constitutional restrictions related to the principles of freedom of expression and of the press would be able to impose *ex-post* as opposed to *ex-ante* controls where medicines are authorized at national level (see also Recital 16 of the amended proposal). **7.82**

The amended proposals must now be scrutinized and approved by the European Parliament in a second reading prior to their final submission to and approval by the Council. If adopted, the proposals will represent another important step towards enhancing patient rights in the EU law on health care. **7.83**

D. Conclusion

Both the Patients' Rights Directive and the proposal for a Directive and a Regulation on pharmaceuticals advertising are based on Articles 114 (harmonization legislation) and 168 (health care) TFEU. As such, they demonstrate the limits to the scope for the Member States to restrict EU involvement in health care in line with the sector-specific subsidiarity clause in Article 168(7) TFEU. These new EU measures on health care combine a common concern for the welfare of patients with the goals of social protection and social cohesion, alongside the more traditional goal of ensuring the functioning of the internal market. This appears to be the tandem that is presently able to trump sector-specific scepticism and subsidiarity, precisely because some level of harmonization is necessary to protect patient welfare in an increasingly globalized market, whether individually, in the case of the Directive on Patients' Rights, or collectively, as in the right to information of the general public in the case of the proposed Directive and Regulation on pharmaceuticals advertising. **7.84**

As regards patients' rights, events appear to have followed a process whereby striking down barriers to the exercise of market freedoms generated the need for elaborating rights and obligations in legislation to strike a new balance between **7.85** private freedoms and legitimate public interests. As mentioned above, we see this as a watershed given the constitutional barriers that, potentially, had been erected in the Lisbon Treaty against harmonization in this field, and which have now been scaled successfully. The proposals on pharmaceutical advertising suggests that straightforward bans imposed by EU law on certain forms of promotional activities are no longer tenable in a globalized market where information on many products is already available through the Internet.

7.86 The proposed measures build on pre-existing harmonization legislation. They mainly appear to strike a new three-way balance between the rights of Member States to monitor information, the promotion of the internal market for pharmaceutical products, and recognition of the rights of public access to pharmaceutical product information. If these measures are adopted then patients' rights will be enhanced by EU regulation that involves reaching out directly to the consumer, alongside the market and public interests traditionally represented by business on the one hand and public authorities on the other.

8

COMPETITION

A. Introduction

8.01 In the previous chapters we have dealt with the internal market dimension of health care of which especially the free movement aspects in relation to services (from *Kohll* to *Watts*) are relatively well-known. The EU competition law dimension of health care is less frequently discussed in the existing literature. At the same time, the relevance of EU competition law has increased because following the modernization of EU competition law since May 2004 the national competition authorities (NCAs) of the Member States have been charged with applying the antitrust provisions in Articles 101 and 102 TFEU where an EU dimension (effect upon trade between Member States) is involved.[1] Moreover, in most cases the Member States have adopted highly similar systems of national competition law in a process of spontaneous harmonization. Both systems can be relied upon in national courts as

[1] Council Reg (EC) No 1/2003 of 16 December 2002 on the implementation of the rules on competition laid down in Articles 81 and 82 of the Treaty [2003] OJ L1/1, Arts 3 and 5.

the relevant provisions of the Treaty have direct effect, and although this is not formally a result of modernization, in practical terms the number of cases based on the EU competition rules before national courts is likely to multiply.[2] Hence, the national competition rules of the Member States must often be interpreted in the light of EU competition law.

8.02 The application of EU Treaty competition law rules and principles to health care at a national level is potentially problematic given the political sensitivities involved. Competition is often assumed to weaken, if not destroy, the foundations of solidarity on which most European health care systems rest. At the same time a dose of competition may invigorate the sector and open new opportunities for more efficient provision by ensuring that health care markets operate freely and without anti-competitive restraints or monopolistic abuse, to the ultimate benefit of the consumer interest.[3]

8.03 Addressing the interplay between competition and health care requires an introduction to the general background of EU competition law and its make-up. The objective of EU competition law is creating a regime of undistorted competition on the internal market. This area of EU law focuses on undertakings, as opposed to the free movement rules, which in general apply only to public authorities. This is why we will first examine the definition of what constitutes an undertaking with specific reference to the health care sector. Next we will look at the three sets of rules which comprise competition law in the strict sense (that is, not including the state aid rules): (i) the cartel prohibition of Article 101 TFEU; (ii) the prohibition on dominance abuse of Article 102 TFEU with respect to the behaviour of undertakings (sometimes jointly called antitrust); and (iii) merger control, based on the Merger Control Regulation 139/2004,[4] with regard to market structure. We will deal with each of these three elements in turn, followed by a brief look at the interaction between the two levels of government, based on the EU law doctrines of *effet utile* and direct effect. Competition law in the broader sense includes the rules on state aid.[5] This will be the topic of the next chapter, which will also examine the concept of services of general economic interest (SGEI). Undertakings entrusted with the duty to perform these types of services may, under certain conditions,

[2] cf HHB Vedder, 'Spontaneous harmonisation of national (competition) laws in the wake of the modernisation of EC competition law' [2004] *Competition Law Review* 5.

[3] cf M Gaynor, R Moreno-Serra and C Propper, 'Death by Market Power: Reform, Competition and Patient Outcomes in the National Health Service' [2010] *NBER Working Paper No. 16164*, July 2010.

[4] Council Reg (EC) No 139/2004 of 20 January 2004 on the control of concentrations between undertakings (the EC Merger Regulation) [2004] OJ L24/1.

[5] cf J van de Gronden, 'Financing healthcare in EU law: Do the European state aid rules write out an effective prescription for integrating competition law with healthcare?' [2009] *Competition Law Review* 5.

claim exemption from all the Lisbon Treaty rules, including competition, state aid and free movement.

B. Undertakings

Because the EU competition rules apply exclusively to (associations of) undertakings, the first question is how to define the concept of undertaking. Would this cover a health care provider or insurer? The case law of the ECJ on this issue is functional in nature: this means that the formal legal definitions used in national law are irrelevant.[6] What is decisive in this context is whether the entity concerned is involved in an economic activity.[7] In this context an economic activity is described as 'any activity consisting in offering goods and services on a given market'. This holds in particular, as was outlined by the ECJ in *Pavlov* (2000), if this activity occurs in return for remuneration and if the provider of the services assumes the economic risk involved.[8] The allocation of risk is sometimes used to identify the relevant entity.[9] The focus on the concept of undertaking also serves to distinguish the application of the competition rules from the Treaty provisions on the free movement of workers. Health care professionals only fall within the scope of EU competition law in so far as they are independent (self-employed) and do not fall under the authority of an employer. **8.04**

Health care providers

The case law on the concept of undertakings and health care providers is relatively straightforward. Below we discuss the main cases. **8.05**

Pavlov

Generally, the ECJ readily assumes that health care providers are engaged in economic activities. In the abovementioned *Pavlov* case, for example, the ECJ held that independent medical specialists perform services in a market (the market for specialized medical services), inter alia because they receive remuneration for these services and assume the financial risks that are associated with their professional activity. The complexity and technical nature of their services and the fact that the practice of their profession is regulated did not affect this conclusion. Because the **8.06**

[6] Case 118/85 *Commission v Italy (transparency directive)* [1987] ECR 2599, para 11. On the methodology of the Court see also W Sauter and H Schepel, *State and Market in European Union Law: The Public and Private Spheres of the Internal Market Before the EU Courts* (Cambridge: Cambridge University Press, 2009).

[7] Case C-41/90 *Klaus Höfner and Fritz Elser v Macrotron GmbH* [1991] ECR I-1979, para 21.

[8] Joined Cases C-180/98 to C-184/98 *Pavel Pavlov* et al *v Stichting Pensioenfonds Medische Specialisten* [2000] ECR I-6451, para 73 ff; with reference to Case 118/85 *Commission v Italy,* supra n 6, para 7; and Case C-35/96 *Commission v Italy (customs agents)* [1998] ECR I-3851, para 36.

[9] cf Case C-22/98 *Criminal proceedings against Jean Claude Becu* et al [2001] ECR I-5665.

medical specialists involved were engaged in an economic activity they were considered to form individual undertakings in the sense of the competition rules.

Glöckner

8.07 Providing goods and services in competition—or in a context where competition is possible (potential competition)—is likewise seen as carrying out an economic activity as an undertaking.[10] This was, for instance, held by the ECJ in relation to ambulance services in *Glöckner* (2001).[11] As services in the market for emergency transport and (non-emergency) patient transport are not always provided by mutual aid organizations or by public authorities, as had so far been the case in the German region involved, these services were held to constitute an economic activity. This was not altered by the fact that some providers of such services might be less competitive, as the result of public service obligations, than other providers without similar obligations.

8.08 Hence the party offering these services (Glöckner) was an undertaking for the purposes of the EU competition rules. However, due the special characteristics of its activities it was also found be a service of general interest (SGEI) providing a proportional exception to the competition rules. Effectively the ECJ found that there was insufficient solidarity to exclude application of the concept of undertaking but subsequently accepted sufficient solidarity was involved to invoke Article 106(2) TFEU. (This approach was pioneered in the *Albany* (1999) pension insurance case law.)[12] In line with the approach in *Glöckner,* the Commission contended in the state aid case *IRIS-hospitals* (2009) that services provided by the public hospitals concerned constituted economic activities because similar services were offered by private health care operators.[13] Hence, in this decision the argument of potential competition was also taken into account.

8.09 This actual or potential 'offering of services in competition' test leads to the conclusion that most, if not all, private bodies and entities that are active in the provision

---

[10] Case C-41/90 *Höfner*, supra n 7, paras 22 and 23.

[11] Case C-475/99 *Firma Ambulanz Glöckner v Landkreis Südwestpfalz* [2001] ECR I-8089.

[12] Case C-67/96 *Albany International BV v Stichting Bedrijfspensioenfonds Textielindustrie* [1999] ECR I-5751; Joined Cases C-115/97, C-116/97 and C-117/97 *Brentjens' Handelsonderneming BV v Stichting Bedrijfspensioenfonds voor de Handel in Bouwmaterialen* [1999] ECR I-6025; and Case C-219/97 *Maatschappij Drijvende Bokken BV v Stichting Pensioenfonds voor de Vervoer- en Havenbedrijven* [1999] ECR I-6121. In more recent cases alongside the solidarity aspect the degree of public supervision involved has been emphasized. cf Case C-350/07 *Kattner Stahlbau GmbH v Maschinenbau- und Metall- Berufsgenossenschaft* [2009] ECR I-1513; and Case C-437/09 *AG2R Prévoyance v Beaudout Père et Fils SARL* [2011] judgment of 3 March 2011 (nyr), Opinion of AG Mengozzi.

[13] Decision of the Commission of 28 October 2009 with regard to state aid NN 54/2009 (ex CP 244/2005)—Belgium—financing of public hospitals of the IRIS-network of the Brussels capital region, para 109.

of health care are likely to be regarded as undertakings, irrespective of the fact whether they operate in Bismarck systems (in which sickness funds or other types of health insurers are the managing bodies) or in Beveridge systems (in which tax funded health care benefits are provided by the state to its population nominally free of charge).

CNOP and CCG v Commission

In 2010 the General Court ruled on appeals against decisions by the Commission to carry out unannounced inspections at the premises of three organizations of undertakings in the pharmacies and medical laboratories branch in France (which gave rise to the *ONP* cartel decision discussed at para 8.29).[14] The abovementioned organizations contested their qualification as 'association of undertakings' which (alongside the qualification as undertaking) is one of the two categories identified as being subject to Article 101 TFEU. The Court found that the fact that not all members of the associations were themselves undertakings (such as some members who were civil servants) was immaterial in so far as the organizations were bodies in which (i) undertakings in the sense of Article 101 TFEU had (ii) organized themselves and (iii) represented them. In this sense they were capable of taking decisions that might infringe Article 101 TFEU and could therefore be subjected to inspections designed to collect proof regarding the existence of such infringements. The fact that the Conseil de la Concurrence, the French national competition authority, had repeatedly concluded these bodies had infringed the competition rules, confirmed by the highest relevant French court, was cited as further evidence of this finding. Associations of health providers who meet the abovementioned test are thus subject to the competition rules. **8.10**

Providers of health insurance

However, the ECJ has adopted a different approach towards (public law) providers of health insurance, in respect of the purchasing activities of (public) health care management bodies. It is apparent from the *AOK* (2004) and *FENIN* (2006) judgments that the activities of these bodies, such as purchasing health care, should be seen in the context of the principle of solidarity.[15] **8.11**

[14] Case T-23/09 *Conseil national de l'Ordre des pharmaciens (CNOP), Conseil central de la section G de l'Ordre national des pharmaciens (CCG) v Commission* [2010] judgment of 26 October 2010 (nyr).

[15] See also J Lear, E Mossialos and B Karl, 'EU competition law and health policy' in E Mossialos et al (eds), *Health Systems Governance in Europe: The Role of European Union Law and Policy* (Cambridge: Cambridge University Press, 2010), 343.

8.12 Financial solidarity and excluding provision on market terms are the requirements for classifying a system as exclusively fulfilling a social function.[16] In this case the entities involved are not regarded as undertakings and are excluded from the scope of competition law altogether (but not from the market freedoms and public procurement rules that apply to public bodies).[17] This conclusion is reached taking into account the objective and compulsory nature of a system, the degree of public involvement, any elements of redistribution, and the manner in which contributions are calculated and entitlements are awarded.[18]

AOK

8.13 The *AOK* (2004) case concerned the fixing of maximum contributions towards the costs of pharmaceutical products by German health insurance funds.[19] The ECJ had been asked whether this was illegal under the competition rules. The German system made it compulsory for employees to join the public law scheme but on the other hand the insurance premiums did not only depend on the income of the insured party but also on the rate set by the insurance company. There was a degree of rate competition between the insurers involved in order to gain the business of both those with compulsory insurance and customers who took out insurance voluntarily, with price differentials of up to 30 per cent and up to five per cent of customers switching insurers each year. The insurance funds also implemented a risk equalization system (similar to the Irish and the Dutch schemes that will be dealt with in Chapter 9 on state aid) which made insurers with less burdensome risk profiles contribute to the financing of the funds that took care of insuring the more expensive risks.

[16] More broadly in the notion of solidarity cf C Newdick, 'Citizenship, Free Movement and Healthcare: Cementing Individual Rights by Corroding Social Solidarity' [2006] *Common Market Law Review* 1645.

[17] In landmark decisions such as Case C-157/99 *B.S.M. Geraets-Smits v Stichting Ziekenfonds VGZ and H.T.M. Peerbooms v Stichting CZ Groep Zorgverzekeringen* [2001] ECR I-5473; and Case C-385/99 *V.G. Müller-Fauré v Onderlinge Waarborgmaatschappij OZ Zorgverzekeringen UA and E.E.M. van Riet v Onderlinge Waarborgmaatschappij ZAO Zorgverzekeringen* [2003] I-4509, the ECJ reviewed the refusal of Dutch sickness funds to reimburse costs of cross-border health care in the light the Treaty provisions on the free movement of services; whereas in Joined Cases C-264/01, C-306/01, C-354/01 and C-355/01 *AOK Bundesverband* et al *v Ichthyol-Gesellschaft Cordes, Hermani & Co.* et al [2004] ECR I-2493, the ECJ held that German sickness funds were not undertakings within the meaning of EU competition law.

[18] Joined Cases C-159/91 and C-160/91 *Christian Poucet v Assurances Générales de France and Caisse Mutuelle Régionale du Languedoc-Roussillon* [1993] ECR I-637; Case C-205/03 P *Federación Española de Empresas de Tecnología Sanitaria (FENIN) v Commission* [2006] ECR I-6295.

[19] Joined Cases C-264/01, C-306/01, C-354/01 and C-355/01 *AOK Bundesverband*, supra n 17. Annotated by S Belhaj and JW van de Gronden, 'Comments – Some Room For Competition Does Not Make a Sickness Fund An Undertaking. Is EC Competition Law Applicable to the Health Care Sector?' [2004] *European Competition Law Review* 682. cf M Krajewski and M Farley, 'Non-economic activities in upstream markets and the scope of competition law after Fenin' [2007] *European Law Review* 111.

The ECJ held that the German health insurance funds fulfilled an exclusively social function based on the principle of solidarity and in the absence of any profit motive. In this context the health insurance funds form a collective that is based on solidarity (or 'Solidargemeinschaft') which shares out costs and risks equitably: **8.14**

> The sickness funds are therefore not in competition with one another or with private institutions as regards grant of the obligatory statutory benefits in respect of treatment or medicinal products which constitutes their main function.

And:

> The latitude available to the sickness funds when setting the contribution rate and their freedom to engage in some competition with one another in order to attract members does not call this analysis into question.[20]

This freedom and that element of competition were only seen as a way of pursuing an efficiency gain 'in accordance with economic principles of sound management'. Therefore the sickness funds were not considered to be undertakings, and as a result they did not fall within the scope of the competition rules.

What seems to have mattered most to the ECJ was that no competition was possible on the benefits to which patients were entitled. These benefits were fixed in national law and, as a result, the sickness funds did not enjoy any discretion when granting them to insured persons (who were moreover subject to compulsory affiliation). Apparently, as long as health insurers have no possibility of influencing the level of contributions, in the ECJ's view it is not of any interest that they do compete on price.[21] It is clear from the outset that the outcome of the *AOK* test is hard to predict. For instance, in the state aid field, a year after *AOK* the Commission found Dutch health insurers did constitute undertakings, although they have limited influence over the level of benefits and have comparable price differentials to those found in *AOK*.[22] **8.15**

FENIN

This 2006 case concerned a complaint about abuse of dominant position (based on systematic late payments to providers of medical goods and equipment by an average 300 days) by the management bodies of the Spanish national health system (SNS), which collectively accounted for 80 per cent of purchases of medical goods **8.16**

[20] ibid, paras 54 and 56.

[21] cf JW van de Gronden, 'The Treaty provisions on competition and healthcare', in JW van de Gronden et al (eds) *Health Care and EU Law* (The Hague: TMC Asser Press, 2011). JW van de Gronden and W Sauter, 'Taking the temperature: EU competition law and healthcare' [2011] *Legal Issues of European Integration* 213.

[22] Decision of the Commission of 3 May 2005 with regard to state aid N 541/2004 en N 542/2004—the Netherlands—risk equalisation system and retention of reserves.

and equipment in Spain.[23] In this case it was accepted (or at any rate not effectively contested) that the provision of health care services by SNS was purely of a social nature. Thereby the main question posed to the ECJ became whether the purchasing activity of the management bodies should be examined as a separate activity with regard to which they would have to be considered as undertakings that were subject to the competition rules. In a summarily motivated reaction the Court held:

> (…) there is no need to dissociate the activity of purchasing goods from the subsequent use to which they are put in order to determine the nature of that purchasing activity, and that the nature of the purchasing activity must be determined according to whether or not the subsequent use of the purchased goods amounts to an economic activity.[24]

Consequently there was no economic activity nor an undertaking involved, and therefore there could be no question of applying EU competition law.

8.17 This case resolved a contentious issue and it should be noted that similar cases under national competition law initially went in the opposite direction.[25] Because the ECJ did not develop the (uncontested) solidarity argument here it seems there is room for further clarification. The link between purchasing markets and the purpose to which goods are subsequently put has been confirmed outside the health care sector in *Selex* (2009) where the purchasing of prototypes was not considered an economic activity where it was linked to technical standardization provided by Eurocontrol in order to meet its the public service task of safety in air navigation.[26]

8.18 Meanwhile the *FENIN* logic, such as it is, clearly has important implications for NHS systems elsewhere in the EU as well, which will similarly combine public provision of care with purchasing private goods and services in the market. On the one hand the scope of EU competition law in health care is thus limited. On the other hand it may be assumed that the rules on public procurement and state aid would discipline the exercise of public purchasing power for the greater part. The two sets of rules thus complement each other. This evidently makes it important that the interface between the competition rules, the state aid rules and the procurement rules is well-managed. As the public procurement rules oblige public bodies to contract the most competitive service providers (or suppliers of goods), these rules are capable of restoring the imbalance between public health bodies and their

[23] Case C-205/03 P *Federación Española de Empresas de Tecnología Sanitaria (FENIN) v Commission of the European Communities* [2006] ECR I-6295.

[24] ibid, para 26.

[25] eg the Competition Commission Appeal Tribunal's (CCAT) ruling in the case *BetterCare Group Limited v DGFT* [2002] CAT 7. cf JW van de Gronden, 'Purchasing care: economic activity or service of general (economic) interest?' [2004] *European Competition Law Review* 84; J Lear, E Mossialos and B Karl, supra n 15.

[26] Case C-113/07P *SELEX Sistemi Integrati SpA v EU Commission and Organisation européenne pour la sécurité de la navigation aérienne (Eurocontrol)* [2009] ECR I-2207.

contractors. Hence, (as is the case for competition law) it is of great importance that in the application of public procurement law the specific features of health care markets are duly taken into account.[27]

AG2R Prévoyance

AG2R (2011) concerned a scheme for supplementary reimbursement of health care costs that was established by collective agreement between employers and unions in the traditional bakery sector in France.[28] This scheme was subsequently declared by law to be universally binding within the sector. It was characterized by compulsory affiliation to a specific insuring body and the express exclusion of any possibility of exemption from affiliation.[29] **8.19**

The ECJ established in the first place that the results of collective agreements are outside the scope of Article 101(1) TFEU and that consequently the same held for their reinforcement by means of legislative measures (which might otherwise be at odds with Article 4(3) TEU on the useful effect of EU law for circumventing or contravening competition rules). **8.20**

The ECJ also examined whether AG2R constituted an undertaking capable of infringing Articles 102 and 106(1) TFEU on dominance abuse and special and exclusive rights. To determine whether the activity concerned was economic in nature the Court examined whether (i) the scheme could be regarded as applying the principle of solidarity, and (ii) to what extent it is subject to supervision by the state. The first requirement was found to be met, but not the second. The Court concluded that: **8.21**

> (...) AG2R, although being non-profit-making and acting on the basis of the principle of solidarity, is an undertaking engaged in an economic activity which was chosen by the social partners, on the basis of financial and economic considerations, from among other undertakings with which it is in competition on the market in the provident services which it offers (...)[30]

Hence state control did not prevail in the organization of the scheme and the competition rules applied. This approach applied by the Court, based on the criteria of solidarity and state supervision, was first found in cases concerning insurance against accidents at work like *INAIL* (2000)[31] and more recently *Kattner Stahlbau* **8.22**

[27] See eg V Hatzopoulos, 'Public procurement and state aid in national health systems', in E Mossialos et al (eds), *Health Systems Governance in Europe*, supra n 7, p 379.

[28] Case C-437/09 *AG2R Prévoyance v Beaudout Père et Fils SARL* [2011] judgment of 3 March 2011 (nyr).

[29] Unlike the pension scheme addressed in Case C-67/96 *Albany International BV v Stichting Bedrijfspensioenfonds Textielindustrie* [1999] ECR I-5751 which allowed for certain exemptions.

[30] Case C-437/09 *AG2R*, supra n 28, para 65.

[31] In Case C-218/00 *Cisal di Battistello Venanzio & C. Sas v Istituto nazionale per l'assicurazione contro gli infortuni sul lavoro (INAIL)* [2002] ECR I-691.

(2009), where the ECJ stated that with respect to compulsory affiliation to a body charged with carrying out this insurance:

> (…) such an entity is not an undertaking within the meaning of those provisions, but fulfils an exclusively social function, where such a body operates within the framework of a scheme which applies the principle of solidarity and is subject to State supervision.[32]

Since the ruling in *AG2R* this approach now clearly applies across the social sphere.

8.23 It is also worth noting that in the end the ECJ determined that AG2R although subject to the competition rules as an undertaking had been charged with carrying out a SGEI. This allowed it to invoke the exception to the competition rules available to undertakings charged with carrying out public service obligations based on of Article 106(2) TFEU (see Chapter 9). This makes clear that although entities active in a privatized environment are likely to be caught by the competition rules they can rely on the SGEI exception to those competition rules provided there is a significant enough element of solidarity within the services they provide. (See also the discussion in the context of Chapter 9 below on state aid and SGEI.)

Evaluation

8.24 In order to determine whether the competition rules are applicable to health care operators one should make a distinction between providers and insurers. The first category offers services or goods on the market and is therefore in principle caught by EU competition law. The second category, however, is only caught in so far as they do not operate in accordance with principles that are predominantly based on solidarity. In case of a mix of solidarity and competition elements health insurers qualify as undertakings within the meaning of EU competition law.[33] Bodies managing a scheme that is based on a mix of solidarity and competition are obliged to observe the EU rules on competition. Because in its case law on the concept of undertaking the ECJ attaches great value to the extent managing bodies can influence the level of benefits it may be assumed that NHS bodies, operating in a Beveridge-type system, are more immune from competition law than are sickness funds or other health insurers, which provide their services in accordance with Bismarck-type systems.

8.25 After all, in a supply-driven, tax-based system, governments are likely to determine the precise levels of benefits, whereas governments that rely on a health insurance scheme are more likely to leave some room for demand driven competition with regard to the benefits that the insured persons are entitled to (for instance, based on

[32] Case C-350/07 *Kattner Stahlbau GmbH v Maschinen- und Metall- Berufsgenossenschaft* [2009] ECR I-1513, para 68.

[33] See eg Case C-244/94 *Fédération Française des Sociétés d'Assurance* et al *v Ministère de l'Agriculture et de la Pêche (FFSA)* [1995] ECR I-4015; Case C-67/96 *Albany*, supra n 29; Joined Cases C-115/97, C-116/97 and C-117/97 *Brentjens*, supra n 12; Case C-219/97 *Drijvende Bokken*, supra n 12.

supplementary insurance). Thus, fixing the level of benefits seems to be inherent to tax based health care systems, but states are more flexible if they operate a health insurance system. The counterpoint to this flexibility is that it leaves the parties involved more exposed to the competition rules. However it should be noted that the effects resulting from the applicability of the EU competition rules can be mitigated by relying upon the exceptions contained in Article 106(2) TFEU on SGEIs.

The ECJ seems to have developed an expansive concept of undertaking for health care providers and a restrictive concept for health insurers/managing bodies. By broadening the meaning of 'undertaking' for health care providers the EU courts have potentially opened the door to a multitude of health care cases arising under EU competition law. Those cases will not only occur at the EU level but also at the national level, as the enforcement of EU competition law is decentralized and because many national competition law systems within the EU are modelled on the TFEU. **8.26**

C. The Cartel Prohibition

We will now discuss the potential implications in terms of the substantive or material norms of EU competition law in relation to health care.[34] This discussion concerns the rules directed at undertakings: Article 101 TFEU, Article 102 TFEU and the provisions of the Merger Control Regulation. After that, the relationship between EU and national competition law will be touched upon. **8.27**

The cartel prohibition of Article 101 TFEU applies to collusive agreements between, and concerted practices of, undertakings, as well as decisions of associations of undertakings. Article 101(1) TFEU contains the relevant prohibition whereas Article 101(3) contains an exception that requires the creation of technical or economic benefits, that are shared with the consumer and do not involve restrictions to obtain the benefits concerned, and finally do not eliminate all competition in the relevant market. A significant body of case law and decisional practice is available on the application of Article 101 TFEU.[35] However, so far there are few EU level **8.28**

[34] cf J Lear, E Mossialos and B Karl, supra n 15; J van de Gronden, 'The Treaty provisions on competition and healthcare' in J van de Gronden, M Krajewski, U Neergaard and E Szyszczak (eds), *EU Law and Healthcare* (The Hague: Asser Press, 2011); For a general discussion of competition law see J Faull and A Nikpay (eds), *The EC Law of Competition* (2nd edn, Oxford: Oxford University Press, 2007), on the economics see M Motta, *EU Competition Policy: Theory and Practice* (Cambridge: Cambridge University Press, 2004).

[35] Apart from general works such as J Faull and A Nikpay, *The EC Law of Competition* (2nd edn, Oxford: Oxford University Press, 2007) and G Monti, *EC Competition Law* (Cambridge: Cambridge University Press, 2007), specialist studies on Article 101 are emerging such as C Townley, *Article 81 EC and Public Policy* (Oxford: Hart Publishing, 2009) and O Odudu, *The Boundaries of EC Competition Law: The Scope of Article 81* (Oxford: Oxford University Press, 2006).

decisions or judgments concerning the cartel prohibition applied specifically to health care outside the pharmaceutical sector.

ONP

8.29 A notable exception is the 2010 Article 101 TFEU fining and prohibition Decision with regard to the Ordre national des pharmaciens (ONP). ONP is the industry body responsible both for pharmacies and clinical testing laboratories for restricting competition in the clinical testing market in France (the Decision followed unannounced on-site inspections, or 'dawn raids', in 2008).[36] This professional body for the pharmacy and clinical testing sector had taken decisions that aimed to fix prices and had obstructed market entry by new laboratories. In particular it had blocked price discounts of over 10 per cent, and slowed down or prevented acquisitions and statutory changes or changes in the capital of the undertakings involved in market entry by outsiders. As regards the price restraints especially state hospital and insurance undertakings had suffered, with the resulting prices for clinical laboratory testing services in France being two or three times as high as in other Member States. In its exclusionary practices the ONP systematically used, as leverage, its various state backed statutory powers over French pharmacists and clinical testing laboratories, notably the exclusive power to register those licensed to practice.

8.30 The Commission distinguished this case from the *Wouters* (2002) case (see para 8.43) on the ground that there was no non-economic ethical and/or deontological justification at play here, or at least not to the extent that the restraints of competition involved were inherent in the pursuit of such public interest objectives.[37] A conclusive argument in this respect was the existence of a comprehensive legal framework which already protected the public health interests concerned.

8.31 This case seems a clear illustration of the pitfalls of abuse and rent-seeking of corporatist state endorsed self-regulation in the provision of health care that are so far not discussed in the free movement case law, in particular in the area of establishment (see Chapter 4 above), where corporatism instead tends to be applauded as protection from free market profit-seeking. In this context it is worth underlining that in its ONP Decision the Commission relied exclusively on the breach of the cartel prohibition in Article 101 TFEU (which applies to formal associations of undertakings as well as informal cartels) and did not address the public patronage of the association or its possible dominance abuse. Hence it trod carefully around the

[36] Commission Decision of 8 December 2010 based on Article 101 TFEU in Case 29510—ONP. <http://ec.europa.eu/competition/antitrust/cases/dec_docs/39510/39510_1203_3.pdf> accessed 24 February 2012. cf EU Commission press release IP/10/1683, *Antitrust: the Commission rules against the Ordre national des pharmaciens for restrictions on competition in the French clinical analysis market* (Brussels, 8 December 2010).

[37] Case C-309/99 *J.C.J. Wouters, J.W. Savelbergh and Price Waterhouse Belastingadviseurs BV v Algemene Raad van de Nederlandse Orde van Advocaten (Wouters)* [2002] ECR I-1577, para 97.

French institutional arrangements. So does the ECJ: when the legality of French ownership restrictions on clinical testing laboratories was tested in *Commission v France* (2010) they were duly found to be acceptable under the freedom of establishment on health protection grounds (see Chapter 4).[38]

Pharmaceuticals

In 2008–09 the pharmaceutical sector was the subject of an industry-wide pan-EU sector inquiry by DG Competition which was concluded with a Commission Communication of 8 July 2009, the Pharmaceutical Sector Inquiry Report.[39] Specifically, the pharmacy sector inquiry found that between 2000 and June 2008, more than 200 settlement agreements, covering 49 medicines (63 per cent of which were best selling medicines that had lost exclusivity) were concluded between originator and generic companies. About half of the settlements restricted the generic company's ability to market the medicine. A number of settlements involved direct payments by the originator company to the generic company (reverse payment settlements, under which the originator pays the generic company in return for agreeing to limit market entry). The Commission concluded that settlement agreements that limit generic entry and include a value transfer from an originator company to one or more generic companies are an example of potentially anti-competitive agreements that are designed to keep competitors out the market. Such agreements raise particular concerns where the motive of the agreement is the sharing of profits via payments from originator to generic companies to the detriment of patients and public health budgets. **8.32**

A second round of monitoring was launched in January 2011, and in July that same year, the Commission published its report on this second monitoring exercise. The Commission found that as many as 89 patent settlement agreements were reached between originator and generic companies in 2010 (compared with 207 such agreements in the 8 and a half years covered by the sector inquiry). However, the number of settlements that are potentially problematic from a competition perspective had decreased significantly. The Commission considers that this reflects increased awareness of possible competition issues. The continued increased use of patent settlements indicates, however, that companies have been able to find solutions to disputes that do not generally raise competition problems.[40] **8.33**

Moreover, the Commission has conducted, in total, three rounds of unannounced on-site inspections ('dawn raids') of pharmaceutical companies in 2008 and **8.34**

38 Case C-89/09 *Commission v France (laboratories)* [2010] judgment of 16 December 2010 (nyr).

39 Communication from the Commission, Executive Summary of the Pharmaceutical Sector Inquiry Report, COM (2009) 0351 final.

40 cf L Hancher, 'The EU pharmaceuticals markets: parameters and pathways', in E Mossialos et al (eds) *Health systems governance in Europe*, supra n 15.

2009 and as a result of the information gathered, it initiated proceedings in relation to:[41]

- a possible abuse of dominance by Les Laboratoires Servier; and
- agreements between Les Laboratoires Servier and a number of generic companies.

8.35 The Commission was concerned that this conduct and these agreements may have the object or effect of hindering entry onto the market of the generic form of a cardio-vascular medicine originally developed by Les Laboratoires Servier. The Commission also initiated proceedings to investigate a suspected breach, by the pharmaceutical company Lundbeck, of Articles 101 and 102 TFEU. The Commission stated that it intends to investigate unilateral behaviour and agreements by Lundbeck which may hinder the entry of the generic form of the anti-depressant drug Citalopram into markets in the European Economic Area.[42]

8.36 There is nevertheless, so far, little specific guidance for health care operators carrying out a self-assessment under Article 101(1) TFEU and Article 101(3) TFEU (as is required under the decentralized system of antitrust). Aside from the recent *ONP* case that was just discussed, the most significant cases which have already been decided and do address the application of the cartel prohibition in health care are the *Bayer* and *GlaxoSmithKline* cases, both of which concern parallel imports of pharmaceuticals. In another case based on a prejudicial reference the ECJ found that Article 101 TFEU read in conjunction with Article 4(3) of the TEU (‘*effet utile*’) did not apply to a Belgian ban on advertising for dentists. This is dealt with below under the relationship between EU and national rules at para 8.91.[43]

Bayer

8.37 The *Bayer* (2004) case concerned the question of whether there were agreements between wholesale dealers and the aforementioned pharmaceutical concern for the purpose of frustrating parallel imports (between Spain and France on the one hand, and the United Kingdom on the other) in the sense of Article 101 TFEU—or whether unilateral conduct by Bayer was involved, and therefore potentially an infringement of Article 102 TFEU on abuse of dominance.[44] In the event of agreements, price differentiation can result in an infringement of Article 101 TFEU. Maintaining a quota system on the other hand only infringes Article 102 TFEU in

[41] Case C-156/03 P-R *Commission of the European Communities v Les Laboratoires Servier SA* [2003] ECR I-6575; Case T-147/00 *Les Laboratoires Servier v Commission of the European Communities* [2003] ECR II-85.

[42] European Commission Press release IP/10/8, *Antitrust: Commission opens formal proceedings against pharmaceutical company Lundbeck* (Brussels, 7 January 2010).

[43] Case C-446/05 *Criminal proceedings against Doulamis (Belgian dentists)* [2008] ECR I-1377.

[44] Joined Cases C-2/01 P and C-3/01 P *Bundesverband der Arzneimittel-Importeure eV and Commission v Bayer AG* [2004] ECR I-23; Case T-41/96 *Bayer AG v Commission* [2000] ECR II-3383.

cases of unilateral conduct and a dominant position. (In *Sandoz* (1990) the fact that the message 'export prohibited' was printed on all invoices was held to constitute proof of the existence of tacit acceptance of anticompetitive conduct.)[45] Hence in *Bayer* Articles 101 and 102 TFEU are mutually exclusive. The ECJ held that only anticompetitive behaviour by Bayer had been proven but that no convincing evidence regarding concurrence of wills between Bayer and its customers was available. Hence, Article 101 TFEU did not apply.

GlaxoSmithKline

This case (2009) concerned the similar practice of the pharmaceutical company GlaxoSmithKline, of maintaining differentiated prices in the Spanish market in order to block parallel imports (tariff arbitrage).[46] The Commission had established a breach of Article 101 TFEU on this basis, but in the view of the ECJ it had neglected to demonstrate that there was (tacit) acceptance and whether, given the degree of regulation in place, there was any room left for restrictions of competition by the private parties involved.[47] It is also worth noting that the General Court had in addition addressed the question of whether restrictions of parallel imports deny the benefits thereof to consumers (or rather, whether these benefits are substantial): given the existence of price regulation at national level the benefits appeared to accrue primarily to the parallel importers themselves. As a result, the General Court was of the opinion that agreements containing the restrictions to parallel trade did not have the object of restricting competition. **8.38**

By putting forward this point of view the General Court derogated from longstanding case law, according to which restrictions to parallel trade were considered to be a severe infringement of the cartel prohibition ('hard core restriction'). The General Court based this decision on the view, which was at that time untested, that consumer welfare is the only goal that matters in EU competition law. Finally, the General Court did find adverse effects on competition (resulting from the agreements under review). However, this did not call into question its change of approach towards restrictions to parallel trade, which used to be based on an absolute ban on such restrictions. **8.39**

The ECJ on the other hand indicated that, apart from consumer welfare, other goals (such as the market structure and competition itself) must be weighed, and emphasized that territorial restrictions must be regarded as a restriction by object **8.40**

[45] Case C-277/87 *Sandoz prodotti farmaceutici SpA v Commission* [1990] ECR I-45.

[46] Joined Cases C-501/06 P, C-513/06 P, C-515/06 P and C-519/06 P *GlaxoSmithKline Services Unlimited v Commission (C-501/06 P) and Commission v GlaxoSmithKline Services Unlimited (C-513/06 P) and European Association of Euro Pharmaceutical Companies (EAEPC) v Commission (C-515/06 P) and Asociación de exportadores españoles de productos farmacéuticos (Aseprofar) v Commission (C-519/06 P)* [2009] ECR I-9291.

[47] Case T-168/01 *GlaxoSmithKline Services Unlimited v Commission* [2006] ECR II-2969.

which is therefore per se illegal. However, ultimately, the findings of the ECJ and General Court did not differ substantially. Both courts agreed that an infringement of Article 101 TFEU was involved, while the Commission would have to collect more information in order to be able to decide whether the exception of Article 101(3) TFEU applied.[48]

8.41 This novel approach adopted by the General Court towards restrictions to parallel trade (which have been considered to be of a hard core nature in the ECJ's settled case law since 1960s) was driven by the need to fine-tune the competition rules to the specific features of health care. The General Court stressed that because insurers usually bear the health care costs involved the paradigm established in the old case law barring restrictions to parallel trade as a matter of principle in order to oppose market partitioning was not appropriate for solving pharmaceutical cases. In other words, the General Court's attempted to accommodate health care-specific features in the application of the cartel prohibition.

8.42 Given the gap between the innovative solution of the General Court and the long-standing settled case law, which dates back to traditional landmark decisions such as *Consten and Grundig* (1966),[49] and strictly forbids restrictions to parallel trade in order to stimulate market integration, the decision of the ECJ to overturn the General Court's ruling did not come as a surprise. However it is a pity that the ECJ did not express its views on how the classic approach towards restrictions of parallel trade could be tailored to health care. Possibly the ECJ's view was precisely that this was a regular market where intervention—if necessary to remedy market failures—should be limited to public authorities and hence normal competition law standards applied. Then again, the ECJ could have at least shed more light on how the circumstance that health insurers usually bear the costs should be taken into account in the assessment under Article 101 TFEU. Should this be taken into account by the Commission when applying the first (prohibition) or third (exemption) section of this Treaty provision?

The pursuit of legitimate objectives

8.43 In other cases in different areas however, the ECJ has developed an approach that takes into consideration the special features of the sector involved. In *Wouters* (2002),[50] for example, it was called upon to review a decision taken by the Dutch Bar Association. The ECJ said that for the purpose of the application of Article 101 TFEU particularly, account must be taken of the objectives of the restrictions

[48] J van de Gronden, *EU Law and Healthcare*, supra n 21.

[49] Case 56/64 *Établissements Consten S.à.R.L. and Grundig-Verkaufs-GmbH v Commission* [1966] ECR 429.

[50] Case C-309/99 *Wouters*, supra n 37.

involved and that it must be examined whether these restrictions are inherent in the pursuit of those objectives:

> (…), not every agreement between undertakings or every decision of an association of undertakings which restricts the freedom of action of the parties or of one of them necessarily falls within the prohibition laid down in Article 85(1) of the Treaty. For the purposes of application of that provision to a particular case, account must first of all be taken of the overall context in which the decision of the association of undertakings was taken or produces its effects. More particularly, account must be taken of its objectives, which are here connected with the need to make rules relating to organisation, qualifications, professional ethics, supervision and liability, in order to ensure that the ultimate consumers of legal services and the sound administration of justice are provided with the necessary guarantees in relation to integrity and experience (…). It has then to be considered whether the consequential effects restrictive of competition are inherent in the pursuit of those objectives.[51]

Hence, the ECJ held that that the decision taken by the Dutch Bar Association was necessary given the professional ethics and deontological rules at stake and therefore not contrary to the cartel prohibition. In *Meca-Medina* (2006)[52] the ECJ even applied the approach developed in *Wouters* to sports. The application to health care such as it is, is uneven. As we have seen in the 2010 *ONP* Decision, the Commission found that the objectives and restrictions of the body organising the French pharmacists was not thus favoured. Outside competition law, in the context of establishment, rules promoting exclusionary industry self-regulation remain favoured and are so far rarely contested successfully under EU law (see Chapter 4). **8.44**

It is worth noting that the ECJ in these cases referred in general wording to the need to achieve legitimate objectives (not public objectives), which meant that competition law was not infringed.[53] Hence, in areas other than health care the ECJ seems to have developed an approach that is capable of accommodating issues of general interest in the application of EU competition law.[54] **8.45**

Evidently in health care such objectives may well be at stake.[55] For instance many health care providers are guided by a specific medical deontology (starting from the Hippocratic oath) and might apply rules that are 'inherent' in the organization of health care. One example may be rules prohibiting doctors from advertising[56] or from using their qualifications in a non-medical setting. Of interest in this regard is the judgment of the General Court in *Institute of Professional Representatives before the European Patent Office* (2001), where it held that a ban on comparative publicity **8.46**

[51] ibid, para 97. cf Case C-3/95 *Reisebüro Broede v Gerd Sandker* [1996] ECR I-6511, para 38.

[52] Case C-519/04P *David Meca-Medina and Igor Majcen v Commission (Meca-Medina)* [2006] ECR I-6991.

[53] ibid, para 45.

[54] J van de Gronden [2011]; and J van de Gronden and W Sauter [2011], supra n 21.

[55] See also J Lear, E Mossialos and B Karl, supra n 15.

[56] Case T-144/99 *Institute of Professional Representatives before the European Patent Office v Commission* [2001] II-1087.

issued by an association of professionals was justifiable in the light of Article 101(3) TFEU. This maybe especially relevant to agreements because dominance related issues are often addressed using the SGEI concept. However, the ECJ has so far not ruled on whether the legitimate objectives approach might apply to health care cases.

D. Abuse of Dominance

8.47 Abuse of dominance concerns cases where a single undertaking has (or in exceptional cases several undertakings acting collusively have) gained such a strong position in the relevant market that it has dominance. It then abuses this dominance by (i) exploiting consumers; and/or (ii) excluding (or foreclosing) competitors (sometimes discrimination is included as a third category of abuse). Dominance means it is able to act independently from competitors, customers, suppliers, and/or ultimately consumers.[57] A tight oligopoly of several large undertakings can lead to a position of 'collective dominance': (i) the members must be able to observe each other's behaviour closely; (ii) there has to be an enforcement mechanism against deviant behaviour (eg punitive price reductions); and (ii) it must be impossible for outsiders such as competitors or entrants to undermine the oligopoly.[58]

Market definition

8.48 In order to determine whether a dominant position exists, the relevant market needs to be defined in two dimensions: the product market (such as hospital care) and the geographic market (for instance, a particular city or local area).[59] It is also required that a significant part of the internal market is concerned. This would be the case for the entire territory of a Member State or part of a larger Member State. Important infrastructural bottlenecks such as a major sea- or airport—and by analogy, a highly specialized clinic, or an electronic network for patient data—can also constitute a significant part of the internal market.[60]

8.49 Logically, the broader the relevant market is, the smaller the chance that dominance will be found and vice versa: the narrower the relevant market is defined, the greater the chance that dominance will be established. When determining the relevant market generally the SSNIP test is used ('small but significant non-transitory increase in price'). This means that by way of a thought experiment (or, hypothetically) the price

[57] Case 85/76 *Hoffmann-La Roche & Co. AG v Commission* [1979] ECR 461. cf A Ezrachi (ed), *Article 82 EC: reflections on its recent evolution* (Oxford: Hart Publishing, 2009).

[58] Case T-342/99 *Airtours plc v Commission* [2002] ECR II-2585.

[59] Commission Notice on the definition of the relevant market for the purposes of Community competition law [1997] OJ C372/5.

[60] cf Case C-179/90 *Merci convenzionali porto di Genova SpA v Siderurgica Gabrielli SpA* [1991] ECR I-5889.

of the product concerned is increased by 5–10 per cent and the reaction of customers is observed. If customers switch to other products and/or providers in significant numbers these products and/or their providers must be added to the market because they discipline the behaviour of the provider who is being investigated. This process is repeated until there is no longer any significant substitution: thus the market is determined.

This system of market definition, based on the SSNIP test, has a number of significant drawbacks: **8.50**

- First, there is the general market definition problem of the so-called 'cellophane fallacy'. This means that if a monopolist has already increased its prices to the maximum level of what the market will bear in order to exploit its market power, a SSNIP test will lead customers to switch to sub-optimal providers that do not really form part of the market. For example they may be induced to seek treatment by a general practitioner or physical therapist instead of a more effective surgical intervention by a specialized consultant. The result would be that the market is defined much too widely by including those other services.
- Secondly, there is a market definition problem that is specific to health care on account of the 'third party pays' principle. This occurs especially in insurance based Bismarck systems as consumers do not directly bear the costs of their treatment but may also occur where national health systems contract with private health care providers. In the case of health insurance, as the General Court pointed out in *GlaxoSmithKline*,[61] the insurer pays the costs of the healthcare consumed and as there is no direct relationship between the insurance rates paid by consumers and their choices in health care consumption the latter are hardly affected by cost considerations (hence the cellophane fallacy is less likely to occur). This means market definition based on a notional price increase as in the SSNIP test is not feasible here.

This second problem is now being addressed at national level by health economists **8.51** who have developed econometric models that are based, for instance, on the willingness of customers to travel to alternative providers (with additional travel time to next preferred options as the equivalent of a price increase), or their willingness to pay in order to include a particular provider in the package of care available to them (which takes account of the role played by insurers).[62] Initially the 'Elzinga Hogarty' test was applied based on the number of consumers that would travel from within a region to outside the region and vice versa. This method has meanwhile been

[61] Joined Cases C-501/06 P, C-513/06 P, C-515/06 P and C-519/06 P *GlaxoSmithKline*, supra n 46.

[62] M Varkevisser, *Patient choice, competition and antitrust enforcement in Dutch hospital markets* (PhD thesis, Rotterdam, 2010); M Varkevisser, C Capps et al, 'Defining hospital markets for antitrust enforcement: new approaches and their applicability to The Netherlands' [2008] *Health Economics, Policy and Law* 7–29; DOJ/FTC, *Improving healthcare: a dose of competition* (US Department of Justice and Federal Trade Commission, 2004).

discredited in US merger practice, not least because in a 2006 case Professor Ken Elzinga himself testified that his method was not useful in health cases. Market definition is not just crucial to determining the existence of dominance for abuse cases but also to determining merger cases (likewise largely based on dominance) and, to a lesser extent, cartel cases (except when hard core restrictions or restrictions by object are involved and the exact definition of the market is less important).

Dominant position

8.52 When determining a dominant position the market share is examined first. If this is 50 per cent or more, the existence of a dominant position may be assumed. According to the ECJ in *AKZO* (1991):

> (...) the view may legitimately be taken that very large shares are in themselves, and save in exceptional circumstances, evidence of the existence of a dominant position.[63]

8.53 Apart from the absolute market share, other factors are taken into account, such as the relative market share (as compared to the next largest competitors), and also countervailing market power, as well as commercial (brands), technical (patents), and financial advantages (such as deep pockets or preferential access to capital). The existence of entry barriers as a result of law and regulation can also be relevant—especially in highly regulated sectors such as health care. This may vary by which segment of the sector is concerned, for example, entry in the hospital market is likely to be much more difficult than it would be for an individual medical practitioner—such as a general practitioner, a dentist or a physical therapist—requiring far lower investments and a much lighter regulatory burden. Finally, the behaviour of the undertaking concerned is relevant as well: if it is in a position to impose unilaterally profitable price increases that may constitute an important proof of the existence of a dominant position.

Abuse

8.54 However, proving that an undertaking enjoys a position of dominance is not enough. The existence of abusive behaviour must also be shown. As mentioned above, two main types of such behaviour are generally distinguished: exploitation and exclusion.

- *Exploitation* may concern charging excessive prices (many times higher than costs and/or comparable prices) with respect to consumers or other customers and having as its purpose the increase in profits of the undertaking enjoying a

[63] Case C-62/86 *AKZO Chemie BV v Commission* [1991] ECR I-3359, para 60. With reference to Case 85/76 *Hoffmann-La Roche*, supra n 57, para 41.

dominant position above competitive levels. Such cases are highly exceptional at EU level.[64]

- *Exclusion* may concern predatory pricing (below costs)[65] or a price squeeze (not leaving a margin between consumer prices and the prices for key inputs)[66] and aims to foreclose competition by pushing competitors out of the market, thereby creating the opportunity to subsequently exploit consumers (then deprived from alternatives).

In recent years antitrust enforcers have generally given combating exclusionary abuses priority over correcting exploitative abuses. Accordingly, the European Commission published an extensive communication on the former at the beginning of 2009.[67] The reason behind this approach is that if exclusion is controlled effectively it will soon become superfluous to address exploitation because the latter problem will generally be solved by the market mechanism itself. In this context, ensuring that effective market entry is not foreclosed is important as well. **8.55**

Another reason for this focus is that using the general competition rules to combat exploitation is also very difficult: the Commission has powers to impose hefty fines but not, for instance, to impose detailed price regulation. In some sectors (such as energy, transport, and electronic communication) there are sectoral regulators who do have such powers, often based on EU Directives. Generally they are empowered to act even in the absence of a prior showing of abuse, although generally only in the event of dominance, or its sectoral equivalent, significant market power (SMP).[68] **8.56**

Finally, it is important to note that fighting exploitation can also be counterproductive: the high margins that could have provoked effective entry are then suppressed by price regulation, and a regulated monopoly may well ensue, giving rise to efficiency concerns. Although regulation may be relatively easy to introduce it can be all the more difficult to abolish: regulation is self-perpetuating and creates dependence. **8.57**

Interestingly, in its Guidance the European Commission has indicated that reasons external to a dominant undertaking may be capable of justifying abusive behaviour. After all, the Commission has expressed its intention to apply an objective necessity test to cases of dominance. In this context the Guidance however does not refer to **8.58**

[64] One such exception is provided by Joined Cases 110/88, 241/88 and 242/88 *François Lucazeau* et al *v Société des Auteurs, Compositeurs et Editeurs de Musique (SACEM)* et al [1989] ECR 2811.

[65] Case C-202/07 P *France Télécom SA v Commission* [2009] ECR I-2369.

[66] Case T-271/03 *Deutsche Telekom AG v Commission* [2008] ECR II-477.

[67] Commission Communication, Guidance on the Commission's enforcement priorities in applying Article 82 of the EC Treaty to abusive exclusionary conduct by dominant undertakings [2009] OJ C45/7.

[68] In the Netherlands, SMP exists in healthcare based on national legislation. cf W Sauter 'Experiences from the Netherlands: the application of competition rules in healthcare' in JW van de Gronden et al (eds), *Healthcare and EU Law* (The Hague: TMC Asser Press, 2011), 337–58.

health care but to cases where product-related risks were involved so there is no explicit suggestion that health care interests, other than those connected with product safety, are capable of justifying abusive behaviour.[69]

Case law

8.59 So far the Commission has not acted against abuse of dominance with regard to health care providers or insurers. However in recent years it has taken action on several occasions in the pharmaceuticals sector.

IMS Health

8.60 This case (2004) revolved around a refusal of access by IMS Health (which was a monopolist based on an intellectual property right) to provide access to its competitors in Germany to a 'brick structure' used for recording data (regional sales figures) for the supply of pharmaceutical products.[70] The ECJ decided that the intellectual property right creates a position of dominance and that the owner of the essential input is obligated to supply it: if the undertaking that has requested a license intends to use this to create a new product; if there is no objective justification for the refusal; and if the refusal eliminates all competition from the market.[71]

AstraZeneca

8.61 In this 2005 case, the Commission found a breach of the prohibition on dominance abuse by this pharmaceutical company which had, in a number of ways, abused licensing and authorization procedures for marketing pharmaceuticals in order to foreclose competition in the market for proton pump inhibitors.[72] Based on its patents AstraZeneca enjoyed a dominant position for proton pump inhibitors on six national markets in the EU (as well as Norway) and manipulated the renewal procedures of its authorizations to the detriment of competing producers of generic substitutes, as well as the form in which its products were marketed, to the detriment of parallel importers.

8.62 On appeal in 2010 the General Court noted that Article 102 TFEU prohibits a dominant undertaking from eliminating a competitor and so strengthening its own position by using methods other than those which come within the scope of

---

[69] Case T-30/89 *Hilti AG v Commission* [1991] ECR II-1439, paras 118–19; Case T-83/91 *Tetra Pak International SA v Commission (Tetra Pak II)* [1994] ECR II-755.

[70] Case C-418/01 *IMS Health GmbH & Co. OHG v NDC Health GmbH & Co. KG* [2004] ECR I-5039.

[71] An interim measure was imposed in: *NDC Health/IMS Health* (Case COMP D3/38.044) Commission Decision 2003/741/EC [2003] OJ L268/69.

[72] *AstraZeneca* (Case COMP/A.37.507/F3) Commission Decision 2006/857/EC [2006] OJ L332/24. This was in line with the norm established by the Court of Justice in Joined Cases C-241/91 P and C-242/91 P *Radio Telefis Eireann (RTE) and Independent Television Publications Ltd (ITP) v Commission* [1995] ECR I-743; which was relaxed by the General Court in Case T-201/04 *Microsoft Corp. v Commission* [2007] ECR II-3601.

competition on the merits.[73] The unlawful acquisition of an exclusive right can constitute an abuse even it does not have the effect of eliminating all competition. Therefore, the General Court concluded that the Commission correctly applied Article 102 of the TFEU in taking the view that the submission to the patent offices of objectively misleading representations by a dominant undertaking which led those offices to grant it supplementary protection certificates (SPCs) to which it was not entitled or to which it was entitled for a shorter period, so resulting in a restriction or elimination of competition, constituted an abuse of dominance.

The General Court also concluded that conduct designed to prevent manufactures of generic products from making use of their right to benefit from the original clinical tests and trials is not based in any way on the legitimate protection of an investment that comes within the scope of competition on the merits. The deregistration of the marketing authorizations by AstraZeneca prevented applicants for marketing authorizations for essentially similar products from being able to use the abridged procedure and so obstructed or delayed the market entry of generic products. Such deregistration may also prevent parallel imports, depending on the relevant factual and legal context. **8.63**

The fact that AstraZeneca was entitled to withdraw the marketing authorizations does not mean that the conduct escapes Article 102 TFEU. Therefore, the existence of alternative procedures for generic competitors to justify their registration did not mean that AstraZeneca's deregistration was not abusive. That conduct solely served to exclude from the market, at least temporarily, competing manufacturers of generic products. For the main part the General Court therefore upheld the Commission's decision, except that it held the Commission failed to establish, to the requisite legal standard, that the deregistration of marketing authorizations was capable of restricting parallel imports in two of the Member States affected. **8.64**

Apart from this the ECJ has addressed a prejudicial reference concerning the application of Article 102 TFEU with regard to pharmaceuticals, discussed below. **8.65**

Sot. Lélos v GlaxoSmithKline AEVE

In this 2008 case the question was raised: to what extent a pharmaceutical company was allowed to defend itself against parallel imports (arbitrage between 'high price' and 'low price' Member States) by means of a refusal to supply.[74] The ECJ took the position that regulation of pharmaceuticals does not remove the abusive character from every refusal by a pharmaceutical undertaking to fulfil the orders from wholesale traders that are involved in parallel exports. However, it should be able to take **8.66**

[73] Case T-321/05 *AstraZeneca AB and AstraZeneca plc v Commission* [2010] judgment of 1 July 2010 (nyr).

[74] Joined Cases C-468/06 to C-478/06 *Sot. Lélos kai Sia EE* et al *v GlaxoSmithKline AEVE* [2008] ECR I-7139.

reasonable and proportionate measures to defend its own commercial interests.[75] In this context the usual size of these orders given the size of the market involved and earlier commercial relations between the parties should be taken into account. Hence a measured response to parallel imports appears possible.

8.67 With this we have given a first indication of what the application of the EU abuse of dominance prohibition in health care implies. So far however it appears likely that, for providers of health care and for insurers, national rather than EU competition law is being applied. However, with the adoption of new and more reliable methods of market definition and the emergence of greater pressure for market entry if liberalization spills over across borders, dominance abuse cases at EU level may well become more frequent over the next few years.

E. Mergers

8.68 The EU system of merger control is based on *ex ante* examination. Mergers between undertakings of which the combined turnover exceeds certain predetermined thresholds have to be notified to the European Commission and must be vetted by it before they can be implemented.[76] Until that time the consummation of the merger concerned is prohibited (by the so-called stand-still clause). If a merger nevertheless goes ahead it can be dissolved at the orders of the Commission. The test applied when deciding if a merger should be prohibited is whether the merger would lead to a significant impediment of competition, in particular as a result of the creation or strengthening of a dominant position:

> A concentration which would significantly impede effective competition, in the common market or in a substantial part of it, in particular as a result of the creation or strengthening of a dominant position, shall be declared incompatible with the common market.[77]

8.69 The evaluation takes place in two phases: in the first, preliminary, phase it is examined whether there are serious doubts about the compatibility of the merger with the internal market. If that is indeed the case then the second and conclusive phase is started, which will determine whether the merger is declared compatible or incompatible with the internal market. The first phase takes up to 25 working days and the second phase 90 working days, although these deadlines can be extended while the undertakings involved are preparing their answers to questions posed by the Commission; and if the undertakings are prepared to give specific commitments

[75] ibid, paras 69–70.
[76] Council Reg (EC) No 139/2004, supra n 4, Art 1(2) and (3).
[77] ibid, Art 2(3).

(eg to spin-off certain branches or place activities at arm's length)[78] in order to remove doubts that have arisen with the Commission then the mergers can go ahead. The Commission can attach conditions and obligations to its decision in order to ensure that the undertakings concerned will meet the commitments that they have engaged in vis-à-vis the Commission in order to ensure that their concentration is compatible with the internal market.

Market definition

As in cases with regard to abuse of dominance, market definition is crucial to merger cases: the Commission has to determine what are, and will be, the competitive conditions on the market, or markets, concerned before and after the merger between the parties involved, and what the position of the merging parties will be. Again, a product market and a geographic market must be defined in order to evaluate the effects on the relevant market. Apart from market shares, other instruments are also used to determine the risk of market power emerging. The most well-known of these is the Herfindahl-Hirschmann (HHI) index, which is based on the sum of the squared market shares. Both the absolute level of the HHI index is studied and the delta—that is to say the change that would result from the merger.[79] **8.70**

The geographical market definition is also relevant for the division of labour between the different competition authorities as well: if a merger has significant effects on a market in a Member State that exhibits all the characteristics of a distinct market and which does not constitute a significant part of the internal market then the national competition authority concerned may ask for a referral in order to handle the case itself. This is also referred to as the 'German clause'.[80] The reverse situation is also possible, where a national competition authority refers a merger that falls below the EU thresholds to the Commission (also called the 'Dutch clause'). A successful referral does require an effect on trade between the Member States which also threatens to significantly affect competition in the Member State or Member States involved.[81] It should be noted that not all merger procedures are based on market definition: for instance, in the event that, even in the most strictly (hypothetically) defined market, no problems would arise the market is left undefined. (See further the remarks on market definition made above under dominance at para 8.48.) **8.71**

---

[78] Commission Notice on remedies acceptable under the Council Reg (EC) No 139/2004 and under Commission Reg (EC) No 802/2004 [2008] OJ C267/1.

[79] Guidelines on the assessment of horizontal mergers under the Council Regulation on the control of concentrations between undertakings [2004] OJ C31/5, paras 14–21. A HHI of 1000 or less is considered harmless, a HHI above 2000 with a delta greaterthan 150 is considered problematic.

[80] Reg 139/2004, supra n 4, Art 9.

[81] ibid, Art 22.

Merger cases: health care (equipment) providers

8.72 Due to a combination of the European turnover thresholds and the relatively small scale of most health care providers in the EU (excepting the pharmaceutical sector where the Commission has vetted over 70 mergers so far) the Commission has taken only a limited number of formal merger decisions in health care. Here we discuss three mergers of health care (equipment) providers.

Blackstone/NHP

8.73 This case (2005) concerned the takeover, by the investment company Blackstone, of the undertaking NHP which leases locations for long term care in the United Kingdom.[82] Blackstone already owned Southern Cross, a provider of long term care to the elderly, likewise in the United Kingdom. In three regions of the United Kingdom there was a combined market share of between 50 and 60 per cent. The analysis of the Commission however focused on the question of whether the merger would have an impact on a significant part of the internal market because the competition authority, the Office of Fair Trading (OFT), in the United Kingdom had requested a referral. Because the three local areas most affected by the operation were found not constitute a substantial part of the internal market, the effects were indeed concentrated in the United Kingdom and the case was referred back to the OFT.

Johnson&Johnson/Guidant

8.74 This second phase merger case (2005) revolved around the takeover of Guidant, a company specialized in the manufacture of medical equipment for cardiology, by Johnson&Johnson, a large provider of medical equipment that also has a strong position in the market for cardiological equipment. Both companies had their business seat in the United States.[83] However, because they would jointly occupy a dominant position on a number of markets, the parties offered commitments—notably divesting certain businesses in the EU. This involved divestiture of all endovascular activities; the activities with regard to steerable guide wires of Guidant in the EEA; and either the activities of Johnson&Johnson with regard to 'harvesting' blood vessels and veins, or the heart surgical activities of Guidant or Guidant's activities with relation to harvesting veins. This served in order to help a competitor into the market and to address the expected problems in a structural manner. On this basis the merger was cleared as compatible with the internal market.

[82] *Blackstone (TBG CareCo)/NHP* (Case COMP/M3669) Commission Decision of 1 February 2005.

[83] *Johnson&Johnson/Guidant* (Case COMP/M.3687) Commission Decision 2006/40/EG [2006] OJ L173/16.

Fresenius/Helios

This (2005) case involved the takeover by Fresenius, a hospital chain operating worldwide, of Helios, a German hospital chain. Both operated emergency aid clinics as well rehabilitation clinics in Germany.[84] The Commission did not proceed to a formal market definition as it found that given the lack of overlapping activities even the narrowest market definition (looking at even more specialized hospitals) would not result in competition issues. On the national market the parties would have a market share of less than five per cent, while both parties were active in a very low number of local markets. Hence the merger was declared compatible with the internal market. 8.75

Evaluation

Although we have discussed only a few mergers the pattern is relatively clear. In all three of these cases, health care providers with worldwide operations were concerned which had cast their eye on markets in the EU. As liberalization in the EU proceeds (as we expect eventually it will) this constellation is likely to appear more frequently. Insofar as this increased frequency would promote effective, efficient, and well capitalized entry that would be a welcome development from a liberalization perspective. 8.76

Pharmaceuticals cases

For the sake of comprehensiveness we will now cover several of the pharmaceutical mergers, of which the Commission has handled a large number, since the coming into force of the original merger control Regulation in 1989 (now superseded by Regulation 139/2004). This is a health care sector where consolidation is already well advanced. 8.77

Astra/Zeneca

This concerned the merger (1999) between two undertakings from, respectively, Sweden and the United Kingdom, that were active in research and development, production, and sales of pharmaceutical products (in addition Astra produced medical equipment and Zeneca produced agricultural chemical products).[85] The definition of the product markets was based on the anatomical therapeutic categorization that is used by the World Health Organization (WHO). The parties made commitments to divest a number of activities (the production of combination beta blockers in the entire EEA and a worldwide license for a certain local anaesthetic) 8.78

[84] *Fresenius/Helios* (Case COMP/M.4010) Commission Decision of 8 December 2005 [2006] OJ C26/9.

[85] *Astra/Zeneca* (Case COMP/M.1403) Commission Decision of 26 February 1999 [1999] OJ C335/3.

or to grant third parties sales licenses (regular beta blockers in Sweden and Norway). On this basis the merger was considered compatible.

Novartis/Hexal

8.79 The merger case, *Novartis/Hexal* (2005), between the Swiss undertaking Novartis and the German undertaking Hexal (and its sister undertaking EON labs in the United States) concerned not just branded pharmaceuticals but also generic pharmaceuticals, and over the counter drugs as well as prescription drugs.[86] Concerning generics this combination would even become the leading market participant in Europe. The conditions that were eventually imposed were that: for calcitonines, Hexal's product Calcihexal had to be sold off in Poland; for topical anti-rheumatics, Hexal's product Diclac had to be sold off in Germany; and, with regard to medicines against gout, Hexal's product Apurin had to be sold off in Denmark (as well as possibly, at the buyer's request, Hexal's product Allopurinol). Just as the *Astra/Zeneca* case did, the *Novartis/Hexal* case demonstrates that the Commission is likely to define pharmaceutical markets painstakingly in product markets and (usually national) geographical markets and to carefully craft its remedies accordingly.

GlaxoSmithKline/Stiefel laboratories

8.80 This case (2009) regarded a merger between an undertaking with its business seat in the United Kingdom, (GlaxoSmithKline (GKS)) and another in the United States (Stiefel).[87] Both were active not just in the area of pharmaceuticals but also in producing other health care products for consumers. The noteworthy aspect of this case is that apart from the limited horizontal overlap between the parties their vertical relationships were also examined. This occurred because both parties were active not only in the production of drugs under contract for third parties but also in marketing drugs to consumers. However the Commission determined there was no risk of a significant restriction of competition and declared the merger compatible with the internal market.

Evaluation

8.81 As is already evident from this limited selection of cases the pharmaceutical sector is at a fundamentally different stage from the other health care providers. Here we find a very large scale industry with a reach that covers the entire EU and/or the rest of the world. The geographical markets however still tend to be national due to the existence of national social security systems and the concomitant price regulation. Hence interaction between national regulatory regimes and EU competition policy occurs.

[86] *Novartis/Hexal* (Case COMP/M.3751) Commission Decision of 27 May 2005.
[87] *GlaxoSmithKline/Stiefel laboratories* (Case COMP/M.5530) Commission Decision [2009] OJ C246/6.

To sum up, in the cases on mergers between pharmaceutical companies the Commission's investigations concentrate on the consequences of the mergers for competition between original and generic medicines and for research and development. Further, a couple of hospital mergers and mergers of companies that offer hospital related products or services were notified to the Commission. Given the low markets shares and the limited overlap of the activities of the parties concerned, the Commission cleared these mergers and was, as a result, not forced to decide on tensions between competition and health care objectives.[88] In some cases, the parties to the merger solved competition problems resulting from overlap of health care activities by relying on a classic method, ie offering remedies.[89] Hence, the Commission was not called upon to deal with tensions between competition and health care issues. What is more, so far the EU courts have not delivered any judgments on merger cases that have involved health care operators. **8.82**

Although the case law of the European courts and Commission Decisions are silent on the relationship between competition and health care objectives, the Guidelines issued by the Commission on horizontal and non-horizontal mergers shed some light on reasons that may be invoked in order to justify restrictions of competition.[90] Would these guidelines be useful in merger cases that involve a clash between competition and health care objectives? **8.83**

In its Guidelines the Commission states that efficiencies may make the Commission decide that a merger is compatible with the internal market, if the consumers are not worse off as a result of the merger.[91] Hence the point of departure is the consumer welfare test. The Commission points out that cost reduction and gains in the sphere of research and development are regarded as efficiencies. In the approach set out by the Commission, in the Guidelines, mainly benefits of an economic nature are regarded as justification for competition restrictions caused by mergers. However we will have to see whether referring to efficiencies will resolve tensions between competition and health care objectives in merger cases that may be related to securing or improving quality, to minimum scale required to perform certain types of operations, or to vertical integration. After all, these kinds of problems are rooted in non-market concerns. **8.84**

[88] See eg *Rozier/BHS* (Case COMP/M.4788) Commission Decision [2007] OJ C276/3; *Nycomed Group/Altana Pharma* (Case Case COMP/M.4418) Commission Decision [2007] OJ C38/1; and European Commission Press release IP/05/1553, *Mergers: Commission approves acquisition of Helios Kliniken GmbH by Fresenius AG* (Brussels, 9 December 2005).

[89] See eg *APW/APSA/Nordic Capital/CAPIO* (Case COMP/M.4367) Commission Decision [2007] OJ C176/2;and *Nordic Capital/ConvaTec* (Case COMP/M.5190) Commission Decision [2008] OJ C206/6.

[90] Guidelines of the Commission on the assessment of horizontal mergers under the Council Regulation on the control of concentrations between undertakings [2004] OJ C31/5.

[91] ibid, point 79.

F. EU and National Competition Rules

8.85 Below we will look at several aspects of the relationship between EU competition law and national (competition) law. This mainly concerns the *effet utile* (or useful effect) as well as the so-called 'CIF' jurisprudence (discussed at para 8.98) and the question of when public involvement in the markets protects the undertakings to which it applies from the competition rules (the 'state action doctrine'). The powers of national competition authorities with regard to the EU competition rules will also be addressed briefly. It should be noted that two Member States, the United Kingdom[92] and the Netherlands, have set up specialized regulatory authorities to supervise competition and protect consumer interests in health care.

National and EU competition law

8.86 All EU Member States now have national competition authorities (NCAs), which are empowered and obliged to apply Articles 101 and 102 TFEU in cases where trade between the Member States may be affected.[93] In such cases the Commission must be notified, and may itself take control of the case at any point where it believes this is warranted.[94] Amicus curiae interventions by the Commission in national court proceedings are also foreseen.[95] The NCAs are also members of the so-called 'network of EU competition authorities' (ECN) that is coordinated by the European Commission. These are the results of the modernization of EU antitrust rules based on Regulation 1/2003 which combines rationalization (a greater emphasis on economic reasoning) and prioritization (more emphasis on hard core cartels) with systemic reform based on a combination of decentralization and coordination. Meanwhile all Member States have also adopted national competition laws, which are often carbon copies of Articles 101 and 102 TFEU (a process called spontaneous harmonization). According to Regulation 1/2003 these national rules may not be stricter than the EU rules, unless they apply to unilateral conduct.[96] (That is, variations on abuse of market power and fair trading rules.) Hence, the national competition authorities have to apply both EU competition law and national competition rules inspired by their Treaty equivalents.

[92] See for a description of the work of the UK body; R Curran and A Taylor 'Regulating the Advertising of Patient Services in the NHS in England' [2011] *European Journal of Consumer Law* 777.

[93] Council Reg (EC) No 1/2003, supra n 1, Arts 3 and 5.

[94] ibid, Arts 11 and 12. cf Commission Notice on cooperation within the Network of Competition Authorities [2004] OJ C101/43.

[95] Commission Notice on the co-operation between the Commission and the courts of the EU Member States in the application of Articles 81 and 82 EC [2004] OJ C101/54.

[96] ibid, Art 3(2).

As discussed, due to the ECJ's settled case law on the concept of an undertaking, the door is wide open for applying competition law to health care cases. This is a significant finding for the NCAs, since they are obliged to interpret the concept of undertaking in the light of this case law. This is not only true for Article 101 and Article 102 TFEU cases but also in matters involving the national competition rules. After all, these national rules are often modelled on EU competition law, which implies that the national concept of undertaking is frequently identical to the one developed in the ECJ's jurisprudence. As the majority of the health care cases are of a national or sub-national nature, the national competition authorities are required to apply the broad concept of undertaking and as a result to develop health care-specific approaches to competition law.[97] **8.87**

Guidance

As mentioned, the European Commission is at the centre of the network of national regulators (ECN) and can trump the procedures of the NCAs by taking over in important cases (provided always that there is an effect on trade between the Member States), or in cases where its views differ significantly from that of the NCA involved. Policy convergence is actively promoted within the ECN. At the same time undertakings have to perform self-evaluation of their agreements and national courts may be called upon to decide issues of EU competition law. Consequently the Commission has taken upon itself to provide extensive and regularly updated guidance on such issues as vertical and horizontal restraints and exclusionary abuses.[98] On vertical and horizontal mergers (even though these are not covered by the modernization of antitrust) the Commission has likewise issued detailed explanatory communications.[99] Market definition has also been the subject of a 1997 Commission Notice, albeit arguably now outdated.[100] **8.88**

So far, sectoral guidance remains relatively rare and where it exists is not always kept up to date,[101] albeit with the significant recent exceptions of distribution agreements **8.89**

---

[97] J van de Gronden and W Sauter [2011], supra n 21.

[98] Commission, Guidelines on the application of Article 81(3) of the Treaty [2004] OJ C101/97; Commission Reg 330/2010 of 20 April 2010 on the application of Article 101(3) of the Treaty on the Functioning of the European Union to categories of vertical agreements and concerted practices [2010] OJ L102/1; Commission, Guidelines on Vertical Restraints [2010] OJ C130/1; Commission, Guidelines on the applicability of Article 81 to horizontal co-operation agreements [2001] OJ C3/2; Guidance on enforcement against exclusionary conduct, supra n 67.

[99] Guidelines on the assessment of non-horizontal mergers under the Council Regulation on the control of concentrations between undertakings [2008] OJ C265/6; Guidelines on the assessment of horizontal mergers under the Council Regulation on the control of concentrations between undertakings [2004] OJ C31/5.

[100] Notice on market definition, supra n 59.

[101] eg Notice from the Commission on the application of the competition rules to the postal sector and on the assessment of certain State measures relating to postal services [1998] OJ C39/2.

in the automobile industry[102] and regarding the insurance industry.[103] Other exceptions are the liberalized network sectors such as electronic communications where, during the initial liberalization phase and the transition period, more guidance tends to be provided.[104] In any event, apart from the general guidance just mentioned, there is no specific guidance available to NCAs applying the EU competition rules to the health care sector, even while the broad application of the concept of undertaking opens the previously sheltered field up to application of the competition rules. Likewise in the state aid field—where by contrast there is a wide range of sectoral guidance documents[105]—the Commission does not provide specifics for health care.

Effet utile

8.90 Given the degree of government involvement in health care the *effet utile* (useful effect) case law is relevant. This is the case law which demonstrates that Member States may infringe their duty of sincere cooperation under Article 4(3) TEU if a Member State, by means of its regulation, requires or encourages the adoption of agreements, decisions, or concerted practices contrary to Article 101 TFEU or reinforces their effects, or where it divests its own rules of the character of legislation by delegating to private economic operators responsibility for taking decisions affecting the economic sphere.[106] The corollary of this doctrine is that if collusive behaviour is imposed on undertakings by public authorities, the private parties concerned accordingly escape liability under the competition rules (because they may invoke a 'state action defence'), unless they had sufficient margin of freedom to engage in some competition but snuffed this out at their own initiative.[107]

8.91 In the *Belgian dentists* (2008) case, a dentist established in Belgium had submitted before the national court that advertising is an indispensable instrument for free

[102] Commission Reg (EU) 461/2010 on the application of Article 101(3) of the Treaty on the Functioning of the European Union to categories of vertical agreements and concerted practices in the motor vehicle sector [2010] OJ L129/52.

[103] Commission Reg (EC) 267/2010 of 24 March 2010 on the application of Article 101(3) of the Treaty to certain categories of agreements, decisions and concerted practices in the insurance sector [2010] OJ L83/1.

[104] Commission, Guidelines on market analysis and the assessment of significant market power under the Community regulatory framework for electronic communications networks and services [2002] OJ C165/6; Notice on the application of the competition rules to access agreements in the telecommunications sector—framework, relevant markets and principles [1998] OJ C265/2; Guidelines on the application of EEC competition rules in the telecommunications sector [1991] OJ C233/2.

[105] With (sometimes multiple) separate documents covering agriculture, audiovisual production, broadband broadcasting, the coal industry, electricity, financial services, fisheries, postal services, shipbuilding, steel, synthetic fibres, and transport.

[106] Case 267/86 *Pascal Van Eycke v ASPA* [1988] ECR 4769.

[107] Joined Cases C-359/95 P and C-379/95 P *Commission and France v Ladbroke Racing Ltd* [1997] ECR I-6265.

economic competition.[108] Hence, invoking the combined provisions of (now) Articles 4(3) TEU and 101 TFEU, he relied on the judgment in *Van Eycke* (1988)[109] to assert that—in view of the obligation upon the Member States not to introduce or maintain in force measures which may render ineffective the competition rules applicable to undertakings—the part of the criminal proceedings brought against him that related to advertising in health care matters was unfounded.

The national court, in its reference to the ECJ for a preliminary ruling, relied on the Opinion of Advocate General (AG) Jacobs in *Pavlov* (2000), that: **8.92**

> Owing to the heterogeneity of the professions and the specificities of the market in which they operate, it is necessary to assess, on a case by case basis, whether a restriction of conduct leads in fact on the market in issue to a restriction on competition within the meaning of Article 81 EC [now Article 101 TFEU].[110]

This assessment is to be carried out in the light of other Treaty provisions, such as Articles 168 and 169 TFEU on the protection of public health and consumer protection, respectively.

In its short judgment the ECJ had no hesitation in ruling that there was no link between the 1958 legislation barring advertising for dental services and a private restrictive agreement. As the AG had confirmed, there was no evidence in the documents before the Court to suggest that the law in question reinforced a pre-existing agreement and the referring court provided no indication as to the circumstances in which the relevant legislation was adopted, that would have supported the assumption that Belgium had delegated to economic operators responsibility for taking a decision on advertising in the dental care sector and that the legislation of 1958 simply codified that decision. **8.93**

Advocate General Bot took the view that a ban on all advertising to promote the provision of health care services was liable to create a greater obstacle for professionals from other Member States than for those from the host Member State. A law of a Member State such as the applicable Belgian Law of 1958 therefore constituted a restriction within the meaning of Article 49 TFEU. However, he opined that the restriction was justified on the ground of the protection of public health: **8.94**

> (...) where the national legislation in question does not have the effect of prohibiting dental care providers from giving, in a telephone directory or other source of information accessible by the public, basic details, free from enticements or incentives, making known their existence as professionals, such as their name, the activities they are permitted to pursue, the place where they pursue them, their hours of business and their contact details.[111]

---

[108] Case C-446/05 *Belgian dentists*, supra n 43.

[109] Case 267/86 *Van Eycke*, supra n 106.

[110] Joined Cases C-180/98 to C-184/98 *Pavel Pavlov et al v Stichting Pensioenfonds Medische Specialisten (Pavlov)* [2000] ECR I-6451, Opinion of AG Jacobs, para 89.

[111] Case C-446/05 *Belgian Dentists*, supra n 43, Opinion of AG Bot, para 124.

8.95 The ECJ however did not examine the application of Article 49 TFEU on establishment at all. This Belgian case shows—in line with settled case law[112]—that for the *effet utile* doctrine to be applicable a link should exist between, on the one hand, the restrictive state measures concerned and, on the other hand, particular practices of undertakings.

8.96 In other Member States, such as the Netherlands, tariff setting based on agreements between the government and bodies of medical practitioners may be vulnerable to the *effet utile* rule if restrictive agreements between the practitioners are promoted by the government in the process. After all, in the light of the *effet utile* doctrine it is questionable whether tariff agreements concluded between undertakings are compatible with EU competition law (in so far as they affect the trade between Member States). The limits of what may be permissible are set out in the *Arduino* (2002) and *Cipolla* (2006) cases on the remuneration of Italian lawyers.[113] These cases show that, apart from the possibility for public authorities to intervene *ex ante* (before a particular measure is taken) in the general interest, it must be possible for public authorities to take a decision in place of the one proposed by market parties as well (eg for judges to adjust rates at a later stage).

The direct effect of the doctrine of *effet utile*

8.97 It is important to note that the EU competition rules have direct effect. This means that they can be invoked by citizens before national courts. In addition, as already mentioned above, the NCAs are obliged to enforce Articles 101 and 102 TFEU at national level in cases that have a European dimension:[114]

> Where the competition authorities of the Member States or national courts apply national competition law to agreements, decisions by associations of undertakings or concerted practices within the meaning of Article 81(1) of the Treaty [now Article 101(1) TFEU] which may affect trade between Member States within the meaning of that provision, they shall also apply Article 81 of the Treaty to such agreements, decisions or concerted practices. Where the competition authorities of the Member States or national courts apply national competition law to any abuse prohibited by Article 82 of the Treaty [now Article 102 TFEU], they shall also apply Article 82 of the Treaty.

Application of EU provisions having direct effect by public bodies is in fact inherent in the concept of direct effect.

---

[112] See eg Case C-245/91 *Criminal proceedings v Ohra Schadeverzekeringen NV* [1993] I-5851; and Case C-2/91 *Criminal proceedings v Wolf W. Meng* [1993] I-5751.

[113] Case C-35/99 *Criminal proceedings against Manuele Arduino* [2002] ECR I-1529; Joined Cases C-94/04 and C-202/04 *Federico Cipolla v Rosaria Portolese and Stefano Macrino and Claudia Capoparte against Roberto Meloni* [2006] ECR I-11421. On the same problem under free movement see: Case C-565/08 *Commission v Italy* [2011] judgment of 29 March 2011 (nyr).

[114] Reg 1/2003, supra n 1, Art 3(1).

The *CIF* (2003) case is relevant here as it creates a supplementary responsibility under EU law for NCAs as well as (arguably) other national regulators.[115] In *Fratelli Costanzo* (1989) the ECJ had already decided that all public bodies, not only domestic courts but also national administrative authorities (such as municipalities), were obliged to apply provisions of EU law having direct effect and to set aside those national (legislative) rules that were at odds with these EU provisions.[116] In *CIF* this was confirmed with regard to the *effet utile* doctrine discussed above, which means that the undertakings that had so far been protected by the state action doctrine would henceforth become liable under EU competition law (albeit not for the period preceding intervention by the NCA). It could be argued that this obligation not only rests with the national authorities (the NCAs), that have powers to apply Articles 101 and 102 TFEU, but also with other authorities such as health care regulators (which may for instance have national powers regarding significant market powers 'SMP') who, when acting within the limits of their procedural autonomy, have the authority and, as result, the duty to take action against national measures that are in violation of Article 4(3) TEU in conjunction with Articles 101 and 102 TFEU. 8.98

In any event, it is clear that on the basis of the *effet utile* doctrine that NCAs may set aside national health care interventions that are of a mixed public-private nature. This possibility raises concerns as EU law does not provide guidance on whether and to what extent health care objectives are accommodated in the application of EU competition law. An NCA and a national health care body that is (partly) of a private nature but also legitimized by public law may be involved in a dispute on the compatibility of a particular national measure with EU competition law. An example could be collectively negotiated doctors' rates (as since *Pavlov* doctors are in principle regarded as undertakings) backed up by a related public adjustment of hospital budgets with a view to containing overall costs. For now the direction that the Commission and the EU courts would take is not clear. Hence it is likely that preliminary questions to the ECJ will play an important role in this field—possibly to provide backing for national authorities that are hesitant to face down both their governments and entrenched lobbies singlehandedly based on EU law. 8.99

G. Conclusion

On the basis of this overview of EU competition law we can draw the following conclusions. The Commission and the EU courts apply the concept of undertaking 8.100

[115] Case C-198/01 *Consorzio Industrie Fiammiferi (CIF) v Autorità Garante della Concorrenza e del Mercato* [2003] ECR I-8055.

[116] Case 103/88 *Fratelli Costanzo Spa v Comune di Milano en Impresa Ing. Lodigani Spa* [1989] ECR 1839.

in a functional and expansive manner. Since *Pavlov* and *Glöckner* this means that most providers of health care are likely to be caught by the competition rules because they provide (economic) services (potentially) in competition. However, whether this also applies to health care insurers and to public law bodies managing health care is much less clear. So far the *AOK* and *FENIN* cases suggest these entities are not covered if they manage a scheme that is predominately based on solidarity. But the precise lines of demarcation are not easy to draw, and these cases remain difficult to square with some of the other case law.

8.101 The combination of this expansive interpretation of the concept of undertaking in EU law, and the decentralization of the application of EU competition policy requires many NCAs to apply EU competition law to health care cases.[117] National courts will also be confronted more frequently with questions involving EU competition law, and undertakings must make self-assessments as to whether the legal exemption from the cartel prohibition of Article 101(3) TFEU applies. Unfortunately however, so far there is limited guidance from the EU when it comes to concrete sectoral issues. This is most likely because, with partial exception of pharmaceuticals, the health care sector in the EU (both insurance and provision) remains composed of tightly regulated national enclaves with limited cross-border activity. Hence the Commission has only had to come into action on few occasions—and may have few incentives to do so on its own account, given the political sensitivity of the sector. A significant exception is the *ONP* Decision (2010), a cartel case which was investigated in tandem with a freedom of establishment case that the Commission had launched in the same sector and Member State, *French Laboratories* (likewise decided in 2010), where the ECJ however found the contested ownership restrictions were justified.

8.102 Given the current division of powers between the EU and its Member States—the organization and delivery of health care is reserved to the Member States, whereas EU law provides for the rules of the market such as the competition rules—it is no surprise that the EU Courts and the Commission have construed health care as a market value. Yet as we have seen above the European institutions have only recently begun to adopt health care specific competition law precedents. Even if the gate to competition law has been opened by a broad interpretation of the concept of undertaking there is still not much sector specific precedent or guidance on the application of the prohibitions.[118] At the same time, some form of guidance could

[117] cf J Lear, E Mossialos and B Karl, supra n 7; A Taylor et al, 'Healthcare and competition law: an emerging area – overview of cases by European national competition authorities' [2011] No33647 E-Competitions, special healthcare issue of 5 January 2011, <www.concurrences.com> accessed 24 February 2012. Monographs on individual Member States are also emerging eg T Lübbig and M Klasse, *Kartellrecht im Pharma- und Gesundheitssektor* (Baden-Baden: Nomos, 2007), for Germany and; D Fornaciari, S Callens and E Schokkaert, *Ziekenhuizen, Mededingingsrecht en Recht op Kwaliteitsvolle Zorg* (Antwerp: Intersentia, 2010), on Belgium.

[118] J van de Gronden (2011); and J van de Gronden and W Sauter [2011], supra n 21.

be important not just for health care but for the other key parts of the welfare state as well (such as education, social services, and pensions) that are similarly likely to be more affected by the internal market and the competition rules in the near future. Hence in their application of the EU competition principles, competition authorities and courts will have to show that these principles are equal to the challenge of offering this key sector a competition law framework that is based on a coherent approach and strikes an adequate balance between competition concerns and health care objectives.

9

STATE AID AND SERVICES OF GENERAL ECONOMIC INTEREST

A. Introduction

Distortions of competition

The EU state aid regime is designed to prevent the distortion of competitive conditions in the EU's internal market that may arise because public authorities grant and finance economic advantages to certain products or undertakings.[1] 9.01

[1] cf J van de Gronden, 'Financing healthcare in EU law: Do the European state aid rules write out an effective prescription for integrating competition law with healthcare?' [2009] *Competition Law Review* 5; W Sauter and J van de Gronden, 'State Aid, Services of General Economic Interest and Universal Service in Healthcare' [2011] *European Competition Law Review* 615. More generally

One can distinguish at least three kinds of distortions of competition induced by state aid. First, state aid, by interfering with the allocation of rents through markets, may have long-term dynamic effects on the incentive to invest and compete. Second, at a more specific level, state aids may affect competition in the product market and trigger different responses by competitors depending on the circumstances. Third, state aid may affect competition in the input markets and in particular the location of investment.

9.02 All these distortions of competition will affect the distribution of economic activities among sectors and between Member States and will have detrimental impact on the internal market, by affecting trade and disturbing the efficient allocation of activities across national borders. In fact, the very possibility of state aid in one Member State being authorized may create incentives for other Member States to also make use of state aid measures in order to strategically attract activity to their territories, thereby prompting the risk of a subsidy race. Given that the health care sector is the recipient of considerable financial support provided either directly or indirectly through state measures or resources such as insurance funds which may be subject to state control, the relevance of the EU state aid regime to the health care sector is potentially of great importance. Nevertheless, as explained in this chapter, the full force of the EU state aid regime is somewhat tempered by the possibility of designating the services in question as 'services of general economic interest'.

Prohibition and exemption

9.03 Article 107 TFEU provides that any aid granted by a Member State or through state resources in any form whatsoever is prohibited. This is not however an absolute prohibition; the Commission may according to Article 107(2) or (3) TFEU declare aid to be compatible with the internal market. The power to do so is exclusive to the Commission. Article 108 TFEU sets out the procedural requirements regarding the notification of new aids to the Commission as well as the duty of the latter, together with the Member States, to keep existing aid under constant review.

9.04 Given the degree of Member State involvement in health care markets the state aid regime is important for any national health care system that relies at least in part on undertakings to provide health care services or health insurance (see Chapter 8 for the definition of undertaking). Although it may be argued that cross-border trade of health care services is not highly developed, the EU state aid rules apply even if their impact on trade is minimal. In *Altmark* (2003), discussed in detail below at para 9.32, the ECJ held that subsidies for local transport services could distort competition and effect trade between the Member States as competitors from other

cf A Biondi, P Eeckhout and J Flynn (eds), *The Law of State Aid in the European Union* (Oxford: Oxford University Press, 2004).

Member States would have less chance of providing those services within that locality.[2]

Similarly in *Heiser* (2005) certain tax exemptions for medical practitioners were considered to affect trade even though the aid was intended to compensate dentists in Austria who had been subject to VAT (value added tax) on their services whereas their competitors in other Member States were exempt from VAT.[3] The argument that medical practitioners who benefited from the aid measure did not face competition based on prices was also rejected. The ECJ held that even if the choice of a medical practitioner by patients may be influenced by criteria other than price, such as quality and trust, the fact remained that the price was likely to have an influence on the choice of practitioner by the patient, particularly when the patient paid most of the cost out of his or her own pocket.[4] **9.05**

Centralization

In contrast to the three policies discussed in Chapter 8 in relation to cartels, abuse of dominance, and mergers, the state aid regime generally does not have a national equivalent, albeit that many of the accession states were required to entrust powers to deal with state aid to national bodies prior to their accession.[5] This is generally logical, not just because national governments would then have to police themselves (although it might be feasible for the national government to police regional or local bodies, or for a specialized body to assume such tasks) but also in view of the political sensitivity of state subsidies in general. Nevertheless EU state aid policy plays an increasingly important role in limiting public intervention in markets as the Commission has developed its policy to promote less, and more effective, aid at Member State level. Furthermore, apart from the centralized enforcement by the Commission, interested parties can rely upon direct effect of Article 108(3) TFEU, and bring actions before national courts, which can in turn establish whether there is aid that has not been notified, or has been granted in breach of the 'standstill' provision (the requirement not to grant aid prior to Commission approval), and hence is per se illegal. Thus, some degree of decentralized enforcement is possible and indeed occurs. **9.06**

[2] Case C-280/00 *Altmark Trans GmbH and Regierungspräsidium Magdeburg v Nahverkehrsgesellschaft Altmark GmbH, and Oberbundesanwalt beim Bundesverwaltungsgericht* (Altmark) [2003] ECR I-7747, para 75.

[3] Case C-172/03 *Wolfgang Heiser v Finanzamt Innsbruck* [2005] ECR I-1627, paras 52–54.

[4] ibid, paras 56–67.

[5] See further, J Rapp, 'State aid in the accession countries' in L Hancher, T Ottervanger and P Slot, *EU State Aids* (5th edn, London: Sweet & Maxwell, 2012) Ch 5.

Services of general economic interest

9.07 Finally, we will briefly address the concept of services of general economic interest (SGEI) in the context of state aid. Such services can be designated by the Member States in accordance with subsidiarity, and in the absence of any limited list or definition existing at EU level. The main legal basis for SGEI is found in Article 106(2) TFEU which provides for an exception to the Treaty rules for undertakings charged with providing SGEI in so far as observing these rules would obstruct the performance of their public service task. The Commission has recently (December 2011) adopted a new package of measures with regard to SGEI and state aid based on Article 106 TFEU.

9.08 Below we will first look briefly at state aid procedures, followed by the concepts of state aid and of SGEI, both with a discussion of the key health care cases.

B. Procedures

Compatible aid

9.09 As noted, the Commission has exclusive competence to declare a state aid measure to be compatible with Article 107(2) or (3) TFEU. Article 107(2) TFEU concerns the so-called automatic exemptions of aid with a social character; aid to repair the damage of natural disasters; and aid to certain regions of Germany that suffered as a result of the post-war partition. Article 107(3) TFEU gives the Commission a discretionary power to assess the compatibility of the national measure as guaranteeing an objective of common interest. Article 108(3)(c) TFEU provides in particular that 'aid to facilitate the development of certain economic activities or of certain economic areas, where such aid does not adversely affect trading conditions to an extent contrary to the common interest' can be declared compatible.

Notification

9.10 A Member State is obliged, in accordance with Article 108(3) TFEU, to notify the measure for clearance and must observe the 'standstill' obligation, that is to say the measure must not be put into effect (thus the aid cannot be granted) prior to a positive decision from the Commission. The Procedural Regulation of 1999[6] codifies the procedural rules and Regulation 794/2004/EC sets out further implementing rules.[7] In addition the Commission has published guidance on simplified

[6] Council Reg 659/1999 of 22 March 1999 laying down detailed rules for the application of Article 93 of the EC Treaty [1999] OJ L83/1.

[7] Commission Reg (EC) 794/2004 of 21 April 2004 implementing Council Reg (EC) 659/1999 laying down detailed rules for the application of Article 93 of the EC Treaty [2004] OJ L140/1.

notification.[8] A detailed explanation of these provisions is outside the scope of this book, however.[9]

Following notification the Commission has, in accordance with Article 4 of the Procedural Regulation, two months to reach a decision on whether the aid as notified is compatible. If it is unable to conclude that the measure is compatible with Article 107(2) or (3) TFEU the Commission is then required to open a formal investigation and it should strive to conclude this phase within 18 months. It may then decide that the measure is compatible or only compatible subject to certain conditions or it may conclude that the aid is incompatible. The time limits do not apply to non-notified aid. **9.11**

The Commission can only require recovery of illegal aid following a formal investigation. A national court however, once it has established that the measure is aid, can order suspension or recovery of aid at any point in time—it need not await the Commission's final decision, and even if the aid is subsequently declared compatible this does not remove the 'illegality' of the measure. A national court may therefore still impose a recovery order and require the repayment of that portion of the aid which had been paid out prior to the final ruling on its compatibility. **9.12**

The Commission may become aware of non-notified aid either as a result of its inquiries or it may be alerted to the potential infringement of the state aid rules as a result of a complaint—usually by a competitor of the beneficiary. The Commission is under a duty to examine a complaint and should take a final position on it. It is not however under a duty to investigate every complaint. **9.13**

Judicial review

It should be noted at this point that when it comes to challenging a Commission decision, before the EU courts, the procedural rights of third parties—in other words competitors as well as beneficiaries of state aid—are generally rather restricted, because state aid decisions are addressed to Member States. In order to challenge a Commission decision, a third party has to satisfy the so-called *Plaumann* (1962) test, meaning that it must show that although the decision is addressed to the Member State, nevertheless that decision is of direct and individual concern to it:[10] **9.14**

> Persons other than those to whom a decision is addressed may only claim to be individually concerned if that decision affects them by reason of certain attributes which are peculiar to them or by reason of circumstances in which they are differentiated

[8] Annex II (Simplified notification form) to Commission Reg (EC) 271/2008 of 30 January 2008 amending Reg (EC) 794/2004 implementing Council Reg (EC) 659/1999 laying down detailed rules for the application of Article 93 of the EC Treaty [2008] OJ L82/1.

[9] See P Slot, 'Administrative procedure', in L Hancher et al, supra n 5, Ch 25.

[10] Case 25/62 *Plaumann & Co. v Commission* [1962] ECR English Spec Ed 95.

from all other persons and by virtue of these factors distinguishes them individually just as in the case of the person addressed.

9.15 The jurisprudence of the EU courts in relation to standing is highly complex, but it suffices to say that the Commission has not been overly keen to be drawn into the politically sensitive area of national health care financing. As a result it has not always been enthusiastic in taking up and investigating complaints by competitors in this sector.[11]

Asklepios Kliniken

9.16 In the German hospitals case, *Asklepios Kliniken* (2007), a number of private hospitals had complained that German public hospitals received state aid by way of regional support—mostly in the form of unlimited guarantees.[12] The complainant asked the Commission in January 2003 to look into the allegedly unlawful conduct on the basis of the information which it had provided to the Commission and to take measures to suspend the aid until such time as the Commission had taken a final decision. The Commission initially refused to take a decision, and ultimately informed the complainants that its position on the matter was covered by the then draft Decision of 2005 on Compensation for SGEIs (discussed below). The complainants challenged the Commission's approach before the General Court. They argued that the Commission had used an unreasonable delay in responding to their complaint, and further that the final position taken by the Commission was not a legitimate method of dealing with their complaint.

9.17 The General Court ruled that the general rules on legal review allowed legal standing against decisions as well as refusals to take a decision:

> Articles 230 EC and 232 EC [Articles 263 and 265 TFEU] prescribe one and the same remedy. It follows that, just as the fourth paragraph of Article 230 EC allows individuals to bring an action for annulment against a measure of an institution not addressed to them provided that the measure is of direct and individual concern to them, the third paragraph of Article 232 EC must be interpreted as also entitling them to bring an action for failure to act against an institution which they claim has failed to adopt a measure which would have concerned them in the same way.[13]

The General Court then added:

> (...) Article 1(h) of Regulation No 659/1999, (...) states that term 'interested party' is to mean 'any Member State and any person, undertaking or association of

[11] A complaint to the Commission concerning the funding of French public hospitals was lodged on 10 December 2003, and an appeal against the Commission's decision was lodged before the General Court: Case T-397/03 [2004] OJ C47/58 but subsequently removed from the Court's register—see Resolution of the General Court [2006] OJ C22/25.

[12] Case T-167/04 *Asklepios Kliniken GmbH v Commission* [2007] ECR II-2379.

[13] ibid, para 45; with reference to Case 15/70 *Amedeo Chevalley v Commission* [1970] ECR 975, para 6; and Case T-395/04 *Air One SpA v Commission* [2006] ECR II-1343, para 25.

undertakings whose interests might be affected by the granting of aid, in particular the beneficiary of the aid, competing undertakings and trade associations'.

Therefore, even a future or simply a potential competitor of the beneficiary of the contested aid must be deemed to be a party concerned within the meaning of Article 88(2) EC [Article 108 paragraph 2 TFEU].[14]

Nevertheless the General Court dismissed the action, as the adoption by the Commission of a decision of general scope, setting out abstract criteria for assessing the legality of state financing, does not by itself constitute a definition of its position by the Commission on a complaint concerning that financing. Only the actual application of those criteria by the Commission to the situations complained of can constitute a definition of position that creates legal standing.[15] Finally, the General Court held that the reasonableness of the duration of the investigation of a state aid complaint must be determined in relation to the particular circumstances of each case, its context, the various procedural stages, and the complexity of the case. Uncertainty about the (national) legal framework concerned may justify the Commission deferring its proceedings pending clarification.[16] **9.18**

Brussels' hospitals

In the *Brussels' hospitals* case,[17] discussed below, the private hospitals had lodged a state aid complaint in 2005 but the Commission again appeared reluctant to take up the case. The complainant therefore initiated an action for the annulment of the Commission's initial position that no aid was involved. Unusually, this action was subsequently suspended and withdrawn, following a request to the General Court by the Commission to provide it with a fixed period within which to finalize the procedures, and take a formal decision (see further below, at para 9.48), which has meanwhile been appealed.[18] **9.19**

Involvement in the initial investigation

These cases seem to show that third parties often face a protracted battle in attempting to engage the Commission in their attempts to challenge national funding measures, and in general the EU courts have not been prepared to relax the abovementioned *Plaumann* test. However, there is an exception to this in cases where the Commission takes a decision at the end of a so-called preliminary examination as **9.20**

[14] ibid, paras 49–50; with reference to Case C-225/91 *Matra v Commission* [1993] ECR I-3203, para 19; and Case T-395/04 *Air One v Commission*, supra n 13, para 39.

[15] ibid, paras 77–78.

[16] ibid, para 81.

[17] Decision of the Commission of 28 October 2009 with regard to state aid NN 54/2009 (ex CP 244/2005)—Belgium—financing of public hospitals of the IRIS-network of the Brussels capital region. cf the pending Case T-137/10 *Coordination bruxelloise d'Institutions sociales et de santé (CBI) v Commission* [2010] OJ C148/38.

[18] See for a description of these procedures, Case NN 54/2009, paras 1–10.

provided for in Article 4 of the Procedural Regulation 659/1999,[19] as opposed to a full or formal investigation as provided for in Article 7 of that Regulation. Here the courts have been prepared to relax the strict *Plaumann* test to a limited extent given that third parties have no right to participate in the preliminary phase. Hence third parties may have more scope to contest decisions to approve the measure as compatible aid or to declare the measure not to be aid following the first phase or preliminary investigation.

9.21 However at best, this will mean that the Commission must then go on to open the full procedure and give the third parties a right to submit observations. Hence involvement in the initial investigations is more like a due process 'right to be heard' than like participation as a party to the proceedings. There is no guarantee that the final decision at the end of this procedure will be in their favour. Once a final decision has been taken then the rights of third parties to subsequently challenge that decision before the EU courts are extremely circumscribed, however, and the *Plaumann* test is still applied strictly.[20]

C. The Concept of State Aid

The prohibition

9.22 The EU courts have interpreted the concept of state aid in Article 107(1) TFEU (which is in principle incompatible with the Treaty, in other words, prohibited) expansively. The concept of state aid encompasses, in the view of the EU courts, not only positive benefits such as subsidies but also interventions which mitigate the charges that are normally included in the budget of the company concerned.[21] Consistent with the goal-oriented or teleological nature of EU law, the form of the measure is irrelevant: it is its effect that is of importance. So, both the concept of state aid and the term undertaking (see Chapter 8) are subject to broad definition and, as a result, many national measures to finance the provision of health care may fall within the scope of the EU state aid regime.

The conditions for state aid

9.23 It is clear that the broad definitions given by the EU courts raise state aid issues in health care. Which conditions must be fulfilled for a measure to be caught by the

---

[19] Council Reg (EC) 659/1999 of 22 March 1999 laying down detailed rules for the application of Article 93 of the EC Treaty [1999] OJ L83/1.

[20] See for a full discussion P Slot 'Administrative procedure', in L Hancher et al, supra n 5, Ch 25.

[21] See Case 30/59 *De Gezamenlijke Steenkolenmijnen in Limburg v High Authority* [1961] ECR English Spec Ed 1; and Case C-39/94 *Syndicat français de l'Express international (SFEI)* et al *v La Poste* et al [1996] ECR I-3547.

prohibition contained in Article 107(1) TFEU (not to grant state aid to undertakings)? It is settled case law that this prohibition is applicable if a national measure (that is to say a measure adopted by any central, regional or local public authority as well as other decentralized bodies under the control of the state, including public undertakings), meets the following four cumulative conditions:

1. aid must be granted by the state or through state resources;
2. it must confer an economic advantage on particular (selected) undertakings (this is increasingly being seen as two separate conditions);
3. the aid must affect trade between the Member States; and
4. it must distort competition in the internal market.[22]

Although all these conditions are evidently important it is especially the second one (advantage/selectivity) that has been most controversial, both in general—in the wake of the *Altmark* (2003) judgment and its follow-up—and for health care in particular, where often payments in exchange for the provision of specific health services are likely to be concerned rather than outright grants to promote production in general. Does a financial measure which compensates for burdens or obligations imposed upon an undertaking amount to an economic advantage to it? This question was answered in varying terms by the Commission, the General Court and the ECJ prior to the landmark *Altmark* (2003) case which consolidated the case law (dealt with in more detail below, at para 9.32). **9.24**

The final two criteria, which are that the measure in question affects trade between the Member State and must distort competition in the internal market, are usually less controversial, and will be applied to health services as a matter of course, as in the *Heiser* case, discussed in the introduction. The first and second tests remain somewhat problematic and have been considered in a large body of case law, albeit outside the health care sector. These two tests will be discussed briefly here before going into the health care case law and the *Altmark* test. **9.25**

State resources

The EU courts have defined the concept of state resources widely to include not only direct subsidies or grants, but to cover any measure, whatever their source or destination. Moreover, resources which are under indirect state control may also be deemed to be 'state resources' for the purposes of Article 107(1) TFEU. This means in effect that public entities owned or controlled by the state, such as a national or regional health board, an independent equalization fund, or even a health care insurance company which is subject to state control, may be seen as providers of state aid. Hence if such a body was to confer an advantage on another undertaking, for example by allowing free medical services for its employees or preferential **9.26**

[22] cf Case C-475/99 *Firma Ambulanz Glöckner v Landkreis Südwestpfalz* [2001] ECR I-8089.

insurance premiums, then this may, assuming all the other conditions of Article 107(1) TFEU are met, be caught by the state aid rules.

9.27 In this context the Transparency Directive[23] is of key importance because it makes the transfers between Member States and undertakings verifiable. The Transparency Directive requires accounting separation as well as justified cost allocation and cost accounting of publicly funded activities; it applies to public funds made available directly by public authorities to the public undertakings concerned as well as public funds made available by public authorities through the intermediary of public undertakings or financial institutions. All undertakings charged with special or exclusive rights are covered—which would include such undertakings entrusted with a SGEI.

9.28 Nevertheless for state resources to be deemed to be state aid, it is necessary to establish that the decision to use those resources in a particular way can be imputed to the state—in other words that the undertaking or entity in question would not have used those resources in that particular way without state persuasion.

9.29 At the same time, Article 107(1) TFEU cannot apply to competitive advantages that were granted by the state but which do not involve any burden on the state or appropriation of private financial resources. For example, a state measure exempting small hospitals from complying with certain provisions of national employment protection legislation could be seen to confer an advantage on such firms in terms of employment costs as compared to larger hospitals but would not be caught by Article 107(1) TFEU.

Selectivity

9.30 Article 107(1) TFEU applies to aid for certain products or undertakings, so that only selective measures are caught by the state aid regime. A general measure reducing the level of health insurance premiums payable to the state or a state-backed fund and applicable across the entire economy would not be selective, whereas a state measure allowing certain sectors to benefit from a reduction in payments of such premiums would be deemed selective.

9.31 In applying the selectivity test it is often important to establish the actual beneficiary of the measure. In *Heiser* it was established that medical practitioners enjoyed a selective benefit in the form of a tax reduction. The argument that this advantage was systematically passed on by them to sickness insurance bodies was rejected.[24]

---

[23] Commission Dir 2006/111/EC of 16 November 2006 on the transparency of financial relations between Member States and public undertakings as well as on financial transparency within certain undertakings [2006] OJ L318/17.

[24] Case C-172/03 *Heiser*, supra n 3, paras 40 and 47.

The concept of advantage and the *Altmark* exception

The *Altmark* case concerned the licensing conditions for regional transport in Germany.[25] In this case the ECJ determined that if the undertaking concerned performed a universal service or public service obligation in exchange for the financing concerned there could be no question of state aid but only of compensation provided for performance of a service. In order to meet the four *Altmark* conditions: 9.32

1. the undertaking must have clearly defined public service obligations (PSO) to discharge;
2. the parameters for compensation must be established in advance in an objective and transparent manner;
3. compensation cannot exceed the costs of the PSO and a reasonable rate of return; and
4. the undertaking must be selected by public procurement procedures, or meet the standard of a comparable efficient undertaking.

Generally undertakings stumble at the hurdle of the 'procurement or efficiency' requirement that is the fourth *Altmark* condition. In the event that these cumulative conditions are not met there may be a finding of state aid, but there is still a possibility that this aid can be declared compatible with the internal market based on the SGEI exception of Article 106(2) TFEU. The Commission has, subsequent to the *Altmark* case, clarified its policy with regard to the application of Article 106(2) TFEU to compensation in the state aid context by means of its so-called SGEI package (at the time also known as the *Monti/Kroes* package, after the two Commissioners for Competition then responsible for its development). This consisted of a Commission Decision and a Framework of 2005,[26] which has meanwhile been updated by the Second *Altmark* package (also known as the *Almunia* package, after the current Commissioner for Competition).[27] 9.33

[25] Case C-280/00 *Altmark*, supra n 2. This pursued the line set out in Case C-53/00 *Ferring SA v Agence centrale des organismes de sécurité sociale (ACOSS)* [2001] ECR I-9067. cf F Louis and A Vallery, 'Ferring revisited: the *Altmark* Case and State Financing of Public Service Obligations' [2004] *World Competition* 53; A Sinnaeve, 'State Financing of Public Services: the Court's Dilemma in the *Altmark* Case' [2003] *European State Aid Law Quarterly* 351.

[26] Commission Decision of 28 November 2005 on the application of Article 86(2) of the EC Treaty to State aid in the form of public service compensation granted to certain undertakings entrusted with the operation of services of general economic interest [2005] OJ L312/67; Community framework for State aid in the form of public service compensation [2005] OJ C297/4.

[27] Communication from the Commission on the application of the European Union State aid rules to compensation granted for the provision of services of general economic interest (Brussels, 20 December 2011) COM(2011) 9404 final; Commission Decision of 20 December 2011 on the application of Article 106(2) of the Treaty on the Functioning of the European Union to State aid in the form of public service compensation granted to certain undertakings entrusted with the operation of services of general economic interest, COM (2011) 9380 final; Communication from the Commission on the European Union framework for State aid in the form of public service compensation (Brussels, 20 December 2011) COM(2011) 9406 final.

9.34 The first *Altmark* package was considered necessary because the *Altmark* ruling was not limited in time and therefore many financial schemes for the benefit of undertakings performing SGEIs were illegal as they could not meet the four cumulative *Altmark* criteria. The Decision and the Framework dispense with the fourth criterion but require individual notification above a turnover threshold, with a number of exceptions.

9.35 In the Decision, the duty to notify potential aid is lifted inter alia for all hospital care and, as of December 2011, all health and long term care (as well as a number of other types of social policy) that is designated as a SGEI, irrespective of the turnover of the recipient undertaking, and irrespective of the amount of aid. Notification is waived for all other undertakings which receive annual compensation for the service in question of less than €15 million. Hence as long as the conditions for exemption are satisfied the aid may be disbursed prior to Commission vetting so the normal standstill rule does not apply here.

9.36 The conditions for the SGEI exemption may be summarized as follows. First, there must be a genuine SGEI, entrusted by way of one or more official acts, the form of which may be determined by the Member State. The act or acts must specify in particular the precise nature and duration of the SGEI, the undertakings and territory concerned, the nature of any exclusive or special rights assigned to the undertaking, the parameters for calculating, controlling and reviewing the compensation, and the arrangements for avoiding and repaying any over-compensation.

9.37 Where a company carries out activities falling both inside and outside the scope of the SGEI, the internal accounts must show separately the costs and receipts associated with the SGEI and those associated with other services, as well as the parameters for allocating costs and revenues.

9.38 The Framework applies to those cases that do not benefit from the special regime of the Decision with regard to notification, and therefore must be notified and assessed individually for compatibility with Article 106(2) TFEU. However, as far as its substantive criteria are concerned the terms of the Framework are identical, that is to say with regard to the amount of compensation, the relevant costs to take into account, the meaning of reasonable rate of return, and over-compensation. Under the Framework, any over-compensation may be used to finance another SGEI operated by the same undertaking but any such transfer must be shown in the undertaking's accounts. The Member States must ensure that such transfers are subject to proper control and in this respect the transparency rules laid down in the Transparency Directive apply.[28] The Second *Altmark* package will be dealt with in more detail in the section on SGEIs.[29]

---

[28] Commission Dir 2006/111/EC, supra n 23.

[29] At the time of writing the *Altmark* package was subject to a review. See <http://ec.europa.eu/competition/consultations/2010_sgei/index_en.html> accessed 25 February 2012; W Sauter

It therefore follows that if a Member State can establish that the compensation for the provision of an SGEI meets all four *Altmark* criteria, the measure need not be notified. If one of these criteria is not met, but all the cumulative criteria of Article 107(1) TFEU are fulfilled, then the measure must be assessed to determine its compatibility with either Article 107(2) or (3) or Article 108 TFEU. This compatibility can be based on Article 106(2) TFEU, in accordance with the Commission Framework. Further guidance to the assessment of the compatibility of the aid with Article 106(2) is provided in a document on frequently asked questions produced by the Commission.[30] **9.39**

D. Case Law

Against this background we will discuss four important recent Commission Decisions concerning health care and state aid. These cases illustrate both the application of the *Altmark* criteria and the Commission's findings as to whether the measure in question can be classified as aid or not, as well as the application of the concept of SGEI and Article 106(2) TFEU to assessing the compatibility of the measure where it had indeed been deemed to be an aid within the meaning of Article 107(1) TFEU. **9.40**

Risk equalization: Ireland

This case concerned the Irish system of risk equalization between private providers of supplementary health care insurance who were subject to a public framework of open enrolment, lifetime cover, community rating, and minimum benefits.[31] According to the Commission the risk equalization system in principle met the four conditions for state aid in Article 107(1) TFEU. Although this concerned transfers between the insurers these were regarded as concerning state resources because it concerned contributions that were imposed by public law and managed and distributed by the State in accordance with those legal instruments.[32] **9.41**

'The Altmark package Mark II: New rules for state aid and the compensation of services of general economic interest' [2012] *European Competition Law Review* 307.

[30] Commission, FAQs concerning the application of Article 86(2) [now Article 106(2)] to State aid in the form of public service compensation granted to certain undertakings entrusted with the operation of services of general economic interest, and of the Community Framework for State aid in the form of public service compensation, SEC (2007) 1516 final. And Commission staff working document of 7 December 2010, Guide to the application of the European Union rules on state aid, public procurement and the internal market to services of general economic interest, and in particular to social services of general interest, SEC(2010) 1545 final. See <http://ec.europa.eu/services_general_interest/sgei_guide_en.htm> accessed 25 February 2012.

[31] Decision of the Commission of 13 May 2003 with regard to state aid N 46/2003—Ireland—risk equalisation scheme in the Irish health Insurance market.

[32] cf Case C-114/91 *Criminal proceedings against Gérard Jerôme Claeys* [1992] ECR I-6559; Joined Cases C-144/91 en C-145/91 *Gilbert Demoor en Zonen NV* et al *v Belgium* [1992] ECR I-6613.

9.42 As this Decision was drafted prior to the ECJ's findings in *Altmark*, the Commission based it on an early version of the compensation doctrine outlined in *Ferring*,[33] which set less strict conditions than *Altmark*. Although an explicit act of entrustment setting out a SGEI was absent from the relevant Irish laws, the Commission was prepared to derive this (implicitly) from the general regulatory context. The public service obligation was found to have been formulated in the obligations cited above, and the Commission also held that apart from the classical SGEI where a single undertaking is charged with providing public services in an entire national territory at comparable rates and quality, it was also possible to impose public service obligations on all the operators in a particular market. This meant the Irish government had not committed a manifest error in designing the relevant aspects of its system of supplementary health insurance.

9.43 According to the Commission, the risk equalization system that was being examined also met the requirements of necessity and proportionality, the latter because a certain incentive towards efficiency had been retained by the fact that compensation was based on the market average (making it attractive to perform better than average) and because new entrants were granted a holiday from contributing during their first three years in the market. Hence the Commission concluded (i) that compensation was involved, rather than a selective advantage, and therefore no state aid was found to exist, but (ii) that if the latter were to be found to exist anyway the aid concerned would be compatible with the internal market based on Article 106(2) TFEU. This decision was to be tested before the General Court in the *BUPA* case that will be discussed at the end of this section, at para 9.56.[34]

Risk equalization and financial reserves: the Netherlands

9.44 In this 2005 case the new Dutch framework for health insurance was under evaluation, specifically the aspects (i) whereby private insurers would cover the entire population in the context of the application of a risk equalization system, and (ii) where moreover the formerly public or cooperative insurers when being transformed into private entities would be allowed to keep their financial reserves.[35] Both problems were tackled by the same Commission Decision. In contrast to the Irish system that was fully based on private insurance premiums, the Dutch insurers receive half their financing from a public fund, which is fed by income related social insurance contributions that are withheld at the source. The relevant framework was that of publicly defined minimum benefits, public supervision, national coverage, open enrolment, and community rating. In this system the risk equalization

[33] Case C-53/00 *Ferring*, supra n 25.

[34] Case T-289/03 *British United Provident Association Ltd (BUPA)* et al *v Commission* [2008] ECR II-81.

[35] Decision of the Commission of 3 May 2005 with regard to state aid N 541/2004 en N 542/2004—The Netherlands—risk equalisation system and retention of reserves.

system compensates for the open enrolment obligation, at 50 per cent of the expected costs, and *ex post*. The Commission took a positive view on this. Normally however only *ex ante* compensation is desirable in order to retain incentives for efficiency and any *ex post* compensation should be limited to the necessary minimum. The Irish scheme was seen as a system of double solidarity: among the insured population and between persons with various income levels (progressive financing). The capital requirements were linked to solvability ratios imposed on private insurers.

The Commission decided that in this case (unlike in *AOK*, discussed in Chapter 8) the risk equalization system did not so much form a restriction of competition but instead promoted competitive health care provision. When it applied the *Altmark* criteria however it found that the fourth (efficiency) condition had not been met, because in principle all insurers received compensation, irrespective of their efficiency. The reserves were (partly) considered as aid. The same applied to the risk equalization system. **9.45**

Therefore this case was dealt with based on the SGEI exception in Article 106(2) TFEU as far as the risk equalization aspect was concerned. Just as in the Irish case, the Commission was prepared to derive a SGEI mission from the general legal and regulatory context, although in this case it explicitly held that the Member State tried to realize its public objectives by means of obligations and objective constraints that it imposed on the undertakings involved.[36] It also held that the risk equalization system was necessary to maintain stability in the market and to guarantee universal access to affordable health care. Because the compensation involved would be limited to the necessary minimum the proportionality test was met as well. **9.46**

The retention of the financial reserves was evaluated based on Article 107(3)(c) TFEU regarding aid for the development of certain types of economic activity. On this count the Commission held that the retention of the reserves, on the one hand, had only limited negative effects on competition and, on the other hand, formed an essential element of the liberalization of the health insurance markets in the Netherlands. Hence the Commission ruled that the Dutch measures were compatible with Article 106(2) and also, respectively, Article 107(3) TFEU, to the extent that aid was involved (and not compensation) with respect to the financial reserves. **9.47**

[36] With reference to Case C-157/94 *Commission v the Netherlands (Almelo)* [1997] ECR I-5699, para 40.

Brussels' hospitals

9.48 This case concerned compensation payments to the public hospitals in the Brussels' metropolitan region (IRIS-H) in order to cover costs that according to the Commission were necessary to cover the costs of SGEIs for intramural (hospital) care that were based on the hospital care legislation of 1987.[37] In this case the hospitals (or more in particular their board which consisted mainly of representatives of the Brussels' municipalities' social services) had entrusted the SGEIs that were alleged to have been involved—especially the commitment to treating all patients who presented themselves irrespective of the degree of emergency, financial considerations of their social situation—to themselves.[38] In exchange the IRIS-H, based on the Belgian hospital care legislation, enjoyed supplementary funding on top of the normal budget that was awarded to private hospitals as well. Because this funding was in practice paid out only after a ten years delay it was granted by way of a temporary advance by the Brussels region.

9.49 According to the Commission all conditions for finding state aid were met, but the (likewise cumulative) *Altmark* conditions were not. It did however find the existence of an SGEI based on the compulsory nature of the service provided to all comers at identical conditions,[39] although only part of the population was covered:

> The compulsory nature of the service and, accordingly, the existence of an SGEI mission are established if the service-provider is obliged to contract, on consistent conditions, without being able to reject the other contracting party, which does not exclude that the undertakings enjoys a certain freedom in the market with respect to the management and the content of the services concerned.[40]

9.50 In line with its previous decisions on the health care schemes operated in Ireland and the Netherlands, the Commission derived the SGEI mission from general obligations and did not enforce the requirement that this mission should have been explicitly entrusted. However, just as in the Dutch case, the fourth *Altmark* condition of public procurement or finding based on the needs of an efficient undertaking was not met. Hence the measures concerned constituted state aid that was next vetted with regard to its compatibility with the requirements of the aforementioned SGEI package. This meant examining the following aspects:

- necessity;
- genuine SGEI;

[37] Decision of the Commission of 28 October 2009 with regard to state aid NN 54/2009 (ex CP 244/2005)—Belgium—financing of public hospitals of the IRIS-network of the Brussels capital region.

[38] The responsible public bodies, the municipal social services administrations, have delegated this authority to the regional board for inter-hospital infrastructural collaboration (IRIS).

[39] Commission Decision NN 54/2009, supra n 17, para 149; with reference to Case T-289/03 *BUPA*, supra n 34, para 190.

[40] Commission Decision NN 54/2009, supra n 17; with reference to Case T-289/03 *BUPA*, supra n 34, para 186.

- parameters for compensation established in advance;
- proportionality;
- accounting separation and no cross-subsidies; and
- availability of adequate mechanisms to check for overcompensation.

On the basis of its assessment of each of these elements, the Commission declared the aid involved to be compatible with the internal market. (This decision is now under appeal.)

Irish risk equalization scheme mark II

This scheme is a temporary replacement for, and very similar to, the previous risk equalization scheme, which as explained at para 9.57 below, was eventually annulled by the Irish Supreme Court.[41] The European Commission has authorized this scheme of levies and tax relief. The objective of the scheme is to promote intergenerational solidarity by decreasing the risk differentials for health insurers between old and young customers. In 2009 the Commission concluded that the measure was in line with the EU Framework for state aid in the form of public service compensation and as such compatible with Article 106(2) TFEU. In particular, after the Irish authorities agreed to amend the scheme, the Commission was satisfied that none of the insurers would be overcompensated for the discharge of the public service. **9.51**

The scheme concerns private medical insurance (PMI), which is subject to special regulation in Ireland, as already discussed above. Insurers are obliged to accept a customer who wishes to conclude an insurance contract (open enrolment), cannot terminate the policy against the will of the insured (lifetime cover), and must apply the same premium for a given insurance policy regardless of the risk (age, health status) represented by the insured. Policies must offer a minimum benefit level prescribed by law (minimum benefit). It follows from these obligations that insurers cannot risk-rate their policies, which in turn can result in imbalances on the market if their risk profiles are different. **9.52**

To address this problem, the scheme introduces tax relief for individuals, the amount of which increases with age. The relief is paid directly to the insurer that the individual chose for taking out PMI cover. It is financed by a flat rate levy on all insurers, payable after each insured life. The combined effect of the levy and the tax relief is that the insurance of older lives becomes cheaper and that of younger lives more expensive for insurers, while community rating is maintained vis-à-vis customers. As a consequence the scheme decreases the incentive of insurers to avoid high risk older lives and cherry-pick low risk younger lives; furthermore it **9.53**

[41] Decision of the Commission of 18 June 2009 with regard to state aid N 582/2008 (IP/09/961)—Ireland—Health Insurance intergenerational solidarity relief.

compensates insurers with a worse-than-average risk profile. Due to its worse risk profile the incumbent state-owned Voluntary Health Insurance Board (VHI) will be a net beneficiary of the scheme, while its competitors will be net contributors.

9.54 The Commission considered that although the tax relief is directed at individuals, it clearly has an effect on health insurers, namely that an insurer with a bad risk profile benefits from it at the expense of those with a better one. Therefore the EU state aid rules were applicable. As in its earlier 2003 decision on the risk equalization scheme, the predecessor of the current measure (see above), the Commission recognized that due to its importance in the overall health system and in particular to the special obligations it is subject to, private medical insurance qualifies as a public service, it constitutes an SGEI.

9.55 In line with the *Altmark* ruling, the Commission concluded that the measure constitutes state aid, in particular as the fourth condition was not satisfied. In the course of the investigation, into its potential compatibility with the state aid rules, the Commission found that the scheme was designed in a way so as not to lead in principle to overcompensation of the insurers. Furthermore the Irish authorities committed to introduce a mechanism to avoid the overcompensation of the net beneficiary of the scheme, the VHI. In light of the design of the scheme and this commitment, the Commission found that the measure was in line with the Framework and as such compatible with Article 106(2) TFEU as compensation for public services. This decision is without prejudice to the Commission's ongoing investigation into the Irish health insurance market and the VHI's continued exemption from the applicable Non-Life Insurance Directives, a matter which is being examined separately by the Commission's Internal Market Directorate General.

The approach of the General Court: the *BUPA* case

9.56 Following on from the Commission Decisions discussed above it is important to address the 2008 judgment of the General Court in the case started by BUPA against the 2003 Commission decision clearing the Irish system of risk equalization between private providers of supplementary health care insurance (discussed above).[42]

The context of the case

9.57 BUPA was a private health insurer that entered the Irish market for voluntary supplementary private health insurance that covered some 50 per cent of the population and was dominated by VHI, a former monopolist. Although BUPA was much

[42] ibid. Annotated by W Sauter, 'Case T-289/03, British United Provident Association Ltd (BUPA), BUPA Insurance Ltd, BUPA Ireland Ltd v. Commission of the European Communities, Judgment of the Court of First Instance of 12 February 2008, nyr' [2009] *Common Market Law Review* 269.

smaller than VHI, the risk equalization system that the Commission had approved in its 2003 Decision, that was discussed above, was triggered to the advantage of VHI. Consequently BUPA both challenged the Commission's Decision before the General Court and appealed the relevant Irish decisions before the Irish courts. The Commission Decision was upheld by the General Court based on a 'belt and braces' approach. First it applied the *Altmark* criteria that at the time of the Commission Decision did not yet exist but the applicability of which had not been limited in time by the ECJ (so they could be applied retroactively).[43] Second, it also based its ruling on the SGEI criteria. Not much later the Irish Supreme Court found the risk equalization system unconstitutional under Irish law. BUPA however was not much aided by this finding as it withdrew from the Irish market.

Adjusting the Altmark *criteria?*

As regards the *Altmark* criteria it is noteworthy that the General Court in relation to the first criterion (the existence of an SGEI) did not demand that the service concerned was available to the entire population of the Member State concerned: instead the obligation to deal with all comers at standard conditions (open enrolment) was considered sufficient to find the existence of a universal service. The fact that different services with price differentiation were concerned did not mitigate this consideration, nor did the fact that not all consumers (in fact almost half of the population) either could or would pay for these services. **9.58**

The second criterion requires clearly defined parameters for compensation and was not contested. The necessity and proportionality of the compensation were more difficulty to establish in the absence of a direct link between the universal service and the need for compensation. Here the General Court accepted that the arrangement was 'consistent with the purpose and the spirit of the third *Altmark* condition in so far as the compensation is calculated on the basis of elements, which are specific, clearly identifiable and capable of being controlled'.[44] This meant applying almost the exact same test as under the second *Altmark* criterion. Likewise with respect to the fourth *Altmark* condition the General Court formulated an alternative version because it would not be possible to determine in advance which insurer had a right to compensation and therefore to compare its costs with those of an efficient competitor. Because compensation was based on the average costs in the market (and not on those of the individual competitor) an incentive toward efficiency would be retained. It follows that it is not sufficient to avoid notification for a Member State merely to assert that the costs of the undertakings concerned are less than the costs of providing the service in question.[45] **9.59**

[43] As the General Court observed in Case T-289/03 *BUPA*, supra n 34, para 158.
[44] ibid, para 237.
[45] Case T-388/03 *Deutsche Post AG v Commission* [2009] ECR II -199, para 116.

9.60 In this manner the General Court substantially amended the relatively recently minted *Altmark* criteria in the first important case where they were applied—in the sense that it broadened their scope. By contrast, several other aspects of the case, such as the scope for market entry, and the undesirable effects of *ex post* compensation, were not addressed. In any event, by moderating the fourth *Altmark* condition, the General Court has put pressure on the approach of the Commission adopted in its health care decisions discussed above. In these Decisions the Commission started from a strict reading of the criterion of the costs of a well-run company in order to determine whether notification was required or not. It is for the Member State to satisfy this test and if the compensation is not awarded by tender, then the Member State must provide evidence that the company is well-run.

9.61 As long as the ECJ has not shed any light on this matter, at least in the health care sector, it remains unsolved whether this condition should be applied in a strict or lenient manner. If the approach adopted by the General Court is upheld by the ECJ, the Member States will enjoy more regulatory freedom than the Commission was prepared to allow them in its decisions discussed above. Although it may take a strict approach to enforcing the *Altmark* criteria in relation to notification issues, the Commission is nonetheless prepared to declare the state measures as compatible with Article 106(2) TFEU on the basis of a cursory examination of the economics of the measure or its effect on competition.[46] Indeed the Staff Working Paper of April 2009 on the economic assessment of state aid measures' indicated that the Commission would be less inclined to apply economic analysis to SGEIs which were intended to address equity objectives.[47]

The approach of the ECJ: *AG2R*

9.62 Finally we move on to the ECJ. So far the ECJ has not returned to its *Altmark* case law itself. It has had to deal with the health care sector in the context of SGEI however, even if not in relation to state aid. In *AG2R* (2011) (see above Chapter 8) the ECJ addressed the applicability of the competition rules and abuse of dominance rules in relation to an exclusive right in the context of SGEI. Here the ECJ held that the provident society, that was charged with the task of managing a supplementary health care scheme set up by employers and unions in the traditional bakery sector in France, was on the one hand an undertaking, so the competition rules applied, but on the other should be regarded as being entrusted with carrying

46 C Koening and J Paul, 'State aid screening of hospital funding exemplified by the German case' [2010] *European State Aid Law Quarterly* 755; L Hancher and P Larouche, 'The coming of age of EU regulation of network industries and services of general economic interest', in P Craig and G De Burca (eds), *The Evolution of Law* (Oxford: Oxford University Press, 2011).

47 See para 3.2 thereof. <http://ec.europa.eu/competition/state_aid/reform/economic_assessment_en.pdf> accessed 25 February 2012.

out a SGEI in the sense of Article 106(2) TFEU.[48] Compulsory affiliation to this managing body was justified due to this SGEI as it would ensure that universal cover was provided and that the undertaking entrusted with the task to provide supplementary insurance for all persons insured would not end up with an increasing share of bad risks. Hence, the compulsory affiliation guaranteed that the managing body concerned was able to carry out its SGEI task under economically acceptable circumstances. As in *Glöckner* (2001), the concept of SGEI led the ECJ to accommodate health care specific concerns in its reasoning.

However, it is noteworthy that in *AG2R* the ECJ did not assign any value to the act of entrustment of the imputed SGEI. It merely derived the relevant task from the fact that the supplementary health care scheme at issue was characterized by a high degree of solidarity with contributions not proportionate to the risks insured and fixed at uniform rates, partly paid by the employer and partly by the employee, without any role for factors such as age or health. Furthermore, the ECJ pointed to the constraints imposed on AG2R that were related to the continuity of the cover granted to the persons insured. This approach is a striking departure from earlier cases where the EU courts have gone to some trouble in order to identify the legal context from which the existence of SGEI could be derived.[49] **9.63**

In *AG2R* it seems that in the view of the ECJ the mere existence of obligations (related to a general interest) imposed upon a managing body suffices to assume this body is engaged in providing a SGEI. Moreover, in this particular case the entities, which decided on the designation of the management of the scheme concerned, were social partners, that is to say the employers and trade unions representing employees in the traditional bakery sector. Although French legislation provides that collective bargaining agreements may be imposed by law on an entire sector, French law does not oblige the social partners to arrange for supplementary health care schemes. Hence, the mission to provide these insurance services originated with the private entities concerned and not from the state. This is in line with the *Albany* (1999) case law where the ECJ seems to have accepted that a SGEI mission may be designated by social partners. At issue in these cases were supplementary pension schemes and the provision of such schemes by private pension funds was found to constitute a SGEI.[50] **9.64**

[48] Case C-437/09 *AG2R Prévoyance v Beaudout Père et Fils SARL* [2011] judgment of 3 March 2011 (nyr).

[49] eg Case T-289/03 *BUPA*, supra n 34.

[50] Case C-67/96 *Albany International BV v Stichting Bedrijfspensioenfonds Textielindustrie* [1999] ECR I-5751; Joined Cases C-115/97, C-116/97 and C-117/97 *Brentjens' Handelsonderneming BV v Stichting Bedrijfspensioenfonds voor de Handel in Bouwmaterialen* [1999] ECR I-6025; and Case C-219/97 *Maatschappij Drijvende Bokken BV v Stichting Pensioenfonds voor de Vervoer- en Havenbedrijven* [1999] ECR I-6121.

Conclusion

9.65 Meanwhile, the ECJ in cases relating to the compatibility of compensation for the performance of SGEIs in other sectors, such as broadcasting (TV Denmark),[51] has only required that the Member States establish that compensation is based on net costs—it has not required the Member States to prove that those costs are either necessary or are efficiently occurred. This has resulted in considerable criticism of the Commission's overall approach, as endorsed by the EU courts, as a 'black hole'.[52] In March 2011, the Commission commenced a review of the first *Altmark* package, as required by the review clause in the 2005 Decision and Framework, and it announced its intention to consider whether a stricter 'efficiency' criteria should be included in any revised version of these measures. This might go some way to meeting the criticisms of the adverse impact of 'deficit compensation' of public hospital budgets, for example, and their distortive effects on competition between publicly-funded and private health care providers, as well as competition on upstream markets (eg for medical equipment) and downstream markets (eg for ambulant care).[53] Following two rounds of consultation, on 20 December 2011, the Commission adopted its Second *Altmark* Package (or '*Almunia* package' after the current Commissioner for competition) which will be discussed in more detail below, at paras 9.77 et seq.

9.66 In the meantime the contours of the state aid regime, unlike that of competition law *strictu sensu*, have been largely clarified in relation to health care. As we have seen this hinges in large part on the use of the idea of a SGEI, a concept that is of broader application and will next be discussed in more detail below at section E. In this respect it should be noted that Commission Guidance on issues of state aid and health care is less urgent than guidance on other competition and health care matters, since at the national level a regime equivalent to Articles 107-9 TFEU is generally absent.

E. Services of General Economic Interest

9.67 The state aid cases discussed here clearly show that services of general economic interest (SGEI) could play an important role in issues of health care and competition generally, and beyond the confines of the state aid regime. SGEI is an EU law concept that serves to bridge the gap between legitimate national public interest objectives on the one hand and the EU Treaty rules on free movement, competition,

[51] Joined Cases T-309/04, T-317/04, T-329/04 and T-336/04 *TV2/Danmark A/S* et al *v Commission* [2008] ECR II-2935.
[52] C Koening and J Paul, supra n 46.
[53] ibid, for a further discussion of the German hospital sector.

and state aid on the other.[54] By entrusting an undertaking with a SGEI, public authorities at national level can charge it with carrying out public service obligations, in particular the provision of a universal service. This may allow for a proportionate exception to the rules of the Treaty, if it can be proven that the entrusted undertaking could not carry out its tasks under acceptable conditions unless the relevant Treaty rules were disapplied. Because SGEI is an exception to the general rules it should be applied—in line with the classic doctrine as developed by the ECJ in areas such as free movement law and competition law—restrictively, but at the same time the ECJ is sensitive to the economic context involved.

The SGEI concept and the universal service obligations that are at its heart have played a key role in the liberalization of the network industries (such as electronic communications and energy). If liberalization of health care spreads within the EU, the SGEI concept is likely to play an important role here as well because, in this manner, mixed regimes that guarantee essential provision on equitable terms can be sustained, while defining the universal service concerned is likely to facilitate allowing a market-based regime for the remaining services. As we have seen above, ambulance transport and health insurance (especially risk equalization between insurers) are areas where the SGEI exemption has so far been applied in health care.[55] Some other areas of health care may likewise be candidates for the application of SGEI. We will first map the main features of the concept of SGEI before discussing some reasons why it may be especially significant for health care. **9.68**

The role of SGEI in EU law

The SGEI concept is derived from Article 106(2) TFEU, which provides a proportionate exception to the free movement, competition, and state aid rules, for undertakings charged with SGEI, if the application of those rules would hamper the performance of the SGEI in question. The legality of a SGEI is tested based on necessity and proportionality. This involves balancing the non-economic interest invoked by the Member State against the (economic) EU interest. **9.69**

[54] cf L Gyselen, 'Public service and EU competition law' [2011] *Journal of European Competition Law and Practice* 572; T Prosser, 'EU competition law and public services' in E Mossialos (ed), *Health Systems Governance in Europe* (Cambridge: Cambridge University Press, 2010); W Sauter, 'Services of general economic interest and universal service in EU law' [2008] *European Law Review* 167; M Krajewski, U Neergaard and JW van de Gronden (eds), *The changing legal framework for services of general economic interest in Europe* (The Hague: Asser Press, 2009).

[55] Case C-475/99 *Glöckner*, supra n 22. On insurance see the previous section. Decision of the Commission of 13 May 2003 with regard to state aid N 46/2003—Ireland—risk equalisation scheme in the Irish health Insurance market; Decision of the Commission of 3 May 2005 with regard to state aid N 541/2004 en N 542/2004—The Netherlands—risk equalisation system and retention of reserves; Decision of the Commission of 18 June 2009 with regard to state aid N 582/2008—Ireland—Health Insurance intergenerational solidarity relief; Case T-289/03 *BUPA*, supra n 34.

9.70 The Commission is charged with supervising the application of Article 106 TFEU as a whole, which also concerns revenue producing monopolies, public undertakings, and undertakings enjoying special and exclusive rights. It can adopt Decisions and Directives to do so: a relevant example is its 2005 Decision on public service compensation in the SGEI package, discussed above.[56] Also relevant are Article 14 TEU, which creates a legal basis for European Parliament and Council Regulations on SGEI, Article 36 of the Charter of Fundamental Rights of the EU, and Protocol No. 26 on Services of General Interest that was added to the Lisbon Treaty. Article 14 TFEU and Protocol No. 26 to the Treaties were intended by the Member States to limit the Commission's powers with respect to SGEI. However the legislative competence given to the European Parliament and the Council in Article 14 has so far not been used. The Protocol concerns the common values that are the subject of SGEI and services of general interest (SGI). Because SGIs are not economic in nature they remain outside the scope of the Treaties.

9.71 The Commission has, as discussed, been more active. It had announced in its 'Single Market Act' that it would issue a Communication and a series of measures on services of general interest,[57] which it in fact presented on 15 September 2011.[58]

Defining SGEI

9.72 Neither a standard definition of SGEI nor a limited list of such services exists. Moreover the element 'economic' in the definition refers to the service involved (as it is provided by an undertaking) and not to the public interest involved. This leaves broad scope for Member States to define SGEI. It is a dynamic concept, which means that services may over time come to be regarded as SGEI, or vice versa cease to be so. This allows technical, economic, and socio-political developments to be taken into account at national, regional, and local level. As the General Court confirmed in *BUPA*, the Commission must confine its assessment to establishing whether the definition constitutes a manifest error—to determine if the tasks are genuine SGEIs. That said, the Court has ruled that an SGEI cannot be derived from the mere fact that the undertakings concerned pursue activities in the public economic interest.[59]

Health care in the first *Altmark* package

9.73 Nevertheless it is important to note that a clear definition of the SGEI and an act of entrustment are required as constitutive elements of creating a SGEI. This had been

[56] Commission Decision of 28 November 2005 on the application of Article 86(2) of the EC Treaty to State aid in the form of public service compensation, supra n 27.

[57] See Commission Communication, Towards a Single Market Act. For a highly competitive social market economy, COM (2010) 608, pp 20–1.

[58] These proposals have meanwhile been adopted in slightly modified form, infra n 61.

[59] Case T-222/04 *Italy v Commission* [2009] ECR II-1877, para 113.

clear well before the 2003 *Altmark* judgment, as the Opinions of AG Leger confirm.[60] These requirements were reiterated in the Commission's 2005 package (discussed in section C on state aid), and have been repeated in the second *Altmark* package of 2011.[61]

Article 2(1)b of the 2005 Decision covers 'public service compensation granted to hospitals (...) carrying out activities qualified as services of general economic interest by the Member State concerned'. The precise nature of the activities concerned is left to the Member States. However point 16 of the preamble elaborates as follows: **9.74**

> Hospitals (...) which are entrusted with tasks involving services of general economic interest have specific characteristics that need to be taken into consideration. In particular, account should be taken of the fact that at the current stage of development of the internal market, the intensity of distortion of competition in those sectors is not necessarily proportionate to the level of turnover and compensation. Accordingly, hospitals providing medical care, including, where applicable, emergency services and ancillary services directly related to the main activities, notably in the field of research (...) should benefit from the exemption from notification provided for in this Decision, even if the amount of compensation they receive exceeds the thresholds laid down in this Decision, if the services performed are qualified as services of general economic interest by the Member States.

It is therefore not sufficient to provide hospital services: in addition it is necessary that the services concerned are designated as SGEI. The conditions that must be met are, first, that the act or acts concerned must specify (i) the nature and the duration of the public service obligations; (ii) the undertaking and territory concerned; (iii) the nature of any exclusive or special rights assigned to the undertaking; (iv) the parameters for calculating, controlling and reviewing the compensation; and (v) the arrangements for avoiding and repaying any overcompensation. Second, compensation may not amount to more than the costs of the services concerned plus a reasonable profit. A mechanism of control for over-compensation with annual checks must be in place although a maximum of 10 per cent excess financing can be carried forward to a following year. In addition the Decision covers availability of information (records kept for 10 years) and transparency requirements with three-yearly reporting to the Commission. **9.75**

[60] Case C-280/00 *Altmark*, supra n 2; cf Case C-53/00 *Ferring*, supra n 25.

[61] Commission Decision of 20 December 2011 on the application of Article 106(2) of the Treaty on the Functioning of the European Union to State aid in the form of public service compensation granted to certain undertakings entrusted with the operation of services of general economic interest [2012] OJ L7/3; Communication from the Commission on the European Union framework for State aid in the form of public service compensation, [2012] OJ C8/15; Communication from the Commission on the application of the European Union State aid rules to compensation granted for the provision of services of general economic interest [2012] C8/4. A Commission Reg on the application of Arts 107 and 108 of the Treaty on the Functioning of the European Union to de minimis aid granted to undertakings providing services of general economic interest was adopted in April 2012 [2012] OJ C8/23.

9.76 For health care services other than hospital services, including health insurance, the general SGEI regime of individual notification (and the standstill obligation) for a clearance decision by the Commission applied. In practice there have been no examples of formal Commission Decisions in this area.

Health care in the second *Altmark* package

The Commission Decision

9.77 As regards health care, the second *Altmark* package consists primarily of a Commission Decision that is a block exemption for certain sectors with a general notification threshold for aid of €15 million and a Framework that sets out how the Commission intends to deal with individual notifications. In addition there will be a *de minimis* Regulation that is currently subject to a further round of consultation. A Communication that spells out certain aspects, such as the incidence of the public procurement rules and the net avoidable cost methodology also forms part of the package.

9.78 In broad terms the package is characterized by three trends:

- a generous *de minimis* regime for smaller amounts of aid granted by local authorities (not discussed here) not considered aid;
- a block exemption from individual notification and standstill for the social sectors provided minimum standards are met and hence the compensation is qualified as compatible aid; and
- a tightening of the regime for services that require individual notification and prior approval to establish compatibility, largely focused at the utilities sectors.

9.79 We will focus on the second of these trends as it singles out health care as one of its key concerns. The block exemption of the Commission Decision of 2005 has been carried over into the 2011 Decision. The former explicitly created the possibility of exempting hospital financing from the state aid notification obligation provided its compensation was proportionate to the costs concerned, and provided these services were designated as SGEI, respectively the undertakings concerned have been entrusted with an SGEI. Under the new regime not only hospital services (and social housing) but all health care services, long term care and several other social services—not however, in our view, including health insurance—are exempted under these same conditions (entrustment with an SGEI and controls on compensation):

(a) compensation for the provision of services of general economic interest by hospitals providing medical care, including, where applicable, emergency services; the pursuit of ancillary activities directly related to the main activities, notably in the field of research, does not, however, prevent the application of this paragraph;
(b) compensation for the provision of services of general economic interest meeting social needs as regards health and long term care, childcare, access to and

reintegration into the labour market, social housing and the care and social inclusion of vulnerable groups.[62]

In these cases the standard maximum amount of annual compensation of €15 million required for exemption under the Decision does not apply: there is no absolute threshold for these social services. The relevant consideration in the preamble (11) is substantively unchanged although in part the text is now incorporated in Article 2(1)b. The most significant extensions are obviously the unlimited inclusion of 'health and long term care' in Article 2(1)c which is somehow incongruous with the specifications in Article 2(1)b as regards the various types of medical services and the status of ancillary activities. Indeed it raises the question whether the more general phrasing in Article 2(1)c could not have sufficed. However, it may yet be that the link between health and long term care with social needs will be construed as a restriction, the scope of which is yet unclear. **9.80**

As under the first *Altmark* package, according to Article 4 of the Decision the act of entrustment must contain: **9.81**

(a) the content and duration of the public service obligations;
(b) the undertaking and, where applicable, the territory concerned;
(c) the nature of any exclusive or special rights assigned to the undertaking by the granting authority;
(d) a description of the compensation mechanism and the parameters for calculating, controlling and reviewing the compensation;
(e) the arrangements for avoiding and recovering any overcompensation; and
(f) a reference to the Commission's 2011 Decision.

This bears repeating because these requirements are so far often ignored in practice but could well become subject to review by national courts, as is normally the case with block exemptions—that is to determine if all the conditions for application of the block exemption in the Decision have been met.

In addition Article 5 of the Decision contains the requirement that the amount of compensation may not exceed what is necessary to cover the net cost incurred in discharging the public service obligations, including a reasonable profit. The Communication that forms part of the package spells out the conditions in further detail but its para 2.11 for aid that meets the conditions of Article 2(1) of the Decision contains an exception inter alia concerning the more detailed rules on the calculation of net costs, using the net avoided cost methodology.[63] This means that even where they are assessed on a case by case basis only a limited regime applies to health care services. **9.82**

[62] Commission Communication of 20 December 2011, supra n 61, Article 2(1).
[63] Commission Communication of 20 December 2011, supra n 61. 'The principles set out in paragraphs 14, 19, 20, 24, 39, 51–59 and 60(a) do not apply to aid which meets the conditions laid down in Article 2(1) of Decision 2012/21/EU.'

9.83 This regime set out in the Decision nevertheless goes well beyond the original *Altmark* package. The calculation of net costs and reasonable profit is likewise addressed for the first time, with profits based on the internal rate of return obtained on invested capital plus 100 basis points regarded as not unreasonable. It is also worth noting that the Decision stresses the need to introduce incentive criteria, in order to ensure a measure of efficiency and to forestall 'gold plating' of inefficient SGEIs by the Member States. More broadly, the Framework provides for the notion that services that can at least potentially be provided in competition at an acceptable level of service and costs should not be eligible to be designated as SGEI, albeit that the Commission will only subject such measures to a test to see whether the designation is manifestly inappropriate.

9.84 So far however even the formal designation of services as SGEI still tends to be more honoured in the breach than in the observance. As we have seen the Commission is as a consequence often prepared to derive the existence of SGEI from the broader regulatory context; whether this will change in the enforcement of the second *Altmark* package remains to be seen. Moreover in *BUPA* the General Court likewise derived a SGEI mission from the legal context, general obligations, and policy measures. Nevertheless the exemption from notification (also enabling disbursement) available under the 2011 block exemption Decision should provide a strong incentive toward formal entrustment, which is also an effective means of enabling the proportionality test that is key to any EU law examination of the scope of a SGEI.

9.85 Not explicitly defining the SGEI mission and not notifying state aid granted to health care operators that are supposed to carry out this implicit mission amounts to an enormous risk. First, deciding upon the validity of the financial measures is placed into the hands of a small group of unelected Commission officials and EU judges. Second, it depends entirely on their willingness to find implicit SGEI missions as to whether the workings the health care system at stake are jeopardized. However, there are a variety of options open to Member States in relation to the types of acts they adopt in order to entrust the tasks to the undertakings in question—a formal law or a centralized approach to entrustment is not mandatory.[64]

The Framework

9.86 Taking the above points into consideration, the block exemption Decision is not the only relevant part of the Second Altmark Package for health care. This is because, as we have seen in the cases discussed above, in principle, health insurance services have been found to be eligible as SGEI. Being excluded from (or not covered by) the Decision, they will instead have to be assessed on a case by case basis under the

[64] Case T-17/02 *Fred Olsen SA v Commission* [2005] ECR II-2031.

Framework, while respecting the standstill requirement.[65] That is to say aid to health insurers (such as may be involved in a risk equalization scheme) may not be granted prior to an individual clearance by the Commission (aside from special circumstances such as a provisional and limited amount of rescue aid).

The Framework is based on the same criteria as the Decision: (i) an entrustment test based on the manifestly inappropriate standard (except where provisions of EU law provide a stricter standard); and (ii) control on the amount of compensation, based on methodologies such as the net avoidable cost methodology and on cost allocation methods (involving all direct costs and an appropriate contribution to common costs); as well as (iii) allocation of no more than a reasonable profit, such as a rate of return on capital that does not exceed the relevant swap rate plus a premium of 100 basis points to compensate inter alia for the liquidity risk inherent in the commitment to an SGEI for the duration of an entrustment act. Where it is available, the expertise of independent entities such as sector regulators are taken into account. When determining their method of compensation the Member States must introduce efficiency incentives unless they can justify why not doing so is appropriate or doing so is not feasible. **9.87**

As regards the potentially contentious issue of whether a service can be provided equally well by the market—in which case assigning an SGEI would be inappropriate—both the Framework and the Commission's Communication state that the Commission's assessment on this point is limited to controlling for manifest error.[66] (Nevertheless it does provide examples of such cases in the broadband communications sector.)[67] **9.88**

In the context of the evaluation under the Framework it is noteworthy that the *BUPA* case,[68] discussed above, already showed that the General Court was prepared to take a more tolerant approach toward the scope of the public service obligation involved than that found in *Altmark*, an issue the Commission will have to address in its decisions on individual cases. At the same time, Commission practice so far has not gone into the details of compensation: both cost and reasonable rates of return remain to be examined in detail, as they will have to be now under the Framework. The consequences of the second *Altmark* package for health insurers providing SGEIs in future are therefore potentially much more far reaching than **9.89**

[65] Decision of the Commission of 13 May 2003 with regard to state aid N 46/2003—Ireland—risk equalisation scheme in the Irish health Insurance market; Decision of the Commission of 3 May 2005 with regard to state aid N 541/2004 en N 542/2004—The Netherlands—risk equalisation system and retention of reserves; Decision of the Commission of 18 June 2009 with regard to state aid N 582/2008 (IP/09/961)—Ireland—Health Insurance intergenerational solidarity relief; supra n 55.

[66] Framework, supra n 61, para 2.2. and Commission Communication of 20 December 2011, supra n 61, para 3.2.

[67] cf Communication for the Commission, Community Guidelines for the application of State aid rules to rapid deployment of broadband networks [2009] OJ C235/7.

[68] Case T-289/03 *BUPA*, supra n 34.

those of the three formal Commission decisions (discussed above) that were handed down so far.

The case law on universal service

9.90 It is apparent from the case law that the scope of a SGEI is predominantly that of the universal service which it covers, along with any ancillary restraints that may be necessary to ensure the universal services is carried out in sustainable economic circumstances.[69]

9.91 The *Ferring* and *Glöckner* cases are illustrative of this.

- The *Ferring* (2001) case concerned the issue of whether state aid was involved in a tax on direct sales of medicines that was imposed in France upon pharmaceutical laboratories but not on wholesale distributors, which corresponded to costs that the latter incurred as a result of public service obligations.[70] According to the ECJ this could be seen as compensation for the additional burdens imposed on wholesale distributors and not as a selective advantage, so the measure involved did not constitute a state aid.[71] In this context it was relevant that the 1992 Council Directive on the wholesale distribution of medicinal products for human use left open the possibility that the Member States could impose public service obligations. However insofar as the tax advantage concerned exceeded the costs of the relevant public service obligation it was not covered by the SGEI exception in Article 106(2) TFEU as it failed to meet the requirement of necessity.
- We have already looked at the *Glöckner* (2001) case above when discussing the concept of undertaking.[72] In relation to the scope of Article 106(2) TFEU this case is noteworthy because the ECJ held that fulfilling a SGEI under economically acceptable conditions presupposes the possibility of compensation between profitable (patient transport services) and less profitable (emergency transport services) segments, or a cross-subsidy—and consequently legitimizes a limitation of competition in the profitable segment. Extending the SGEI to the profitable segment however is only allowed for services that are closely related and provided that the undertaking benefiting from a dominant position as a result of the SGEI is capable of meeting demand.[73]

9.92 The more recent *BUPA* case (likewise discussed above) added several important qualifications with respect to SGEI and universal services. The *BUPA* (2008) case

---

[69] Case C-320/91 *Criminal proceedings against Paul Corbeau* [1993] ECR I-2533, paras 16–17. cf Case C-475/99 *Glöckner*, supra n 22, para 57.

[70] Case C-53/00 *Ferring*, supra n 25.

[71] Council Dir 92/25/EEC of 31 March 1992 on the wholesale distribution of medicinal products for human use [1992] OJ L113/1.

[72] Case C-475/99 *Glöckner*, supra n 22.

[73] cf Case C-41/90 *Klaus Höfner and Fritz Elser v Macrotron GmbH* [1991] ECR I-1979.

involved voluntary private supplementary health insurance in Ireland.[74] The General Court held that in order to qualify as a SGEI the service involved needs not to be a universal service in the strict sense of meeting a demand for the entire population or throughout the national territory. It is acceptable that the services concerned have only a limited territorial or material scope and benefit only a relatively limited group of users. Even the fact that some potential users may not have the necessary means to enjoy the service does not affect its universal nature, insofar as the service in question is offered at uniform and non-discriminatory rates and on similar quality conditions for all customers.[75] Hence the scope of universal service is sufficiently broad in nature to cover a range of different national interpretations. Harmonized definitions are not required. We now move on to a brief discussion of the question to clarify further why SGEI may be particularly useful in health care.

Market failure and SGEI in health care

Health care markets are characterized by several types of market failure that may justify intervention by means of a SGEI. These are adverse selection, information asymmetry, and producer as well as consumer moral hazard (see Chapter 1). They can lead to problems of under-insurance and over-consumption, low quality, and high prices. **9.93**

These economic problems can also be formulated in terms of solidarity and resolved as such. For instance, as we have seen, in some Member States the adverse selection problem is addressed by means of insurance based on open enrolment, lifetime cover and community rating as well as defined benefits backed up by risk equalization schemes, which the EU Commission has recognized as constituting SGEI.[76] (In addition, a duty of care on insurers and collecting and exchanging data on quality of treatment would tend to be required.) What we observe here is the pursuit of public policy objectives (affordable 'universal' health insurance) by mobilizing undertakings, as well as a means of opening up (the remainder of) markets to competition by allowing certain proportional restrictions. **9.94**

Asymmetric information, moral hazard, and principal-agent problems also cause problems in other health care markets. Most of these problems can be addressed in a market-based manner, such as by insurers pooling the interests of consumers in their interaction with health care providers and acquiring the necessary expertise. New entrants may introduce quality-based competition and intermediaries may start providing comparable information on quality and performance of health care providers. However, it may well be that where public authorities are likely to look to undertakings to solve such problems, they may wish **9.95**

[74] Case T-289/03 *BUPA*, supra n 34.
[75] ibid, paras 202–203.
[76] Decision of the Commission N 541/2004 and N 542/2004, supra n 56; Decision of the Commission N 46/2003, supra n 56; Case T-289/03 *BUPA*, supra n 34.

to entrust them with a SGEI. Emergency care, highly specialized care, academic care, care of multiple-handicapped persons, rare and highly expensive pharmaceuticals, and immunization may be examples. In addition, where such solutions already exist, expressly classifying them as SGEI by means of an act of entrustment, as well as ensuring proportional compensation, would be highly expedient from a state aid perspective.

9.96 However, is the concept of SGEI, as it has so far developed in the case law of the ECJ, capable of addressing the market failures that are common in health care? It should be noted that the ECJ has developed the test of the economically acceptable circumstances in order to assess whether the restrictions caused by a SGEI mission are proportionate.[77] It has acknowledged that the provision of a SGEI may be put under pressure, if commercially oriented enterprises were to apply themselves only to the most profitable activities, such as providing services in densely populated areas. This would leave the undertaking to which the SGEI mission is attributed with the less attractive activities and may prevent it from financing the universal provision. Hence the test of the economically acceptable circumstance is well suited to tackling problems of cherry picking.[78]

9.97 However, as we pointed out, in health care other market failures such as adverse selection and moral hazard are in fact more common than cherry picking. With the cases on risk equalization (which could also be described as barring cherry picking) the Commission and the General Court have made a start on addressing these issues.

Other competition issues in health care

9.98 It should be noted that not all difficulties presented by the application of the EU competition rules to health care could be construed in terms of problems related to the provision of an SGEI—not least since the implication of using SGEI is that the services that are not covered are open to competition, and hence subject to the competition rules. We have already mentioned the problems concerning the geographical market definition and the three-sided interaction between consumers, providers of care, and (public or private) third party payers (such as insurers). Access, affordability, and quality are often referred to as key general health care concerns. More specific issues are how to treat integrated care, which often combines horizontal and vertical integration to provide managed care of usually chronic ailments. Equally complex is the role of gatekeepers, such as general practitioners with the power of referral to a hospital or specialist, or medical specialists referring

[77] see eg Case C-320/91 *Corbeau*, supra n 69, para 16.

[78] see JW van de Gronden, 'The internal market, the state and private Initiative. A legal assessment of national mixed public-private arrangements in the light of European law. Private initiative, general interest and EC law' [2006] *Legal Issues of Economic Integration* 125.

complex cases to top-clinical care, or ambulance coordination systems that have to decide which emergency ward casualties are taken to.

To put it differently, not all health care services are suitable to constitute a SGEI. At the same time there may still be a public interest in not exposing them to the full force of the competition rules. In this respect, the 'legitimate interest' approach developed in *Wouters* and *Meca-Medina* could be useful (see Chapter 8).[79] After all, this approach starts from the context of a particular agreement and bases its assessment on the function of this agreement in the light of the peculiarities of the sector concerned. Consequently, this approach could well complement the concept of SGEI. **9.99**

F. Conclusion

In state aid the Commission (with some decentralization to national courts) remains directly in charge of a centralized system. For the state aid cases related to health care that were reviewed, at least since the *Altmark* case (2003), the *Altmark* package (2005), and a fortiori with the exemption in the second *Altmark* package, the solution to balancing national public service objectives and the EU interest is now generally likely to be based on the concept of a SGEI. This is significant for health care. In fact the first *Altmark* package even contained a block exemption from the state aid rules for hospital services—provided they were entrusted with a SGEI and there was no over-compensation. This approach was retained and is now extended to health care services as a whole, long term care, and indeed social services at large, in the second *Altmark* package. It should be noted however that this exemption applies only if SGEIs are formally entrusted, which involves specifications on compensation, and controls on compensation. It should be noted moreover that national courts can check whether the conditions of the block exemption are met. **9.100**

Moreover, since the health insurance case *BUPA*, universal service covers all compulsory public interest provision. As a result we observe the beginnings of health care sensitive rulemaking and guidance by the EU courts and Commission based on the recognition that the proportionate pursuit of public policy objectives by means of universal service obligations in line with state aid obligations can be secured by the SGEI exception. However, this implies that Member States, in order to secure that *Altmark* can be invoked successfully, and notification avoided, should define the SGEI mission entrusted to a particular health care operator as clearly as possible. So far the EU courts have been prepared to derive entrustment acts from the general context of policy, law, and regulation involved. Explicit acts of **9.101**

[79] Case C-309/99 *J.C.J. Wouters, J.W. Savelbergh and Price Waterhouse Belastingadviseurs BV v Algemene Raad van de Nederlandse Orde van Advocaten* [2002] ECR I-1577; Case C-519/04P *David Meca-Medina and Igor Majcen v Commission* [2006] ECR I-6991.

entrustment are likely to provide greater certainty and therefore legal protection. However providing such clarity on the trade-offs involved may involve changes to longstanding health care policies of the Member States. In any event accounting separation, as well as justified cost allocation and cost accounting are necessary.

9.102 Acts of entrustment are also significant because the weak point of state aid control in general and of the first *Altmark* package in particular has been enforcement. As for the second *Altmark* package, this is likely to focus on individual notifications in the utilities sector, so it is unlikely that strict enforcement with regard to health care will occur. Here, as before, too much rides on the Commission services. Against this background, even judicial review that is limited to the formal requirements set for entrustment acts would be a welcome development.

10

CONCLUSION: EU LAW AND HEALTH CARE IN ACTION

A. Introduction

10.01 In this concluding chapter we endeavour to bring together, and comment in general terms on, the main EU law developments that we have described in greater detail in the preceding chapters.

10.02 We have seen that at present EU law concerning health care still primarily consists of the general EU rules being applied to health care. As we stressed in our introductory chapters, the health care sector enjoys no special status under the Treaty: the Treaty rules on competition and free movement apply in full. At the same time the Member States generally claim the right to organize the sector as they see fit. Tensions between national and EU objectives are therefore inevitable, so it is not unremarkable that conflicts have reached the national as well as EU courts.

10.03 This is of course due to the sensitivity of the subject matter. In its *DocMorris* (2009) ruling the ECJ stated:

> (...) account must be taken of the fact that the health and life of humans rank foremost among the assets and interests protected by the Treaty and that it is for the Member States to determine the level of protection which they wish to afford to public health and the way in which that level is to be achieved. Since the level may vary from one Member State to another, Member States must be allowed discretion.[1]

10.04 It is not our concern here to adjudge the merits of these rulings but rather to assess how the 'toolbox' discussed in Chapter 2 has been put to use in practice. To this end we have examined in some depth the three areas of EU law—internal market, competition, and social and employment law—that have significant implications for national health care systems and underline the multiple aspects of EU law concerning health care that are of significance for the arrangements at national level.

10.05 Furthermore, a considerable body of secondary legislation impacts on national health care provision, even if this legislation is not addressed to the health care sector as such. We have reviewed the scope and impact of EU Directives which are intended to promote free movement of goods and services through further harmonization of relevant procedural and substantive rules, such as the rules on procurement. We have also examined the impact of secondary legislation which addresses specific health care related products, such as medical devices, pharmaceutical marketing and pricing, and specific health care related services, including professional qualifications. While many of these measures have their roots in the drive to create a single or internal market and to promote trade across the EU it would be a mistake to perceive more recent, as well as future, EU initiatives in many of these areas through the narrow lens of internal market law and policy.

10.06 As Professor Monti stated in his 2010 Report to Commission President Barroso on 'A New Strategy for the Single Market':

> If the *market* and the *social* components do not find an appropriate reconciliation, something has to give in. Following the crisis, with the declining appetite for the market and the increasing concern about inequalities, it is by no means clear that it would be the market, i.e. the single market, to prevail. A distinct category of social concerns has to do with services of general economic interest and the real or perceived threats posed to them by the single market.[2]

---

[1] Joined Cases C-171/07 and C-172/07 *Apothekerkammer des Saarlandes and Others (C-171/07) and Helga Neumann-Seiwert (C-172/07) v Saarland and Ministerium für Justiz, Gesundheit und Soziales* [2009] ECR I-4171, para 19. With reference to Case C-322/01 *Deutscher Apothekerverband eV v 0800 DocMorris NV, Jacques Waterval* [2003] ECR I-14887, para 103; Case C-141/07 *Commission v Germany (hospital pharmacies)* [2008] ECR I-6935, para 51; Case C-169/07 *Hartlauer Handelsgesellschaft mbH v Wiener Landesregierund and Oberösterreichischer Landesregierung* [2009] ECR I-1721, para 3.

[2] 'A new strategy for the single market at the service of Europe's economy and society: Report to the President of the European Commission José Manuel Barroso', by Mario Monti (Brussels, 9 May 2010), p 26.

Professor Monti also recommended, in order to address those concerns, that supporting actions should be taken in order to foster market integration in the health care sector.[3]

We have also seen that in some areas, most recently patients' rights, the EU law concerning health care can be seen as EU health care law. In this respect, and given the past emphasis on the Member States' prerogatives and due respect to the principle of subsidiarity in this sector, the Patients' Rights Directive can be seen as a watershed. Patients are increasingly viewed as consumers of health services who should be entitled not only to determine the quality of the care they receive and where they receive it so that they are entitled to select their health care service provider, but they must also be entitled to access to the information to exercise a meaningful choice. Patients are thus no longer the passive recipients of the services that public authorities deem appropriate but active—and potentially critical—consumers. They are active players in the internal EU health care market. Obviously, health care providers are faced with new challenges in addressing these new developments not least because overall cost constraints remain in place at national level. Developments in health care may also well be harbingers of what is to come in other areas of social policy. For all these reasons EU health care law is in this respect a fascinating if complex and fragmented field of EU law. **10.07**

At the same time, it must be acknowledged the EU institutions are keen to achieve the full economic potential of the EU's health care sector in a time of recession, and to maximize its economic as well at its social value. The health sector is driven by innovation and a highly qualified workforce. Health-related research and development has the potential to reach 0.3 per cent of European GDP. The health care sector is one of the largest in the EU and it is growing: it presently accounts for approximately 10 per cent of the EU's gross domestic product and employs one in ten workers, with a higher than average proportion of workers with tertiary-level education. In most Member States it is the single largest employer and the same often holds true at municipal level: **10.08**

> With an ageing population and changing family structures, the demand for formal, professionalized care is increasing as the availability of informal care in the family environment is declining. Healthcare has also become more specialised and requires more intense work and longer training. By 2020 there will be a shortage of one million health workers in the EU and, should no action be taken, 15% of necessary care will not be covered.[4]

Given these facts and figures, health care provision cannot be considered to be an exclusively or even a predominantly national prerogative within a EU that not only **10.09**

[3] ibid, at p 56.

[4] Commission Proposal for a Regulation of the European Parliament and of the Council on establishing a Health for Growth Programme, the third multi-annual programme of EU action in the field of health for the period 2014–2020, COM (2011) 709 final.

aspires to creating an internal market with free competition but also to a being a community based on social justice, cohesion and solidarity and a highly competitive social market economy, as stipulated Article 3(3) TEU. While some commentators may criticize EU intervention in health policy as 'being made, or constrained, by people who know little and perhaps care little about health' they are also forced to acknowledge that 'the European Union institutions, especially the ECJ and the European Commission [have] powerfully and effectively created EU health policy without any demand for it'.[5] Others may argue that a more coordinated approach is indeed inevitable especially if some value is attached to exercising individual rights under EU law.

10.10 This book has sought to explain the dynamics of EU law concerning health care and to trace the seeds of an evolving EU health care law. In this concluding chapter we aim to bring together these different legal dynamics and from this perspective we will look at the evolving trends as they affect the EU toolbox from different angles:

- the tools for the Member States to challenge the Commission and vice versa;
- the tools for consumers, patients and/or citizens; and
- the tools for market actors versus the Member States and versus one another.

10.11 We will first map out the most important legal dynamics which we have identified in the preceding chapters. The detailed discussion of the relevant case law has established that the application of the Treaty rules by the EU courts is by no means static: the ECJ has developed new ways of balancing competing national and EU interests to meet the policy challenges presented by this complex sector (see section B of this Chapter). In this context we will also recall the impact if any, of the new constitutional framework and compromises established by the Lisbon Treaty (see section C of this Chapter) and we comment on the impact of Article 168 TFEU on national prerogatives. We will then move on to a more detailed consideration of both the potential strengths and weaknesses of the EU toolbox in the light of these legal dynamics (see section D of this Chapter). In our final concluding section (section E) we shall offer some thoughts on the further development of EU health care law as an important area of European social service law, and especially in the context of the evolving approach to reconciling social service provision in general with the Treaty rules on competition in relation to state aid and on free movement, in the area of procurement.

B. The Dynamics of EU Law and Health Care

10.12 As we remarked by way of introduction to the EU toolbox in Chapter 2, it is unique, being more restricted than any comparable national toolbox, but of higher rank

[5] SL Greer, The politics of European health policies (Buckingham: Open University Press, 2009), 3.

(in that EU law can trump national rules), yet at the same time it is more extensive than that at the disposal of any other international or inter-governmental organization. EU law comprises a dynamic set of rules, fashioned by a considerable body of case law which is not necessarily specific to the health care sector, but the implications of which must be kept in view in order to understand how EU law concerning health care is evolving, even if the evolution of EU internal market law regarding health care itself is fairly well charted.

From vertical to horizontal enforcement

A first and foremost trend is the shift in focus from vertical enforcement—that is away from the enforcement of EU primary and secondary law by private individuals against Member States and vice versa—to allow for enhanced horizontal enforcement by private parties against other non-state actors, be these private companies, professionals or indeed professional organizations, as we have seen, for example, in our review of the case law on freedom to provide services and application of the freedom of establishment to the health care sector. **10.13**

The horizontal impact of Directives

A second and related trend is the willingness of the ECJ to acknowledge that even if Directives do not have full horizontal direct effect, even in situations where the Directive in question has not been properly implemented into national law, many of its provisions can be still invoked before national courts in order to realize rights conferred or obligations imposed on other private or non-State actors—as for example in the area of procurement law. Even if the doctrine of direct effect has certain limits and the EU courts continue to refuse to endorse the concept of full horizontal direct effect, the doctrine of state liability may function as a backstop, as we have seen in our examination of the implementation of the Working Time Directive. **10.14**

Both these developments strengthen the potential for horizontal enforcement and are of key importance in mixed health care systems where public and private provision exist side by side; this underlines the relevance of the EU toolbox irrespective of how national health care provision is organized. **10.15**

Balancing national prerogatives with the internal market

A third trend relates to evolving judicial techniques in balancing national prerogatives in the health care sector with EU aspirations of free movement and workable competition. On one hand, the EU courts have widened the reach of the concept of a restriction on free movement and have embraced non-discriminatory national rules and measures which nevertheless inhibit market access. On the other hand, the ECJ has fashioned new concepts to assess the necessity and suitability of these national measures. **10.16**

In this context it is significant that in *Duphar* (1984) the ECJ affirmed both the right of the Member States to organize their own social security systems and their **10.17** duty to align these systems with EU law where necessary.[6] Yet it is the definition of 'what is necessary' that seems to be subject to periodic redefinition—as we have seen in the evolution of the services case law from *Kohll* (1998)[7] to *Watts* (2006).[8]

Proportionality

10.18 This also leads us to the fourth trend—the growing impact of the constitutional principle of proportionality which requires that measures must be suitable, necessary in the sense of the least intrusive effective means, and applied after balancing the interests involved. In this context we have seen the development of the consistency requirement when testing the proportionality of national arrangements such in as the recent establishment cases *Dermoestética* (2008) and *Hartlauer* (2009).[9] In these cases both prohibitions on over the air pharmaceuticals advertising at national level that did not cover local and regional emissions, and respectively, planning permission requirements for outpatient dental clinics that did not apply for highly similar group practices, fell foul of this requirement. Hence systems that can no longer justify their inherent contradictions in line with EU law can be picked apart using the consistency requirement. The counterpart to the consistency requirement is that restrictions can be justified to safeguard the 'unity and balance' of the national health care system as in the *German hospital pharmacies* (2008) case.[10] Although so far applied as a defensive argument, this test also appears to suggest that the logic and functionality of national health care systems may be questioned in the application of the proportionality principle.

Transparency

10.19 A fifth trend is the increased insistence on transparent procedures. For example, although the EU courts may accept that it is necessary to reserve the provision of a particular service to a single provider, for example, it will require that the grant of the concession or licence to that provider meets certain requirements in order to ensure that out-of-state actors are able to compete for that concession or licence on fair, transparent, and non-discriminatory terms. Thus procedures that gave a role to potential competitors in determining market entry,[11] or that awarded extra points to an incumbent in a competition for new licenses,[12] or that did not contain any

---

[6] Case 238/82 *Duphar* et al *v The Netherlands* [1984] ECR 523.

[7] Case C-158/96 *Raymond Kohll v Union des caisses de maladie* [1998] ECR I-1931; Case C-120/95 *Nicolas Decker v Caisse de maladie des employés privés* [1998] ECR I-1831.

[8] Case C-372/04 *The Queen, ex parte Yvonne Watts v Bedford Primary Care Trust and Secretary of State for Health* [2006] ECR I-4325.

[9] Case C-500/06 *Corporación Dermoestética SA v To Me Group Advertising Media (Dermoestética)* [2008] ECR I-5785; Case C-169/07 *Hartlauer Handelsgesellschaft mbH v Wiener Landesregierung and Oberösterreichischer Landesregierung (Hartlauer)* [2009] ECR I-1721.

[10] Case C-141/07 *Commission v Germany (hospital pharmacies)* [2008] ECR I-6935.

[11] Case C-169/07 *Hartlauer*, supra n 9.

[12] Joined Cases C-570/07 and C-571/07 *Blanco Pérez and Chao Gómez* [2010] ECR I-4629.

transparent award criteria at all,[13] have fallen foul of the internal market rules. Similarly, although a health care provider may be entitled to compensation for providing social services in the general economic interest, here too enhanced procedural guarantees are insisted upon.

The impact on secondary legislation

A final trend, which we will explore in the last section, is the consolidation of these trends in the jurisprudence into secondary legislative provisions and soft law targeted at the social services sectors with a view to establishing a more stable and predictable reconciliation of market and social components. **10.20**

The impact of these trends cannot be doubted. When assessing the ECJ's recent record on the application of the fundamental freedoms to the health sector, for example, we should not forget that just over a decade ago, in *Sodemare* (1997) the ECJ found no infringement of Article 49 TFEU at all, given that the measure at issue did not discriminate against out of state actors. By 2009, in *DocMorris*, a public health defence was required even for non-discriminatory measures, involving a proportionality test based on consistency and rationality.[14] This should be seen as a significant development for increased opportunities for private individuals to test the legality of many national measures in the health care sector before national courts. **10.21**

These types of developments are, of course, contentious because, although the manner in which health care is organized differs widely between the Member States, (while they can broadly be divided into insurance based Bismarck systems and National Health Services or Beveridge systems funded by taxation), in all cases public authorities are deeply involved in regulating not just entitlements but also the market structure at all levels.[15] Common problems (such as spiralling costs) due to ageing populations, rising expectations, and technical developments, are also shared, albeit from different starting points. In this respect the constitutional framework to which we turn in the next section is of key importance. **10.22**

Together, these various dynamics have proved an important force for the process of what is often called negative integration—using Treaty provisions to remove disparities in national regimes. Increasingly these tools can be invoked to deepen policy integration, especially in relation to the scope of secondary legislation. As such they have provided an important counter-balance to the relative lack of **10.23**

[13] Case C-372/04 *The Queen, on the application of Yvonne Watts v Bedford Primary Care Trust and Secretary of State for Health (Watts)* [2006] ECR I-4325.

[14] Joined Cases C-171/07 and C-172/07 *Apothekerkammer des Saarlandes* et al *v Deutscher Apothekerverband and Helga Neumann-Siewert v Saarland* [2009] ECR I-4171.

[15] cf E Mossialos, G Permanand, R Baeten and T Hervey (eds), *Health Systems Governance in Europe: The Role of European Union Law and Policy* (Cambridge: Cambridge University Press, 2010); T Hervey and J McHale, *Health Law and the European Union* (Cambridge: Cambridge University Press, 2004).

momentum for, as well as progress on, positive integration (finding agreement on common norms, often of a sectoral nature) in politically sensitive sectors. These processes can have a profound impact on the organization and delivery of health care services. Once policy integration based on common norms is introduced in a certain sector, and often as a response to judicial activism striking down barriers, then in a further stage primacy and direct effect will give teeth to such secondary legislation.

10.24 This results in a broader relevance of EU law for health care: policy integration norms are more often invoked by individuals before national courts than market integration norms. That may well justify the claim that EU law on health care has become a charter not just of economic rights but also of consumer rights, social rights, and citizenship rights, all of which are of considerable importance to this sector.[16] An obvious example of this trend is the Patients' Rights Directive, which codifies but also expands on the case law on the freedom to provide and receive services,[17] and which may prove the harbinger of a new EU health care law.

C. The Constitutional Framework

Health care in the Treaties

10.25 Among EU lawyers, taking a constitutional perspective on the Treaties has become commonplace—even if this concept is not yet widely accepted by the public or in national political discourse.[18] In this context the directly effective internal market and competition provisions of the TFEU (that can be invoked directly by private parties in national courts) are seen as elements of an economic constitution that underpins the less developed political one. However these two objectives seem to be growing closer; thus, Article 3(2) TEU now states that the EU shall pursue a social market economy, reflecting the need to reconcile economic and social objectives.

10.26 At the same time the constitution deals with the allocation of public powers and responsibilities. The Member States can enforce this balance politically within the institutional setting but also by legal means, such as an action against the EU institutions for exceeding their powers. Examples are the 2000 and 2006

---

[16] See N Reich, 'A European Constitution for Citizens. Reflections on Rethinking of Union and Community Law' [1997] *European Law Journal* 131; B De Witte, 'Direct Effect, Primacy and the Nature of the Legal Order' in P Craig and G De Burca (eds), *The Evolution of EU Law* (Oxford: Oxford University Press, 2011), 359.

[17] Dir 2011/24/EU of the European Parliament and of the Council on the application of patients' rights in cross-border healthcare [2011] OJ L88/45.

[18] M Poiares Maduro, *We The Court: the European Court of Justice and the European Economic Constitution: A Critical Reading of Article 30 of the EC Treaty* (Oxford: Hart Publishing, 1998); W Sauter, 'The economic constitution of the European Union' [1998] *Columbia Journal of European Law*, 27–68.

Tobacco cases.[19] These actions could be described as forming part of the EU law toolbox of the Member States.

Subsidiarity

10.27 The constitutional principles of proportionality and transparency have already been covered in the previous section. We now focus on the principle of subsidiarity. Article 168 TFEU on health care plays an ambiguous role in this context: on the one hand, it enshrines a sector-specific subsidiarity clause at Treaty level (acting at the lowest effective level of government), reserving the organization and delivery of health care to the Member States; on the other hand, it has been used as part of the legal basis for the Patients' Rights Directive that is the single most significant incursion into national sovereignty regarding health care so far. It appears therefore that subsidiarity is not determined once and for all for the entire health care sector but is dependent on the setting and the individual subject matter at stake. This also means that the Member States, in spite of what Article 168 TFEU states as to the organization and delivery of health care, do not have a fixed position and will on occasion be forced to move toward further harmonization on common norms and policy.

Competition and SGEI

10.28 Noteworthy constitutional changes made by the Lisbon Treaty have been the relegation of the principle of free competition on open markets from the body of the Treaty to become Protocol 27 to the TFEU, as well as the introduction of a Protocol 26 on services of general economic interest (SGEI) to the TFEU alongside Article 14 TFEU (formerly Article 16 EC). At first sight this seems like a straightforward promotion of state intervention to the detriment of competition. In practice we have not seen the Commission field a proposal for a European Parliament and Council Regulation on the principles and conditions of SGEI as required by Article 14 TFEU. Instead the Commission has twice, in 2005 and 2011, proposed legislation based on its own powers under the state aid rules and Article 106(3) TFEU, in which it regulates SGEI more closely and embarks on promoting both competition (notably in terms of procurement) and, at least in principle, efficiency.

10.29 It is not clear whether this reflects Commission recalcitrance or a lack of focus on account of the legislative actors, or a combination of both. In any event the Commission in its SGEI frameworks of 2005 and 2011 establishes mechanisms for balancing competition with social objectives. Likewise, the Protocol on competition does not appear to have frustrated the application of the EU competition rules, decentralized since 2004, rules which may if anything have intensified in their

[19] Case C-376/98 *Germany v European Parliament and Council of the European Union* [2000] ECR I-8419. The new directive was upheld in Case C-380/03 *Germany v European Parliament and Council of the European Union* [2006] ECR I-11573.

application. Meanwhile we also see the Commission using its internal market and competition tools in tandem in the health care sector, as in the *ONP* (2010) case.[20]

The Treaty freedoms and competition law as constitutional provisions

10.30 As mentioned above, the Treaty provisions on free movement and competition are also constitutional in nature, especially from the perspective of the economic constitution. Moreover they are directly effective and thus open to enforcement by individuals and/or undertakings against the Member States, in the case of free movement; and against other undertakings in the case of the competition rules. The state aid rules occupy a halfway house between them. This means that the constitutional framework in material or substantive, rather than in institutional, terms is characterized by a strong trend toward market dynamics. The institutional and the material provisions of the EU constitution can therefore pull in different directions, with the potential—due to the presence of vertical or private enforcement—towards greater dynamism on the market side. The internal market thus acts as a constitutional bulwark against backtracking by the Member States seeking to defend their sovereignty in the social sectors, including health care.

10.31 At the same time as we have seen that the internal market is a broad concept that covers not just the directly effective four freedoms but also general (that is applicable across sectors) and specific (sectoral) rules. In all of these aspects the relevance of EU law to health care is increasing, even despite Article 168 TFEU, as it turns out that a degree of harmonization is necessary to enable the internal market to work in line with health care interests.

Citizenship

10.32 Article 20 TFEU formulates the Treaty basis for EU citizenship, of which the freedom of movement and residence are most relevant here. Some commentators have analysed the patient mobility, or patients' rights case law, and more recently legislation, as expressions of this citizenship.[21] This is in line with social science theories about the emergent nature of a new 'open' type of citizenship which would require a rethinking of citizenship at national level and possibly a distribution of social tasks between the different levels of government within the EU.[22] Again, this can be seen

[20] Commission Decision of 8 December 2010 based on Article 101 TFEU in Case 29510—*ONP*; Case C-89/09 *Commission v France (laboratories)* [2010] judgment of 16 December 2010 (nyr).

[21] G Davies, 'Legislating for patients'rights' in JW van de Gronden et al (eds), *Health Care and EU Law* (The Hague: TMC Asser Press, 2011), 191.

[22] cf M Ferrera, 'Towards an "open" social citizenship? The new boundaries of welfare in the European Union' in G de Búrca (ed), *EU law and the welfare state: In search of solidarity* (Oxford: Oxford University Press, 2005), 11; M Fererra, *The Boundaries of Welfare: European Integration and the New Spatial Policies of Social Protection* (Oxford: Oxford University Press, 2005).

in the context of negative integration (striking down barriers) spawning positive integration (new common norms). The latter appears to be a clear trend within which we can, however, only see the very first traces of citizenship being applied in the case law without so far determining concrete outcomes.[23] But this may change.

The European Charter of Fundamental Rights

Following the entry into force of the Lisbon Treaty, the European Charter of Fundamental Rights (by force of Article 6(1) TEU) is read as forming part of the Treaties and is consequently enforceable by the EU courts in principle. As we have seen, Article 35 of the Charter contains both an expression of individual entitlements to health care and a mainstreaming requirement: health care is to be taken into account in the definition and implementation of all EU policies and activities.[24] So far however, like Article 20 on citizenship, the role of Article 35 of the Charter has been muted in terms of the development of the constitutional framework for EU law on health care.[25] **10.33**

Conclusion

In summary, although several recent changes have modified the constitutional framework, in particular the changes introduced by the Lisbon Treaty, its application remains relatively stable. That does not mean there is no movement. While constitutional guarantees of the powers and competences of the Member States are in place, the dynamics on the internal market pull the EU in the direction of greater economic freedom. This is an autonomous source of momentum for change fuelled by the individual rights of market participants, not least patients, or consumers. Meanwhile the Commission, using its Article 106(3) TFEU powers, is likewise striking a new balance with a greater role for competition and efficiency. It seems likely that faced with further negative integration (removing barriers) the Member States may become more reconciled to positive integration—to common norms and a degree of policy integration. **10.34**

D. The EU Toolbox for Health Providers and Patients Revisited

The EU toolbox is complex, varied, and dynamic, and at first sight, may be challenging for both patients and health care providers to use in practice. Before **10.35**

[23] Case C-345/09 *J.A. van Delft* et al *v College van zorgverzekeringen* [2010] judgment of 14 October 2010 (nyr).

[24] J McHale, 'Fundamental rights and health care' in E Mossalios et al (eds), *Health Systems Governance in Europe: The Role of European Union Law and Policy* (Cambridge: Cambridge University Press, 2010) 282.

[25] cf AG Ruiz-Jarabo Colomer in Case C-444/05 *Aikaterini Stamatelaki v NPDD Organismos Asfaliseos Eleftheron Epangelmation (Stamatelaki)* [2007] ECR I-3185.

discussing in detail how the different instruments can be deployed by these different parties, we first summarize a number of the key features.

10.36 First, it should be recalled that primary Treaty law, and in particular the rules on free movement and competition, apply in full to the health care sector and to national health care systems. The Treaty provides no general exception for the sector as such. The Treaty rules form part of the EU's economic and social constitution, and are underpinned by the principles of supremacy and direct effect. This allows individuals to invoke the rights guaranteed by the Treaty to challenge not only restrictions on the exercise of those rights imposed by governments and other emanations of the state, but also restrictions resulting from the actions of third parties. As explained in Section B above, as a result of developments in the case law, it is clear that the toolbox can be invoked to ensure the vertical enforcement of private rights as well as the horizontal enforcement of those rights.

10.37 Second, as we have shown, the doctrines of direct effect, as well as indirect effect, and the related doctrine of triangular direct effect, allow individuals to invoke the rights given to them under the relevant secondary legislation, in particular Directives, and to challenge national laws which do not properly implement these Directives. This particular tool is an important complement to the right of the Commission, as guardian of the Treaty, to bring infringement actions against errant Member States. It is also an important gateway for individuals and associations to raise actions in their national courts and to have those courts refer questions of interpretation (preliminary ruling requests) to the EU courts.

10.38 Third, as we have stressed, *no rights are absolute*. The Treaty Articles on the four freedoms, competition, and state aid, all make provision for those defending a restriction on the right in question to invoke an exception. For example, Article 38 TFEU provides that the Treaty does not preclude restrictions on imports of goods justified on the grounds of protecting the health and life of humans. A similar exemption is available for restrictions on freedom to provide services, freedom of establishment, and freedom of persons, on the basis of 'protection of public health', although the EU courts have interpreted these exemptions restrictively. These explicit exceptions for public health in the Treaty potentially modify the scope of the free movement provisions in relation to health care, provided the measures concerned are appropriate, necessary, and proportionate.

10.39 Furthermore, the EU courts have not been prepared to allow the internal market objective to maintain the upper hand and have been sensitive to national petitions in the name of social cohesion. Member States are entitled, in accordance with Article 106(2) TFEU, to protect undertakings providing universal service from competition and to finance providers of services of general economic interest (SGEI); this area is discussed further in the final section of this chapter.

10.40 At the same time, the EU courts have not been prepared to give carte blanche to the Member States at the expense of internal market goals. As we indicated in section B, new legal principles have been fashioned—including the overriding principles of transparency, non-discrimination, and consistency—and imposed as requirements on Member States if they attempt to invoke the various exceptions.

The fourth key feature is that the instruments discussed vary in scope of their impact on residual powers of Member States, although soft law is gradually making room for hard law in health care, and maximum harmonization (uniform rules) is now generally preferred over minimum harmonization (more flexible rules) for market building purposes. This sharply reduces the remaining scope for invoking exceptions (whether Treaty based or overriding reasons). At the same time, at the level of secondary rules a mild regime specifically for health care has been foreseen in the context of the procurement rules and in the *Altmark* packages on state aid and public service compensation,[26] and there are public interest exceptions that apply to health insurance in the Third Non-Life Insurance Directive.[27] Indeed, ongoing codification of the case law—in the form of secondary, soft law instruments or special regimes within general legislation, can enhance legal certainty but can also offer an opportunity to fine tune Commission control—a theme we return to in the final section. **10.41**

Finally, we have examined how the EU toolbox has originally been applied to the supply side of the health care market so that trade in goods and services has been optimized albeit subject to the residual rights of Member States to invoke the relevant exceptions to defend certain elements of their national health care systems. As we have demonstrated, especially in Chapters 3 and 7, the toolbox is now increasingly applied to the demand side of the market, to underscore the rights of patients—as both consumers and citizens—to health care service provision throughout the EU. This in turn exposes the many organizational and regulatory obstacles to market access that face out-of-state health care providers. Although a cornerstone of the EU's legal framework, the internal market for health care remains fragmented. This has important implications for the practical reach of the EU toolbox. **10.42**

The patient's toolbox

We have looked at the freedom to provide and receive services, primarily from the demand side of patients crossing borders. This has demonstrated how the ECJ has developed a parallel regime for patient mobility, based on the freedom to provide services of Article 56 TFEU, alongside the pre-existing rules based on the free **10.43**

[26] Commission Decision of 28 November 2005 on the application of Article 86(2) of the EC Treaty to State aid in the form of public service compensation granted to certain undertakings entrusted with the operation of services of general economic interest [2005] OJ L312/67; Community framework for State aid in the form of public service compensation [2005] OJ C297/4.

[27] Council Dir 92/49/EEC of 18 June 1992 on the coordination of laws, regulations and administrative provisions relating to direct insurance other than life assurance and amending Dirs 73/239/EEC and 88/357/EEC (Third Non-Life Insurance Directive) [1992] OJ L228/1.

movement of workers provided by Regulation 1408/71 (now Regulation 883/2004).[28] It successively determined that restitution-based insurance systems,[29] benefits-in-kind-based insurance systems,[30] and national health service systems [31] were obliged to enable the reimbursement of cross-border health care provision.

10.44 Greatly simplified, this case law can be summed up as follows. The scope of social security coverage is determined by the Member State of affiliation (the 'home' Member State) alone and therefore is not at issue. This is the key principle derived from *Duphar* (1984) that is still generally adhered to and reflected in Article 168(7) TFEU as well as Article 2(2) of the Patients' Rights Directive.[32] In addition, the right of individual patients to seek treatment abroad and pay for it themselves is not at stake: they are free to do so. Instead the focus of both the Article 56 TFEU regime and that of Regulation 883/2004 is on *the conditions for the reimbursement of treatment abroad*, when a patient is in principle entitled to the treatment involved in his Member State of affiliation.

- When Article 56 TFEU is relied on reimbursement is at the level of domestic treatment in the Member State of affiliation, based on Regulation 883/2004 reimbursement is at the level of the Member State of treatment. Where the latter is lower than the former, the difference may be claimed based on Article 56 TFEU.[33]
- More complicated is the question of whether prior authorization may be required. Based on Regulation 883/2004 prior authorization of treatment abroad is always required as a condition for reimbursement. Based on Article 56 TFEU, prior authorization (which is in principle a barrier to the freedom to provide services) may be required for hospital services. This is considered justified to safeguard the financial balance of the national social security system of the Member States and their planning in the hospital sector.
- So far, the ECJ has never required evidence before allowing this justification. Over time it has come to accept that prior authorization may be justified provided that material and procedural due process guarantees are respected concerning the

[28] Reg (EEC) No 1408/71 of the Council of 14 June 1971 on the application of social security schemes to employed persons and their families moving within the Community [1971] OJ L149/2; Reg (EC) No 883/2004 of the European Parliament and of the Council of 29 April 2004 on the coordination of social security systems [2004] OJ L166/1.

[29] Case C-158/96 *Raymond Kohll v Union des caisses de maladie* [1998] ECR I-1931; Case C-120/95 *Nicolas Decker v Caisse de maladie des employés privés* [1998] ECR I-1831.

[30] Case C-157/99 *B.S.M. Geraets-Smits v Stichting Ziekenfonds VGZ and H.T.M. Peerbooms v Stichting CZ Groep Zorgverzekeringen* [2001] ECR I-5473; Case C-385/99 *V.G. Müller-Fauré v Onderlinge Waarborgmaatschappij OZ Zorgverzekeringen UA and E.E.M. van Riet v Onderlinge Waarborgmaatschappij ZAO Zorgverzekeringen* [2003] ECR I-4509.

[31] Case C-372/04 *The Queen, ex parte Yvonne Watts v Bedford Primary Care Trust and Secretary of State for Health* [2006] ECR I-4325.

[32] Case 238/82 *Duphar* et al *v The Netherlands* [1984] ECR 523.

[33] cf Case C-368/98 *Abdon Vanbraekel* et al *v Alliance nationale des mutualités chrétiennes* [2001] ECR I-5363.

objective and proportionate nature of the authorization process, notably fleshing out the concept of 'undue delay' by requiring due regard to the individual circumstances of each patient. These requirements are similar if not identical for the Article 56 TFEU setting and that of Regulation 883/2004.

In this manner the ECJ has balanced the public interest justifications invoked by the Member States with the rights of individual patients based on free movement. It is this case law that was recently codified because the Member States, up to that point, had failed to implement it properly or consistently, and raised questions of coherence. The Patients' Rights Directive sets out a new framework for cross-border health care in the EU and forms a watershed in the approach to health care under EU law which had long been conditioned by the subsidiarity provisions in the Treaty. Older rights to reimbursement of costs are supplemented by new, more consumer-based rights to transparency and accountability, and are being combined with a formalization of the open method of coordination (OMC)-based cooperation. The transparency and accountability rights will lead to new data on prices, costs, and quality that will exceed what is now available nationally—even if only because they will be compared across systems, and may be produced and/or adjusted to do so. We believe these rights will not be restricted to consumers crossing borders but also within the confines of the individual Member State, because it is not conceivable that they will be granted to citizens from other Member States but not nationally. **10.45**

As a result, even if actual benefit levels are not harmonized, the conditions for access to cross-border health care are now harmonized to a significant extent. Hence the leading development concerning patient mobility is in the area of secondary law, with the Patients' Rights Directive adopted on 9 March 2011 that came into force on 29 March 2011 and with implementation at national level required by 25 October 2013.[34] **10.46**

From Treaty rights to citizenship

As we have seen above the main technical content of the Patients' Rights Directive can be divided into three parts: **10.47**

- First, the Directive is based on the planning exception related to access and cost control. For the Member State of affiliation this concerns a system of prior authorization as well as other requirements that can be imposed; and the possibility to limit the application of the rules on reimbursement. For the Member States of treatment the planning exception can be invoked for safeguard measures. The norm applied is in line with standard principles of EU law, that is to say whether recourse to this exception is objectively justified, necessary, and proportional.

[34] Dir 2011/24/EU of the European Parliament and of the Council of 9 March 2011 on the application of patients' rights in cross-border healthcare [2011] OJ L88/45.

- Second, the Directive is clearly based on the concept of 'undue delay', that had been developed in the case law. This means looking at the individual health characteristics of the patient such as the degree of pain and the development of the illness. Also, the job implications for the patient must be taken into account. Such considerations trump the exception invoked by the Member State. This is also more in line with Regulation 883/2004 which contains similar provisions.
- Third, and finally, other due process guarantees are imposed as well, such as the right to a decision on a case by case basis that is subject to judicial review.

10.48 Based on these three elements the Directive shapes a coherent system that as such forms an improvement on the preceding case law. However, apart from leaving less room for uncertainty, it also leaves less room for secondary effects such as exposing the underlying costs of treatment. We may conclude that the European Commission's proposal follows the familiar interaction between negative and positive integration. Striking down barriers to the market freedoms breeds the need for elaborating rights and obligations in legislation that strikes a new balance between private freedoms and legitimate public interests. For health care this is no less than a watershed given the constitutional barriers that had been erected in the Treaty against harmonization in this field and which have now been breached. Could this mean the scope for applying the EU law concept of citizenship has increased?

10.49 It appears that so far citizenship has played a limited role in this context. The main instance where citizenship rights per se, rather than consumer rights under the free movement rules, has been invoked is the *Van Delft* (2010) case concerning allegations of discrimination as regards the applicant's health insurance status against pensioners resident in another Member State.[35] The ECJ held that Article 20 TFEU did not bar the Member States from subjecting such citizens to the same insurance requirements but did block unjustified discrimination—which would frustrate the right to reside throughout the EU. In this context citizenship is thus, so far, an extension of free movement. Will this develop in the direction of migration and/or solidarity rights?

10.50 It remains to be seen whether other EU integration mechanisms such as spill-over, the interaction between liberalization and regulation, as well as the increasing role of individual EU citizenship rights, will have a similar impact on this sector in the coming years. It also remains to be seen whether the degree of harmonization achieved leaves room for further case law in this area that is based directly on the freedom of services. For the time being however the momentum seems to have shifted from the sphere of primary law to that of secondary law. This does not mean that the application of the other Treaty freedoms is now plain sailing.

[35] Case C-345/09 *J.A. van Delft and Others v College voor zorgverzekeringen* [2010] judgment of 14 October 2010 (nyr).

Health care providers and the EU Toolbox

It is generally acknowledged that compared to the comparatively simple command and control systems of public provision, health markets need more regulation as a framework for efficient transactions (to reduce transaction costs). The need for new national rules is therefore likely to be inescapable in systems that are in transition to a more market-based system, and in search of a balance between solidarity, social cohesion, and efficiency. The EU law toolbox may be especially relevant in this situation—if a Member State opens its health care services even to limited competition, then it must comply with its EU law obligations in full. Health care providers have a variety of tools with which to attempt to gain access to new markets; but even if a national health care sector continues to be organized along more traditional solidarity based lines, EU law is not without relevance. Secondary legislation, including the EU Procurement Directives, can play an important role in securing market access. **10.51**

Vertical and horizontal enforcement and the EU competition regime

Competition law applies as soon as governments introduce a modicum of competition, meaning both mixed-markets and a solidarity-based approach to health care provision and its funding. However, in the application of the competition rules to the health sector, the scope for competing private undertakings operating in the sector may be limited by public service requirements. Prominent examples are the *BUPA* (2008) case where an Irish risk equalization scheme between private health insurers was held to not to constitute state aid by the Court of First Instance;[36] *AG2R Prévoyance* (2010),[37] where private health insurance was considered a SGEI as defined by the social partners; and *Ambulanz Glöckner* (2001), where awarding exclusive rights to private ambulance services in the interest of universal service provision was in principle considered to be acceptable.[38] **10.52**

It should be noted however that the dividing lines between solidarity-based and market-based health care provision are no longer clearly drawn, and as a result the boundaries of EU competition law remain untested in some important respects. For example, the interaction between public and private insurance is evolving: private health insurance is not necessarily a mere substitute for cover that would otherwise be provided by social security, but has an increasingly important supplementary function. (For instance in Ireland, the supplementary private health insurance services at issue in the *BUPA* case covered 50 per cent of the population.) **10.53**

---

[36] Case T-289/03 *British United Provident Association Ltd (BUPA)* et al *v Commission* [2008] ECR II-81. Noted by W Sauter [2009] 46 *Common Market Law Review* 269.

[37] Case C-437/09 *AG2R Prévoyance v Beaudout Père et Fils SARL* [2011] judgment of 3 March 2011 (nyr).

[38] Case C-475/99 *Firma Ambulanz Glöckner v Landkreis Südwestpfalz* [2001] ECR I-8089.

10.54 Despite this overall ambiguity, it is important to stress the basic distinction between public authorities and undertakings.

Public authorities and public and private rules

10.55 The organization of health care delivery (the supply side) is primarily determined by Member State rules and through national regulations. Obstacles to market access, entry barriers, are also likely to originate from these types of measures. In theory, the Treaty competition rules can be applied to the Member States' rules and regulations—eg if those rules confer an exclusive right on an undertaking which is unable to meet demand. The government measure in question could be challenged under the rules concerning exclusive rights and dominance abuse in Articles 106(1) and 102 TFEU. Agreements between health professionals, to organize access to treatment in a restrictive manner, that are sanctioned by public regulation may also be challenged, (under certain conditions) under Article 4(3) TEU (formerly Articles 3, 5 and 10 EC) in combination with Article 101 TFEU.[39] So far however, the ECJ has been reluctant to apply these provisions to the health care sector, such as national legislation prohibiting advertising by dentists in *Doulamis* (2008).[40] In other cases, notably *Wouters* (2002), the ECJ has been even more deferential to state-backed self-regulation by professional organizations.[41]

Undertakings

10.56 The application of the competition rules is restricted to situations where 'undertakings' are involved.[42] As discussed in Chapter 8, the ECJ has tended to construe this concept rather broadly by taking a functional approach. What is important is whether or not an entity is engaged in an economic activity.

10.57 The main exclusion from the concept of economic activity from the perspective of the health care sector is that of 'organization based on social solidarity'—as opposed to being active in the market subject to competition.[43] This characteristic can feed through in the different functions in which an entity is engaged. Thus in

[39] Case 267/86 *Pascal Van Eycke v ASPA NV* [1988] ECR 4769; Case C-198/01 *Consorzio Industrie Fiammiferi (CIF) v Autorità Garante della Concorrenza e del Mercato* [2003] I-8055; Case C-35/99 *Criminal proceedings against Manuele Arduino* [2002] I-1529.

[40] cf Case C-446/05 *Criminal proceedings against Ioannis Doulamis* [2008] ECR I-1377.

[41] Case C-309/99 *J.C.J. Wouters, J.W. Savelbergh and Price Waterhouse Belastingadviseurs BV v Algemene Raad van de Nederlandse Orde van Advocaten* [2002] ECR I-1577.

[42] In Case C-67/96 *Albany International BV v Stichting Bedrijfspensioenfonds Textielindustrie* [1999] ECR I-5751, para 72 ff; and Case 222-/98 *Hendrik van der Woude v Stichting Beatrixoord* [2000] ECR I-7111. Contrast with Case C-350/07 *Kattner Stahlbau GmbH v Maschinenbau- und Metall-Berufsgenossenschaft* [2009] ECR I-1513.

[43] Generally contrasted in this context are Case C-41/90 *Klaus Höfner and Fritz Elser v Macrotron GmbH* [1991] I-1979 (defining the concept of undertaking); and Joined Cases C-159/91 and C-160/91 *Christian Poucet v Assurances Générales de France and Caisse Mutuelle Régionale du Languedoc-Roussillon (Poucet)* [1993] I-637 (defining solidarity).

AOK (2004), price fixing in relation to maximum reimbursements for pharmaceuticals by German health insurers fell outside the scope of competition law as they were not considered to be undertakings—in spite of the fact that the insurers competed on certain key parameters, such as the amount of contributions.[44] The ECJ based its findings on the existence of a 'Solidärgemeinschaft' in the form of risk equalization, and of obligatory statutory benefits. Similarly, in *FENIN* (2006), the ECJ held that Spanish health care management bodies were incapable of infringing Article 102 TFEU in their role as purchasers because they could not be regarded as undertakings in their role as managers of the public health care system—and the two identities were not separable.[45] Conversely, in *Pavlov* (2000), medical specialists contributing to a single occupational pension fund were held to be acting as undertakings.[46]

The restriction in scope to undertakings applies equally to the Treaty state aid rules, Articles 107 and 108 TFEU, as these rules only apply where a selective economic benefit (funded by state resources) is conferred upon an undertaking (as opposed to another part of the state).[47] It cannot however be dismissed that the concept of an undertaking may evolve further as the scope of both liberalization and competition in national health sectors increase in tandem. **10.58**

State action and the Treaty competition rules

So far the EU precedents in this particular area of the law fail to map out a clear path as to how and when the Treaty competition rules can be used (either by public or private parties) to challenge state measures instead of the behaviour of undertakings. In so far as challenges to state measures are concerned, the Treaty competition rules are regarded as having been infringed only in two types cases: where a Member State requires or favours the adoption of agreements, decisions, or concerted practices contrary to Article 101 TFEU, or reinforces their effects; or, alternatively, where that State divests its own rules of the character of legislation by delegating to private economic operators responsibility for taking decisions affecting the economic sphere. This case law has been the subject of critical academic commentary. In addition, opinions of several Advocate Generals have suggested a further refinement to it. The limitations of the case law have been summarized as follows:[48] **10.59**

(i) inability to cope with state measures restricting competition without mandating an anti-competitive conduct on the part of economic operators;

[44] Joined Cases C-264/01, C-306/01, C-354/01 and C-355/01 *AOK Bundesverband* et al *v Ichthyol-Gesellschaft Cordes* et al [2004] ECR I -2493.

[45] Case C-205/03 P *Federación Española de Empresas de Tecnología Sanitaria (FENIN) v Commission* [2006] ECR I-6295. This can be contrasted with a bolder approach by national authorities. cf the UK competition authority's in its 2002 ruling in *Better Care* [2002] CAT 7, para 234.

[46] Joined Cases C-180/98 to C-184/98 *Pavel Pavlov* et al *v Stichting Pensioenfonds Medische Specialisten* [2000] ECR I-6451.

[47] Case T-289/03 *BUPA*, supra n 36.

[48] See AG Maduro in Joined Cases C–94/04 and C–200/04 *Cipolla* [2006] ECR 1-11421.

(ii) inconsistent application of the 'active supervision' criterion across cases;
(iii) failure to account for the legitimate results that can motivate the mere codification or approval of measures decided by industry actors; and
(iv) lack of concern for the impact of the relevant state measures on out of state economic actors in terms of access to the national market.

10.60 Finally, the 'state action' doctrine creates uncertainty as to the possible justification for anti-competitive conduct.[49] EU competition law does not allow for 'public interest' type justifications unless these can be fitted into Article 101(3). It is therefore hardly surprising that attempts by health providers to rely on the combined application of Article 4(3) TEU and Article 101 TFEU to strike down a state measure have met with little success to date.

The competition and the free movement rules compared

The standard for free movement

10.61 The threshold for applying the free movement rules to health care appears now to be lower than that for the competition rules. This offers improved opportunities for market actors to use this part of the toolbox to challenge obstacles to market entry. The fact that the provision of health care is a service activity within the meaning of the EU Treaty means that health care providers established in one Member State can exercise their fundamental freedom to establish themselves or provide services in another. The interpretation of what constitutes a barrier to free movement has been gradually extended to cover national measures which are not directly discriminatory (which expressly exclude or militate against service providers from other Member States) but which put domestic providers at an advantage. As restated in *Kattner* (2009) concerning the legality of compulsory accident insurance rules:

> (…) the freedom to provide services requires not only the elimination of all discrimination on grounds of nationality against providers of services who are established in another Member State, but also the abolition of any restriction, even if it applies without distinction to national providers of services and to those of other Member States, which is liable to prohibit, impede or render less advantageous the activities of a provider of services established in another Member State where he lawfully provides similar services.[50]

10.62 In Case C-518/06 *Commission v Italy*,[51] (motor insurance) the ECJ ruled that a restriction would arise where the imposition of a national measure could lead to substantial additional costs for companies in terms of organization and investment

---

[49] D Gerard 'EU Competition Policy after Lisbon: Time to Review the 'State Action' Doctrine [2010] *1 JBCL & Pract* 202

[50] Case C-350/07 *Kattner*, supra n 42.

[51] Case C-518/06 *Commission v Italy* [2009] ECR I-03491, paras 66–69.

inter alia, because the companies involved would have to re-think their business strategies and considerably expand the range of services offered.

Hence, any national measure which requires a service provider to amend their services or business model in order to provide or to continue to provide those services in another Member State is a restriction on the free movement of services within the meaning of Article 56 TFEU. The concept of a restriction is wide, and covers all rules which although applicable without distinction, affect access to the market for undertakings from other Member States and thereby hinder intra-community trade. **10.63**

Similarly, the ECJ has held in its more recent judgment in Case C-565/08 *Commission v Italy*,[52] (lawyers' fees) that a restriction on the freedom of establishment exists, in particular, if parties are deprived of the opportunity of gaining access to the market of the host Member State under conditions of normal and effective competition.[53] As Advocate General Sharpston has confirmed in her review of the ECJ's recent case law in her Opinion in Case C-400/08 *Commission v Spain*, the restriction in question does not have to result in a 'serious' interference—it is sufficient that market access is less attractive.[54] **10.64**

Given this extensive interpretation, it is hardly surprising that the ECJ can also cast its net very widely to cover not only national rules and practices but also various implementation procedures. Of particular interest here is Case C-400/08 and the ECJ's approach to the constitution and role of the so-called 'Retail Facilities Committee', a committee set up to advise on planning licence applications, but composed of potential competitors of the economic operator wishing to set up a new large retail establishment in Catalonia. It should be noted that the only sectoral interest represented in that committee was that of the existing local trade. Parallels with cases such as *Hartlauer* and *French laboratories* are immediately apparent. In Case C-400/08 the ECJ held that 'a body composed of potential competitors of the applicant for a licence, cannot constitute an appropriate instrument for pursuing objectives relating to consumer protection'.[55] **10.65**

Market access, at the level of the provider of services or undertaking that intends to establish itself in a Member State, is the key issue in the context of non-discriminatory barriers.[56] At the same time, as the ECJ has pointed out, blocking establishment **10.66**

[52] Case C-565/08 *Commission v Italy* [2011] judgment of 29 March 2011 (nyr).

[53] Case C-442/02 *CaixaBank France v Ministère de l'Économie, des Finances et de l'Industrie* [2004] ECR I- 8961, paras 13–14; Joined Cases C-94/04 and C-202/04 *Cipolla and Others* [2006] ECR I-11421, para 59; and Case C-384/08 *Attanasio Group* [2010] ECR I-0000, para 45.

[54] Case C-400/08 *European Commission v Kingdom of Spain* [2011] Opinion of AG Sharpston delivered on 7 October 2010.

[55] Case C-400/08 *Commission v Spain* [2011] judgment of 24 March 2011 (nyr), at paras 111–13.

[56] Case C-442/02 *CaixaBank France v Ministère de l'Économie, des Finances et de l'Industrie* [2004] ECR I- 8961, paras 13–14.

deprives consumers of greater choice.[57] Consumer choice thus adds a second, and even more powerful, rationale for acting against non-discriminatory measures that favour domestic incumbents.

10.67 Furthermore, the EU courts have recognized that these Treaty articles may be invoked in certain horizontal situations: that is, in disputes between non-state actors and not just vertically, between a state and a market actor.[58]

Advantages and disadvantages to relying on free movement

10.68 These combined developments greatly enhance the potential attraction for health care providers to use the market freedoms to challenge national rules (and/or related organizational arrangements) in relation to health care provision and its financing, that constitute entry barriers and can also serve as a major source of market power for incumbent providers. At the same time, there are disadvantages to relying on free movement which should not be overlooked.

10.69 A complaint to the European Commission that a national rule violates Articles 49 or 56 TFEU may lead the Commission to open infringement proceedings against the offending Member State, and can eventually lead to the restrictions that were challenged being removed. However, this is invariably a long and unpredictable process. The Commission has far more discretion regarding these procedures and cannot be required to take a formal position on a complaint, as it is required to do under Regulation 1/2003 on the application of Articles 81 and 82 EC (now Articles 101 and 102 TFEU).[59]

10.70 It should be noted however that the Commission may reject competition related complaints based on the *Automec* case law, assigning priority based on its assessment of the Community interest.[60] Where the Commission rejects a complaint, the complainant is entitled to a decision of the Commission without prejudice to Article 7(3) of the Procedural Regulation 773/2004 where a complaint is deemed

[57] Joined Cases C-94/04 and C-202/04 *Federico Cipolla v Rosaria Fazari, née Portolese (C-94/04) and Stefano Macrino and Claudia Capoparte v Roberto Meloni (C-202/04)* [2006] I-11421, paras 59–60.

[58] cf eg Case C-176/96 *Jyri Lehtonen and Castors Canada Dry Namur-Braine ASBL v Fédération royale belge des sociétés de basket-ball ASBL (FRBSB)* [2000] ECR I-2681; Case 36/74 *Walrave and Koch* [1974] ECR 1405; Case C-309/99 *Wouters*, supra n 42; Joined Cases C-51/96 and C-191/97 *Christelle Deliège v Ligue francophone de judo et disciplines associées ASBL, Ligue belge de judo ASBL, Union européenne de judo (C-51/96) and François Pacquée (C-191/97)* [2000] ECR I-2549; Case C-411/98 *Angelo Ferlini v Centre hospitalier de Luxembourg* [2000] ECR I-8081; and Case C-281/98 *Roman Angonese v Cassa di Risparmio di Bolzano SpA* [2000] ECR I-4139.

[59] Council Reg (EC) No 1/2003 of 16 December 2002 on the implementation of the rules on competition laid down in Articles 81 and 82 of the Treaty [2003] OJ L1/1.

[60] Case T-64/89 *Automec Srl v Commission* [1990] ECR II-367; and Case T-24/90 *Automec Srl v Commission* [1992] ECR II-2223.

withdrawn if time limits are not respected by the complainant.[61] The final decision to proceed with infringement proceedings is inevitably a political one, and there are many reasons (eg impending elections), which can dissuade the Commission from tackling sensitive cases.

The exceptions to free movement

Although there is a relatively low threshold for the application of the free movement rules, the EU Treaty is not to be seen as an instrument of deregulation nor does it give prospective entrants unconditional access to any particular domestic health care market. Barriers to free movement can be maintained if these are in the public interest. Justification consists in meeting a four part test generally traced back to *Gebhard* (1995) where the ECJ accepted that non-discriminatory rules could constitute obstacles to free movement.[62] The first part of the test is whether the measure is *non-discriminatory* and applies to domestic and non-domestic providers alike; and second, is in pursuit of a legitimate *(overriding reason of) public interest* then; in the absence of harmonization at least, third, Member States have to prove that it is *appropriate* (or 'suitable') for ensuring the attainment of a public interest objective; and the fourth and final part of the test is that the contended measure does not exceed what is *necessary* to attain the objective (often framed as a test of whether the result can be achieved in a less restrictive way). **10.71**

As we have seen in the internal market chapters (Chapters 3 and 4), this 'public interest' test is frequently applied in a casuistic manner and often based on implicit and ready assumptions about the goals of the (national) system in question, and the ways in which those goals can be pursued.[63] These judicial assumptions are not subject to any form of economic testing as regards their plausibility (allowing, eg the mere formal existence of deontology rules to become a trump card). This lack of regard for economic analysis is currently one of the most important areas of divergence between the free movement and the competition rules. A clearer definition of the public interest as a basis for strictly proportionate regulatory intervention would be of considerable assistance to those seeking to challenge such rules and would provide greater legal certainty for all concerned. At present, when applying the free movement rules, and in the absence of harmonization, the ECJ appears to leave it entirely up to the national authorities to strike this balance and only demands **10.72**

---

[61] Commission Reg (EC) No 773/2004 of 7 April 2004 relating to the conduct of proceedings by the Commission pursuant to Articles 81 and 82 of the EC Treaty [2004] OJ L123/18; See Commission Notice on the handling of complaints by the Commission under Articles 81 and 82 of the EC Treaty [2004] OJ C101/05.

[62] Case C-55/94 *Reinhard Gebhard v Consiglio dell'Ordine degli Avvocati e Procuratori di Milano (Gebhard)* [1995] ECR I-4165, para 37; citing Case C-19/92 *Kraus v Land Baden-Wuerttemberg (Kraus)* [1993] ECR I-1663, para 32. cf E Spaventa, 'From *Gebhard* to *Carpenter*: towards a (non-) economic European constitution' (2004) *Common Market Law Review* 743.

[63] cf point 89 of his Opinion of AG Jacobs in Joined Cases C-180/98 to C-184/98 *Pavlov*, supra n 46 as cited there in the body of the text.

that they do so consistently. While this cautious approach may be understandable given the sensitivities involved, it should not be overlooked that in practice this primarily means that it essentially serves vested national interests best. In this respect it is illustrative that many of the free movement cases have resulted from challenges lodged by professional organizations keen to defend the status quo.

10.73 Thus in *German hospital pharmacies* the ECJ held that the German system did not go beyond what is necessary. In addition it pointed out that the system proposed by the Commission (with separate supplying and monitoring pharmacies) would be financially wasteful. The Court then went on to emphasize first, the need for planning the hospital system, and second, the need to avoid financial waste.[64] The 'unity and balance' of the system may approximate to the 'consistency' criterion in *Dermoestética* and *Hartlauer*, or the financial balance of the medical systems in the earlier patient mobility cases. However, it is by no means evident why the process of contracting for medicines through *in situ* pharmacists by individual hospitals should be seen as forming part of a system that required coherence and balance: there simply was no system here that required unity and balance.

10.74 We have suggested that a more positive reading of this judgment could be seen as allowing a Member States to plan a gradual reorganization (eg to move former internal services to an external setting) without the risk of having that controlled transformation threatened by the free movement rules. At the same time the ECJ gave little credence to the Commission's attempts to demonstrate that public health objectives need not have been put at risk if the requirement that the pharmacist should be local had been eliminated, and that other measures were realistically possible and would not have imposed unnecessary costs on the system. This important ruling therefore appears to be based on the implicit assumption that if a system of organization of certain health care activities is inextricably linked with a certain standard or level of protection, then any further attempted analysis of the different components of that system can be avoided by assuming a need for unity and balance.

10.75 In the case law involving the application of the fundamental freedoms to the supply side of markets such as the health care market, invariably it is a private interest in market access that has to weighed against a public interest in regulation and its stated objectives (even if the latter has the effect of protecting an incumbent's privileged position on that market). In this context the party seeking market access is assumed to be driven by profit motives, which could result in 'cherry-picking' of low risk cases for example. This is then viewed as a threat to the public values that national health sector regulation is expected to uphold. Obviously when a patient

---

[64] Referring to Case C-157/99 *Smits and Peerbooms*, supra n 30; Case C-385/99 *V.G. Müller-Fauré v Onderlinge Waarborgmaatschappij OZ Zorgverzekeringen UA and E.E.M. van Riet v Onderlinge Waarborgmaatschappij ZAO Zorgverzekeringen (Müller-Fauré)* [2003] ECR I-4509; Case C-372/04 *Watts*, supra n 8.

exercises her rights to choose a supplier, these assumptions do not readily come into play. It is assumed that choice in and of itself brings benefits. On the supply side of the health care market, however, there is very little consideration given in the case law as to whether market access or market exclusion can or could bring clear benefits to consumers. This may indicate that for the time being at least, the potential reach of the EU toolbox is more limited for health providers, for instance when seeking cross-border establishment, than for patients seeking treatment.

E. Social Services Law and EU Health Care—New Trends?

We want to conclude this chapter with some comments on a final item in the EU toolbox, the Treaty rules on state aid; this is because we believe the impending developments in this area to be of particular interest. In contrast to the competition rules on antitrust, in state aid law the Commission remains in charge of a centralized system so that enforcement here is mainly vertical—in that it is a process where the Commission adopts Decisions addressed to Member States to abolish aid measures. The latter should then recover the aid from the beneficiary. Private parties may bring a complaint before the Commission but the Commission is not obliged to act on that complaint—it must however provide the complainant with a summary of reasons for not doing so.[65] National courts are competent to interpret and apply the Commission's block exemption regulations on certain types of state aid. In its jurisprudence on Article 108(3) TFEU the ECJ often refers to the fact that the national court must ensure the protection of individual rights 'under national law'. At the same time this protection must be effective and must take account of the direct effect of the standstill obligation and the EU interest. **10.76**

As Article 108(3) TFEU is directly effective, competitors may also seek to enforce that provision before national courts. A national court may have cause to interpret and apply the concept of aid as set out in Article 107(1) TFEU in order to determine whether the aid ought to have been notified, and if so, whether the 'standstill' provision as laid down in Article 108(3) TFEU has been respected. The national court may have to make certain findings in fact, for example to ascertain whether the measure in question may distort competition and affect trade between Member States or whether the measure in question complies with the 'market investor principle'. This allows for potential 'horizontal' enforcement: a competitor could seek to challenge the grant of aid before the national courts. The national court cannot however rule on the compatibility of an aid measure.[66] This falls within the exclusive competence of the Commission and the Council. **10.77**

[65] Case C-521/06 *P Athinaiki v Commission* [2009] ECR I-5829.

[66] Furthermore a national court cannot ask the ECJ on a reference for a preliminary ruling under Art 267 TFEU for guidance as to the compatibility with the internal market of a given state aid measure or scheme.

10.78 There is still some doubt as to whether a national court is competent to apply the exemption from the Treaty rules, including the state aid rules, as provided under Article 106(2) TFEU.[67] Following the ECJ's landmark ruling in the *Altmark* case, a national court should be satisfied that each of the four '*Altmark* criteria' have been met before ruling that a national measure is not aid within the meaning of Article 107(1) TFEU.[68] If any one of those conditions is not met, however, the national court should rule that the measure ought to have been notified, unless it falls within the scope of SGEI Decision of 2005[69] as replaced by the recent Decision of 2011.[70] It is not clear whether the national court is then competent to judge whether the conditions set out for exemption in the Decision are met.

How effective is the state aid tool?

10.79 For the state aid cases related to health care that we reviewed in Chapter 9, at least since the *Altmark* case (2003)[71] and with the subsequent '*Altmark* packages' (2005 and 2011), the solution to balancing national public service objectives and the EU interest is now generally based on the concept of SGEI. Moreover, since the health insurance case *BUPA* (2008), the concept of an SGEI can include universal service and covers all compulsory public interest provision.[72] This is significant for health care services where some degree of public interest provision is frequently involved but recourse to the SGEI concept is not yet commonplace—given that many Member States do not explicitly or formally entrust health care providers with such services. This means that the SGEI must be derived from the regulatory context—complicating, at a minimum, the application of the proportionality test required. In a worst case scenario from the perspective of the Member State (albeit one that it can remedy by taking legislative action), the Commission will not find an SGEI to exist in the absence of a formal assignment of a public service obligation in order to establish compatibility under Article 106(2) TFEU.

10.80 In fact the '*Monti/Kroes* package' of measures—also referred to as the '*Altmark* package' of 2005, already included a block exemption from the state aid rules for

[67] See AG Geelhoed's Opinion in Case C-172/00 *Ferring Arzneimittel GmbH v Eurim-Pharm Arzneimittel GmbH* [2002] ECR I-6891.

[68] Case C-280/00 *Altmark Trans GmbH and Regierungspräsidium Magdeburg v Nahverkehrsgesellschaft Altmark GmbH, and Oberbundesanwalt beim Bundesverwaltungsgericht* [2003] ECR I-7747.

[69] Commission Decision of 28 November 2005 on the application of Article 86(2) of the EC Treaty to State aid in the form of public service compensation granted to certain undertakings entrusted with the operation of services of general economic interest [2005] OJ L312/67.

[70] Commission Decision of 20 December 2011 on the application of Article 106(2) of the Treaty on the Functioning of the European Union to State aid in the form of public service compensation granted to certain undertakings entrusted with the operation of services of general economic interest [2012] OJ L7/3; Commission Communication on the application of the European Union State aid rules to compensation granted for the provision of services of general economic interest [2012] OJ C8/4.

[71] Case C-280/00 *Altmark*, supra n 68.

[72] Case T-289/03 *BUPA*, supra n 36.

hospital services—provided they are entrusted with a SGEI by formal legal act and that the rules on calculating compensation are respected. As a result, as we concluded in Chapter 9, we could observe the beginnings of health care sensitive rulemaking and guidance by the EU courts and Commission, based on the recognition that the proportionate pursuit of public policy objectives by means of universal service obligations in line with state aid obligations can be secured by invoking the SGEI exception in this area. We also noted in Chapter 5 that a 'mild regime' had been adopted in relation to the application of the public procurement directives in the health care sector, even if this approach has not worked entirely satisfactorily. Two recent developments in relation to both these regimes may indicate that a more consolidated, coherent, as well as focused approach, to the application of the Treaty state aid rules, as well as to the Treaty free movement rules to what are now known as social security services, is now emerging.

The so-called '*Altmark* package' of 2005 expired in November 2011 and consulta- **10.81**
tion on its revision coincided with a review of the current EU procurement regime for the purpose of aligning the two—that is in relation to selection of provider and calculation of compensation—in order to ensure a consistent approach.[73] The reforms are aimed at increasing legal certainty as well as flexibility for Member States. Both legal certainty and flexibility will be needed as the health care sector is increasingly subjected to EU law and the balance between national solidarity and EU-wide competition is to be re-established in this context.

The second *Altmark* package

In December 2011 revisions to the 2005 '*Altmark* package', now referred to as the **10.82**
so-called 'second *Altmark* package' were adopted.[74] The Commission has extended the block exemption Decision to a wider category of social security services including health services and long term care generally (Article 2(c)), and not only to hospital care and social housing as was previously the case. As of 31 January 2012, these sectors are to be exempt from the general notification and standstill requirements imposed under Article 108(3) TFEU and would not be subject to any thresholds on the amount of compensation they may receive in order to escape notification (the general threshold, which does not apply here, is €15 million annually).

[73] Commission Communication, Reform of the EU State Aid Rules on Services of General Economic Interest COM(2011) 146 final. cf also 'A new strategy for the single market at the service of Europe's economy and society: Report to the President of the European Commission José Manuel Barroso', by M Monti (Brussels, 9 May 2010), pp 73–4.

[74] Commission SGEI Decision, supra n 71; Communication SGEI Framework, supra n 71; Communication from the Commission, European Union framework for State aid in the form of public service compensation [2012] OJ C8/15; and Draft Commission Regulation on the application of Articles 107 and 108 of the Treaty on the Functioning of the European Union to *de minimis* aid granted to undertakings providing services of general economic interest [2012] OJ C8/23.

If it meets the requirements of the Decision, the compensation to health care services concerned is *ipso facto* compatible with the internal market.

10.83 The new Decision maintains essentially the same requirements as the earlier 2005 Decision. The aid must be granted for a genuine and correctly defined SGEI, and as regards the act of entrustment, this must set out inter alia the parameters for compensation as well as the arrangements for avoiding and recovering any overcompensation. The duration of the entrustment should be limited and should be justified by the need to depreciate the main assets required to provide the SGEI. At the same time the Decision imposes stricter requirements on how that compensation is to be calculated. In particular the Commission is attempting to take a closer look at the costs to be compensated and to build in certain safeguards to ensure that those costs are incurred efficiently.

10.84 An important innovation of the new framework for state aid, in the form of public service compensation[75] which applies to aid which would not fall within the scope of the exemption Decision, is the requirement for Member States to hold a public consultation to establish public service needs. Finally the Commission considers that contracts for the performance of SGEIs should be awarded in compliance with the procurement principles, as well as the EU procurement Directives in so far as these apply. If such procedures have not been followed, then the aid cannot be deemed compatible. If in its subsequent enforcement, the Commission succeeds in its attempt to restrict 'gold plating' of public services by the Member States, this may indicate that the Commission is prepared to embark on a more economic approach to examining the trade off between national public interests on the one hand and competition and free movement objectives on the other.

10.85 At the same time in *BUPA* (2008),[76] private provision of an SGEI relating to supplementary health insurance according to public standards was found to be consistent with the *Altmark* criteria. The Commission declared public provision of social and hospital services based on SGEI defined by a governing body staffed by representatives of municipal social services compatible with the internal market in its *IRIS-H* Decision of 2009.[77] In *AG2R Prévoyance* (2010) the ECJ accepted the existence of an SGEI in supplementary health insurance formulated by the social partners.[78] Together with the revision of the SGEI rules just discussed, these developments could have a profound effect on the way health care services are organized and delivered in the EU, relying on private provision, public entrustment, and EU

[75] Commission Communication, European Union framework for State aid in the form of public service compensation, COM(2011) 9406 final.

[76] Case T-289/03 *BUPA*, supra n 36.

[77] Decision of the Commission of 28 October 2009 with regard to state aid NN 54/2009 (ex CP 244/2005)—Belgium—financing of public hospitals of the IRIS-network of the Brussels capital region.

[78] Case C-437/09 *AG2R Prévoyance*, supra n 37.

supervision, if not on the basis of *ex ante* notification then on the basis of the onerous *ex post* reporting requirements now imposed on Member States who wish to invoke the new exemption decision.

The proposed procurement regime

On the same date that the new or 'second *Altmark* package' was adopted, the Commission announced its proposed reforms to the EU procurement regime. The new proposals, discussed in Chapter 5, can be summarized as follows. **10.86**

First, the Commission intends to publish a separate measure for a Directive on services concessions—albeit that social service concessions get special treatment. Second, the current distinction between Annex A and B services is to be abolished, and a new 'light regime' approach to social services, including health care services will be introduced. Third, a new, clearer definition of contracting entity is to be adopted and the definition of the term 'bodies governed by public law' is to be clarified. Fourth, new criteria for the award of contracts will be recognized—so that a cost- effectiveness approach is firmly recognized. Fifth, the right of contracting authorities to deploy a strategic use of the procurement rules, to improve public health for example, will be explicitly acknowledged. Finally, the proposal recommends the establishment of a designated national authority to monitor and review observance of procedures. **10.87**

As noted, a new separate procurement regime for social services, including health services is to be introduced. The Commission considers that social, health, and education services have specific characteristics which make them inappropriate for the regular procedures used to award public service contracts. These services are considered to be typically provided within a specific context that varies widely between Member States due to different administrative organizational and cultural circumstances. Therefore, once again the Commission confirms that such services have, by their very nature, only a very limited cross-border dimension. Member States should have the discretion to organize the choice of service providers. The proposed Directive provides: **10.88**

(i) a higher threshold for social services of €500,000, and
(ii) that above this threshold, the only procedural obligations that will apply are the so-called procurement principles, discussed in Chapter 5, that is respect for the basic 'procurement principles' of transparency and equal treatment.

F. Conclusion

As we have demonstrated throughout this book, the health care sector does not enjoy special status, in spite of the existence of a sector specific subsidiarity regime set out in Article 168 TFEU. In addition we note two contrasting trends, both of **10.89** which regard health care in particular. On the one hand, the patients' rights legislation and the legislation on pharmaceuticals advertising show that a new role for EU rules is emerging, to protect both individual and collective rights, based on the interest of the health care consumer, and perhaps ultimately the citizen. This means the creation of a new sphere of EU health care law that goes beyond national standards and rules to create common EU norms.

10.90 On the other hand, we have noted the carve-out for social services including health care in the proposed new procurement regime and in the newly adopted 'second *Altmark* package', which is based on the contrasting assumption that these services so far have a limited cross border dimension. This suggests that the remaining scope for the Member States to organize health care provision and delivery, and to finance it in accordance with national prerogatives, remains significant but at the same time confirms that their choices are not immune from the application of EU law. In this context it is important to remember that these specific regimes apply to health care and social service activities and not to the general economic activities undertaken by health care providers which may well have cross border effects. If a hospital which is contracting entity within the meaning of the Directive, buys a large quantity of tables or chairs it will be subject to the full procurement regime, whereas if it buys specialized beds or other health related equipment, it will fall under the proposed new simplified specific regime. If a hospital receives compensation for performing patient-related services it should fall within the new exemption Decision but if it receives state support to develop a new pharmaceutical product it probably will not.

10.91 These latest developments may seem ironic given the Commission's findings in its latest health strategy document, that coordinated action on public health policy is necessary to realize the full economic potential of the EU's health sector. It appears that for the time being these contrasting trends will play out in the health care sector in the EU, with pull and push factors (and/or supply and demand) at cross-purposes. While the Member States try to retain, and/or adjust themselves to, the present balance however the internal market and competition principles of the EU constitution are likely to continue generating an independent momentum toward further, if limited, integration. At the same time, the cost crisis in health care will inevitably lead to further experiments with new types of payment, insurance, and provision. It is the interaction between these trends that suggests that the EU internal market and competition rules will be of increased rather than diminished significance to health care in the years to come.

BIBLIOGRAPHY

Akkermans, B and Ramakers, E 'Article 345 TFEU (ex Article 295 EC), Its Meanings and Interpretations' [2010] *European Law Journal* 292.

Altenstetter, C 'Regulation of Medical Devices in the EU' in McKee, M, Mossialos, E and Baeten, R (eds), *The Impact of EU Law on Healthcare Systems* (Brussels: P.E.I.-Peter Lang, 2003).

—— and Permanand, G 'The EU regulation of medical devices and pharmaceuticals in comparative perspective' [2007] *Review of Policy Research* 385.

Arrow, K 'Uncertainty and the welfare economics of medical care' [1963] *American Economic Review* 941.

Baeten, R 'EU pharmaceutical policies: direct-to-consumer advertising' in Degryse, C (ed.), *Social Developments in the European Union* (European Trade Union Institute, 2009) 173–200.

—— and Palm, W 'The quality and safety paradox in the patients' rights Directive' [2011] *European Journal of Public Health* 271.

Belhaj, S and van de Gronden, JW 'Comments – Some Room For Competition Does Not Make a Sickness Fund An Undertaking. Is EC Competition Law Applicable to the Health Care Sector?' [2004] *European Competition Law Review* 682.

Barnard, C 'Fitting the remaining pieces into the goods and persons jigsaw?' [2001] *European Law Review* 35.

—— 'EU 'Social' Policy: From Employment Law to Labour Market Reform' in Craig, P and De Burca, G (eds), *The Evolution of EU Law* (Oxford: Oxford University Press, 2011).

—— *The substantive law of the EU: The four freedoms* (2nd edn, Oxford: Oxford University Press, 2007).

Beck, U *Risk Society: Towards a New Modernity* (London: Sage, 1992).

Biondi, A, Eeckhout, P and Flynn, J (eds), *The Law of State Aid in the European Union* (Oxford: Oxford University Press, 2004).

Bradley, K *A Handbook of EU Institutional Law* (Oxford: Hart Publishing, 2012).

de Búrca, G (ed.), *EU Law and the Welfare State: In Search of Solidarity* (Oxford: Oxford University Press, 2005).

Cabral, P 'Cross-border medical care in the European Union—bringing down a first wall' [1999] *European Law Review* 387.

Campolini, M 'ECJ Ruling Confirms Complete Harmonisation of Drug Advertising Rules in Europe' [2008] *RAJ Pharma* 519.

Chalmers, D, Davies, G and Monti, G *European Union Law* (2nd edn, Cambridge: Cambridge University Press 2010).

Cousins, M 'Patient Mobility and National Health Systems' [2007] *Legal Issues of Economic Integration* 183.

Crosby, S 'The new Tobacco Control Directive: an illiberal and illegal disdain for the law' [2002] *European Law Review* 177.

Culyer, AJ and Newhouse, JP (eds), *Handbook of Health Economics, Parts 1A and 1B* (Amsterdam: Elsevier, 2000).

Curran, R and Taylor, A 'Regulating the Advertising of Patient Services in the NHS in England' [2011] *European Journal of Consumer Law* 777.
Damman O, 'Public reporting about healthcare users' experiences: the Consumer Quality Index' (PhD thesis, Tilburg University, April 2010).
Dashwood, A 'From Van Duyn to Mangold via Marshall' [2006] *Cambridge Yearbook of European Legal Studies* 81.
Davies, G 'The effect of Mrs Watts' trip to France on the National Health Service' [2007] *King's Law Journal* 158.
—— 'Legislating for patients' rights' in van de Gronden, JW et al (eds), *Health Care and EU Law* (The Hague: TMC Asser Press, 2011) 191.
Delnoij, D and Sauter, W 'Patient information under the EU patients' rights Directive' [2011] *European Journal of Public Health* 271.
Dougan, M 'When Worlds Collide: Competing visions of the relationship between Direct Effect and Supremacy' [2007] *Common Market Law Review* 931.
—— 'Remedies and Procedures for Enforcing Union Law' in Craig, P and De Burca, G (eds), *The Evolution of EU Law* (2nd edn, Oxford: Oxford University Press, 2011) 408.
—— and Spaventa, E (eds), *Social welfare and EU law* (Oxford: Hart Publishing, 2005).
DTB 'How medical devices are regulated in the UK' [2010] *Drugs Ther Bull* 48.
Ezrachi, A (ed.), *Article 82 EC: reflections on its recent evolution* (Oxford: Hart Publishing, 2009).
Faull, J and Nikpay, A (eds), *The EC Law of Competition* (2nd edn, Oxford: Oxford University Press, 2007).
Ferrera, M 'Towards an "open" social citizenship? The new boundaries of welfare in the European Union' in de Búrca, G (ed.), *EU law and the Welfare State: In Search of Solidarity* (Oxford: Oxford University Press, 2005), 11.
—— *The Boundaries of Welfare: European Integration and the New Spatial Policies of Social Protection* (Oxford: Oxford University Press, 2005).
Flear, M 'Case C-385/99 V.G. Müller-Fauré v. Onderlinge Waarborgmaatschappij O.Z. Zorgverzekeringen U.A. and E.E.M. van Riet v. Onderlinge Waarborgmaatschappij Z.A.O. Zorgverzekeringen' [2004] *Common Market Law Review* 209.
Fornaciari, D, Callens, S and Schokkaert, E *Ziekenhuizen, mededingingsrecht en recht op kwaliteitsvolle zorg* (Antwerp: Intersentia, 2010).
Fraser, AG et al, 'Clinical evaluation of cardiovascular devices – principles, problems and proposals for European regulatory reform' [2011] *EUR Heart Journal* 1673.
Gaynor, M, Moreno-Serra, R and Propper, C 'Death by Market Power: Reform, Competition and Patient Outcomes in the National Health Service' [2010] *National Bureau of Economic Research (NBER) Working Paper No. 16164*, July 2010.
Georgakopoulos, NL *Principles and methods of law and economics: basic tools for normative reasoning* (Cambridge: Cambridge University Press, 2005).
D Gerard 'EU Competition policy after Lisbon: time to review the "State Action doctrine"?' [2010] *Journal of European Competition Law and Practice* 202.
Giddens, A 'Risk and Responsibility' [1999] *Modern Law Review* 1.
Giesen, R 'Case C-120/95, Nicolas Decker v. Caisse de maladie des employes prives, Judgment of 28 April 1998, Case C-158/96, Raymond Kohll v. Union des caisses de maladie, Judgment of 28 April 1998' [1999] *Common Market Law Review* 841.
Gosalbo Bono, R 'L'arrêt "Tabac" ou l'apport de la Cour de justice au débat sur la délimitation des compétences' [2001] *Revue trimestrielle de droit européen* 790.
Greer, SL *The politics of European health policies* (Buckingham: Open University Press, 2009), 3.

—— and Vanhercke, B 'The hard politics of soft law: the case of health' in Mossialos, E et al (Cambridge: Cambridge University Press, 2010).

van de Gronden, JW 'Purchasing care: economic activity or service of general (economic) interest?' [2004] *European Competition Law Review* 84.

—— 'The internal market, the state and private Initiative. A legal assessment of national mixed public-private arrangements in the light of European law. Private initiative, general interest and EC law' [2006] *Legal Issues of Economic Integration* 125.

—— 'Financing healthcare in EU law: Do the European state aid rules write out an effective prescription for integrating competition law with healthcare?' [2009] *Competition Law Review* 5.

—— 'Cross-border healthcare in the EU and the organization of the national health systems of the Member States: The dynamics resulting from the European Court of Justice's free movement and competition law' [2009] *Wisconsin International Law Journal* 705.

—— 'The Treaty provisions on competition and healthcare' in van de Gronden, JW, Krajewski, M, Neergaard, U and Szyszczak, E (eds), *EU Law and Healthcare* (The Hague: Asser Press, 2011).

—— and Sauter, W 'Taking the temperature: EU competition law and healthcare' [2011] *Legal Issues of European Integration* 213.

Gyselen, L 'Public service and EU competition law' [2011] *Journal of European Competition Law and Practice* 572.

Hancher, L 'The Pharmaceuticals market: Competition and free movement actively seeking compromises' in McKee, M, Mossialos, E and Baeten, R (eds), *The Impact of EU Law on Healthcare Systems* (Brussels: P.I.E.-Peter Lang, 2002), 235–75.

—— 'The EU pharmaceuticals market: parameters and pathways' in Mossialos, E et al (eds), *Health Systems Governance in Europe: The Role of European Law and Policy* (Cambridge: Cambridge University Press 2010).

—— and Sauter, W 'One Foot in the Grave or One Step Beyond? From *Sodemare* to *DocMorris*: The EU's Freedom of Establishment Case Law Concerning Healthcare' [2009] TILEC Discussion Paper No 2009-28 <http://ssrn.com/abstract=1429315> accessed 23 February 2012.

—— and Sauter, W 'One step beyond? From *Sodemare* to *DocMorris*: The EU's freedom of establishment case law concerning healthcare' [2010] *Common Market Law Review* 117.

—— and Larouche, P 'The coming of age of EU regulation of network industries and services of general economic interest', in Craig, P and De Burca, G (ed.), *The evolution of law* (Oxford: Oxford University Press, 2011).

—— and Földes, ME 'Push or Pull? – Information to Patients and European Law' [2011] *European Journal of Consumer Law* (forthcoming).

Hatzopolous, V 'Health Law and Policy: the Impact of the EU' in De Burca, G (ed.), *EU Law and the Welfare State: In Search of Solidarity* (Oxford: Oxford University Press, 2005), 125–27.

—— 'Public procurement and state aid in national healthcare systems' in Mossialos, E et al (eds), *Health Systems Governance in Europe: The Role of European Union Law and Policy* (Cambridge: Cambridge University Press, 2010).

—— 'Killing national health and insurance systems but healing patients? The European market for healthcare services after the judgments of the ECJ in *Vanbraekel* and *Peerbooms*' [2002] *Common Market Law Review* 683.

—— and Stergious, H 'Public procurement law and healthcare: from theory to practice' in van de Gronden, JW, Szyszczak, E, Neergaard, U and Krajewski, M (eds) *Healthcare* and

EU Law. Legal Issues of Services of General Interest (The Hague: TMC AsserPress/ Springer Verlag, 2011).
Hervey, TK 'Up in smoke? Community (anti)-tobacco law and policy' [2001] *European Law Review* 101.
—— 'The legal basis of European Community public health policy' in McKee, M, Mossialos, E and Baeten, R (eds), *The Impact of EU Law on Health Care Systems* (Brussels: PIE.-Peter Lang, 2002), 46–47.
—— 'Mapping the contours of European Union health law and policy' [2002] *European Public Law* 69.
—— 'The current legal framework on the right to seek healthcare abroad in the European Union' [2007] *Cambridge Yearbook of European Legal Studies* 261.
—— and McHale, J *Health Law and the European Union* (Cambridge: Cambridge University Press, 2004).
Hilf, M and Frahm, K 'Nichtigerklärung der Richtlinie zum Tabakwerbeverbot: Das letzte Wort?' [2001] *Recht der internationalen Wirtschaft* 128.
Kaczorowska, A 'A review of the creation by the European Court of Justice of the right to effective and speedy medical treatment and its outcomes' [2006] *European Law Journal* 345.
Kaldellis, EI 'Freedom of establishment versus freedom to provide services: an evaluation of the case – law developments in the area of indistinctly applicable rules' [2001] *Legal Issues of European Integration* 23.
Koening, C and C Paul, C 'State aid screening of hospital funding exemplified by the German case' [2010] *European State Aid Law Quarterly* 755.
Krajewski, M, Neergaard, U and van de Gronden, JW (eds), *The changing legal framework for services of general economic interest in Europe* (The Hague: Asser Press, 2009).
—— and Farley, M 'Non-economic activities in upstream markets and the scope of competition law after *Fenin*' [2007] 111.
Lear, J, Mossialos, E and Karl, B 'EU competition law and health policy' in Mossialos, E et al (eds), *Health Systems Governance in Europe: The Role of European Union Law and Policy* (Cambridge: Cambridge University Press, 2010), 343.
Loozen, EHM, Schut, EJ and Varkevisser, M 'Verticale integratie tussen zorgverzekeraars en zorgaanbieders' [2010] *Markt en Mededinging* 5.
Louis, F and Vallery, A '*Ferring* revisited: the *Altmark* Case and State financing of public service obligations' [2004] *World Competition* 53.
Lübbig, T and Klasse, M *Kartellrecht im Pharma- und Gesundheitssektor* (Baden-Baden: Nomos, 2007).
Lundvall, K, Ballebye Okholm, H, Marcusson, M, Jespersen, ST and Birkeland, ME 'Can Public Procurement spur Innovations in healthcare' (*Copenhagen Economics*, 2009) <www.vinnova.se> accessed 23 February 2012.
McKee, M, Mossialos, E and Baeten, R (eds), *The Impact of EU Law on Healthcare Systems* (Brussels: P.I.E.-Peter Lang, 2003).
McHale, J 'Fundamental rights and health care' in Mossalios, E et al (eds), *Health Systems Governance in Europe: The Role of European Union Law and Policy* (Cambridge: Cambridge University Press, 2010), 282.
van der Mei, AP 'Cross-border access to medical care: Non-hospital care and waiting lists' [2004] *Legal Issues of Economic Integration* 57.
Meny, Y 'De la democratie en Europe: Old Concepts and New Challenges' [2003] *Journal of Common Market Studies* 1.
Motta, M *EU competition policy: theory and practice* (Cambridge: Cambridge University Press, 2004).

Monti, G *EC Competition Law* (Cambridge: Cambridge University Press, 2007).
Moravcsik, A 'In defence of the democratic deficit: reassessing legitimacy in the European Union' [2002] *Journal of Common Market Studies* 603.
Mossialos, E, Permanand, G, Baeten, R and Hervey, TK (eds), *Health Systems Governance in Europe: The Role of European Union Law and Policy* (Cambridge: Cambridge University Press, 2010).
Newdick, C 'Citizenship, Free Movement and Healthcare: Cementing Individual Rights by Corroding Social Solidarity' [2006] *Common Market Law Review* 1645.
Odudu, O *The Boundaries of EC Competition Law: The Scope of Article 81* (Oxford: Oxford University Press, 2006).
—— 'Are state owned healthcare providers that are funded by general taxation undertakings subject to competition law?' [2011] *European Competition Law Review* 231.
Paolucci, F, den Exter, A and van de Ven, WPMM 'Solidarity in competitive health insurance markets: analysing the relevant EC legal framework' [2006] *Health Economics, Policy and Law* 107.
Peeters, M, McKee, M and Merkur, S 'EU law and health professionals' in Mossialos, E et al (eds), *Health Systems Governance in Europe: The Role of European Union Law and Policy* (Cambridge: Cambridge University Press 2010) 589.
Pelkmans, J 'The New Approach to Technical Harmonization and Standardization' [1987] *Journal of Common Market Studies* 249.
Pennings, F 'Inclusion and exclusion of persons and benefits in the new co-ordination Regulation' in Dougan, M and Spaventa, E (eds), *Social Welfare and EU Law* (Oxford: Hart Publishing, 2005).
—— *European social security law* (5th edn, Antwerp: Intersentia, 2010).
Poiares Maduro, M *We the court: the European Court of Justice and the European Economic Constitution: a critical reading of Article 30 of the EC Treaty* (Oxford: Hart Publishing, 1998).
—— 'Harmony and dissonance in free movement' in Andenas, M and Roth, W-H (eds), *Services and Free Movement in EU Law* (Oxford: Oxford University Press, 2002).
Posner, R *Economic analysis of law* (8th edn, New York: Aspen Publishers, 2010).
Prechal, S 'Joined Cases C-397/01 to C-403/01 Bernhard Pfeiffer et al' [2005] *Common Market Law Review* 1445.
—— 'Direct Effect, Indirect Effect, Supremacy and the Evolving Constitution of the European Union' in Barnard, C (ed.), *The Fundamentals of EU Law Revisited: Assessing the Impact of the Constitutional Debate?* (Oxford: Oxford University Press, 2007), 35.
Prosser, T 'Regulation and social solidarity' [2006] *Journal of Law and Society* 364.
—— 'EU competition law and public services' in Mossialos, E (ed.), *Health Systems Governance in Europe: The Role of European Union Law and Policy* (Cambridge: Cambridge University Press, 2010).
Rapp, J 'State aid in the accession countries' in Hancher, L, Ottervanger, T and Slot, PJ *EU State Aids* (London: Sweet & Maxwell, 2012 forthcoming).
Reich, N 'A European Constitution for Citizens. Reflections on Rethinking of Union and Community Law' [1997] *European Law Journal* 131.
Sauter, W 'The economic constitution of the European Union' [1998] *Columbia Journal of European Law* 27.
—— 'Services of general economic interest and universal service in EU law' [2008] *European Law Review* 167.
—— 'The Proposed Patient Mobility Directive and the Reform of Cross-Border Healthcare in the EU' [2008] TILEC Discussion Paper No 2008-034 <http://ssrn.com/abstract=1277110> accessed 23 February 2012.

Sauter, W 'Case T-289/03, *British United Provident Association Ltd (BUPA), BUPA Insurance Ltd, BUPA Ireland Ltd v. Commission of the European Communities*, Judgment of the Court of First Instance of 12 February 2008, nyr' [2009] *Common Market Law Review* 269.
—— 'Experiences from the Netherlands: the application of competition rules in healthcare' in van de Gronden, JW et al (eds), *Healthcare and EU Law* (The Hague: TMC Asser Press, 2011), 337–58.
—— 'Harmonization in health care: The EU patients' rights directive', in Cantillon, B, Verschueren, H and Ploscar, P (eds), *Social Inclusion and Social Protection in the EU: Interactions between Law and Policy* (Antwerp: Intersentia, 2012), 105.
—— 'The Altmark package Mark II: New rules for state aid and the compensation of services of general economic interest' [2012] *European Competition Law Review* 307.
—— and Schepel, H *State and Market in European Union Law, the Public and Private Spheres of the Internal Market before the EU Courts* (Cambridge: Cambridge University Press, 2009).
—— and van de Gronden, J 'State Aid, Services of General Economic interest and Universal Service in Healthcare' [2011] *European Competition Law Review* 615.
Sbragia, A and Stolfi, F 'Key Policies', in Bomberg, E, Peterson, J and Stubb, A (eds), *The European Union: How Does it Work?* (2nd edn, Oxford: Oxford University Press, 2008).
Scharpf, FW 'The Joint-Decision Trap. Lessons From German Federalism and European Integration' [1988] *Public Administration* 239.
—— 'Negative and Positive Integration in the Political Economy of European Welfare States', in Marks, G, Scharpf, FW, Schmitter, PhC and Streeck, W (eds), *Governance in the European Union* (London: Sage, 1996).
—— 'The European social model: coping with the challenges of diversity' [2002] *Journal of Common Market Studies* 645.
—— 'The Joint-Decision Trap Revisited' [2006] *Journal of Common Market Studies* 845.
Schoonderbeek, C and Lisman, J 'EU member states and the Transparency Directive', in *PLC Cross-border Life Sciences Handbook 2009* pp 33–8.
Senden, L *Soft Law in European Community Law* (Oxford: Hart Publishing, 2004).
Sinnaeve, A 'State financing of public services: the Court's dilemma in the *Altmark* Case' [2003] *European State Aid Law Quarterly* 351.
Slot, PJ 'Harmonisation of law' [1006] *European Law Review* 378.
—— 'Administrative procedure' in Hancher, L, Ottervanger, T and Slot, PJ *EU State Aids* (London: Sweet & Maxwell, 2012 forthcoming).
Spaventa, E 'From *Gebhard* to *Carpenter*: towards a (non-)economic European constitution' (2004) *Common Market Law Review* 743.
Smulders, BMP 'Institutional aspects of European Commission guidance in the area of antitrust law' [2009] *Competition Policy International* 25.
Stöger, K 'The freedom of establishment and the market access of hospital operators' [2006] *European Business Law Review* 1545.
Taylor, A et al, 'Healthcare and competition law: an emerging area – overview of cases by European national competition authorities' [2011] No33647 E-Competitions, special healthcare issue of 5 January 2011, <www.concurrences.com> accessed 24 February 2012.
Thomson, S and Mossialos, E 'Private health insurance and the internal market' in Mossialos, E et al (eds), *Health Systems Governance in Europe: The Role of European Union Law and Policy* (Cambridge: Cambridge University Press, 2010), 427.
Townley, C *Article 81 EC and Public Policy* (Oxford: Hart Publishing, 2009).

Trepte, P *Public Procurement in the EU: A Practitioner's Guide* (2nd edn, Oxford: Oxford University Press, 2007).

Varkevisser, M *Patient choice, competition and antitrust enforcement in Dutch hospital markets* (PhD thesis, Rotterdam, 2010).

—— Capps, CS et al 'Defining hospital markets for antitrust enforcement: new approaches and their applicability to The Netherlands' [2008] *Health Economics, Policy and Law* 7.

Vedder, HHB 'Spontaneous harmonisation of national (competition) laws in the wake of the modernisation of EC competition law' [2004] *Competition Law Review* 5.

Weatherill, S 'After *Keck*: some thoughts on how to clarify the clarification' [1996] *Common Market Law Review* 885.

—— 'European private law – Is there a future after the Tobacco Advertising decision?' [2003] *Europäisches Integrationsrecht im Querschnitt* 93.

—— 'Harmonisation: How much, how little?' [2005] *European Business Law Review* 533.

de Witte, B 'Direct Effect, Primacy and the Nature of the Legal Order' in Craig, P and De Burca, G (eds), *The Evolution of EU Law* (Oxford: Oxford University Press, 2011), 359.

Wyatt, D 'Community competence to regulate medical services' in Dougan, M and Spaventa, E (eds), *Social Welfare and EU Law* (Oxford: Hart Publishing, 2005), 131.

INDEX